I0816818

MISERABLE LITTLE CONGLOMERATION

MISERABLE LITTLE CONGLOMERATION

A SOCIAL HISTORY OF THE PORT HUDSON CAMPAIGN

CHRISTOPHER THRASHER

VOICES OF THE CIVIL WAR,
Michael P. Gray, Series Editor

THE UNIVERSITY OF TENNESSEE PRESS | KNOXVILLE

The Voices of the Civil War series makes available a variety of primary source materials that illuminate issues on the battlefield, the home front, and the western front, as well as other aspects of this historic era. The series contextualizes the personal accounts within the framework of the latest scholarship and expands established knowledge by offering new perspectives, new materials, and new voices.

Manufactured in the United States of America.
First Edition.

Library of Congress Cataloging-in-Publication Data
Names: Thrasher, Christopher David, author.
Title: Miserable little conglomeration : a social history of the Port Hudson campaign / Christopher Thrasher
Other titles: Social history of the Port Hudson campaign | Voices of the Civil War series.
Description: First edition. | Knoxville : The University of Tennessee Press, [2023] | Series: Voices of the Civil War | Includes bibliographical references and index. | Summary: "The siege at Port Hudson, largely overshadowed by the longer, large-scale siege of Vicksburg, nevertheless had many parallels to it. Like Vicksburg, Port Hudson involved logistical challenges, an overmatched Confederate defense, and a rough slog in usually adverse conditions. Among many interesting features, the Port Hudson campaign featured widespread participation of African American Federal troops. Drawing on a large body of primary sources and secondary scholarship, Thrasher presents a 'bottom-up' portrayal of the campaign" —Provided by publisher.
Identifiers: LCCN 2023022294 (print) | LCCN 2023022295 (ebook) | ISBN 9781621907916 (cloth) | ISBN 9781621907923 (pdf) | ISBN 9781621907930 (Kindle edition)
Subjects: LCSH: Port Hudson (La.)—History—Siege, 1863. | United States—History—Civil War, 1861-1865—Social aspects. | United States—History—Civil War, 1861-1865—African Americans.
Classification: LCC E475.42 .T47 2023 (print) | LCC E475.42 (ebook) | DDC 973.7/34—dc23/eng/20230526
LC record available at https://lccn.loc.gov/2023022294
LC ebook record available at https://lccn.loc.gov/2023022295

*My work is dedicated to the
loving memory of my mother
Theresa Thrasher
(1953–2021).*

Contents

Illustrations

Figures

Maps

Foreword

The Civil War history of Port Hudson, due to its strategic location, has recently earned more attention from scholars. Located on the Mississippi River some twenty-five miles upriver from Baton Rouge and guarded by eighty-foot bluffs with a tricky bend in the river, the region had served as a nexus for transportation. To the south of Port Hudson, the mouth of the Red River flowed from the rich hinterlands of Texas, west to east, and with the Mississippi running north to south, a properly fortified Port Hudson could protect these supply routes. The installation of river batteries would be in line with the defense system of Vicksburg, about 120 miles upriver; and with New Orleans about one hundred miles downriver already taken in the spring of 1862, it was paramount for the Confederacy to control this vital area full of watersheds, bayous, swamps, and marshland.

The University of Tennessee Press is steadfast in its commitment to publishing books about the Western Theater of the American Civil War. Our mission statement for the Voices of the Civil War series affirms that we offer "a variety of primary source materials that illuminate issues on the battlefield, the home front, and the western front, as well as other aspects of this historical era." Furthermore, it states, "The series contextualizes the personal accounts within the framework of the latest scholarship and expands established knowledge by offering new perspectives, new materials, and new voices." Christopher Thrasher's *Miserable Little Conglomeration: A Social History of the Port Hudson Campaign* resoundingly meets those criteria. Thrasher goes even further by framing his work around heretofore silenced voices, utilizing a social history methodology that investigates the "longest siege" in American military history from the bottom up. We now have the voices from slaves to civilians, from privates to commanders.

Thrasher's new book is the perfect complement to the work of another author associated with the press. A foremost scholar of the Western Theater and author or editor of several volumes published by the University of Tennessee Press, Lawrence Lee Hewitt probably knows more about Port Hudson than any living person. Hewitt served as the first manager of the

Port Hudson State Historical Site, then went onto a career in academia, ultimately becoming professor emeritus of history at Southeastern Louisiana University. He co-edited two exhaustive series with the press, *Confederate Generals in the Western Theater: Essays on America's Civil War* (four volumes, 2010–17) and *Confederate Generals in the Trans-Mississippi: Essays on America's Civil War* (three volumes, 2013–19). Hewitt also contributed to the Voices of the Civil War series in co-editing *To Succeed or Perish: The Diaries of Sergeant Edmund Trent Eggleston, Company G, 1st Mississippi Light Artillery Regiment* (2015). And most recently, Hewitt's *Port Hudson: The Most Significant Battlefield Photographs of the Civil War* (2021), was published by the press, which utilized Hewitt's four decades of Port Hudson expertise and an extraordinary collection of photographs by six contemporary cameramen to document the changing landscape of war in some 170 images of the campaign—a number of the vivid exposures not readily available before.

In addition to the press's histories related to Port Hudson, the Voices of the Civil War specifically has offerings—from soldiers, sailors, and civilians to decision makers and diplomats—on the operations on, near, or related to the Mississippi River and its tributaries. Hewitt's co-edited book on Eggleston describes the Confederate sergeant stationed at Vicksburg, which ties into the Port Hudson campaign, as well as describing his surroundings, especially watercraft such as the *Essex.* Another vessel of more notoriety was the subject of Chester D. Berry's *Loss of the Sultana and Reminiscences of Survivors* (2005). Berry excavates that tragic event, the deadliest maritime disaster in our history. Nearly 1,700 passengers, mostly Federal prisoners of war, endured captivity in Southern prisons, but could not survive scalding boiler blasts nor the powerful currents of the Mississippi, just north of Memphis. *The Memoirs of Winfield Scott* (2015), edited by Timothy D. Johnson, offers contextualization of operations out west and the Mississippi River Valley. The reader gains a better understanding of Old Fuss and Feathers's military mind in embracing combined soldier and sailor operations, something practiced in the Mexican War, and further cultivated in the Civil War with his Anaconda Plan. An integral facet of that strategy was taking control of the Mississippi River, thereby strangling the South and cutting the Confederacy in half—New Orleans, Vicksburg, and Port Hudson were all barriers in this objective.

Yankee sailor Bartholomew Diggins proved to be one of the "players" in helping carry out Scott's plan. George S. Burkhardt's *Sailing with*

Farragut: The Recollections of Bartholomew Diggins (2016) recounts Admiral David G. Farragut's miscues during the Port Hudson campaign, and his resurrection with his victory in the capture of Mobile Bay. Diggins, on Farragut's flagship the *Hartford*, writes about gun boats, iron clads, supply ships, monitors, submarines, and semi-submarines on rivers, bays, and oceans; he also explains weaponry, tactics, and strategy. In *Miserable Little Conglomeration*, the *Hartford*, Farragut, and Diggins are all entangled in the Union's "Brown-water navy," as Thrasher provides substantial analysis with ground force personnel and the planning between Union General Nathaniel Banks and Rear Admiral Farragut in taking Port Hudson. For even wider context, on the diplomatic front, we offer *Ruined by This Miserable War: The Dispatches of Charles Prosper Fauconnet, a French Diplomat in New Orleans, 1863–1868*, edited by Carl A. Brasseaux and Katherine Carmines Mooney (2013). Fauconnet provides insight on Port Hudson as well as other strategic points in the region in his official correspondence with the French Ministry of State. From his home in New Orleans, the French diplomat believed that, with the capture of Vicksburg and Port Hudson, the Confederacy would resort to guerrilla warfare, shifting from battlefield action to "pillaging, seizures, and devastation."

While *Miserable Little Conglomeration* has few predecessors, an earlier volume in the series, *Little to Eat and Thin Mud to Drink: Letters, Diaries, and Memoirs from the Red River Campaigns, 1863–1864* (2007), is close to it in style and location. Ably edited by Gary D. Joiner, a leading expert on the Trans-Mississippi conflict, and others, it offers a profound, extended look into the innermost thoughts of the soldiers and civilians who experienced the events that took place in Louisiana, Texas, and Arkansas. Gleaning from a rich body of rare journals, diaries, and letters, this groundbreaking book demonstrates the significant impact that military operations in this region had on the local population in years between 1863 and 1864.

Christopher Thrasher's 2021 book, *Suffering in the Army of Tennessee: A Social History of the Confederate Army of the Heartland from the Battles for Atlanta to the Retreat from Nashville*, set a new standard in the Voices of the Civil War series by marrying social history with many voices. It differed from previous volumes in the series, since it is not the letters of one, two, or a few contemporaries. Rather, it is a full-length narrative interwoven with an "army" of primary source materials that include common soldiers, officers, and civilians—from letters and diaries to official reports. Also threaded into the story is the historiography and the memory of these participants, as Thrasher's discerning editorial pen analyzes postwar accounts in light of battle reports of the day. The result was a book that won the 2022 Douglas Southall Freeman History Award.

Thrasher's latest volume brings the reader on a journey farther south, to the environs of Port Hudson, and also further down the social rung of the time period, as voices of people of color are cited heavily in the book. Thrasher also has the ability to weave new interpretation into his projects, which are sometimes void in many primary source volumes. He argues that the Confederate defenders of Port Hudson were not passive, as previous scholars had thought, but rather very active in their defense. The editor offers an array of primary sources, bringing unheard voices like those of civilians, slaves, and soldiers all together. He especially highlights the Federal use of African American troops, those in bondage, and those trying to escape slavery. Thrasher also opens with a historiographical scrutiny of the role of African Americans in the campaign, as well as a consideration of their memories of it.

Although Thrasher's main attention is on the 1862 to 1863 Port Hudson campaign, he starts his narrative by describing prewar Port Hudson. He provides details about its history and its unique geography, gifted by "mother nature," and ultimately enhanced by "man" in army fortifications and batteries. He begins with the start of war, moves to the Battle for Baton Rouge, draws out implications of the capture of New Orleans, and iron clad and gunboat fighting. As the campaign continued, the death toll rose. Among the dead was rebel A. H. Todd, half-brother of Mary Todd Lincoln. There is commentary from top-of-commanders, such as Benjamin Butler, an "ineffective general but a clever lawyer and an astute politician," and his successor Nathaniel Banks. Confederate leaders are represented as well, including Port Hudson defender Franklin Gardner, among others. While the rebels hoped to recapture New Orleans, some women of that city fled to Port Hudson. One observer noticed how soldiers met up with "the fastest set of girls I have seen." Alcohol was highly sought after, and both soldiers and civilians were creative in providing it to troops, such as brewing "corn beer," while others distilled their own liquor. Of particular delight was rum made from local sugar-cane, to the point that military officials had to send out patrols to obliterate stills. The more temperate soldiers found solace in other occupations while off duty, such as camp religion, musical entertainment, and game playing.

The so-called hairpin turn on the Mississippi, complemented with fortifications, posed a substantial obstacle for Federal gunboats, particularly when Confederate forces were able to hide artillery on the forested high bluffs. Once shelling began, captains would find it hard to reverse engines in time, once they committed to moving downriver. One contemporary observer commented that Port Hudson's position was stronger than that of Vicksburg, and "doubted that any navy could run the gauntlet." If Port Hudson were to be captured, ground forces would have to support any naval operation. Thrasher emphasizes the Confederate design in defending Port Hudson, the building of lunettes and Fort Desperate. With summer temperatures reaching 110 degrees, weather would make labor intense, and heat stroke was only one of the many issues that both sides had to deal with, as one soldier claimed it was "hot as hell." The environment was a breeding grounds for gnats, lice, ticks, fleas, and mosquitos. In turn, it seemed sickness was always a problem. Yellow fever and malaria fevers were especially contagious, but diarrhea, dysentery, smallpox, and eventually malnutrition would also be prevalent.

Medical care was underwhelming, and more than one combatant felt that it was healthier to stay away from doctors. A Port Hudson patient believed "medicines were poisonous, particularly in the large doses favored by many physicians, and wondered how many men the doctors killed or permanently disabled." Interestingly enough, since the North recruited African American troops from the region, many of whom were either free or former slaves who lived in Louisiana, some were relatively immune to such maladies compared to their Federal counterparts. One medical report found that Maine troops especially suffered, but another report found malarial fevers did not discriminate and wreaked havoc on all populations.

Thrasher's investigation of people of color is an important piece to the story. There is commentary on escaped slaves who sought refuge on the USS *Diana,* while USS *Essex* was able to shuttle escaped slaves across the Mississippi River to Federal lines. One Northerner wrote to his wife, "The blacks are coming in very fast." Union officers and even some of the enlisted soldiers employed former slaves as servants, while those still in bondage worked for Confederate officers as "body servants." Other runaway slaves or those who were a part of the free black populace from New Orleans and made it to Federal lines, wanted to fight. The Northern high command vehemently felt that each slave taken and put to service, whether digging trenches or gathering food, was one less worker for the Confederacy. Some Union commanders argued these men could be used as cooks, teamsters, or laborers, while others contended they could serve on the battlefield, especially in helping with defensive operations. However, the Louisiana "Native Guards" defied that mindset by striking forward in an assault. The First and Third Native Guards, two of the first black regiments to fight in the Civil War, comprised African American soldiers across the ranks, from officers to privates. Many of the men previously came from the liberated Black or mixed population of New Orleans. They showed their bravery as the First and Third Native Guard supporting the Union right flank charge on the Confederate garrison near Fort Desperate. General Banks wrote that the Native Guards were "heroic" men and that they were "excellent soldiers." Commander Henry W. Halleck maintained that the "north must conquer the slave oligarchy or become slaves themselves." Black soldiers would figure into Port Hudson—and for that matter, the rest of the war—those opposed to their participation, no matter what side, had better get used to them actively engaging in combat.

Miserable Little Conglomeration also reveals the use of bulletproof or metal vests that were used to protect soldiers' bodies. A private mentioned that some officers had ordered them, but when they were in the field, they had the "misery of carrying 'an iron foundry' in the Louisiana heat and left their body armor on the roadside." The reader will find information about raids, partisan rangers, cavalry skirmishes, grenades, and sharpshooters. Details about mine-shaft digging and counter-shaft maneuvering at Fort Desperate, reminiscent of what would later happen in the Petersburg campaign, are included. And there are stories about the unsolved mystery of the "Buried Treasure of Port Hudson." Just as at Vicksburg, the siege warfare waged by the Federals at Port Hudson devolved into starving out the garrison. After a wounded mule was butchered to be eaten, Southerners compared their meal to venison. General Gardner admitted to his Confederates that their desperate situation might perhaps get worse and inquired if they would they prefer mule meat over surrender. The unbowed rebels replied, "Yes! give us dog, if necessary!" Indeed, dog was the next item necessary to dine on, as well as horse meat, and then rats. One Port Hudson defender recalled, "When I look back to these times, I wonder how any of us lived." The starving time during the forty-eight-day siege on Port Hudson was longer by one day compared to Vicksburg, 120 miles upriver, which surrendered on July 4, 1863. When Confederate Generals William Beall and Franklin Gardner learned about the Vicksburg surrender, they came to the grim conclusion that a similar fate awaited at Port Hudson, and Gardner surrendered five days later. Beall, like most of the Confederate officers, would find a new home at the Federal prison in Johnsons Island, Ohio, while the enlisted Confederate would have the fortune of being placed on parole. Thrasher's new book will fascinate readers who appreciate both narrative and analysis, adding to the social history scholarship of the Civil War from the "bottom up." According to Port Hudson expert Lawrence Hewitt, "It is the best 'Historical Memory' work I have read since Carol Reardon's *Pickett's Charge in History and Memory*."

Michael P. Gray
East Stroudsburg University

Acknowledgments

I THANK THE ENTIRE TEAM at the University of Tennessee Press, including Scot Danforth and Michael Gray, for their help transforming a rough manuscript into a finished book.

I express my gratitude to all the archivists and librarians who helped me. In the words of my dearly departed friend Jim Sanderson archivists are "the keepers of the treasures." I am particularly thankful for Guy Lancaster and his wife, Anna Lancaster, at The Butler Center for Arkansas Studies for their research help. I thank Mary K. DiRisio at the Paul H. Thompson Library of Fayetteville Technical Community College for her supportive comments during the final phases of this project.

I appreciate all my friends and colleagues who helped me with this book. Lawrence Lee Hewitt, who is the true expert on Port Hudson, generously served as one of my peer reviewers and even took the time to chat with me on the phone. Richard Holloway gave excellent feedback in his peer review of my manuscript. Abby Hanks helped me track down several of the more obscure sources I used and checked the manuscript for errors. Several members of the Historians of the Western Theatre provided helpful comments on the manuscript at our annual meeting. I appreciate my dearly departed friend Gene Barnett, who taught me most of what I know about the Confederate cavalry. I am sorry I could not share this book with him before he passed away unexpectedly.

I appreciate my supportive family. I am thankful for my father, David Thrasher, who reads everything I publish and always encourages me to write more. I reserve my deepest thanks for my wife, Barbara Thrasher. Her constant encouragement and support made this book possible.

Introduction

> As to what they called the town of Port Hudson—a miserable little conglomeration of two or three wooden buildings and a nondescript church among them—the destruction is so complete that I cannot see how they escaped being utterly swept away.[1]
>
> —John R. Hamilton, reporter and artist for *Harper's Weekly*

SHORTLY AFTER THE SIEGE of Port Hudson ended, journalist John Hamilton described Port Hudson, with its odd mix of buildings, as "a miserable little conglomeration." He could have just as easily described the people who endured the siege as the place itself. The Federals who approached Port Hudson were an eclectic conglomeration of men that included abolitionists from New England, Midwestern farmers, New York draft dodgers, recent immigrants who fled European wars only to get caught up in America's most horrific conflict, former slaves fighting for their freedom, and even southern men who wore gray before changing sides and fighting for the Union. An equally odd conglomeration of people including French-speaking Louisianans, sharpshooting "wrackensackers" from the Arkansas hills, heavy artillerymen from the Alabama Gulf Coast, northern men who fought for the Confederacy, and a diverse array of civilians, burrowed into the slippery Louisiana mud and tried to resist the mighty blue tidal wave that swept up the Mississippi River.

Union forces at Port Hudson enjoyed an overwhelming superiority in men, ships, artillery, and logistics, but they struggled to translate their superiority into victory. Federal soldiers flung themselves at Confederate positions in suicidal charges against rebels who met them with improvised landmines and loads of buckshot. Men in blue pounded Port Hudson with heavy artillery barrages from ship and shore that often did little more than create new rifle pits for the Confederate defenders and supply them with metal to fire back at the Federal forces. In desperation, the Federals even constructed tunnels under rebel lines only to discover counter tunnels built by men in gray who fought as well under the earth as on it. Confederate defenders never lost their offensive spirit and launched desperate raids from Port Hudson against Union forces while southern guerillas outside the lines harassed Union supply networks until at least one Federal soldier began to wonder who was besieging whom.

This book is titled "miserable conglomeration" because misery is the most common theme in accounts of the conglomeration of soldiers and civilians who participated in the campaign. Every Civil War campaign was horrific, but Port Hudson inflicted unique miseries. Louisiana was hot and wet, even by southern standards. Sun and rain conspired with insects to turn the area around Port Hudson into a disease-infested hellscape. Within Port Hudson's lines, Confederate soldiers and civilians quickly ran out of medicine and food. Desperate defenders and the town's civilians survived on a meager diet of horsemeat, rats, and peas sprinkled with shards of glass from shattered windows. When their medical supplies ran out, Confederate doctors turned to improvised home remedies until they too ran out. In the Union lines ringing the town, heat stroke and disease killed more men than Confederate bullets. Confederate raiders attacked Federal supply lines. By the end of the siege, many Union soldiers wore little more than rags, licked the bottoms of supply crates in search of crumbs, and worried that the medical department would be unable to evacuate them if they got sick. Perhaps nobody said it better than Private Frank Flinn of the 38th Massachusetts Infantry, who concluded, "camping in Louisiana is very much more disagreeable than in Virginia."[2]

Despite the horrors, the Federals refused to withdraw, and the Confederates refused to surrender. A relentless Union force battered an immovable Confederate object. On July 4, 1863, Vicksburg's Confederate garrison surrendered to Union forces. Alone, without a stronghold to the north, Port Hudson was of little value to the Confederacy. Reluctantly, most of the Confederate garrison laid down their arms on July 9, 1863. A few defenders refused to accept defeat and slipped away to fight another day. More than 10,000 Union and 1,000 Confederate troops lost their lives during the longest siege in American history. An unknown number of civilians also died.

Modern scholars have written comparatively little about the battles for Port Hudson. In most overviews of the Civil War, including the excellent works of James McPherson and Joseph Glatthaar, the July 1863

Confederate defeats at Gettysburg and Vicksburg overshadow the Port Hudson campaign.[3] This trend is both understandable and unfortunate. With almost 50,000 casualties, Gettysburg was the costliest battle of the war, it was the Confederacy's most ambitious invasion of the North, and it was probably the worst defeat suffered by the Army of Northern Virginia. Like Gettysburg, the battles for Vicksburg involved far more troops than the fights for Port Hudson. While only about 40,000 Union and 7,500 Confederate troops fought at Port Hudson, more than 75,000 Union and 30,000 Confederate soldiers participated in the Vicksburg campaign. Paul de Gournay, who commanded the 12th Louisiana Heavy Artillery at Port Hudson, explained "the relative strength of the two places considered, Port Hudson was looked upon as an outpost of Vicksburg; hence public attention was centered in the latter, whose stupendous fall gave such a shock that there was no interest left to be spent on minor calamities."[4] Several of the war's most notable figures, including Ulysses Grant, William Sherman, Joseph Johnston, and Nathan Bedford Forrest, all played major roles in the Vicksburg campaign. In contrast, the commanders at Port Hudson, such as Frank Gardner, William Beall, and Nathaniel Banks, are less famous. As a result of the smaller forces, smaller losses, and lesser-known commanders at Port Hudson, the historical record has left historians with far fewer documents to examine and made a detailed study of Port Hudson more difficult.

Historiography

The first histories of Port Hudson were written during the conflict and included a wide assortment of letters, diaries, and newspaper accounts produced in midst of the war by soldiers, sailors, and civilians. After the war ended in 1865, several Union and Confederate veterans as well as a handful of civilians published works that included accounts of the siege.[5] With rare exception, each of these primary sources told the story of Port Hudson from a single perspective. This book will weave many primary sources together so that the reader will understand the campaign from many points of view. It is often said that "history is written by the victors," but this is often incorrect. Many of the men who suffered defeat at Port Hudson wrote their stories. It is probably far more correct to say, as Gettysburg battlefield guides Jim Hessler and Eric Lindblade once remarked, that "history is written by the survivors." This book will acknowledge the imperfections in even the best primary sources and present a history both of the campaign as it actually happened and of the campaign as the survivors remembered it.

A century after the battles for Port Hudson, scholars wrote the first academic histories of the campaign. In 1963 Edward Cunningham wrote the first significant scholarly history of the battles for Port Hudson, *The Port Hudson Campaign: 1862–1863*. Cunningham's work provided an excellent brief overview of the campaign. Cunningham deserves praise for his argument that Port Hudson was a vital battle. However, his work's two hundred pages barely scratched the subject's surface. Cunningham relied almost exclusively on published accounts by major leaders and made little use of archival collections or materials produced by ordinary Americans. This book will build on Cunningham's work by providing a more thorough examination of the campaign with an emphasis on the stories of ordinary people preserved in archival collections. This work will also take issue with Cunningham's suggestion that the Confederate garrison's defense was "passive."[6] This book will argue that the Confederate defenders were remarkably active and that their aggression played a major role in their ability to hold out longer than any other besieged force in American history.

David Edmonds expanded on Cunningham's work with a two-volume series on Port Hudson titled *The Guns of Port Hudson*. Volume 1 was published in 1983 and Volume 2 in 1984. The two books drew on archival sources and provided a great deal of information in their combined total of 726 pages, but unlike Cunningham's tightly focused analysis, Edmonds's work provides little context or analysis. To his credit, Edmonds admitted, "I make no claims here to having written the definitive Civil War history of Port Hudson" and "the complete Confederate story of Port Hudson has yet to be written."[7] This book will provide much of the context and analysis that Edmonds did not.

Lawrence Lee Hewitt wrote two important books on Port Hudson. In his 1987 book *Port Hudson, Confederate Bastion on the Mississippi*, Hewitt attempted to fill in important gaps left by Cunningham and Edmonds by striking a balance between Edmonds's detailed narrative and Cunningham's thoughtful analysis. Hewitt argued that the battles for Port Hudson may have led to the fall of the Confederacy through two indirect processes. Firstly, Hewitt argued that the Union's inability to quickly capture Port Hudson may have prevented Nathaniel Banks, the Union commander at Port Hudson, from superseding Ulysses Grant as overall commander of Union forces during the war. Hewitt argued that, since Grant was the superior general, the long siege at Port Hudson may have led to the eventual Confederate defeat during the war. Secondly, Hewitt argued that the impressive performance of African American soldiers at Port Hudson ensured that the Union would use large numbers of black soldiers, who played a vital role in the conflict and helped ensure that the Union won the war.[8] In 2021 Hewitt built on his earlier work to publish *Port Hudson The Most Significant Battlefield Photographs of the Civil War.* Hewitt's new work published many rarely seen photographs from before, during, and after the battles for Port Hudson. More importantly, by conducting a detailed analysis of the images and archival resources about the images, he provided new insights into the campaign. This book will build on Hewitt's two books, providing additional insights into the images and ideas he shared.

In the last several years, a series of scholarly books have discussed Port Hudson within broader studies of the campaign for the Mississippi River. Dennis Dufrene's 2012 *Civil War Baton Rouge, Port Hudson, and Bayou Sara: Capturing the Mississippi* contextualizes Port Hudson within the broader struggle for the Louisiana banks along the Mississippi River. In 2015 Donald Frazier published the evocatively titled *Blood on the Bayou: Vicksburg, Port Hudson, and the Trans-Mississippi*, which emphasized the importance of small unit actions, particularly by Texas cavalry units, during the struggle to control the Mississippi River. These books do an excellent job of contextualizing Port Hudson, but they all spend little time on the battles for Port Hudson. This book will build on this recent scholarship while focusing primarily on the experiences of ordinary Americans at the crucial battles for Port Hudson.

Several scholars have explored the racial component of the fight for Port Hudson. In 1998 James Hollandsworth's *The Louisiana Native Guards* claimed that abolitionists wildly exaggerated the performance of African American soldiers at Port Hudson as part of their campaign for racial equality. In 2011 William A. Dobak's *Freedom by the Sword: The US Colored Troops 1862–1867* argued that the first combat experiences of African American troops at Port Hudson were a "disaster" but that the survivors learned and became successful largely because of their initial failures at Port Hudson.[9]

This book will contribute to this scholarship by revealing often ignored Confederate perspectives on African Americans at Port Hudson.

This book will provide insight into the technology of warfare. In *America Goes to War*, Bruce Catton argued that "the Civil War was the first modern war," largely because of technological innovations such as rifled small arms and armored warships. Barton Hacker's *Astride Two Worlds* provides a far more nuanced explanation of technology during the Civil War. Hacker acknowledges the war's important innovations but also points out that "more innovations failed than succeeded" and that during the Civil War "horses still mattered more than steam engines, and disease still killed more soldiers than did weapons." Kenneth Rutherford's *America's Buried History: Landmines in the Civil War* presented a great overview of the improvised explosives used at Port Hudson and throughout the Civil War.[10] This book will argue that Port Hudson provides a glimpse of postmodern warfare, where armored machines creep forward in fear of improvised explosives, underfunded revolutionaries snipe at better funded attackers, and quick moving guerillas nip at the heels of powerful armies before disappearing into difficult terrain.

Confederates loved to brag that one southerner could whip ten Yankees. Port Hudson is a rare example where they did, at least for a little while. This book will highlight the key factors that allowed Confederate defenders to hold out longer than any other besieged force in American history and to inflict horrific losses on their opponents. It will also help explain why Union soldiers chose to remain, many even volunteering to extend their enlistments, and their misery, rather than return home.

Port Hudson's defenders enjoyed geographic and biological advantages. Perched on a high bluff overlooking a tight bend in the Mississippi River, Confederate heavy artillerymen enjoyed excellent fields of fire against enemy boats. Ravines, underbrush, and swamps dominated the countryside near Port Hudson, which made overland attacks slow and difficult. Confederate soldiers and slaves, under the watchful eye of professional military engineers, built an impressive system of interconnected fortifications on nature's foundation. The Confederacy's greatest allies might have been the wildlife that called Louisiana's swamps home and spread disease through Union camps, ensuring that far more Federals died of disease than gunfire. Many Confederates also suffered in the harsh environment, but it was often easier to defend difficult terrain when sick than to cross it.

This book will demonstrate that Port Hudson held out for so long in large measure because Confederate soldiers developed a culture of invincibility. This was not the blind faith of men who ignored all reason but the cold analysis of veterans who understood their advantages and who felt justifiable pride in each small victory and in each day of successful resistance. They knew that they faced difficult odds, but they believed that somehow courage and determination could weigh more heavily on the scales of history than numbers. Confederate soldiers could have deserted to the enemy or tried to slip through enemy lines to return home, and some did, but most Confederate soldiers simply refused to surrender until their officers ordered them to lay down their arms. Some did not surrender even when ordered, slipping away from Port Hudson to fight again another day.

Despite every advantage the Confederates enjoyed, they failed. The Federals refused to retreat in the face of battlefield defeats, illness, and heatstroke, demonstrating that they were just a courageous and determined as their adversaries. Union soldiers remained at Port Hudson for many reasons. Some, particularly white abolitionists and former slaves, believed that God would deliver victory to their army, which fought to make all men free. Others remained with the army because they were bound by patriotism, even when that duty was hard. Regardless of their religion or politics, some men believed that their larger number of troops, greater quantities of supplies, and overwhelming firepower made their victory inevitable. Federal soldiers often blamed defeats on the temporary mistakes of their leaders, not on any fundamental flaw in themselves, their comrades, or their cause. They seemed to think that victory was just a few more days of patience or one more good charge away. History proved them right and rewarded the men who remained faithful to their nation with one of the most important victories in American history. At Port Hudson, the unstoppable force overwhelmed the immovable object.

Methodology

This book will build on the existing scholarship of Port Hudson with a unique social history emphasis. In his famed memoir *Co. Aytch*, Sam Watkins lamented "the histories of the Lost Cause are all written out by 'big bugs,' generals and renowned historians." Watkins believed that, despite his humble station in life, he too had a story worth telling and wrote one of the most enduring personal accounts of life during the Civil War. In the decades since Watkins published his work, authors have produced an endless stream of material on the Civil War, including some good books on this campaign. However, most scholarship on the campaign still focuses on the "big bugs" rather than ordinary people. A careful reader can see the flickering ghosts of common people in the existing books on Port Hudson—a quote from a nameless private, a comment on the army's morale, a newspaper account from some forgotten correspondent, or a footnote from some mostly ignored civilian's diary. Port Hudson, like the Civil War in general, was primarily a story of ordinary people who did extraordinary things. This book is the first to emphasize the stories of common people at Port Hudson. While this book provides some scholarly insights, the primary goal of this work is to share stories from ordinary Americans who participated in the Port Hudson campaign. Their stories are worth remembering, and this book will share them.

This is an unconventional book. It not a story of a single participant nor is it a typical campaign narrative. Eyewitnesses to the campaign like Lawrence Van Alstyne, Daniel Smith, and Sarah Morgan wrote wonderful memoirs, but they wrote the story as seen from one person's perspective. This book draws on many primary sources to reveal how the story looked to numerous people at Port Hudson. This book is a grand overview of the campaign, like Cunningham's *The Port Hudson Campaign*, but if Cunningham's book is a photograph, this book is a photographic negative of that same image. The pictures are similar but reversed and highlight different aspects of the picture. Cunningham focused on the "big bugs," and this work shares tales from ordinary people. J. Tracy Power's *Lee's Miserables* is an outstanding history of ordinary soldiers in Virginia, and this work provides a counterpoint focused on the men who decided the fate of Port Hudson. Like James McPherson's *For Cause and Comrades*, this book emphasizes the stories of numerous common soldiers, but this book focuses on a single, often ignored campaign and not the entire war. Like the work of Alex Mendoza on the Chickamauga campaign, this book weaves the stories of ordinary people into a broader overview of the strategic picture. Like *Diehard Rebels: The Confederate Culture of Invincibility* by Jason Phillips, this book explains why men continued to fight in the service of a cause that seemed hopeless and will focus on the Port Hudson Campaign, which Phillips did not discuss. To tell the story of many people, the work allows as many people as possible to speak. This book is built on a diverse collection of sources, including archival sources, newspapers produced during the war, and published primary sources. This book does not provide a seat at the general's table where a single officer speaks and others listen. Instead, it offers a moonlit walking tour through the camps, ships, homes, and trenches around Port Hudson where countless muttered voices grumble, argue, joke, and weep for the dead as the listener slips past faces obscured by darkness. This story is confusing, but confusing stories are worth sharing.

Confederate soldier John Henning Woods implored the readers of his handwritten 1863 memoir to "let the battles of Port Hudson tell it."[11] Woods did not participate in the battles for Port Hudson. During the battles for Port Hudson, Woods was far away in an Atlanta prison awaiting execution for his plot to desert from the Confederate army and flee north. Even though he was not at Port Hudson, Woods felt that what happened on that field could "tell it." This book will reveal what "it" meant to Woods and countless other Americans. This story will emphasize the lives and experiences of common people because common people decided the outcome. It was the ordinary Confederate soldier who claimed he was invincible, the ordinary Union soldier who taught him the error of his ways, and the ordinary civilian who was caught in the middle.

—1—

Prepared for Anything

THE WAR COMES TO LOUISIANA

There is no word in the English language that can express the state in which we are, and have been, these last three days. Day before yesterday, news came early in the morning of three of the enemy's boats passing the Forts, and then the excitement began. . . . Nothing can be positively ascertained, save that our gunboats are sunk, and theirs are coming up to the city. Everything else has been contradicted until we really do not know whether the city has been taken or not. We only know we had best be prepared for anything.[1]

—SARAH MORGAN, Louisiana civilian

Memory calls up for review the familiar features and forms of the thrifty, bustling, scheming guild of old Port Hudson merchants who were shaping, with so much sagacity, the commercial rise of their young town by the side of the great river; and who were like skillful alchemists converting the streams of commerce which touched their wharves into golden bars.[2]

—HENRY SKIPWITH, 27th Louisiana Infantry

When de Yankees come to New Orleans dey go on to Port Hudson and have de big fight dere. Massa order everybody be ready to travel nex' mornin'. Dey 'bout 300 peoples in dat travel wagon and dey camps dat night at Camp Fusilier, where de 'federates have de camp. Dey make only five mile dat day. Dey stops one night at Pin Hook, in Vermilionville. My brudder die dere. Dey kep' on dat way till dey come to Trinity River. I stay dere five year.[3]

—LOUIS LOVE, slave

Port Hudson before the War

Before the Mississippi River brought death to Port Hudson, it brought life. Like many cities in the growing nation, the city of Port Hudson rested on the banks of a river. The Mississippi River was the most important inland waterway in America. Originating in northern Minnesota, the Mississippi River meanders south for over two thousand miles, connects to eight major tributaries and many smaller bodies of water, and drains water from over a million square miles of watershed in territory that eventually became forty-one states before flowing into the Gulf of Mexico near New Orleans, Louisiana. The steep, eighty-foot-tall bluff that overlooked the Mississippi River at Port Hudson provided the city's residents with a degree of safety from unpredictable flood waters. Near the bluff, the Mississippi River took a sharp turn from east to south through a deep channel along the eastern bank, which ensured that riverboat captains did not miss Port Hudson, even if they were asleep or drunk at the wheel, which some probably were. There were no bridges across the Mississippi River at that time, but ferries at Port Hudson transported a steady flow of people and products across the river. At the bottom of the bluff, the wide riverbank provided an ideal location for riverboats to load and unload their cargo onto wagons and, later, trains that ran along roads that punched through the bluff and into the countryside beyond.

Port Hudson rested on ideal location for a transportation hub. It was about eighty miles from New Orleans to the Louisiana state capital at Baton Rouge and from there it was only another twenty miles to Port Hudson. About sixty miles north of Port Hudson, the Mississippi River intersected the Red River, which flowed deep into Texas, with tributaries that went all the way to New Mexico. A hundred miles north of Port Hudson sat the riverboat and railroad hub of Vicksburg, Mississippi. Much of the countryside just outside of Port Hudson was crossed by steep ravines, murky swamps, and prickly undergrowth, but a few roads connected Port Hudson with inland communities and the plantations that made a few Louisianans rich. New inventions made Port Hudson even more valuable to the growing nation. In 1833 the twenty-seven-mile-long Clinton & Port Hudson railroad connected the Port Hudson docks to the interior town of Clinton, Louisiana, and to the countryside beyond. A year later, three

View of the river with Port Hudson on the bluff in the distance.
Library of Congress.

steamboat companies began regular service to Port Hudson, slowly replacing the keelboats that preceded them.[4]

A growing community coalesced around the rail- and riverboat-centered transportation industry, and in 1838 Louisiana formally incorporated Port Hudson as a town. The community grew steadily in population and commercial importance for the next several decades, and in 1860, thirty thousand bales of cotton, 125,000 gallons of sugar, and countless other goods flowed through the town. Port Hudson was a southern town, but like most towns on the Mississippi River, it benefited from trade networks that crossed regional boundaries. Port Hudson enjoyed strong ties to southern plantations, midwestern family farms, New England factories, and even international shipping companies. Henry Skipwith, a member of the 27th Louisiana Infantry, described the prewar merchants of Port Hudson as "skillful alchemists converting the streams of commerce which touched their wharves into golden bars."[5]

In 1860 Port Hudson was a bustling "small village" of several hundred residents. The down's demographics are unknown, but 708,002 people, including 331,726 slaves and 18,647 free blacks, lived in Louisiana. Port Hudson's population may have included a similar mix of people. Port Hudson's residents lived in fifty or so solid little houses arrayed along the town's twenty-eight streets, worshiped in the community's several churches, and grew vegetables in their backyard gardens. Most of the town's workers made a living working on the wharves, in the warehouses, railroad yards, and stores that supported a constant flow of people and merchandise through the city. Port Hudson was a place of business but also a place of entertainment where liquor flowed freely in numerous saloons and games of draw poker never stopped in the city's hotel lobbies.[6] Port Hudson was the kind of Mississippi River town Mark Twain described as "comely, clean, well built, and pleasing to the eye, and cheering to the spirit." The buzzing little town was an important center of commerce for the region, but there is little evidence that it was important enough for most Americans to notice it over the background noise of American life. Port Hudson was a prosperous riverboat town in a nation dominated by commerce along mighty rivers.

The Civil War Begins

The war remained far away from Port Hudson during that first year of bloodshed. The riverboat town left the Union with the rest of Louisiana on January 26, 1861. A few men from Port Hudson joined the Confederate army assembling a thousand miles away in Virginia, but most stayed home, seemingly content to work and read about the war in the newspapers. The opposing armies clashed at Bull Run, Virginia, on July 21, 1861, and a few men from Port Hudson, serving with the 8th Louisiana Infantry, shared in the glory of the Confederate victory, but the battle didn't end the war, and the conflict raged across the Confederacy's borders. A handful of irregular militia units formed in the region and patrolled the riverbanks around Port Hudson for signs of Union raiders.[7]

When the first few battles failed to end the Civil War, the conflict became a war of attrition. Union commanding general Winfield Scott, a Virginia-born professional soldier almost as old as the nation he was sworn to defend, unleashed the Anaconda Plan to slowly choke the Confederacy into submission. With a blockading fleet in place if not in force by the late summer of 1861, the Union navy began using their ships to capture footholds on the Confederate Atlantic coast.[8] Like the Union armies marching south, the Union fleet remained far away from Port Hudson. The war raged for a year, but Port Hudson was deep in the interior, five hundred miles away from the nearest Union city, and it looked like an unlikely location for a battle.

The War for the Mississippi

Normally, soldiers see rivers as obstacles, but the Union used its industrial and naval might to transform the Mississippi River and its tributaries into grand highways for pouring men and material from countless farms and factories south into the Confederate heartland. Opening the Mississippi River would also allow midwestern farmers, many of whom were reluctant supporters of the war, to sell their products once again on lucrative international markets through the port of New Orleans. For the rebels, the "father of the waters" was the Confederacy's most valuable transportation hub and one of the weakest links in its defensive chain. Eight Confederate states lay east of river, two were west of the river, and Louisiana precariously straddled the body of water. As long as the Confederacy retained their grasp on the river, or at least a section of it, the Confederacy could act as a single unit that shared information, soldiers, workers, and supplies across its entire two-thousand-mile width from Richmond, Virginia, to the Texan border with Mexico. If the Union captured the Mississippi River, it would tear the Confederacy in half and the Confederacy would fall as the Union destroyed each isolated section at their leisure.

The people living near Port Hudson watched the war inch ever closer to their homes in the spring of 1862. On May 1, 1862, Federal troops captured New Orleans and raised the United States flag over the city to the sounds of Yankee Doodle. The most important city in the Confederacy was in Union hands, and the war came within a hundred miles of Port Hudson. Sarah Morgan, a wealthy, twenty-year-old resident of Baton Rouge with three brothers in the Confederate military, was horrified when she heard reports that New Orleans had fallen. She wrote in her diary "there is no word in the English language that can express state in which we are." Countless, contradictory rumors circulated through the Louisiana countryside until people were in "delirium." Nobody seemed to know exactly what was happening, and Morgan concluded "we had best be prepared for anything." Eliza McHatton wrote that, when the news of New Orleans's fall came to her family's planation outside Baton Rouge, "we boasted and bragged of what we could do and what we were going to

Sarah Fowler Morgan,
A Confederate Girl's Diary, frontispiece.

do" as "nothing but war to the knife was spoken of." She referred to her friends and neighbors as behaving "like children whistling in the dark to keep their courage up."[9]

General Benjamin Butler, commanding the Federal army at New Orleans, wanted more troops than the north could provide, so he recruited white southerners to fill the ranks. Butler claimed that he filled the new Louisiana regiments with southern men who eager to serve the Union. Reality was a little more complicated than Butler admitted. The 1st Louisiana Infantry's field and staff officers were from across New England and even foreign countries, including Ireland, Denmark, Saxony, and Canada, but none listed themselves as southerners. George Smith gave up his post as a sergeant with the 13th Connecticut Infantry to become an officer in the 1st Louisiana Union Infantry because he wanted a promotion and did not foresee getting an officer's slot in his old regiment. Smith claimed that the southerners who joined the Union cause were unemployed former Confederate soldiers who joined the Union army because they had "no alternative." Howard Hunter's study of the 2nd Louisiana Union Infantry found that 61 percent of the regiment's men were born in Ireland, Germany, or France. Algernon Badger, of the 26th Massachusetts Infantry, requested permission to join a unionist cavalry unit he heard was forming, explaining that he had "a preference for that arm of the service and the active life which must ensue." Badger got his wish and became a captain in the 1st Louisiana Union Cavalry, later rising to the rank of lieutenant colonel in the regiment. Regardless of their motives, men quickly filled four Louisiana regiments of infantry and two regiments of cavalry.[10]

Flush with success on the battlefield and at the recruiting desk, Federal forces in Louisiana advanced north, inching ever closer to Port Hudson. Some Louisianans evacuated to avoid Union forces. Confederate governor Thomas Moore fled the state capitol in Baton Rouge just ahead of Union forces and set up a new Confederate government of Louisiana in Opelousas, Louisiana, about fifty miles west of Baton Rouge. Unlike Baton Rouge, which was vulnerable to Union gunboats, Opelousas was far more secure, nearly fifty miles inland. In 1936 ninety-one-year-old former slave Louis Love told an interviewer that, after the Federals captured New Orleans, her master Donaltron Cafrey, sent her and about three hundred other slaves to Texas to keep them out of reach of the "invaders." Sarah Morgan and her sisters sewed their jewelry into their clothing and prepared to flee. They then went down to the river docks where they watched workers burn endless bales of cotton and then throw the precious fiber into the water where "the cotton floated down the Mississippi in one sheet of living flame." Returning home, Morgan watched tavern owners pour out barrels of alcohol into the streets. Morgan noted that "if the Yankees are fond of strong drink, they will fare ill."[11] The destruction came just in time.

Federal ships arrived at Baton Rouge on May 7, 1862. Eliza McHatton, who lived on a plantation a few miles south of Baton Rouge, watched from her porch with her family as the once placid river was suddenly "ablaze with the grandeur of Federal gunboats." Sounds of bands playing Yankee Doodle drifted over the water, filling McHatton's soul with "bitterness unspeakable" for the arrival of "the enemy." James Palmer, commanding the USS *Iroquois*, ordered Baton Rouge mayor B. F. Bryan to surrender the undefended city. Bryan responded, "the city of Baton Rouge will not be surrendered voluntarily to any power on earth." Sarah Morgan considered Bryan's defiant response "worthy of a Southerner." Palmer's next official communication noted that his men had taken possession of the town and hoisted the United States flag over the arsenal in the city. Palmer noted that he would not leave any men ashore to protect the flag or enforce Federal control over the town; however, he did state, "I warn you Mr. Mayor that this flag must remain unmolested." Palmer urged Bryan to leave the flag alone since "the rash act of some individual may cause your city to pay a bitter penalty."[12] Having raised the flag and warned the townsfolk, Union forces resumed their voyage north. The capture of Baton Rouge left Port Hudson as the southernmost Confederate stronghold on the Mississippi River. This made the quiet riverboat town a vital piece of real estate for Confederate forces trying to maintain their hold on the region's most important inland waterway. The Federal fleet steamed past Port Hudson on their voyage to Vicksburg, Mississippi without incident, although they did not attempt to land there or take possession of the Port Hudson's docks. Considering Port Hudson's lowly status at this early stage in the campaign, the Union navy may have considered Port Hudson unworthy of a landing party's time.

The noose tightened around Port Hudson and danger threatened from multiple directions. While the Federal forces on the Louisiana Gulf Coast moved north, Union forces in the upper Mississippi River valley fought their way south. Union forces captured New Madrid, Missouri, on March 14. Confederate defenders surrendered Island Number 10, a short distance from New Madrid, on April 8. Confederate forces evacuated Fort Pillow, about fifty miles north of Memphis, Tennessee, on June 5. Memphis, Tennessee, surrendered to Union forces on June 6.[13]

By mid-June 1862 the Confederacy was barely hanging on to a tiny stretch of less than a hundred miles of the two-thousand-mile-long Mississippi River, from Vicksburg in the north to Port Hudson in the south. It was not much, but it might be enough, if the Confederacy could hold it. To reinforce their hold on the river, the Confederacy reorganized their leadership in the area. On July 2, 1862, General Earl Van Dorn took command of the Confederate defenses around Vicksburg.[14] Van Dorn built up the fortifications at Vicksburg, and under his leadership the garrison successfully thwarted initial Union efforts to run up the Mississippi River and capture the Mississippi stronghold. After failing to capture Vicksburg, Union forces retreated. Their plan was to reequip and reinforce at Baton Rouge in preparation for a later offensive. On May 29, 1862, General Thomas Williams led about five thousand Federal troops into Baton Rouge. Most of Baton Rouge's residents had fled, but many of those who remained were defiant. Sarah Morgan carried a knife and a pistol when she left the house and promised herself that she would test her mettle on "the first one who says an insolent word to me." Morgan still considered herself a good Christian who pledged to repent in "sackcloth and ashes" after committing murder.[15]

Few men remained near Baton Rouge to help Morgan kill men in blue. On July 13, 1862, Confederate provosts A. G. Carter and John Miller, who were near Baton Rouge, informed the Confederate high command that Union troops had fanned out into the countryside surrounding the city. Union authorities ordered civilians to take an oath of allegiance to the Federal government. Anyone who resisted the demand faced the possibility of arrest and confiscation of their property. Because six hundred of the men from the area were serving with the Confederate military and "the blood of her sons has stained nearly every battlefield," almost no Confederate troops were present to defend civilians. The Confederate provosts urged the Confederate army to send troops, protect the countryside, and retake Baton Rouge.[16]

The Battle of Baton Rouge

After stabilizing the situation along the Mississippi, the aggressive Van Dorn decided that the best defense was a strong offense. Van Dorn told Jefferson Davis, "I want Baton Rouge and Port Hudson." Van Dorn requested artillerymen and heavy cannons to secure the Confederacy's hold on Port Hudson and mobile troops to recapture Baton Rouge and then New Orleans. He wanted to strike quickly, while the Federals along the Mississippi River were suffering from heat and disease.[17] Like most of Van Dorn's plans, it was ambitious. The Confederate government sent Van Dorn reinforcements and endorsed his planned offensive.

General and former vice president John Breckenridge moved south toward Baton Rouge on July 27 with 4,000 Confederate troops. It was a small force, but they were the only men Van Dorn could spare. Roughly 5,000 Union soldiers under the command of General Thomas Williams

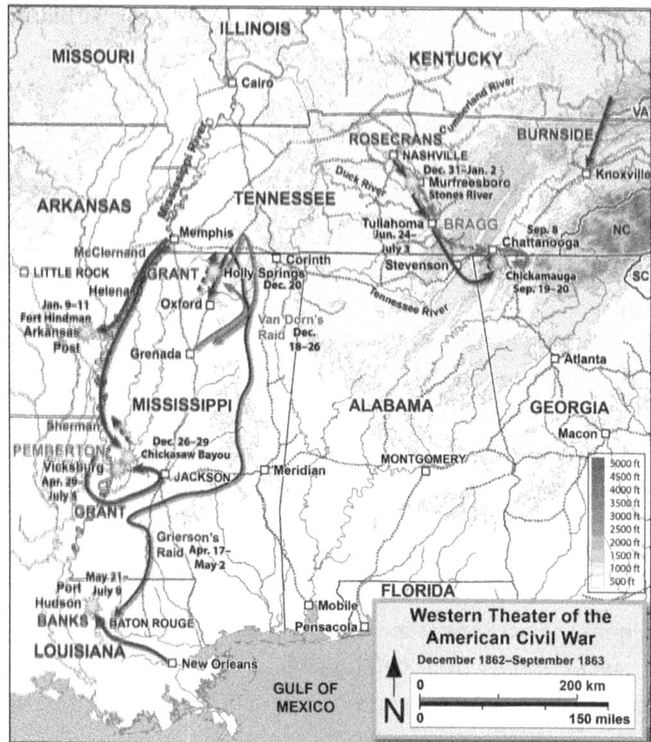

Map 1. Western Theater, December 1862–September 1863.
Hal Jespersen.

garrisoned Baton Rouge with the help of ten warships. Van Dorn realized that the Federals enjoyed an advantage in both men and firepower, but he thought that a rapid attack might catch the Union defenders by surprise and knock them out of the fight before they could bring their superior manpower into action. Breckenridge was willing to give it a shot, but disease proved more damaging than enemy action, and only a few days later, the Confederate army advancing on Baton Rouge had only 3,400 men.[18]

Despite the army's misery, Breckenridge still thought an attack might work, if the fearsome ironclad CSS *Arkansas* could sail south to brush aside Union gunboats and bombard Federal positions onshore. Van Dorn agreed and ordered the *Arkansas* to attack Baton Rouge, but the *Arkansas*'s commander, Isaac Brown, protested Van Dorn's orders from his sick bed, pointing out that the *Arkansas* was undergoing repairs. According to

Charles Read, a twenty-one-year-old sailor on the *Arkansas*, the conflict between Brown and the army's leadership put the *Arkansas*'s crew in a tough spot. The sailors did not want to go into battle in a damaged ship or without their commander. However, they also felt that "no Confederate could refuse to comply with the wish of one so universally loved and respected as General Breckenridge." The *Arkansas* sailed south toward Baton Rouge at 2:00 a.m. under the command of Lieutenant Henry Stevens, who left his sick commander behind.[19]

According to James Harmon of the 35th Alabama Infantry, the rebels who marched south endured "a great deal of hardships." They respected Breckenridge and considered him a "noble and gallant officer" but their respect for the general did little to improve their morale. The men's clothing and shoes "were worn out." Rain fell in torrents and drenched the men to their skin. Harmon suffered horribly from a toothache, but he was grateful for the surgeon who pulled the tooth shortly after they made camp for the evening.[20]

While Confederate soldiers marched overland, the *Arkansas* sailed down the Mississippi River toward Baton Rouge. Initially, the ship made good progress, cruising along at fifteen miles per hour. From his post on the *Arkansas*'s deck, Charles Read observed destroyed homes and farms along the riverbank. People along the shore cheered the *Arkansas*. Everything was going great, until it wasn't. The boat's engines suddenly gave out, and Read sat by helplessly while the Confederate engineers tried to restart them. Each engineer had a different idea of how to repair the engines. Read believed that the engineers were all "good men" who were doing their best, but he concluded that they were also "incompetent." Read wished the *Arkansas* had better engineers, but they were the best men available.[21]

The Confederate army arrived on the outskirts of Baton Rouge at daybreak on August 5. The lumbering *Arkansas* was nowhere to be seen, and illness left the rebels with only about 2,600 effective troops, but Breckenridge ordered the assault anyway. They had not come all this way to retreat without testing the Union defenses. Confederate camps echoed with the sounds of drums and trumpets that called the men into action. Confederate soldiers formed lines at the double quick and advanced through the sugar cane fields on the edge of town. William Dixon of the 4th Louisiana Infantry wrote in his diary, "Oh! What feelings of anxiety were ours, words would fail to describe." The men shouldered rifles and "hastened to the scene of carnage."[22]

The crew of the *Arkansas* heard the opening salvos and pushed their newly repaired engines to the breaking point in hopes of helping with the attack. Initially, the attack looked promising, pushing the Federals to the outskirts of town. Confederate morale soared as Union soldiers retreated. The Federal commander, Thomas Williams, was shot in the chest and fell dead while leading his men. As Williams died, Colonel Thomas Cahill took command of the Union defenders. He ordered his men to withdraw to defensive lines around the state penitentiary. Union gunboats in the river helped cover the retreat, pounding the Confederate attackers with their artillery. According to James Harmon of the 35th Alabama Infantry, the Federals "made an obstinate stand" as the fire from the gunboats caused "havoc in the ranks" of the Confederate attackers. William Dixon of the 4th Louisiana Infantry wrote in his diary, "we were in the fiery path of Mars," a reference to the Roman god of war.[23]

At about this time, the *Arkansas* finally came within sight of the battle and prepared to ram the USS *Essex*. Just before getting into the fight, the *Arkansas's* engine quit again. Lieutenant Read ordered his gunners to open fire with every gun they could aim at the *Essex*, and the boat's engineers tried and failed to get the boat moving again. Stuck between the Federal fleet on their flank and entrenched Union attackers to their front, Confederate soldiers faltered.[24]

Breckenridge conceded defeat and ordered his men to withdraw. The Confederate attack failed, and the survivors in gray retreated north in search of defensive positions. As the Confederate army withdrew, Lieutenant Stevens ordered the crew of the *Arkansas* to gather their small arms, prepare to evacuate, and destroy their immobilized boat rather than allow her to fall into Federal hands. The Union suffered roughly eighty dead and three hundred wounded or missing at Baton Rouge. The Confederates suffered roughly the same number of dead and wounded, but slightly more were taken prisoner. Most notably, the Confederate dead included A. H. Todd, the half-brother of Union first lady Mary Todd Lincoln. William Stubblefield of the 7th Kentucky Mounted Infantry wrote in his diary that "all was accomplished that can be done where the gun boats are." The Confederates had suffered a repulse, and the Union retained control of the ground. However, according to Stubblefield, some of the

Ironclad USS *Essex* at Baton Rouge, Louisiana. Library of Congress.

retreating men in gray believed that they could "claim the victory" because they fought with "such character." Stubblefield wrote that the Confederates had much smaller losses than their opponents and had only retreated because "it was not possible for infantry to fight gun boats."[25] Stubblefield's comment highlighted a common theme in the accounts of Confederate soldiers in which victory was as much a matter of character or honor as strategic or tactical success.

Confederates and Federals Regroup in Louisiana

As the Confederates under Breckenridge moved north toward Port Hudson, the Confederate militia along the Mississippi struck at the Federals. On August 14, 1862, the USS *Sumter*, which had been a Confederate gunboat until the Federals captured it in April, traveled north to scout Confederate positions along the river and quickly ran aground at Bayou Sara, about twelve miles north of Port Hudson. The Confederate militia gathered their shotguns and boarded the disabled *Sumter* without firing a shot. The crew had escaped on a Federal steamer without bothering to remove or damage most of the *Sumter*'s precious cargo. They also left at least five escaped slaves behind. The Confederate militiamen knew that they could not hope to hold the *Sumter* against the inevitable Federal counterattack, so with barely a pause to celebrate, they looted the ship of muskets, accouterments, pistols, swords, shoes, clothing, signal flags, medical supplies, and most importantly two heavy cannons. Both cannons and some of the other goods captured from the *Sumter* eventually made their way to Port Hudson.[26]

The normally well-equipped Union army suffered from supply shortages in Louisiana and could little afford the loss of supplies to their adversaries. In a letter dated August 14, 1862, General Butler complained that he had not received any .54 ammunition and as a result "our .54 rifles are useless."[27] It is unclear how many Union soldiers might have suffered from empty cartridge boxes. The Union produced far more military goods than the Confederacy, and Union soldiers were typically far better supplied than their Confederate counterparts, but Federals in Louisiana suffered from unique obstacles. Union forces in Louisiana were at the end of supply lines that were both long and vulnerable to Confederate raiders. Tenuous supply lines made life difficult for Union forces in Louisiana throughout the campaign.

As the Confederate militia returned to shore, a Union gunboat and a transport approached Bayou Sara. Union troops made landfall and began to march inland with the aid of a local resident described in a Mississippi newspaper as a man "who had proven himself a traitor." When the Union troops and their local guide were about halfway up a steep incline, Confederate militia greeted them with blasts of buckshot from their shotguns. Several Federals fell to the ground, and the rest fled down the hill toward the relative safety of their boats. Confederate militiamen chased their adversaries until Union sailors opened fire on the pursuing militia. A handful of militiamen with rifles took cover and harassed the Federal sailors while the rest of the militia retreated out of range of the Union artillery. A local journalist was "pleased to learn that the traitor" who had helped the Federals was badly wounded in the gunfight.[28]

Confederate soldiers retreating toward Port Hudson from Baton Rouge suffered in the rain. According to Kentuckian William Stubblefield, men lit cook fires but had few cooking utensils, having lost most of their baggage on the retreat from Baton Rouge several days before. Soldiers shared the few utensils they had, taking turns with the precious cookware to prepare their food. The men had no tents to protect them from the "very hard and long" rain. Some of the Kentuckians constructed improvised shelters of palmetto leaves. Others made both beds and shelters from the abundant leaves. Most men refused to bother with leaves, sleeping on wet ground underneath a sky that poured rain on them all night long.[29]

The Federal government sent reinforcements to Louisiana. William Aldis joined the 131st New York Infantry on August 11, 1862. Born in England, the thirty-two-year-old New Yorker was a husband and father to five young children. He stood five feet seven inches tall, his eyes were blue, his hair was brown, and his complexion was light. On his enlistment record, he listed his occupation as painter. However, in at least one letter, he referred to himself as a policeman before the war. In a letter to his wife on October 29, 1862, Aldis reminded her that, while she was clearly unhappy with his decision to enlist, he felt that he had little choice. The Union draft did not take effect until several months later, but in 1862 New York State passed legislation authorizing a draft to fill state regiments. Aldis wrote his wife that police officers like himself were not exempt. Even if he avoided the draft, Aldis believed that business was bad in New York and that he was unlikely to find a good job if he left the police force. In a section of the letter marked "private," he asked, "you did not do what you threatened, did you?" He did not specify what the threat might have been, but he urged her to "take care what you are about, you have a young family that demands your care." Clearly, Aldis was a man dealing with difficult personal and economic problems. William Aldis was probably not unique. James McPherson argued that many men who enlisted in 1862 were motivated, at least in part, by a desire to avoid the draft.[30]

Desperate for reinforcements and facing an increasingly aggressive Confederate presence in Louisiana, Butler redoubled his recruiting efforts. General Hallock refused to send the numbers of northern units that Butler insisted he needed. Butler continued to recruit southerners, but the flow of white southern men could not fulfill Butler's need for troops. In desperation, on August 14, 1862, Butler informed Secretary of War Stanton, "I shall call on Africa to intervene, and I do not think I shall call in vain." Butler made an important decision. While African Americans had served unofficially since the first days of the war, the Union government did not officially authorize the recruitment of black men until the Emancipation Proclamation became active on January 1, 1863.[31]

Entered according to Act of Congress in the year 186[illegible], by Frank Leslie, in the Clerk's Office of the District Court for the Southern District of New York.

No. 385—Vol. XV.] NEW YORK, MARCH 7, 1863. [Price 8 Cents.

SCENES IN LOUISIANA.

Our Artist has sent us some sketches which illustrate, in a striking degree, the novel phases of life, both military and civil, which the present struggle is evolving. The fact of black regiments being actively employed is not a novelty, since they have been for some time part of the British military system, which, with its usual common sense, avails itself of every aid in the pursuit of its objects. Our Artist says that among the cypress swamps of Louisiana negro soldiers are invaluable, and accompanies his sketch of the pickets of the First Louisiana native troops, guarding the New Orleans, Opelousas and Great Western Railroad, with some remarks which we quote:

"In this swamp in the wilderness the 'nigger soldiers' are eminently useful. The melancholy solitude, with the spectral cypress trees, which seem to stand in silent despair, like nature's sentinels waving in the air wreaths of gray funeral moss, to warn all human beings of the latent pestilence around, though unendurable to our soldiers of the North, seems an elysium to these sable soldiers, for the swampy forest has no horrors to them. Impervious to miasma, they see only the home of the coon, the possum and the copperhead, so that with 'de gun dat Massa Sam gib 'em,' they have around them all the essential elements of coloured happiness, except ladies' society."

The Old Slave Laws.

In strange forgetfulness of the use to which the coloured race may be put, the new *régime* has empowered Provost Marshal Col. French to put in force the old Slave Laws of Louisiana. Our Artist says: "The first result of the Emancipation Proclamation has been attended with a paradoxical effect, namely, a revival of the old Slave Laws of Louisiana. On the evening in question, all the negroes found in the streets after nine o'clock wit

Pickets of the First Louisiana "Native Guard" guarding the New Orleans, Opelousas and Great Western Railroad, published in *Frank Leslie's Illustrated Newspaper*. Library of Congress.

Butler was an ineffective general but a clever lawyer and an astute politician. Butler informed Secretary of War Edwin Stanton that he would recruit men who had served in the Louisiana Native Guards. The Native Guards were an unusual unit composed of free men of African and mixed-race ancestry who volunteered for service with the Confederacy before the fall of New Orleans. Despite their willingness to service to the Confederacy, Butler believed that they would be loyal Union men. Butler argued that, since the Native Guards were all free men accepted into service by the state of Louisiana and the Confederacy, their enlistments would not violate any Union obligations to respect slave property. Commanding general Halleck agreed with Butler's argument and authorized use of the Native Guards.[32]

In the Native Guards, the officers as well as the enlisted men were black. Most Native Guard officers were members of New Orleans free black and mixed-race population, which enjoyed freedom, status, and wealth that was highly unusual in the antebellum South. Butler had no objection to using black men as officers in black military units, but many other Union officers, even those willing to use black men as enlisted soldiers and laborers, believed that black men were incapable of serving as officers. Resistance against black soldiers, and particularly black officers, simmered as Butler accepted the Native Guards into Federal service.[33]

Some Union soldiers expressed mixed emotions about recruiting black men into the ranks. Henry Cross, with the 48th Massachusetts Infantry, wrote home that he considered "the negro" to be inferior to "the white" and adamantly opposed "social intermingling of the two races." However, he also considered blacks human and therefore capable of service to the Union. James Peck of the 173rd New York believed "it looks comical to see all the black faces in a line." William Aldis told his wife that the colonel of the 3rd Native Guards offered Aldis an officer's commission in the regiment. Aldis referred to the unit as a "nigger regt [*sic*]" but explained that he was unlikely to be promoted within his own regiment anytime soon, that the officers in the 3rd Native Guards were all white, and that an officer's pay would allow him to send more money home to the family. Aldis hoped to transfer into the Native Guards soon, but he needed his current commanding officer to approve the transfer application, and Aldis worried that his commander might be reluctant to let him leave. It does not appear that Aldis ever transferred to out of the 131st New York Infantry or became an officer, possibly because his commander rejected Aldis's request for a transfer. Aldis's letter supports William Dobak's argument that "opportunists would outnumber abolitionists in the officer corps" of black units. Dobak quoted an Illinois soldier who was amused "to see men who have bitterly denounced the policy of arming Negroes . . . now bending every energy to get a commission."[34]

Some Union soldiers were unhappy with the recruitment of African Americans. Henry T. Aiken was a twenty-six-year-old carpenter from Charlestown, Massachusetts, who joined the 4th Independent Battery of Massachusetts Light Artillery on August 30, 1862. Aiken told his parents that "three companys [*sic*] of niggers [*sic*] soldiers" were camped near his unit. He criticized their sloppy appearance, noting that many wore feathers in their hats and others tucked their trousers into their boots. Aiken believed that "the government are bringing the white soldier down to the level of the black slave." He noted with apparent disdain, "they wear the same uniform, and we must fight side by side." William Park, serving on the Union gunboat *Essex,* believed that the men might "put up with the nigger regiments as a necessary evil, they certainly have a strong dislike to them and the white officers which belong to them."[35]

Union soldiers also disagreed about the draft, the other method the Union used to bolster the army's ranks. William Aldis disliked the draft and volunteered in large measure to avoid getting drafted. Solon Perkins, a globetrotting merchant turned Union cavalry lieutenant, supported the draft and wanted it "strictly enforced" so that every able-bodied man in the country would be forced to "fight or emigrate," with no exemptions and no opportunity for paying a fine instead of serving. Perkins was so disgusted with America's "weak government" that he supported a new national government founded on "military despotism." He knew that many men feared a strong despot, but he believed that a dictatorship was preferable to the "weakness" that he believed had led to war.[36]

On the afternoon of August 15, 1862, General Breckenridge took steps to defend Port Hudson from the growing Union army in Louisiana. Breckenridge ordered Brigadier General Daniel Ruggles, a Massachusetts-born professional soldier married to a Virginia woman, to lead the 3rd and 4th Kentucky Infantry, a section of Cobb's Kentucky Battery, and the 4th Louisiana Infantry to Port Hudson. Ruggles was an experienced battlefield commander who had performed well at Shiloh and Baton Rouge. He was best known for assembling the largest collection of field artillery in the history of the western hemisphere to punch through Union positions at Shiloh, but he was not an engineer, so Breckenridge sent Captain James Nocquet, an experienced engineer who claimed that he served with the French army in Algeria, to supervise construction of fortifications at Port Hudson.[37]

It is unclear exactly how many men Breckenridge planned to station at Port Hudson, but he ordered the commissary department to provide daily rations for four thousand men, which suggests a garrison of roughly that number. Breckenridge directed Ruggles and his troops to build fortifications at Port Hudson as quickly as possible, to improve Port Hudson's connections by railroad to the interior of Louisiana, and to throw out pickets toward Baton Rouge. Breckenridge felt confident that the men he sent to Port Hudson would soon transform it into a nearly impregnable bastion.[38] The offensive had failed, but a defensive approach might be more successful. Although they did not know it, the Confederates preparing to march toward Port Hudson were not the only men with a sudden interest in the previously ignored riverboat town.

—2—

We Are Obliged to Stay and Fight

THE CONFEDERACY PREPARES TO DEFEND PORT HUDSON

Our brigade is at work on the breastworks. We are still pushing them on as fast as we can. We are a little more than half done [with] them, when they are finished they will be the best I have ever see. I recon our lead officer thinks we have run often enough, and they will fix this place so the Yankees can't get to us. . . . In the present state of affairs we are obliged to stay and fight. If I fall, I fall fighting for you and for the South which I feel is nothing more than my duty and if I survive this war, and we succeed in driving back the invading hosts, and return home to you, then I shall think I am fully paid for all the privations we are now under.[1]

—SAMUEL THOMPSON, 23rd Arkansas Infantry

"I am now in the hospital recovering from a fit of sickness. I came here the twenty third of last month but ere this reaches you I expect to be in Fort Pike at the mouth of Lake Ponchatrain [*sic*] to spend the winter our battery has been split up and part of it has been turned over to the regulars so that I have had nothing to do or in fact I haven't been able to do much. Our camp was in a very bad place. There are quite a number of our men sick."[2]

—HENRY AIKEN, 4th Independent Battery,
Massachusetts Light Artillery

THE RIVER THAT BROUGHT LIFE to Port Hudson for decades brought death in the predawn darkness of August 15, 1862. Master Spencer Kellogg Brown of the USS *Essex* had heard that Confederates were using a ferryboat to transport goods across the river to Port Hudson. Brown approached Captain Porter, his commanding officer, and asked for permission to lead a raid and destroy the ferry boat. Porter hesitated. Hit and run raids in enemy territory were tricky affairs, even for professionals. Porter and most of his crew were sailors, not commandoes. Porter was uncomfortable with unconventional warfare, but Brown felt at home in the shadows.[3]

Brown was born to a prominent New York family in 1842. The family moved to Kansas in 1854 to support abolitionist forces, and Brown came of age during the guerrilla warfare of Bloody Kansas. In 1856 proslavery forces captured the fourteen-year-old Spencer Brown because they erroneously thought he was the son of infamous abolitionist John Brown. Eventually his captors figured out that Spencer Brown was unrelated to John Brown and let him go. Perhaps to prevent future kidnappings, Spencer Brown began going by the name Spencer Kellogg, although his legal name remained unchanged. In spite of his captivity, or perhaps because of it, Brown did not hide from conflict with proslavery forces. When the Civil War broke out, he began his military career with the Union army in Kentucky and later transferred to Missouri. In early 1862 Brown joined the Union navy. Brown volunteered for special service, and the navy detached him for duty as a spy along the Mississippi River. He conducted several successful espionage operations while pretending to be a day laborer, and he briefly joined the Confederate army to scout fortifications along the river. After almost getting captured, he returned to the Union navy and became a junior officer on the USS *Essex*.[4] In spite of Porter's reservations about unconventional warfare, he authorized Brown's raid.

Spencer Brown led a group of forty Union sailors in rowboats from the USS *Essex* along the muddy bank, looking for the ferryboat. Initially, the operation went well. Brown and his sailors sank the ferry boat without firing a shot. The Federals could have returned to the *Essex* to receive accolades for a job well done, but Brown decided to push his luck and look for additional targets of opportunity. As Brown and his men slipped up the shore, two civilians on the riverbank called out to Brown and his sailors, claiming to be Union men and encouraging the sailors to come ashore. Brown probably wasn't surprised to see what appeared to be friendly faces. Union supporters were common in the South, even in Louisiana, and southern loyalists often helped Union troops. As Brown and four of his men stepped onto the shore, Confederate militiamen emerged from the bushes and ordered the Federals to surrender. The men who had claimed to be Unionists were Confederate supporters, luring Federal sailors into an ambush. Caught by surprise and hopelessly outgunned, Brown and his men surrendered without a fight.[5]

Confederate authorities accused Brown and his men of being spies. They later dropped the charges against the enlisted men and exchanged them. However, they retained Brown because he was the commander of the expedition and because he had briefly enlisted in the Confederate army to spy on the rebels earlier in the war. Confederate authorities put Brown on trial and found him guilty of desertion and espionage. As he walked to the gallows, Brown reportedly smiled and said, "my death is dark, but beyond all is light and bright."[6]

When Commodore Porter learned of Brown's execution, he asked General Butler to retaliate by executing Confederate prisoners. Despite of his reputation for harshness, Butler refused, explaining, "I do not believe the report made by Commodore Porter." Butler made it clear that he would not execute Confederate prisoners, even if Porter's report proved accurate, because the whole situation demonstrated the dangers of engaging in unconventional warfare.[7] As Confederate militiamen took Brown and his men into captivity, Confederate soldiers marched toward Port Hudson.

The sun rose over Port Hudson on August 15, 1862, revealing a long line of men meandering into the city up the Baton Rouge Road. The city's residents flocked to the roadside to see the visitors. The men were members of the 4th Louisiana Infantry, a unit formed in 1861 and tested in battle at Shiloh and Baton Rouge. Observers noticed that the Louisianans marched with the easy gait of men who had walked endless miles and carried little except for rifles and bedrolls. When the townsfolk realized that these were Confederate soldiers sent to protect Port Hudson, they cheered. They failed to realize what that long, dirty, gray line brought to their door. An officer with the 4th Louisiana paused in a cornfield and asked a resident, "Whose place is this?" The man replied, "It is Slaughter's field." The officer glanced over the ground with a veteran's eye for terrain and replied, "It will be the field of slaughter yet or I am very much mistaken."[8] The revolution had come, and Port Hudson would not be spared.

William Dixon of the 4th Louisiana Infantry reported in his diary that, after the troops arrived in Port Hudson, "coffee was issued to us that evening by counting the grains, 13 grains to each."[9] A grain is equivalent to roughly .065 grams, which means that each soldier received roughly

.845 grams, or a little less than one gram, of coffee. A typical, small cup of coffee is about ten grams of coffee. This means that after a long day of marching, the Louisianans' only luxury was a small cup of watery coffee.

The officers and crew of the CSS *Arkansas* rendezvoused in Jackson, Mississippi, where they reunited with their recuperated commander, Captain Brown. Other members of the crew who had suffered from wounds or an illness also rejoined their comrades until the unit was four hundred strong. After a brief period of recuperation, the boatless sailors made their way to Port Hudson. General Ruggles ordered the sailors to man a battery of four rifled 24-pound guns and a single 42-pound smoothbore as soon as the engineers could build emplacements for the heavy artillery.[10]

A garrison was beginning to arrive in Port Hudson, but it would take more than men to defend the town. Port Hudson provided an excellent natural foundation for defenses. Now men would transform that foundation into a fortress. Captain James Nocquet considered three very different fortification plans. Each option had advantages and disadvantages.

The Confederates could have built a conventional a fort on the river in the style of the famous French military engineer Sebastien Vauban. This approach might have been particularly appealing to the French Nocquet. Along the riverside, artillery emplacements would follow the line of the riverbank to provide maximum firepower against any ships that got within range. The fort's walls facing the overland approaches to Port Hudson would loop around the garrison in a semicircular salient of sharp angles that would catch overland attackers in a deadly crossfire. Because the fort would be small and entirely self-contained, Confederate defenders could hold it with a small garrison. However, because it was small, it would also allow attackers to pummel the entire fort from multiple, overlapping fields of fire, from both ship and shore batteries. Traditionally, engineers constructed Vauban-style forts with reinforced masonry casemates. Unfortunately for Nocquet, the Confederacy had few sources of masonry production, and Port Hudson was isolated far from those few sources. Perhaps the most important reason not to build Vauban-style fort was that rifled artillery had made masonry forts largely obsolete by the fall of 1862. On April 10–11, 1862, Union forces demolished Fort Pulaski, a masonry fort guarding Savanah, Georgia, in a horrific, thirty-hour bombardment by heavy artillery.[11] There was little reason to think that a masonry fort at

Port Hudson would hold up any better. Masonry was strong, but by 1862 it could not withstand rifled artillery.

Alternatively, the Confederates could dig a long and irregularly shaped ditch, backed by a parapet. After engineers mapped out a line shaped to provide converging fields of defensive fire, workers with simple hand tools would dig a ditch. They would pile the dirt they removed into a parapet behind the ditch. Workers could reinforce the dirt with local timber and stone. This was by far the simplest option. It would provide defenders with a large and continuous line of defense made from local materials.[12] The longer lines would make it more difficult for Union gunners to develop overlapping fields of fire, and this would ease the pressure on the garrison and hopefully prevent fortifications from getting hit from multiple angles. Because the fortifications would consist of local materials, engineers could repair damage to a ditch and parapet far easier than to a masonry fort.

Finally, the rebels could build a string of detached earth and timber fortifications around Port Hudson. Each position would consist of a V-shaped lunette with a point facing toward the anticipated enemy advance and an open rear facing Port Hudson. Defenders would leave a gap of several hundred yards to the right and left of each work. There was an obvious danger in leaving open areas between positions. Attackers might exploit the gaps to circumvent defensive positions and attack their openings to the rear or bypass them entirely. Therefore, the defenders would maintain a large reserve force to counterattack any Federals that slipped through. The detached lunette system's need for this reserve force would require a much larger garrison than the fort or ditch and parapet plans, both of which relied almost entirely on static defenders. The lunette system's greater manpower needs were a disadvantage for the often-outnumbered Confederate army. However, because of the gaps between each position, a line of lunettes could cover more ground than a fort or a ditch system, making it more difficult for attackers to concentrate their fire. Detached works would also allow Confederate engineers to take advantage of the existing terrain, since it would not require them to fortify every inch of the defensive perimeter. Engineers could build lunettes on the best ground for construction and leave gaps in areas with ravines or bayous that would be difficult to cross.[13]

After laying out their options, the Confederate leadership made a momentous decision. It is not entirely clear who made the final decision or how it was made. Lieutenant Howard Wright of the 30th Louisiana Infantry stated only, "the plan of detached works was the one decided upon." The final decision was General Ruggles's prerogative as the ranking officer, although he probably relied on Nocquet's advice. A Vauban-style masonry fort was impractical. There was little stone near Port Hudson, no realistic way to import much more, and it was unclear if even the strongest masonry works could withstand rifled artillery. Therefore, the only real choice was between a ditch and parapet line or a series of detached lunettes. If the Federals attacked with a heavy siege train, a parapet and ditch would offer a superior defense. The continuous line would allow defenders to quickly move under cover from one threatened sector to another without leaving any gaps that attackers could exploit. Work crews could also move under cover to repair damage caused by heavy artillery. However, a detached lunette system would be far better if the attackers came without heavy artillery and instead planned to capture Port Hudson with infantry assaults. If the attackers punched through the ditch at a single point, they could get in the Confederate rear and might bring the whole position down. However, a single puncture would be a minor setback for defenders secure within a system of semi-independent detached lunettes. Defenders could launch unpredictable counterattacks from their detached works to retake captured lunettes, strike unwary Federals in the flanks, and keep the attackers off balance. This system might have been less effective on open ground with good visibility, but in the tangled undergrowth and ravines near Port Hudson, Confederates in concealed fortifications would enjoy the twin benefits of geography and engineering. The Confederates selected a lunette system because they believed that the Union forces would try to capture Port Hudson with infantry assaults.[14]

Construction began immediately. Confederate engineers outlined the first lunette on the Baton Rouge Road, roughly four miles south of Port Hudson. They may have focused on this location first since the road was the most obvious avenue of attack for Federals who had just repelled a Confederate counterattack on Baton Rouge. The engineers next planned a broadly semicircular line of lunettes that would loop north toward the mouth of Big Sandy Creek on the Mississippi River, just north of Port Hudson. Other positions would face the Mississippi River to defend against Union gunboats and possible amphibious assaults. The proposed line facing landward would be about eight miles long. Recalling the standard

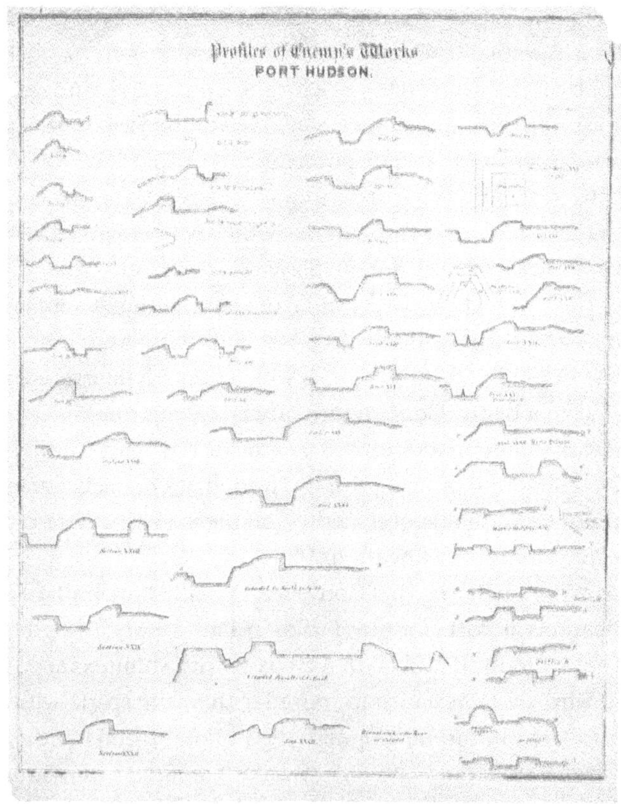

Side profiles of Confederate defensive works
at Port Hudson, image produced by engineers,
New York Public Library.

military doctrine of the time, the Confederate officers at Port Hudson calculated that their defensive plan would require a 35,000-man garrison. Roughly 28,000 of those defenders would take positions in the lunettes, while another 7,000 men remained in reserve, prepared to counterattack. The defenders would also need at least seventy pieces of artillery. It is unclear if Confederate officers at Port Hudson expected to have 35,000 men and seventy cannons. If they did, it was an optimistic hope in a region where the Confederacy mustered only 3,000 men to defend New Orleans and barely 2,600 effective troops for the counterattack on Baton Rouge just a few days before.[15]

According to Howard Wright, "a small force of negroes" did most of the work on the fortifications. Most of these men were probably slaves from area plantations forced to work for the Confederate military under a policy known as slave impressment, which was authorized by the Confederate congress and by several state governments. A spiderweb of conflicting and evolving regulations led to conflicts between slave owners, military officers, state leaders, and Confederate officials to create chaos that limited the value of slave impressment. Slave overseers were generally exempt from both the Confederate draft and from labor impressment laws. Some slave owners and the overseers who worked for them were not inclined to support the Confederate government, which they felt interfered with their ability to make a living. Confederate officials along the Mississippi River struggled with planters who refused to provide slaves for Confederate service, and Confederate official John C. Humphries publicly lamented that he "could not find a single overseer to volunteer to supervise the work of slaves on Port Hudson fortifications."[16]

Howard Wright believed that Confederacy could have built much stronger fortifications at Port Hudson if soldiers had pitched in right away, but "a rifle is much more popular than a spade with volunteers." Wright did not reveal why the rifle was more popular than the spade with the Port Hudson garrison, but in his popular 1854 book Virginia author George Fitzhugh argued that even non slave owners benefited from slavery in part because "few of our whites ever work as day laborers . . . or in other menial capacities." Most Confederate soldiers were farmers in civilian life and almost all were probably accustomed to hard work, but they may have felt that building fortifications was beneath them. It is unclear if Confederate soldiers at Port Hudson explicitly refused to perform manual labor alongside slaves or if their officers understood how their men felt and decided not to press the issue. What is clear is that the slaves worked constantly and built fortified batteries on the bluff along the Mississippi River, lunettes facing the landward approaches to Port Hudson, and bunkers in the town.[17]

On August 18, 1862, General Breckenridge visited Port Hudson. He found that work crews under Nocquet's leadership were making good progress fortifying the town and that some of the positions were ready to receive artillery. The cannons had not arrived yet, but Van Dorn assured Breckenridge that they were on the way. General Richard Taylor, commanding troops at Opelousas, Louisiana, about sixty miles west of Port Hudson, across the Mississippi River, promised to send any siege guns he could find to Port Hudson.[18]

General Breckenridge and many of the men he led near Port Hudson did not stay in Louisiana long. In August 1862 Confederate forces launched a counteroffensive in Kentucky. Breckenridge believed he would be more useful rallying Confederate support in his home state than commanding troops in Louisiana. Breckenridge requested a transfer to Kentucky. Van Dorn initially resisted, noting that he needed every man he could gather to help him hold what was left of the Mississippi River in Confederate hands. Van Dorn only conceded after Secretary of War George Randolph intervened. Breckenridge marched toward Kentucky with 2,500 troops. Ruggles remained behind with 1,500 men at Port Hudson.[19]

In mid-August 1862 the Federals in Louisiana suffered serious setbacks. Confederate forces harassed Union troops along the Mississippi River. Guerillas from Texas and Indian Territory picked off Union soldiers and sailors with long-range rifle fire, cavalry raids, and occasional artillery bombardments from the west bank of the river. As was so often the case during the Civil War, disease proved more deadly than combat. Yellow fever broke out among the Federals in Baton Rouge. Civilians loyal to the Confederacy informed Port Hudson's garrison that Union troops were sick, tired, and demoralized. General Ruggles sent scouts south to test Federal strength near Baton Rouge. On August 20 a Confederate reconnaissance force drove in Federal pickets north of Baton Rouge, capturing twenty head of cattle and forty horses in the process. Federal gunboats "shelled furiously" as the rebels retreated with their captured livestock.[20]

In response to the deteriorating situation in Louisiana, Butler evacuated Baton Rouge on August 21 and pulled his forces back toward New Orleans. The withdrawal forced escaped slaves to choose between evacuating with their blue-clad liberators or remaining near Baton Rouge and taking their chances with the Confederate army. Almost every former slave evacuated. The Federals provided escaped slaves with passage on the large steamer *Diana*.[21]

On August 21 Ruggles heard a rumor that the Federals were evacuating Baton Rouge and sprang into action. Ruggles ordered Brigadier General Jeff Thompson, stationed at Ponchatoula, Louisiana, west of Baton Rouge, to repair the Manchac Bridge southwest of Baton Rouge, rebuild the railroad tracks in the area, and push scouts toward Baton Rouge. Ruggles could have tried to cut the Federals off from their gunboats and push them toward the Confederate-held interior, but Ruggles told Thompson that, if the Federals were still in Baton Rouge, he should push his men "forward toward the Mississippi to encourage that idea."[22] If Ruggles trapped the Federals, they would be forced to fight or surrender. Given those options, the Federals might lay down their arms or cornered men might decide to fight and inflict serious casualties on the Confederates, even if the Confederates eventually won. However, by pushing from the west and leaving an open path toward Union gunboats and transports, the Confederates would allow the Federals to retreat rather than fight, allowing the Confederacy to recapture Baton Rouge at little cost.

The Federals withdrew from Baton Rouge, but they did not want the Confederacy to recapture it. On August 22 Major J. De Baun of the 9th Louisiana Battalion of Partisan Rangers informed Ruggles that the Union army had evacuated Baton Rouge, but that the Federal gunboats *Essex* and *No. 7* remained just offshore. Captain Caldwell, commanding the Federal gunboat *No. 7*, informed Baton Rouge's city council that the Union sailors meant the city's residents no harm and would not fire a single shot on the town if the residents remained peaceful. However, Caldwell warned the town's leaders that, if the Confederate army attempted to occupy Baton Rouge, the gunboats would shell it. Stuck between two opposing forces determined to kill each other, Baton Rouge's city council sent a formal request to De Baun, asking him to keep all Confederate troops outside the city. Unsure of how to proceed, De Baun asked the town's civilians to evacuate the city and sent a report to Ruggles.[23]

On August 23, 1862, Confederate forces took possession of Baton Rouge. William Dixon of the 4th Louisiana Infantry noted that "the Yankees had evacuated the place in great confusion." The 4th Louisiana made their camp near the state penitentiary and drilled for battle. Dixon visited a nearby graveyard, littered with shallow graves, many of which contained the remains of men killed on August 5, 1862, at the Battle of Baton Rouge, where the 4th Louisiana had been hotly engaged. The shallow graves left corpses exposed and, according to Dixon, "the stench was so great that it rendered our visit very unpleasant." Despite their threats, it does not appear that the Union navy bombarded Baton Rouge, choosing instead to withdraw peacefully. A writer for the *Weekly Arkansas Gazette* reported that the recapture of Baton Rouge gave the Confederacy control of the Mississippi from Vicksburg to Baton Rouge and made the "Red River secure."[24]

Commodore Porter sailed the *Essex* north up the Mississippi River on August 23. His first stop was Bayou Sara, about twelve miles north of Port Hudson, where Porter planned to refill his coal bunkers from a stash left there by Union forces earlier in the year. Porter was disappointed to find Bayou Sara deserted and the coal depot on fire. Porter sent a shore party inland. Confederate guerillas ambushed the Federals from houses on the edge of town. A firefight ensued, and the Federals burned several houses before retreating to the *Essex*.[25]

The *Essex* arrived off Port Hudson on August 24. Porter had heard rumors that Confederate forces were fortifying the town, and he wanted to investigate. From the *Essex*, Porter could see that Confederates were building shore batteries, but they did not appear to have mounted any cannons. Confederate soldiers laughed at the "scampering of the negro laborers," who raced to safety as soon as they saw the *Essex*. The slaves escaped just in time. The *Essex* bombarded the growing earthworks in hopes that it might end, or at least slow, the construction project. The Confederate garrison did not return fire. After a brief shelling, the *Essex* returned to Bayou Sara, north of Port Hudson, where Union sailors once again clashed with Confederate guerillas and militia along the riverbank.[26]

The *Essex's* bombardment did not slow the fortification of Port Hudson and served only to fill Confederates with a newfound sense of urgency. Confederate engineers pushed slaves to the breaking point and began mounting artillery. Confederate sailor turned Port Hudson artilleryman Charles Read later recalled that he and his comrades who had once crewed *CSS Arkansas* were pleased to learn their old nemesis, the *Essex*, was nearby. Read and his comrades sighted in their artillery as soon as the engineers mounted the cannons and kept a close lookout for Union warships. They were particularly interested in destroying the *Essex* and hoped it would stumble within range of their growing fortress.[27]

While the Confederates at Port Hudson prepared for action, the Federals continued their recruiting efforts across Louisiana. On August 27 General Butler sent a report to General Halleck in Washington, asking for approval to expand his recruitment of Louisianans. Butler claimed that earlier that day the 1st Louisiana Union Infantry marched to Carrollton on the outskirts of New Orleans to repel a Confederate foray toward

New Orleans. After the skirmish, Butler reviewed the Louisianans and reported that they were "as fine a looking body of men as I have ever seen." He concluded that "the enlistments of white men have succeeded."[28]

George Smith, a lieutenant with the 1st Louisiana Union Infantry, remembered August 27 quite differently than Butler. Smith did not mention a Confederate advance on New Orleans that day. According to Smith, shortly after daybreak Colonel Holcomb shot John Dramond, a soldier in the regiment, for "disobedience." The single pistol bullet penetrated Dramond's chest, killing him instantly. After the summary execution, Butler arrived and inspected the regiment. Butler complimented the Louisianans on their "soldierly appearance" and gave them a rousing speech. It is not clear if Butler was aware that the regiment's colonel killed a man shortly before he arrived or if the Louisianans tried to maintain a "soldierly appearance" because they did not want Holcomb to murder them. After Butler left, members of the regiment tried to make themselves comfortable on their campground that was "full of standing water," which the men did not care for but which the wildlife apparently liked because the campsite was the "habitation of every unclean and hateful bird." Sadly, Smith did not explain what the birds did that was so "unclean and hateful," but it was clearly unpleasant enough to make an impression on the veteran soldier. Clouds of mosquitos also enjoyed the standing water and spread diseases that sent half the regiment's men to the hospital.[29]

Union gunboats dueled with Port Hudson's garrison the last week of August 1862. On August 28 the Federal gunboat *Anglo-American* approached Port Hudson. Confederate lookouts misidentified it as the *Essex* in the darkness. Gunners who had once served on the CSS *Arkansas* rose from their slumber and manned their cannons in silence. They were eager to take vengeance on the ship that hammered them at the battle of Baton Rouge. As the *Anglo-American* approached Port Hudson, the Federal crew could see earthworks but no artillery. Like the *Essex* a few days before, the *Anglo-American* opened fire on the Port Hudson fortifications in hopes of interrupting Confederate work crews. However, in the few days since the *Essex* last visited, the Confederates had emplaced several heavy cannons, and the garrison was now ready for a fight. When the *Anglo-American* got within point blank range of Read's battery, the men in gray opened fire. According to Charles Read, "our men worked lively, and we pounded away in fine style." Two army batteries joined the Confederate sailors, adding their weight to the bombardment. R. K. Riley, commanding the *Anglo-American*, reported taking fire from two 32-pound guns and eighteen smaller cannons. The *Anglo-American* fired a few "wild shots" at the Confederate batteries before sailing north out of range. By the time the *Anglo-American* escaped, the Confederate gunners had hit the gunboat seventy-three times, wounded two Union sailors, and caused significant damage to the boat.[30]

Perhaps pleased by the Port Hudson garrison's successful firefight with the *Anglo-American*, on August 29, 1862, Van Dorn ordered Ruggles to leave 2,500 men at Port Hudson and bring every other man he could gather to Jackson, Mississippi, where Ruggles would help Van Dorn defend Mississippi. Van Dorn suggested that the 2,500 men would be enough to defend Port Hudson. It is unclear how Van Dorn arrived at that number, which was barely 7 percent of the 35,000 men that Ruggles estimated he would need to defend the planned defenses of Port Hudson. Ruggles left Port Hudson on August 31, handing over command of the strategic bluff to Brigadier General William Beall.[31]

William Beall had little experience defending fortifications, but he was a competent professional officer with ties to the region. Born in Kentucky in 1825, he moved with his family to Little Rock, Arkansas, as a boy and graduated from West Point in 1848, barely missing service in the Mexican American War. Like many professional officers of his generation, he served on the frontier, mostly fighting the Kiowa and Comanche, until 1861. When the Civil War broke out, he resigned from the US Army and accepted a Confederate commission. Beall commanded a series of cavalry units in the Trans-Mississippi Theatre under Van Dorn until Ruggles left him in command of Port Hudson. Perhaps most importantly, Beall appears to have been popular with his men. According to one newspaper report, Beall was "a well-liked Christian soldier" who was popular with his men. A report in another Arkansas newspaper described Beall as a "brave and skillful officer." Louisiana soldier Howard Wright claimed the men approved of Beall's promotion since he was "a gallant officer" with "an honorable reputation."[32]

Beall was in a tough spot. He probably already knew that, but like a true professional he compiled a report to document the problems. Beall took a census of the Port Hudson garrison. Van Dorn estimated that 2,500 men could defend Port Hudson, but Beall had only 1,175 men on the roster and only 946 were present for duty. Roughly 46 percent of the garrison was infantry, mostly in the 30th Louisiana Infantry, which was the largest single unit at Port Hudson; 43 percent of the garrison were artillerymen; and the remaining 11 percent were mounted partisan rangers. It was a tiny force to defend the important position. Nocquet designed the Port Hudson series of lunette defenses for a 35,000-man garrison. When Beall took command, he his 946 men present for duty were less than 3 percent of the planned manpower. While Beall had never commanded a major defensive position before, he was a professional solider who knew that 946 was far less than 35,000. He could have begged for the more than 34,000 men needed to fill his ranks, but even the politically inexperienced Beall probably realized that he was unlikely to get anything approaching 34,000 more men.[33]

Beall had very little control of what took place outside of Port Hudson but tremendous authority within Port Hudson. Therefore, he wisely revised the defensive plan. He decided to build a ditch and earthen wall system that could be held with 20,000 men. While 20,000 was more than 946, it was also far less than 35,000, and Beall correctly concluded that he was far more likely to get 19,000 than 34,000 more men. Beall ordered the engineers to survey the shortest possible ditch and parapet line that could effectively defend the town while taking advantage of the terrain. The revised line began about two and a half miles south of Port Hudson and gradually curved to Sandy Creek, about a mile west from the edge of town. From there the line crossed a series of ravines and ridges, following the natural terrain to put the Confederate defensive positions on the best possible ground. It then curved north across a wide plain that included both Gibbon's and the aptly named Slaughter's fields. The rest of the line curved toward the Mississippi River through difficult terrain before coming to rest on the river banks. While the engineers and work crews built a revised system of fortifications, Beall also went on the offensive. He sent detachments of light artillery to take up positions along the Mississippi River and ordered them to fire on any enemy ship that came within range.[34]

Confederate reinforcements trickled into Port Hudson, replacing some of the men that left the garrison for Kentucky and Mississippi. Secretary of War G. W. Randolph ordered Paul de Gournay and all but one company of de Gournay's Artillery Battalion, also known as the 12th Louisiana Heavy

Artillery Battalion, to leave the fortifications around Richmond and move to Port Hudson. The heavy artillerymen were veteran gunners with experience at Yorktown, Virginia. Randolph selected de Gournay's men for service in Port Hudson primarily because they were mostly from southern Louisiana and Randolph believed they were therefore less likely to suffer the heat stroke and tropical illnesses that had caused problems for other Union and Confederate troops in Louisiana.[35]

Paul de Gournay was probably one of the most colorful officers in Confederate service. Born into the French nobility, as a young man de Gournay moved to Cuba to manage his father's estates. The young nobleman was not content to enjoy his family's wealth and got involved in politics. In 1851 the Frenchman joined the Cuban independence movement. The revolution failed, and de Gournay fled to New Orleans just in time to avoid execution by Spanish authorities. In Louisiana, de Gournay spent the next decade as a sugar planter, newspaper editor, and militia officer. When the war came in 1861, de Gournay supported secession, believing that the Confederacy was fighting for the same ideals as the failed Cuban independence movement. He formed an artillery unit which later became known as the 12th Louisiana Heavy Artillery. The unit served in Florida and then Virginia. By the time they received the orders sending them to Port Hudson, de Gournay and his men were well-disciplined veterans.[36]

The bulk of de Gournay's battalion arrived at Port Hudson in the first week of September 1862. A seemingly disappointed de Gournay found "the work of fortifying it was progressing slowly." Howard Wright described de Gournay's men as "a hardy and well drilled body of men" and de Gournay as a fine officer known for "gallant and meritorious service." The Louisianans left their artillery in Virginia and did not receive new cannons for several weeks. Surviving records provide only vague descriptions of how the Louisianans looked, however, on April 1, 1862, just before the artillerymen left for Louisiana, de Gournay obtained new clothing for his men that included jackets, pants, undershirts, socks, shoes, overcoats, and caps from the Richmond Depot. These jackets may have been the type known to historians as Richmond Depot Type 1, notable for their shoulder straps, belt loops, cuffs, and stand up collars decorated with dark trim.[37]

Additional slaves arrived in Port Hudson in early September, and the Confederates made rapid improvements to their fortifications. Despite claims that Confederate soldiers refused to help the slaves build fortifications at Port Hudson, J. W. Minnich, serving with de Gournay's Artillery Battalion, reported that members of his unit helped build fortifications and mount cannons as soon as they arrived in early September 1862. The difference between Wright's and Minnich's observations might indicate a distinction between the infantrymen, who preferred to fight on the move, and the artillerymen with experience defending fortifications in Virginia. The Louisianans might have also enjoyed better tools. On April 1, 1862, just before the artillerymen left Virginia, de Gournay obtained tools, including twenty axes, which the troops may have brought with them to Port Hudson.[38]

At 4:15 a.m. on September 7, 1862, the USS *Essex* returned to Port Hudson on a scouting expedition. The Confederates greeted the *Essex* with a rapid bombardment from their newly mounted shore batteries. The *Essex* returned fire, pounding rebel positions with multiple broadsides. Captain Porter, in command of the *Essex*, reported that the Port Hudson defenses consisted of thirty-five to forty heavy cannons in three batteries that controlled five miles of the river. The Confederate artillery struck the *Essex* fourteen times without making any serious impact, but Porter believed that he "considerably damaged" the Confederate defenders. After doing all the damage he believed possible, Porter withdrew the *Essex*, and the fight ended. While Porter believed that his sailors had inflicted far more damage than they received, his official report warned the Union high command that naval gunfire alone would not eliminate Port Hudson's fortifications. He believed that only a land force could capture the town. Porter warned his superiors that, if they did not destroy the Confederate positions at Port Hudson, shore batteries would seriously interrupt Union use of the river.[39]

Confederate sources dispute Porter's claim that the *Essex* "considerably damaged" Port Hudson's defenders and suggest that the brief bombardment might have improved Confederate morale. J. W. Minnich, serving as an artilleryman during the exchange, later ridiculed Porter's published account, claiming the Confederates fired on the *Essex* with only three small cannons. In contrast to Porter's claims that the *Essex* inflicted "considerably damage" to the Confederate defenders, Minnich reported that the only victim of the *Essex*'s bombardment was a single unlucky mule, peacefully grazing in a field behind the lines until a Union shell killed it. Paul de Gournay reported, "the whole affair lasted but a few minutes" and "half the men on duty in the batteries didn't tumble out of bed quick enough to see the boats." The *Natchez Daily Courier* of Natchez, Mississippi, claimed "the biter got bit" during the attack and was "severely crippled" by Port Hudson's defenders. The newspaper predicted that if the *Essex* ever again came within range of Port Hudson, Confederate artillerymen "will make a finish of her."[40]

The gunfire from Porter's men might not have killed any Confederates, but Confederate soldiers suffered at Port Hudson. Confederate civilians visited Port Hudson in the fall of 1862 to care for sick soldiers, and Sarah Morgan wrote, "there is very little we would not do for our soldiers." Captain John Utley of the 16th Arkansas Infantry requested a medical discharge because he was suffering from "chronic diarrhea of a persistent character" that made it impossible for him to perform his duties. The regiment's assistant surgeon supported Utley's request, and Utley received his discharge.[41] Considering how common diarrhea was among Confederate soldiers, Utley must have been far sicker or far better connected politically than most soldiers suffering from diarrhea.

Suffering led to death. On September 3, 1862, Sergeant W. A. Hay of the 20th Tennessee Infantry arrived in Port Hudson's Confederate hospital, suffering from a bayonet wound to his left lung. The twenty-nine-year-old wagon driver turned soldier suffered his wound in the Battle of Baton Rouge on August 5, 1862. Hay's departure from this world was the first documented death in Port Hudson's Confederate hospital. On September 15, 1862, the Confederate army at Port Hudson purchased three coffins from E. W. Barnes, a local civilian, for twelve dollars each. Surviving records include detailed invoices showing that, in addition to the coffins he sold to Port Hudson's garrison, Barnes also buried the dead for five dollars a body. The most notable Confederate death that fall might have been Brigadier General John Villepigue, who distinguished himself by commanding the defense of Fort Pillow before coming to Port Hudson. Unfortunately for the men in gray, General Villepigue died of typhoid pneumonia before any major fighting took place at Port Hudson.[42] It is unclear how many graves Barnes and others might have dug near Port Hudson that fall, but the limited evidence available proves that death stalked the Confederate camps in the fall of 1862.

Emboldened by the successful reoccupation of Baton Rouge, General Ruggles, now stationed in Jackson, Mississippi, requested permission from Inspector General Samuel Cooper in Richmond for an offensive against New Orleans. Ruggles had heard there were no more than ten thousand troops in New Orleans and that the forces were "demoralized and enfeebled by sickness." Ruggles believed that most residents of New Orleans were loyal to the Confederacy and would rush to the aid of Confederate forces. Ruggles argued that, if the Confederacy could gather twenty thousand men, they could march south, defeat all Federal troops in southern Louisiana, and recapture New Orleans. General Beall supported an offensive posture and requested permission to send additional artillery units to Baton Rouge.[43]

General Cooper did not respond directly to Ruggles's plan to recapture New Orleans. Instead, Major Jasper Whiting, who served as Cooper's assistant, informed Ruggles that New Orleans fell within General Richard Taylor's area of responsibility and was no concern of Ruggles. Whiting also scolded Ruggles for his decision to "give publicity through the medium of the telegraph to suggestions that should have been regarded by him as private." Ruggles did not take either of those statements well, responding a few days later that, according to his most recent orders, he was in command of the area that included New Orleans, not Taylor. Ruggles also fired back at Whiting's suggestion that he should refrain from sending sensitive information over the telegraph lines, arguing, "[I]f the agents are disloyal the plans of the government are at their mercy."[44]

Cooper, and not Whiting, responded directly to Ruggles's comments. Cooper assured Ruggles that "no reproach was intended" by the previous communications from his office. He explained that, when Whiting suggested that New Orleans fell within Taylor's area of control, "neither the department nor this office was informed of the extent of your command." Cooper also told Ruggles that the comment on not using the telegraph for confidential communications was "intended more as a caution than a reproach."[45] It is unclear if Ruggles appreciated that no offense was intended or felt alarm at the realization that the Confederate high command in Richmond was seemingly unaware of who oversaw the vital area, which included New Orleans.

Ruggles's plan for the recapture of New Orleans vastly overestimated both Confederate strength and Union weaknesses in the region. While many Federals in Louisiana were sick, the healthy ones were ready for action. On September 14 three Union regiments attacked Ponchatoula,

Louisiana, roughly halfway between Port Hudson and New Orleans. A small force of Confederate defenders killed sixteen Federals before the Union forces won the day and captured almost the entire Confederate force, including a battery of artillery. Ruggles ordered Beall to counterattack with all available forces. On September 16 Colonel Witt of the 10th Arkansas Cavalry led a counterattack, which retook Ponchatoula, recaptured the Confederate artillery lost the day before, and captured Union prisoners. The Confederates counterattack was successful, but the Confederate commanders in the region, including Ruggles, now realized that the Federals in Louisiana were not as weak as some reports indicated.[46]

On September 17 Ruggles ordered Beall to realign his troops into a more defensive posture, indicating that he had given up on any hopes of capturing New Orleans, at least for the moment. Ruggles told Beall to send a small detachment to Bayou Sara, the scene of several clashes between Confederate militia and Union sailors. Ruggles also ordered Beall to guard Baton Rouge with a company of infantry, a two-gun section of artillery, and fifteen mounted men. Ruggles was particularly interested in protecting unspecified machinery in Baton Rouge.[47]

While Ruggles's letter to Beall was vague, he was clearly referring to the textile production equipment located at the state prison. Production facilities at the prison produced more than three million yards of textiles in 1861. Between the time the war broke out in April 1861 and the fall of Baton Rouge in March 1862, the prison's factory also produced additional goods including brass buttons, uniforms, shoes, fuse caps, belt clasps, tents, knapsacks, and saddles. If Beall could get the prison factory up and running once more, it could produce essential equipment for the Confederate military in Louisiana.[48]

Despite the growing danger, southern civilians continued to visit Port Hudson in the fall of 1862. On September 24, Sarah Morgan and her sister Miriam Morgan visited Port Hudson as guests of Colonel Breaux with Mrs. Badger serving as a chaperone. The Morgan sisters arrived in Port Hudson in a "Confederate carriage." Sarah Morgan explained that the word Confederate was used an adjective for anything "rough, unfinished, unfashionable, or poor." For example, Confederate dresses were old dresses, Confederate silver was tin, Confederate flour was corn meal, and the Confederate carriage that conveyed the Morgan sisters was a jersey wagon, covered with leather and drawn by four mules.[49]

Shortly after arriving in Port Hudson, the ladies observed a parade by the 4th Louisiana Infantry. The soldiers impressed Morgan. The men were mostly veterans, tested in battle at Shiloh and Baton Rouge. Many of them were barefoot, wearing ragged uniforms in "all varieties of colors and cuts" and hats in "every style and shape." Despite their deficiencies, Morgan described the men as "happy." After the parade ended, Sarah Morgan and her companions visited the camp of the 30th Louisiana Infantry. The camp rested on a "large open common," and the men lived in tents. Morgan described the camp as a "pleasant" place where men raced around like schoolboys tossing hats and rocks at birds that flew too close to their tents. Overall, Morgan thought the camp was "a very pretty picture" but she wondered how the men could be happy living in such simple tents. Some Confederate soldiers enjoyed the company of women Morgan described as "the fastest set of girls I have seen." One lady in "a short dress complained that she had not seen her sweetheart." In reply, "a pert little miss of thirteen cried you can bet your head I never went to any place where I did not see one of my sweethearts."[50]

Not every civilian who visited Port Hudson supported the rebellion. After the fall of New Orleans, an increasing number of southerners took the oath of allegiance to the Union. Some of these civilians visited Port Hudson, scouted the growing Confederate fortifications, and shared their observations with Federal commanders when they returned to the city. A writer for the *Weekly Mississippian* in Jackson, Mississippi, urged Confederate officers to ban southerners loyal to the Union from visiting Port Hudson.[51] It is unclear if the Confederate army took the threat seriously or made any efforts to limit spying on their positions by southern unionists.

Watchful spies may have noticed that additional Confederate reinforcements joined the Port Hudson garrison and sent word to the Union army. On October 1, 1862, the 1st Alabama Infantry (also known as the 1st Alabama Heavy Artillery) received orders to join the garrison at Port Hudson. Formed in 1861, the regiment initially saw service across Alabama, Florida, and Tennessee. On April 8, 1862, most of the soldiers of the regiment became prisoners after the fall of Island No. 10. Like many units forced to deal with the dysfunctional Confederate logistical system, the Alabamians took a circuitous path to their new post. The trip began in Vicksburg, where the Alabamians arrived after they were exchanged from a prisoner of war camp. The Alabamians took a train to Tangipahoa, Louisiana, about a hundred and thirty miles southeast of Vicksburg. Next, the Alabamians marched to Clinton, Louisiana. With the precision of a man who walked every step, Daniel Smith of Company K noted that it was a thirty-three-and-a-half-mile march from to Tangipahoa to Clinton. The Alabamians rode the Clinton and Port Hudson Railroad for twenty miles to complete their journey to Port Hudson. Smith was not impressed with the Clinton and Port Hudson Railroad, noting that the "road was not first class, either in road-bed or equipment." The flattened rails rested on rotten ties. Only a single engine was available, and it could only haul half the regiment at a time with its meager collection of one passenger car and six flatbed and cargo cars. Upon arriving in Port Hudson, the regiment set up camp on the bluff between the village of Port Hudson and the depot. James Goble, a New York–born, thirty-three-year-old painter who was living in Auburn, Alabama, at the start of the war wrote in his diary, "Port Hudson is an old dilapidated town with a few old houses standing and nothing but soldiers and horses an can be see [*sic*] going about all day long."[52]

Daniel Smith's 1885 memoir provides a unique snapshot of a Confederate unit at the start of the battles for Port Hudson. Smith reported that, when the regiment entered Port Hudson, they "numbered nearly 700 muskets" and a brass band. However, Beall's report of October 22 listed the 1st Alabama as having only 312 men present for duty, suggesting that many of the Alabamians were too sick for service. Smith reported that the regiment was well clothed in new uniforms, provided by the citizens of Mobile, Alabama, after the regiment was exchanged in September 1862. Smith did not provide any details on the uniforms but was more specific about the regiment's eclectic weapons, which included a mix of "rifles, Springfield muskets, altered flintlocks, and flintlocks." Smith's unit, Company K, received archaic flintlocks. While the firearms were inconsistent, Smith was proud to report that all the regiment's weapons were in good order and equipped with bayonets, "which gave them a uniform appearance." Smith reported that the regiment was "well drilled" and "made a good military appearance on parade."[53]

Smith reported that the 1st Alabama quickly fell into a routine at Port Hudson.

First Lieutenant William R. Felton of Co. H, 1st Alabama Infantry Regiment. Felton was a prisoner of war on April 18, 1862, at Johnson's Island and on July 9, 1863, at Port Hudson. Library of Congress.

Daybreak—Reveille, Roll Call, Inspection of Arms, and Policing of Camps
6 AM—Drill in the School of the Soldier
7 AM—Breakfast
8:30 AM—Guard Mounting
9 AM—Non-Commissioned Officers' Drill
10 AM—Drill in the School of the Company
Men assigned to the guns drilled with their guns instead of with their companies.
Noon—Dinner
1 PM—Skirmish Drill
3 PM—Battalion Drill
5 PM—Dress Parade
Sunset—Retreat
9 PM—Taps

In addition to the schedule laid out by Smith, Edward McMorries, who also served with the 1st Alabama, recalled that "Companies A, B, G, and K, began the construction of their batteries on the river." It is not clear exactly when the men worked on the fortifications or what McMorries meant by "began the construction," considering claims by other Confederate soldiers that most of the work was done by slaves. It is possible that the slaves had focused on other areas Port Hudson's defenses and that the Alabamians of Companies A, B, G, and K built their own works. In contrast, James Goble of Company H in the 1st Alabama Infantry wrote in his diary that "hundreds of negroes [were] working on the entrenchments and batterys [*sic*]." Samuel Thompson of the 23rd Arkansas Infantry wrote home that his brigade was improving the breastworks as quickly as possible. He believed that "when they are finished they will be the best we have ever seen." In contrast to the hectic pace of work and leisure described by other soldiers, a Confederate named M. Hart of an unspecified unit stationed at Port Hudson wrote his brother and sister that he "had nothing to do." Hart reported widespread rumors that "we will have a fight here before long," but Hart was skeptical, explaining, "I don't much think so."[54]

On October 1, 1862, the Confederate high command once again reorganized control of the area that included Port Hudson's growing garrison. They created the Department of Mississippi and East Louisiana, which incorporated both Vicksburg and Port Hudson. The War Department placed John Pemberton in command of the new department on October 14 and set up his headquarters in Jackson, Mississippi. Van Dorn took command of cavalry forces in the department. The Pennsylvania-born Pemberton was an odd choice to command Confederate forces in Mississippi. He was a professional soldier who graduated from West Point in 1837 and saw service during the Mexican War. In 1848 he married Martha Thompson of Norfolk, Virginia. Pemberton's Pennsylvania family expected him to remain loyal to the region of his birth and his oath to the US Army, but his Virginia wife and his many years of service in the southern states pulled him into the Confederate army. Before taking command at Vicksburg, Pemberton's service to the Confederacy was uninspiring. His "abrasive" personality and refusal to cooperate with local leaders forced Jefferson Davis to remove him from command in Charleston, South Carolina. Many southerners were inclined to dislike and distrust anyone born in the North, even a general, and Pemberton's tendency to remain aloof from his men exacerbated the problem. Edwin Hay, a Louisiana sergeant who met Pemberton shortly after he arrived in Mississippi, told his wife that Pemberton was "the most insignificant puke I ever saw" and predicted that the men would hate him. In spite of his talent for alienating many southerners, Jefferson Davis liked him and called him "one of the best generals in our service."[55]

Pemberton organized the Department of Mississippi and East Louisiana into three districts. General Ruggles would command District 1, which included the state of Mississippi east of the Mississippi and Tennessee Railroad and the New Orleans and Jackson Railroad except for the counties of Mississippi that bordered the Gulf of Mexico, from his headquarters in Jackson Mississippi. From Vicksburg, General M. L. Smith would command District 2, which included the state of Mississippi between the Mississippi and Tennessee Railroad, the Mississippi River, and the Big Black River. From his post in Port Hudson, General Beall would command District 3, which included territory in Mississippi from the Big Black to the Mississippi River, Mississippi counties that bordered the Gulf of Mexico, and Louisiana east of the Mississippi River.[56]

As part of the reorganization, additional Confederate soldiers joined the Port Hudson garrison. On October 15, 1862, the 16th Arkansas Infantry received orders detaching them from the 1st Missouri Brigade and sending them to Port Hudson. Lieutenant Joseph Bailey described Port Hudson as "a village of perhaps a hundred and fifty people, mostly women and children" and a rapidly growing garrison of five to six thousand soldiers. A line of partially completed "earthen breastworks" stretched for three or four miles around the town, with both flanks resting against the river.[57]

The Confederacy turned to conscription to fill the army, but conscription forced southern leaders to seek a difficult balance between civilian and military needs. H. Rives, a Mississippi lawyer serving as a commissary officer at Port Hudson, wrote the office of Mississippi governor John Pettus to explain that he wanted to leave the army but did not want to leave his current position if the government would draft him as soon as he arrived home. Rives asked for the governor's assurance that, if he resigned his commission and returned to practice law, he would be exempt from the draft. It is unclear what happened to Rives, but his letter provides helpful insights into conscription policies that affected Port Hudson's garrison. On October 3, Ruggles asked Inspector General Cooper to relax conscription in Mississippi and Louisiana. He explained that so many white men were forced to serve in the army that "slaves are being left without the ordinary and necessary control of the white man." Ruggles worried that the lack of overseers might result in "some serious disturbance in the sections most densely populated by the servile race." Ruggles urged Cooper to intervene and relax conscription policies for slave overseers.[58]

Confederate forces in and around Port Hudson grew stronger in the fall of 1862. On October 22, Beall reported that he now commanded a much larger force than when he initially took command on August 31 and that his force was more broadly distributed than Ruggles suggested. Because Beall's manpower reports on August 31 and October 22 provide different information, an exact comparison of the two figures is impossible, but they do suggest that Beall's forces were growing larger and more capable. The report of August 31 lists 946 men, all of whom were at Port Hudson. On August 31, 46 percent of the Port Hudson garrison was infantry, 43 percent were artillerymen, and the remaining 11 percent were irregular partisan rangers. The October 22 report lists 2,385 men at Port Hudson and another 1,241 men in the area. On October 22, the Port Hudson garrison was 63 percent infantry, 29 percent artillery, including both heavy and light artillery units, and 8 percent cavalry. Most of Beall's 1,241 troops outside Port Hudson occupied the strategic locations of Baton Rouge, Ponchatoula, and Covington in a roughly east-to-west line, with a few cavalrymen on picket duty and thirty-four provost guards at Camp Moore, northeast of Port Hudson. Beall's forces outside Port Hudson included 57 percent infantry, 10 percent artillery, 15 percent cavalry and mounted rangers, 3 percent provost guards, and 15 percent irregular partisan rangers. The Confederates did not commit to a static defense and continued to prepare for a war of maneuver. Field batteries practiced pushing their horses at the double quick across the ravines that surrounded Port Hudson.[59]

On October 24, 1862, Major George Mayo submitted a detailed report on the artillery in and around Port Hudson. Mayo reported that the artillerymen and their equipment were "in good order generally" but also in need of improvement. Mayo reported that the heavy batteries were all located along the steep bluff, which was from forty to eighty-five feet above the river. These were excellent positions to bombard enemy boats. Several cannon carriages were made of unseasoned lumber that warped and shrunk, which made it difficult to use the cannons to their best potential. Two 24-pounder cannons looked through narrow embrasures cut in the works, which provided excellent cover for the crews but also limited their fields of fire. Mayo encouraged Beall to fill in the embrasures, raise the platforms, and set up the guns to fire over the fortifications, which would leave the crews more vulnerable but would also provide superior fields of fire. Mayo thought the tradeoff was worth it, but he was not one of the gunners who would be far more vulnerable to enemy fire. Mayo also noted that one 24-pounder rifled cannon was placed about six feet above and thirty feet behind another 24-pounder rifled cannon. Mayo felt that this placed the crew of the lower gun in danger of friendly fire, and he urged Beall to move one of the cannons. In addition to the siege batteries facing the Mississippi River, Mayo also inspected four light artillery batteries guarding the overland approaches to Port Hudson and mostly gave them high praise as well, although he noted some problems.[60]

Mayo saved his harshest criticism for the bridges that artillerymen used to transport cannons within Port Hudson, which needed repair.[61] This would be particularly important in a siege. If the bridges and roadways within Port Hudson were in good condition, the defenders could use interior lines of transportation to concentrate their men and artillery to the specific section of the works under attack and confront the attackers with superior force as the attackers struggled with much longer exterior lines of transportation. If the garrison failed to repair the bridges within Port Hudson, they would largely lose the vital advantage of interior lines of communication.

Desperate to complete Port Hudson's fortifications and repair the area's roads, Beall asked for permission to declare martial law. He claimed that many of the area's planters refused to furnish slaves to help build fortifications, and Beall believed that only martial law could fix the problem. J. A. Campbell, Acting Secretary of War, replied that he understood Beall's frustration but pointed out that the government must balance military needs with a respect for existing institutions. Campbell declined Beall's request to implement martial law and urged him to cooperate with plantation owners.[62]

The Union faced obstacles just as formidable as any encountered by their gray-clad adversaries. Federal reinforcements trickled into Louisiana, but many of the men were sick and confined to hospitals after their arrival. Captain Nicholas Dederer of the 114th New York Infantry wrote to his son that many men in his regiment were suffering from an outbreak of measles and were quarantined on ship, unable to come ashore. Massachusetts artilleryman Henry Aiken wrote home to his mother from a bed in the Marine Hospital in New Orleans to explain that he was "recovering from a fit of sickness" that included "fever and chills," which the doctors treated with quinine. The symptoms and treatment suggest that Aiken might have had malaria. Aiken detailed a long list of men in his regiment who were also in the hospital, some of whom were so sick that the army had already discharged them from the service. He assured his mother that he was feeling much better and would recover soon. Although not as well documented, mental illness may have also slowed the Union army's advance. On October 16, 1862, army surgeon Jacob Bocker declared Private George Beedenham, a German-born soldier in the 1st Louisiana Union Infantry, as "insane" because he was "constantly under some hallucination." The army sent Beedenham to a mental hospital in Washington, DC. Beedenham later escaped from the mental hospital and disappeared from the historical record.[63]

On November 13 Pemberton informed Adjutant General Cooper that "neither Vicksburg nor Port Hudson is as strong as I desire to make them."

Pemberton wanted to keep seven regiments of unarmed Texans in Mississippi even though he was supposed to send the Texans to General Lee in Virginia. Pemberton's forces included five thousand unarmed men, although it is unclear if the seven unarmed Texas regiments were included in that number. Pemberton dispatched fifty gunsmiths from his command to help at the Briarfield Arsenal at Columbus, Mississippi, but Pemberton feared Briarfield would be unable to meet his needs and requested more small arms from Cooper, as well as ammunition. Almost as soon as Pemberton arrived in Mississippi in October, he requested twenty siege cannons for Vicksburg and Port Hudson. None of those cannons had arrived by November 13, and Pemberton repeated that request. Pemberton also reported that his men were "very deficient" in clothing, blankets, and shoes and that, as a result, "the men suffer greatly." Pemberton reported that he was trying to fill these needs from local sources, but those sources were insufficient. Before Pemberton took command, the Confederate forces in Mississippi had obtained medical supplies through an illicit trade with Union suppliers. Pemberton put an end to the trade and attempted to buy supplies from Mexico, across the Texas border.[64]

As Port Hudson became an increasingly prominent military post, it also remained a busy commercial port. Planters on the west bank of the Mississippi River ferried sugar across the river on flatboats, which workers then loaded onto the railroad to Clinton. From Clinton, teamsters then transported the sugar on wagons to the Jackson railroad. Salt workers in St. Mary's parish transported salt in the same way. Tobacco came to Port Hudson from the east and made its way west across the Mississippi River. Texans sent cattle east across the river, sometimes on boats but more often by forcing the long-horned beasts to swim. James Goble noted in his diary that railroad cars arrived daily from Clinton and that "soldiers and horses can be see [*sic*] going about all day long." Merchants, teamsters, and family members of Confederate soldiers visited Port Hudson. The constant flow of people and merchandise provided an opening for Union spies, who also visited the city and kept the Federals well informed about Confederate work in Port Hudson.[65]

While goods flowed through Port Hudson, precious little of that abundance remained behind to supply the garrison. According to Howard Wright, "men high in military position in the department were more interested in their share of sugar speculations than in provisioning Vicksburg and Port Hudson." Port Hudson's provost marshal, H. C. Miller, tried to build large warehouses and fill them with a year's worth of provisions for the garrison, siphoned off from the flow of goods that passed through Port Hudson. Howard Wright reported that Miller's plan was excellent but never implemented because the Confederate high command jealously guarded its right to handle logistical matters. Edward McMorries lamented that, while plenty of food flowed through Port Hudson, "no bacon and only a few of the poorest cattle were left for our garrison."[66]

Despite the cynicism of some soldiers, the Confederate departmental headquarters did provide Port Hudson's defenders with supplies. Four boats made regular stops at Port Hudson, mostly bringing supplies from the Red River Valley. Private George Waterman of Captain Fenner's light artillery battery later recalled that one of the four boats was named *Nina Simms*. It was crewed by three mates who "were of a flesh-eating, Texas-steer, cattle-train, carnivorous persuasion." Waterman and his comrades joked that the *Nina Simms* was even older than she looked and was the famed *Nina* of Christopher Columbus's 1492 voyage. Other boats, including the *Homer*, a 194-ton displacement sidewheel steamer, brought supplies to Port Hudson. According to Daniel Smith, the food "was generally good" in the fall of 1862. Men lived on "plentiful rations" of corn meal, beef, potatoes, sugar, salt, and molasses. Each unit assigned several men from the ranks as cooks or hired "negro cooks" to prepare their rations. Ladies from Port Hudson visited the Confederate camps and helped the soldiers improve their cooking methods.[67]

Surviving records of junior officers give an incomplete but helpful glimpse into the goods needed by Port Hudson's defenders. Lieutenant Francis Proctor of the 14th Arkansas Infantry wrote that his company received a camp kettle, a mess pan, "jeans jackets," nine pairs of underwear, pants, shoes, shirts, and socks on December 7, 1862. Lieutenant William Moseley in Company C of the 23rd Arkansas Infantry requested tents, camp kettles, and mess pans, as well as clothing for his men. Captain Calvin Roberts, commanding a battery of the Seven Stars Mississippi Artillery, requested shoes, pants, underwear, and socks for his men, as well as stationary for himself, in a series of requisitions from November 1862 to early spring 1863. On December 15, Captain John Stubbs of the 1st Alabama Infantry requested clothing, camp kettles, and "short handled spades."[68]

The Confederate commissary department might have delivered more supplies to Port Hudson, but they were hampered by sickness that struck Confederate sailors as well as soldiers. A Confederate sailor identified only as Evan served on the supply boat *Drover.* Evan complained in a letter home that he was unable to work for "six or seven weeks" because he suffered from "rheumatism."[69] Evan did not explain his symptoms, but people diagnosed with rheumatism often suffered from inflammation and pain in the joints and muscles. It is unclear how many of Evan's shipmates may have also been sick, but the manpower-poor Confederacy suffered every time a worker was unable to rise from his sickbed, and desperate soldiers at Port Hudson felt the loss of every delayed shipment.

Some food continued to flow into Port Hudson, but without the warehouses Miller proposed, much of the food that the men did not consume quickly spoiled. Daniel Smith later recalled that the Confederate government shipped in cattle from Texas and "great herds of long-horned oxen swimming the Mississippi was a curious but not uncommon sight." Cows that arrived in the prime of life quickly "became skeletonized" by the poor pastures near Port Hudson. Tennessee chaplain J. H. McNeilly watched men boil the tough beef for hours without making it any more palatable. He wondered aloud if the cattle slaughtered for Port Hudson's garrison were "the only animals in existence without a single particle of fat in their composition." In 1919, fifty-seven years after his service, McNeilly explained that his memory of the beef he ate at Port Hudson "is still nauseating."[70]

The Confederate army stored some corn in open sheds, which provided little protection. Boatloads of corn sat in the open on damp landing docks until it became musty and inedible. A large shipment of pork spoiled after it remained in the cargo hold of a steamship for too long. Quartermasters, eager to protect pork from moisture, sometimes used so much salt on the meat that they inadvertently ruined it. Soldiers became so hungry that they ate spoiled food rather than go hungry, and many suffered from food poisoning. Angry men grumbled in the ranks and concluded, "if Port Hudson falls, we will have to thank the commissary department for it." Confederate soldiers took matters into their own hands to supplement their rations. Daniel Smith wrote that men purchased food from farmers in the countryside and went fishing in the river and cypress ponds. According to J. H. McNeilly, the Tennesseans at Port Hudson lived mostly on molasses, sweet potatoes, and pumpkins from nearby farms in the fall of 1862. William Porter of the 16th Arkansas Infantry enjoyed both fishing and hunting alligators while camped near Port Hudson.[71]

At least one group of Confederate soldiers engaged in an unconventional protest against their poor rations. According to a story published in the *Memphis Daily Appeal,* in November 1862 the unidentified mounted colonel of an unnamed Arkansas regiment was drilling his regiment as several carriages full of ladies looked on. Hoping to impress the ladies, the colonel ordered his men to shout out a war cry of "Butler the Beast!" This proposed war cry referred to Benjamin Butler, who became infamous for Order No. 28, which stated that Union forces under his command would treat any woman who insulted Federal soldiers as "a woman of the town plying her avocation." The Arkansas colonel was shocked when, instead of yelling "Butler the Beast!" his men cried out "Bull Beef!" in protest of the spoiled beef that made up the bulk of their rations. According to the newspaper, the war cry startled the colonel so badly that his horse bolted away for parts unknown, and drill ended for the day.[72]

Confederate soldiers found time for recreation. Edward McMorries claimed that many members of the 1st Alabama enjoyed "Kangaroo Courts," in which a soldier attempted to convince a jury to convict a comrade of some farcical crime for the delight of spectators. Aspiring journalists in the ranks published humorous newspapers filled with camp gossip. Tennesseans amused themselves by pulling sticky strands of locally grown molasses into candy. Officers with access to horses rode out to plantations in the countryside to visit the area's young ladies. According to Edward McMorries, "if there was anything on earth that a Southern woman, during these days, could not resist it was a Confederate soldier with brass bars and stars on his coat collar." Corporal McMorries also claimed, perhaps with a wink, that "there was some fascination even with a corporal's stripes."[73]

Alcohol became a problem in the Confederate camps. Many men brewed and drank corn beer. Some men were not content with corn beer brewed in camp and developed a taste for distilled liquor. Louisianans produced uniquely flavorful and intoxicating varieties of rum made from local sugar. Confederate officers saw rum as a threat to military order and ordered handpicked soldiers to fight a war on liquor. Army patrols fanned out into the countryside to destroy stills. It is not clear how the civilians responded to the soldiers who destroyed their valuable property. Camp guards poured out any rum they found in camp and, according to Edward McMorries, "the thirsty men would dip it in cups or drink it out of the ditches until driven off by the guards."[74]

Alcohol led to conflict. Robert Patrick of the 4th Louisiana Infantry noted in his diary that his friend Batchelor got drunk and tried to climb into an ambulance for some unknown reason. The ambulance driver objected and struck Batchelor with a stick. Batchelor responded by stabbing the driver in the head with a knife. It was a minor wound but one that ended the conflict. Batchelor was just one of many members of the garrison who drank too much and then got into trouble for fighting or disobeying orders. Robert Patrick struggled with alcohol and explained, "I attribute all my faults and short-comings to that awful habit of drinking which has truly proved the bane of my existence." Patrick confessed in his diary, "sometimes I look back upon my past life with much regret, being conscious (as I now am) of what I could have been and what I could have done if I had only pursued the right course." He had promised his mother that he would not drink any more. Patrick lamented that, the last time he "got on a bender," he lost $220, which was all the money he had saved. Confederate officers tried to keep order, and courts martial became a common feature of life in the Confederate camps around Port Hudson.[75]

Religion provided men with an alternative outlet for their energy. There were several Catholic chaplains in camp but few Protestant chaplains. To fill the gap, several officers who had been preachers before the war worked as unofficial chaplains. J. H. McNeilly led daily church services in the Port Hudson hospital. On Sundays he led two services on the town's parade ground, and "usually the attendance was good." Confederate officers tried "setting the example" for their men. W. C. Porter attended many church services and participated in classes that focused on reciting Bible passages.[76]

Some soldiers enjoyed music at Port Hudson. The 1st Alabama Infantry's brass band of ten musicians played during regimental drills, and, according to Edward McMorries, "they played us to sleep" every night. Officers of the regiment took up a collection to pay band members an additional wage for their services in the band. The 1st Alabama also included several fiddle players, the most famous of whom was Jack Gibson, who gave free concerts from his tent. He was wounded in the right arm, "resulting

A row of log structures at Port Hudson, presumably used by Confederate troops during the siege at Port Hudson. Library of Congress.

in a permanent deflection in the arm." When he healed, members of the regiment asked Gibson if he could still play his fiddle. Gibson replied, "why yes, my arm now has exactly the right crook for the business."[77]

Soldiers built homes near Port Hudson. Robert Patrick convinced a friend working a government workshop to make him a pair of benches. Patrick then laid an old door on top of the benches to form a bed that kept him off the wet ground. His blankets provided additional comfort. Patrick pitched a tent over his bed. Every night he made a fire just outside his tent, where he assembled with friends and "while[d] away the long hours" by "telling long yarns and eating roasted potatoes." Later, Patrick dug a drainage ditch around his tent to keep the ground under his tent dry. Eliza Goble, wife of James Goble of the 1st Alabama Infantry, came to Port Hudson and took up residence with her husband in a house within the Confederate lines. The couple's new home was on the northwestern end of town, not far from the section of the line held by the 1st Alabama Infantry. It was a one-story "old house" near a church.[78]

Port Hudson was surrounded by water, but the men struggled to keep clean. Soldiers suffered horribly at the hands of "gray backs," which infested their clothing and bodies. Men struggled to free themselves from the biting insects that tormented them. They bathed whenever they had access to clean water and soap. However, most men found that the best way of killing the pests was to hold their clothing just close enough to the campfire to kill the insects without getting so close that they damaged their clothing. Members the 10th Tennessee Infantry passed the time listening to the chatter of the "Cajan" [*sic*] French-speaking 30th Louisiana and their washerwomen. A Tennessean claimed that the women "can give one flutter of her tongue and say more than you can say in a week."[79]

—3—

My Thoughts Are Always of You

THE FEDERAL ADVANCE STALLS

You are my hearts [*sic*] dearest hope and I do not think you realize I feel the separation. My thoughts are always of you and my dear children. When I first left home I worried very much about you, but I have learned to trust in our savior and I have found confidence and feel that you will always be true to one who loves you so dearly. As for me dearest love I never see or think of any females since leaving you. In Annapolis there were ladies enough but I was always in camp and there is none here in Baton Rouge. I am closely pinned to my duties and only go out once a week (Sunday to church) so you see I am strictly a lone man, so dear wife have faith in God and me and someday (I hope not very distant) he will restore to you your ever affectionate husband.[1]

—WILLIAM ALDIS, 131st New York Infantry

We have to work on the fortifications every two days and then perhapse [sic] we will have to leave them after all our hard labor. Yesterday we were down there and we got as wet as you need want to see any person and when we came home we found every thing [*sic*] wet as usal [*sic*] when it rains. We are verry [*sic*] comfortably fixed as regards sleeping and so on. We have good tints with flys [*sic*] and have chimneys to them we have beads [*sic*] mad up off the ground and straw on them but that is not like home."[2]

—WILLIAM MAGEE, 39th Mississippi Infantry

THE FALL OF 1862 was a rough time for the Union. The Army of the Potomac in Virginia lost the battles of Second Bull Run (August 29–30, 1862) and Fredericksburg (December 11–15, 1862). On the western frontier, Native Americans fought back against mistreatment by white settlers, forcing the Federal government to divert troops west to put down the uprising

Major General Nathaniel P. Banks.
Library of Congress.

in the Dakota War of 1862 (August 17–December 26, 1862). Along the Gulf of Mexico, Federal forces failed to capitalize on their capture of New Orleans, and their offensive against what was left of the Confederate-controlled Mississippi River stalled. Voters voiced their displeasure with President Lincoln and the Republicans in the midterm elections. The Democratic Party won gubernatorial elections in New York and New Jersey, took control of the state legislatures in New Jersey, Indiana, and the president's home state of Illinois. The Democrats also picked up thirty-five seats in the House of Representatives.[3]

Stinging from political and military setbacks, the Lincoln administration made important changes to Union military leadership in the winter of 1862, particularly along the Mississippi River Valley. On November 9, 1862, Lincoln ordered General Nathaniel Banks to take command of the Department of the Gulf and remove Benjamin Butler. Like his predecessor Butler, Banks was a political general and not a professional soldier. Banks's political career was marked by a savvy ability to remain one step ahead of the voters. Initially a Democrat, he joined the Know Nothings, and became a Republican just as the new party became prominent. Banks resigned from politics in 1861 to accept a general's commission in the Union army.[4]

Banks was a better politician than a soldier. In his first major campaign, Banks suffered defeat at the hands of Stonewall Jackson's troops in Virginia's Shenandoah Valley. Banks was not a great general, but Lincoln understood that politics were just as important as military science. Butler's autocratic rule of New Orleans had alienated many southerners. Lincoln may have hoped that Banks, well known for his political versatility, could play the peacemaker, rallying southerners to the Union banner. Lincoln made Banks "the ranking general in the Southwest" and ordered him to rip the Mississippi River from the Confederacy. As Banks pushed north up the Mississippi River from New Orleans, General Grant would lead the Army of the Tennessee down the Mississippi River toward Vicksburg. To help Banks achieve his objective, Lincoln sent another ten thousand men from Boston and New York to join the Union army in Louisiana.[5]

Lawrence Van Alstyne of the 128th New York Infantry sailed south alongside General Banks. The New Yorkers boarded the cargo ship *Arago* and departed New York Harbor on December 4, 1862. The New Yorkers heard that General Banks was on the *Baltic*, another ship in the flotilla. Van Alstyne recorded in his diary that "anything by way of excitement is good and I am glad something is going to happen." Van Alstyne may have changed his mind a few days later, noting that "the sea is very rough." Van Alstyne and many of his comrades became seasick, disease broke out, several members of the regiment died, and Van Alstyne declared, "it is a wonder so many are alive." The enlisted men like Van Alstyne were only allowed to drink distilled water, which many men blamed for their illnesses. When Van Alstyne discovered the barrels of fresh water reserved for the officers, he built a straw, snuck into the storeroom, and drank all he could hold. He expected to get caught, but the desire for good water weighed more heavily than the fear of punishment. One of the few bright spots on the trip for the New Yorkers might have been when the men watched porpoises "skip out of the water" and dive back again as they chased flying fish.[6]

Massachusetts infantryman Frank Flinn was pleased that the ship he boarded was fitted with bunks but disappointed that the ship carried "one thousand men and millions of gray-backs." He described the regiment's first battle as a fight against the tiny pests that infested the ship. After making a determined assault, "it was a drawn battle." Flinn reserved greater scorn for the "laughable" officers who kept the ship's destination secret, worried that someone would tell the Confederates about the army's plans and spoil the grand surprise.[7]

John Whitehead sailed south on board the *Che Kiang*. The thirty-eight-year-old farmer turned soldier complained in a letter home that the boat did not provide nearly enough beds. He considered himself lucky to make his bed on the mess hall table. Most men slept on the floor, which was "too nasty for hogs to lie in." Other men took their chances on the boat's open decks, where they were exposed to the weather. Whitehead claimed the boat barely avoided capsizing in a "perfect gale." He told his wife that "I feel that you have almost been persuaded to be a Christian, that I have kept you back, but I will do it no longer," because he believed that God saved him from the storm.[8]

Captain Orton Clark of the 116th New York Infantry later recalled that the men's joy at the start of the voyage quickly turned to despair. The "jar and clatter of the engine" made it hard for the men to sleep. A storm hit the fleet, battering the boat and turning the sea into "raging billows." Men became so sick that "organs were cleaned as they had probably never been before." Matthew Andrews of Company G suffered from "congestive chills" and died within a few hours of becoming ill. A chaplain held an Episcopal funeral service, and the men buried their comrade at sea.[9]

In a letter home to his family, John Barnard admitted that the voyage was rough but mocked his comrades who failed to accept the hardships he felt everyone should expect when joining the army. Barnard called many of the men in his regiment "old grannies" because they complained endlessly about the difficult passage. He claimed that a few even proclaimed that "if they had known that they were to be so badly used they would not have enlisted." Barnard was far more sympathetic to other men who did not complain even though they became so sick that surgeons predicted they would be unfit for duty for weeks.[10]

As Union reinforcements streamed south toward New Orleans, Federals already in Louisiana tried to make themselves comfortable and find time for relaxation. Massachusetts artilleryman Henry T. Aiken was stationed at Fort Pike, positioned to protect New Orleans. Aiken asked his father to send a care package of luxuries, including butter, dried apples, sugar, a jackknife, applesauce, and two woolen shirts. George Thomson, serving in the 38th Massachusetts Infantry posted on Ship Island, wrote home to his mother that he and his comrades enjoyed hunting alligators during their leisure hours. Samuel Ellis and his comrades made beds from moss and tried, unsuccessfully, to attract the attention of young southern women who wore "secesh cockades" and greeted Union soldiers with "a curl of the lip." Despite the hostility, Ellis wrote in his diary, "the country charms with its magnificent lemon and orange groves," and declared, "I am in love with the sunny south." He announced plans to return to the South after the war and live the rest of his life in "this beautiful country."[11]

While the Union army in Louisiana waited for reinforcements and reorganized under new leadership, the Federal navy remained active. On November 15, 1862, at about 10:30 p.m., the *Kineo, Sciota, Katahdin,* and *Itasca* steamed north up the Mississippi River from Donaldsonville, Louisiana, about seventy miles north of New Orleans. The sailors planned to gather intelligence on Confederate positions between Donaldsonville and Port Hudson, to find the best place to land troops for an attack on Port Hudson, and to determine the condition of any fortifications at Port Hudson. They passed Baton Rouge without incident at 7:00 a.m. At 10:35 a.m. the sailors arrived at Profit Island, about twenty miles south of Port Hudson, and saw the first signs of Confederate defenders. The Confederates sheltered behind a well-constructed earthwork on the east bank, eighty feet above the river, studded with at least five heavy cannons. Soon after spotting the earthwork, Lieutenant Commander Ransom, commanding the USS *Kineo,* noticed Confederates on the west bank using signal flags to communicate with their comrades behind the earthworks. Ransom ordered his men to fire on the signalers with a rifled cannon. The artillery fire interrupted but did not end the communication, as the rebels dove for cover with every incoming shot only to pop back up again while the sailors reloaded. Ransom then saw Confederate cavalrymen on the east bank who appeared to be studying the Union ships. Ransom ordered his men to fire on the gray-clad equestrians. The cavalrymen were not as stubborn as their comrades on the west bank and disappeared behind the earthworks after the first shot flew in their direction.[12]

As the rebel cavalrymen disappeared, escaped slaves approached the bank. Ransom sent a boat to pick them up and bring them back to the *Kineo.* The former slaves provided Ransom with information on the river channel and the rebel activity in the area. One of the escaped slaves had worked on the rebel positions and provided the Federal sailors with information on Confederate defenses. Intrigued by the former slave's report, Ransom ordered the ships to move north and scout the Confederate positions at Port Hudson.[13]

When the Union sailors arrived near Port Hudson, they immediately noticed a series of Confederate earthworks at irregular intervals. Numerous tents were scattered among the earthworks. Members of the 1st Alabama struck their tents and packed their knapsacks when the Federals arrived. The Alabamians prepared for what they thought would be their first fight since arriving at Port Hudson and deployed along the bank as sharpshooters. The Alabamians loaded their guns and waited for the order to open fire.[14]

Federal sailors sailed forward cautiously. Lieutenant Commander Francis Roe of the USS *Katahdin* did not like the looks of the Confederate positions as they came into view. His dislike turned to worry as the *Katahdin* came deeper into the curve and he realized that the Confederates had used the curving bank and thick woods to conceal many of their cannons so that they were invisible to boats on the river until the boats were within point blank range. Commander Ransom tried to aim the *Kineo*'s 11-inch cannon at the rebel positions, but the Confederates had situated their earthworks at odd angles from the tightly twisting channel, which made bringing the naval artillery to bear more trouble than Ransom thought it was worth. Ransom concluded that the Confederate positions at Port Hudson were far stronger and a far greater threat to Union control of the Mississippi than Vicksburg. Francis Roe believed that the rebels controlled about nine miles of the river near Port Hudson with positions so strong that "I do not believe any navy can pass through it." Lieutenant Fredrick

Rogers agreed with Roe and argued that only troops landed well below Port Hudson could hope to capture Port Hudson.[15]

After completing their reconnaissance, the Union ships withdrew to the south. Ransom reported that "not a shot, not even a musket was fired at us at any time during the reconnaissance." Roe believed that the Confederates did not fire because they were trying to lure the Federal ships deeper into their network of mutually supporting batteries, where they could destroy the Union ships. However, the Federals refused to take the bait and withdrew before getting into the heart of the Confederate positions. The twisting river and narrow channel made returning south easier said than done as the Federal sailors slowly maneuvered down the river. On the way back, Ransom reported that he was both surprised and pleased when he realized that Confederates had done nothing to set up batteries on the west bank of the river, which would have allowed them to catch Union fleet in a deadly crossfire from both banks. Roe reported that steep banks and thick woods made landing troops impossible at most spots along the river between Baton Rouge and Port Hudson. However, there was one opening just across from Profit Island, about five miles south of the first Confederate battery, in a thinner bit of forest, near a road into the interior, where Roe thought that it might be possible to land troops.[16]

On December 12 the *Kineo*, *Katahdin*, *Winona*, and Port Hudson's old nemesis the *Essex* made another reconnaissance in force of Port Hudson. The Union ships arrived near the Port Hudson batteries at 2:00 p.m. Two men greeted the sailors from the bank, and the *Kineo* sent a small boat toward the shore. When the *Kineo*'s boat got within about thirty yards of the shore, Confederate soldiers emerged from cover and poured small arms fire into the unarmed Union boat. The Confederates failed to hit any of the Union sailors, but bullets punctured the Federal boat. In response, Union gunboats returned fire with loads of grapeshot and canister. The Confederates disappeared as quickly as they emerged. Later, the Federals learned that their cannon fire killed four and wounded five Confederates.[17]

The following day, the *Kineo* and *Katahdin* steamed back down the river, leaving the *Essex* and the *Winona* at anchor near Port Hudson. The *Kineo* and the *Katahdin* traded sporadic fire with Confederate forces as they traveled south down the river. F. L. Allen may have referred to this incident in a letter he wrote on December 16. According to Allen's account, a Confederate captain "gave a Negro twenty dollar and he looled [*sic*] 6 of them to the bank in a canoe." When the Federals approached the bank, "they were instantly killed." In response, the Union navy "shelled them terribly" but inflicted no casualties on the Confederates.[18] It is also possible that Allen's account referred to another incident, which would suggest that the technique of luring Union sailors into ambushes was common.

Early on the evening of December 13, the *Essex* and *Winona* anchored for the night near Port Hudson. A stretch of river in enemy-held territory, near strong works, was not an ideal place to spend the night, but it was probably less dangerous than traveling at night on the ever-shifting Mississippi River without charts or reliable river pilots. Federal sailors traveling the river typically anchored just before dark, waited for nightfall, and then moved a short distance away. The simple technique usually protected Union riverboats from Confederate harassing fire overnight since Confederates tended to fire on the last place they saw the gunboats rather than on new positions that the rebel gunners could rarely see. Shortly after nightfall, Winfield Schley, the *Winona*'s executive officer, asked the ship's captain if he would like to move the *Winona* for the evening. The captain declined Schley's suggestion without explanation and sent most of the crew to bed.[19]

While the Union sailors slept, Confederate soldiers near Port Hudson crossed the river and moved into position for a daybreak ambush on the anchored Federal ships. Captain Boone's Louisiana Battery took a pair of smoothbore 6-pounder cannons and a single 12-pound howitzer across the river and placed them behind a levee, directly across from the *Winona* and the *Essex*, anchored just yards away. Companies D and F of the 1st Alabama Infantry prepared to provide infantry support for the artillerymen. The new Confederate positions were less than 250 yards from the unsuspecting Federal ships.[20]

At daybreak on December 14, Confederate batteries and infantrymen opened a "terrific fire" on the *Winona*. A 12-pounder cannon ball cut a Union officer in two, killing him instantly and wounding another sailor. Cannon balls punctured the *Winona* twenty-seven times. The fire on the *Winona* was so intense that the vessel took refuge behind the metal hull of the *Essex*. Sailors lashed the two ships together with the *Essex* on the western side, facing the Confederate batteries, and the damaged *Winona* facing the far safer east bank.[21]

Now operating as a single unit, the *Essex* and the *Winona* drifted down the river stern first as the Confederates continued to fire on them, although their fire had made little impact on the *Essex*'s armor. After arriving near Profit Island, the *Essex* and *Winona* turned around and began steaming south bow first. This put the ships in a better position to maneuver, but it also meant that the wooden-hulled *Winona* no longer enjoyed the protection of the *Essex*'s armored hull. The Confederates noticed that the *Winona* was vulnerable, and 1,500 infantrymen opened fire on the already damaged Federal ship, keeping up a withering small arms fire for two miles. Confederate soldiers cheered when the *Essex* and *Winona* finally departed out of range of their positions.[22]

Both Union and Confederate sources described the foray as a Confederate victory. The *Natchez Daily Courier* announced "gunboats repulsed at Port Hudson" and praised the "great gallantry" of the Confederate gunners. The *Memphis Daily Appeal* published essentially the same story, describing the Federal retreat in response to the excellent work of Captain Boone's artillerymen. Union naval officer Francis Roe believed that the expedition had been a costly failure. He argued that the navy had failed to gather any new intelligence on a trip that resulted in the death of an officer and severe damage to the *Winona*. Roe argued, "we are losing all confidence in Admiral Farragut," who Roe believed displayed "no judgement or prudence" and was "wasteful of life and blood to a criminal degree."[23]

On December 14, 1862, General Nathaniel Banks arrived in New Orleans and formally took command of the Union Army of the Gulf. General Butler accepted the orders removing him from command without public complaint and promised to help Banks with the transition of power. Before leaving New Orleans, he wrote an open letter to the "Soldiers of the Army of the Gulf," which praised them while blaming the stagnated offensive on the government for failing to provide the transportation required for a successful offensive. Butler praised Banks and bid the men a fond farewell. Some men did not accept Butler's excuses or share his fond regards. Francis Roe reported that the government should have removed Butler long ago. After getting in his final word with the men and helping Banks take command, Butler left the Gulf and took a new position with the Union Department of Virginia and North Carolina.[24]

Union newspapers generally approved of Banks's promotion and predicted that he would accomplish great things. In Pennsylvania, the

Raftsman's Journal claimed that Banks "is the greatest general officer that has been taken from the ranks of civil life."[51] The *Urbana Union* in Ohio wrote that Banks's promotion was "a valuable change" because Butler was "not suited" for command.[52] The *New York Herald* praised Banks as "a statesman and a man of sound discretion," who would not repeat Butler's mistakes.[53] The *Chicago Tribune* referred to Banks as a man with "common sense and cool determination." The paper predicted "place him anywhere and he will do well . . . put 25,000 troops at his back and he will find an enemy for them to punish."[25]

Banks took up residence in the St. Charles Hotel and made the building his headquarters. As he set up his office, Banks reorganized Federal forces and appointed a general staff to help him conduct operations. Banks informed Halleck that he was unsure of exact Confederate strength in the region, but he did share a report, from a Confederate captain spying for the Union who Banks thought was credible, that the rebels had 23,000 men dug in at Port Hudson and that a division of Confederates were on route to Port Hudson from California. These reports were incorrect. At that time, the Confederates had no more than 5,000 men in a series of positions from Port Hudson to Baton Rouge. No Confederate division was coming from California. It is unclear if the unnamed Confederate captain was misinformed or if he was intentionally spreading misinformation to the Federals. Banks informed Halleck that, regardless the strength of the Confederate presence on the lower Mississippi River, he would go on the offensive immediately, assuring Halleck that "whatever may happen we shall not be idle."[26]

While it appears that Banks believed Port Hudson's defenders were strong, Banks and his men may have felt pressured to act by newspaper reports that Port Hudson's defenses were weak. A writer for the *Louisville Daily Journal* in Kentucky described Port Hudson's garrison as consisting of "about 5,000, most of them sick." The *Daily Delta* of New Orleans, now under Union control, published reports from southern civilians in Louisiana that "the rebel army about Port Hudson is actually rotting." The press described Port Hudson's soldiers as "without blankets," wearing "tattered garments," without shoes or hats, and "living on half rations." The unnamed writer for the *Daily Delta* believed that the Confederate defenders were "dupes" deceived by "traitorous leaders." The press predicted that soon "the scales will fall from their eyes" and the Confederate garrison of Port Hudson would turn against the Confederacy.[27] While it is true that many Confederate soldiers lacked basic supplies and that some men deserted to the Federals, there is no evidence that most men ever considered themselves "dupes" or that the majority ever turned against their leaders.

Banks was determined to "not be idle," but many of the soldiers defending Port Hudson seemed happy to remain in place and focus on comfort. Jabez Cannon and the rest of the 27th Alabama Infantry had few tents, but they found "stately magnolias" near their campground and the men quickly transformed the trees into "very respectable houses." Cannon and his comrades next made beds from "the long hanging moss which grew abundantly on all the trees." William Magee of the 39th Mississippi Infantry informed his friend William Allen, "we are verry [*sic*] comfortably fixed" in Port Hudson. The Mississippians constructed hybrid shelters of tents and dirt that were equipped with chimneys. Within their new homes, the men slept on raised platforms covered with straw.[28]

Despite the relative comforts he enjoyed, William Magee lamented, "that is not like home." Robert Patrick noted in his diary, "our rations are right slim now." The men had nothing but beef and cornmeal. He thought that the poor diet "is what causes so much sickness in camp." The water was bad, so Patrick preferred to drink homebrew corn beer, even though the beer was "almost vinegar." Perhaps Patrick should have taken his chances with the water. Several days after he began drinking the vinegar-like beer, he reported in his diary, "my stomach is a little deranged from drinking corn beer." Smallpox broke out in the Confederate camps around Port Hudson, but Patrick took comfort in the fact that he was vaccinated shortly before coming to Port Hudson. The twenty-seven-year-old Robert Patrick wished that the war was over so "I could be making something for old age, if I ever live long enough to be an old man." He considered his time in the army "worse than thrown away." Jabez Cannon noted in his diary that the men did laundry in the creeks. The men washed only a single garment at a time, "having no change." Many of the Alabamians suffered from infestations of "gray backs" when they came to Port Hudson, but they eliminated them after a few good washings at Port Hudson. Cannon had heard that even boiling water would not kill "gray backs," but he was happy to prove that rumor incorrect. An officer caught F. L. Allen of the 39th Mississippi

Admiral David Farragut.
Library of Congress.

Infantry with a bottle of whiskey. Allen expected to be punished, but for some unspecified reason, the officers did not punish Allen and simply put him back to work on the fortifications with the rest of his regiment.[29]

On December 15, 1862, Banks ordered his men to prepare for an offensive. For the first move of the new campaign, Banks directed Brigadier GeneralCuvier Grover, a tough Maine-born professional solider, to take 4,500 soldiers up the Mississippi River and recapture Baton Rouge. Banks expected an easy victory against the 500 to 1,000 Confederate soldiers he believed were guarding the former Louisiana capitol. Admiral Farragut rounded up a flotilla of fifteen ships, including the *Essex*, and sent them to New Orleans. The ships would transport soldiers and provide fire support on the expedition to Baton Rouge.[30]

US sloop of war *Richmond*. Library of Congress.

At 4:00 a.m. on December 16, the Federal forces began to move north up the Mississippi River. According to Commander Alden on the USS *Richmond*, "the levees were crowded with people watching the arrival of the great expedition" in New Orleans. The sailors saw camps of Union soldiers all along the riverbanks as the boat moved north. The once-destroyed sugar mills along the river were again grinding sugar, under the watchful eye of Union troops. Sergeant William Tiemann watched from the deck of his northbound transport as "the negroes waved their hats and aprons." In contrast, whites "stood by in sullen silence and with scowling looks." Tiemann suspected that the whites he saw did not like "their country's invaders." The transport was overloaded so most men did not have beds and slept on the exposed decks. The army made no arrangements for men to prepare their uncooked rations, and many men went hungry for most of the trip. Tiemann reported that most men remained healthy, which attributed to the good weather and the fact that most of the men on the campaign were vaccinated against smallpox before leaving New York. James Ewer, a seventeen-year-old bugler, later remembered that, late on the evening of December 16, Colonel Chickering assembled his men on the eve of the "serious work" that would be the regiment's first encounter with the enemy. Chickering ordered the men to load their guns and asked the chaplain to say a prayer for what was "a solemn moment for all present."[31]

The Union forces arrived at Baton Rouge early on the morning of December 17. At 8:30 a.m. the *Essex* shelled the city in preparation for an amphibious assault. Shortly after the bombardment ended, the Federal transports began unloading soldiers at Baton Rouge. Henry Gardner reported that he did not see any Confederate flags in Baton Rouge as he entered the town, but he did see the flag of France flying over the former French city. The small Confederate garrison of less than five hundred men retreated without a fight, and the Federal infantry did not fire a single shot. At 9:00 a.m. the USS *Richmond's* crew sent a landing party ashore, which advanced directly to the state capitol building and hoisted the flag of the United States over the building. Francis Roe, commanding the USS *Katahdin*, believed that "we are now upon the eve of great events," since the capture of Baton Rouge was "the first real movement of a good military character I have witnessed."[32]

William Aldis wrote his wife that "the people seem delighted" by the arrival of the Union army. If th at seems hard to believe, his next line pointed out that "they have not seen so much money or provisions for many a day." The people of Baton Rouge might not have liked Uncle Sam's soldiers, but according to Aldis they were very fond of "Uncle Sam's greenbacks." Soldiers who ran out of official US currency paid for goods in "railroad shin plasters and every other style" of money. Some soldiers spent their money on women, and Aldis acknowledged that there were "ladies enough in camp," but Aldis assured his wife that "I never see or think of any females since leaving you." He asked his "dear wife" to "have faith in God and me." He longed for the day God would "restore to you, your ever affectionate husband."[33]

Massachusetts infantryman William Smith painted a slightly different picture of Baton Rouge in a letter to his wife. He explained, "there looks as though there has been a war here." He saw "a great many vice houses" in the city, but they "are burned to the ground." Smith claimed that "most of the people have gone away" and "everything is scarce." Smith gave no impression that he was aware of men spending money on women, but he did delight in trading army issued hard tack and salt pork for sweet potatoes.[34]

News traveled almost as quickly as the Union transports. Before nightfall on December 17, the rebels were aware that the Federals were moving north up the Mississippi River. Orders circulated through the Confederate camps north of Baton Rouge, canceling all leaves and telling the men to prepare for a fight. Some of the men might have been worried, but Robert Patrick was not. He felt that the Confederate garrison had made the Union troops timid by "thrashing" them during their previous visits to Port Hudson.[35]

General Cuvier Grover was not optimistic. His 4,500 Union troops, many of whom were fresh troops who had never seen action, were a far larger force than the few hundred rebels they sent fleeing north from Baton Rouge but far fewer than the 23,000 Confederate troops rumored to be just a few miles north at Port Hudson. Grover urged Banks to send reinforcements. While Grover waited for additional troops to arrive, he ordered his men to "throw up earthworks" and prepare to defend Baton Rouge from a possible Confederate counterattack. According to William Smith, the army hired "contrabands," who flooded into Baton Rouge to do most of the work on the fortifications. Sergeant William Tiemann wrote that "the men were thoroughly drilled" every day. Worried that the Confederates might counterattack, the officers often woke men in the middle of the night and sent them to their posts to await "a possible onslaught by the enemy." The nights were cold and the air was heavy with "thick mist" that drenched the men and made it impossible to see, but Tiemann claimed, "we took it cheerfully, however, as a soldier's duty and were soon used to it." Many men began to "think the enemy was not coming at all." Reinforcements flowed into the Union camps at Baton Rouge until roughly 10,000 troops camped near Baton Rouge.[36]

On December 22, 1862, General Johnston sent Jefferson Davis his plan to defend the remaining Confederate territory on the Mississippi River. Johnston believed that the Confederacy would need about 40,000 men to hold Vicksburg and Port Hudson. He noted that Beall commanded about 5,500 men around Port Hudson, but Johnston believed that it would take at least 11,000 men to protect Port Hudson. Johnston argued that taking troops from Bragg's command in Tennessee would free Rosecrans to reinforce Federal forces in Virginia. Therefore, he wanted to pull reinforcements from Arkansas.[37]

On Christmas Eve 1862, the Union navy conducted another reconnaissance in force of Port Hudson. The *Essex* left Baton Rouge early that morning and found that the Confederate garrison had made substantial improvements to their earthworks. Just a few weeks before, the southernmost Confederate positions near Port Hudson were little more than "an irregular mound of earth," but now they had "extensive preparations" crowned with heavy artillery. The Confederates did not fire on the *Essex*, possibly because they were still not entirely ready for action. Charles Caldwell, commanding the *Essex*, saw the reinforced position as evidence that the Confederacy was focusing all their defensive power at Port Hudson. Caldwell suggested that this would make a Union victory easier since Union forces could concentrate all their efforts in one place, instead of having to root out countless little positions all along the Mississippi River.[38]

Confederate soldiers in Port Hudson tried to enjoy the Christmas holiday. The officers gave everyone the day off from duty and, according to Jabez Cannon, "it was a warm and pleasant day." Cannon lamented that they had none of the turkey, cake, or eggnog that many of them had enjoyed in the past because there were no such luxuries at Port Hudson, at least not for common soldiers. There was plenty of sugar, but "we are sick and tired of it." Some soldiers purchased jugs of "Louisiana Rum," which sold for one dollar for each ounce of drink. Cannon did not drink any of the liquor, which he considered "the vilest stuff a man ever tried to drink." He noted that many of the men seemed to enjoy the rum, but he predicted in his diary that the drinkers would not enjoy the headache that would follow the next day. Samuel Thompson wrote a letter home to his wife on Christmas in which he thanked her for supporting his decision to serve in the army and assured her, "peace will come." He hoped it would come soon. He wanted to go home, but felt he was "obliged to stay and fight," both "for you and the south." William Porter noted in his diary that the men tried to celebrate but "it makes me think of home." He and many of his comrades had "the blues." William Dixon visited family members near Jackson, Louisiana, which was roughly fifteen miles northeast of Port Hudson. While on leave, Dixon had two ambrotypes taken as gifts for his mother and cousin, paying thirteen dollars in Confederate currency for each picture.[39]

Several Confederate officers resigned their commissions and returned home during the Christmas season. On December 18, 2nd Lieutenant Isaac Guest submitted his resignation from the Confederate army. He explained that his family was in northwest Arkansas, "a place which has been repeatedly occupied by our armies." Guest's family was unable to "procure for themselves the necessities of life" and had "no one to assist them." Guest wanted to go home and care for his family, believing that the duties of a husband and father were even more sacred than the duties of a solider. Jasper Woodruff resigned his commission on January 2, 1863. Like Guest, he wanted to care for his family, which was "compelled to flee from home by the country being overrun by the Federals." However, he stated that he was resigning because declining manpower in his regiment had forced him to command a consolidated unit composed of his company and the fragments of several other companies, and "I am satisfied that my presence creates dissatisfaction and distrust."[40]

Some Confederate soldiers did not get permission to leave Port Hudson but left anyway. Newspapers reported that men were absent without leave from Port Hudson and that the army urged them to return immediately. When the pleas fell on deaf ears, the army offered cash rewards to anyone who delivered a deserter to Port Hudson's commanders. Captain E. G. Mitchell received permission to return home and recruit new soldiers for the garrison. He never returned, and the army declared that he was a deserter. William Park, on the *Essex*, wrote that several Confederate deserters from Port Hudson decided to surrender to the ship's crew rather than return to the Confederate army. Captain Whitfield remained with the army at Port Hudson but confessed in a letter to his wife, "what a struggle have I to encounter between my duty to my country and sincere regard for those tender relations that still engross my affections, nor less earnestly appeal to my manhood for defense."[41]

William Thurman remained at his post, but he worried about his wife and children at Christmas time. In a letter to his wife, Margaret, he expressed his homesickness and boredom. He also gave his wife instructions on managing the family farm near Lynnville, about sixty miles south of Nashville, Tennessee. William told his wife to sell livestock, collect debts owed to the family, and get rid of any Confederate money in case the Federals returned to Middle Tennessee. In a letter written two days later, Thurman threatened his children, perhaps with a friendly paternal smile, that "if you don't mind and do right I will paddle you when I come home."[42] Thurman's letters clearly indicate that he wanted to be at home, managing his farm and raising his children, and not in Port Hudson, where he was bored and homesick. Thurman was not alone.

Like many of their counterparts in gray, Union soldiers also tried to enjoy the Christmas holiday season. A few days before Christmas, William Smith worried that his young daughter might have forgotten him and asked his wife if the little girl ever said anything about him, wondering, "has Hattie forgot her papa yet?" William Aldis wrote a letter home to his family from his camp near Baton Rouge in which he reminded them that he loved them and reminisced about previous Christmases. John Barnard wrote home to his sister on Christmas that he was "in good health" and that his only sorrow came from all the times he reported to mail call and was not one of the lucky men to get a letter. He begged his family to write more often. Louis Boyd, a Floridian serving as 3rd Assistant Engineer on the Union gunboat *Albatross*, had not received a letter from his wife since September. He later concluded that she was intentionally ignoring him because other men were getting letters and told her that he would not write again until she began writing him again.[43] Orton Clark spent Christmas on Ship Island, which he later claimed "is the most desolate and God-forsaken spot upon this footstool." However, Clark and the other officers gave the enlisted men "a great deal of sport" by agreeing to play the role of enlisted men for the day. Officers spent the holiday cooking and cleaning for the delight of their subordinates. At the end of the day, the officers gave the men another present. Each man received a dress coat and "shoulder scales," which "added very much to their appearance."[44]

Perhaps nobody in Louisiana had more to celebrate that Christmas than the former slaves, who enjoyed freedom on the fringes of the Union army camps. Union solider William Smith visited a Christmas Eve celebration held by former slaves at Baton Rouge. He told his wife that it began with a dance of "four or five hundred of them." Then they had a "prayer meeting," which was "such a one as I never attended before." Smith was apparently surprised "one of them would speak at the top of his voice and the rest would sing and respond to him in prayer." The participants "all sing one tune, and that tune is adapted to all words." After the service ended, "they all turn in together, men, women, and children." Smith acknowledged that "there is some of them that are quite intelligent" but also believed many were stupid. He also complained that they smelled bad.[45]

On December 27, 1862, Major General Frank Gardner arrived in Port Hudson with orders to take command of the Confederate garrison. Born on January 29, 1823, in New York City, Gardner was a professional soldier who graduated from West Point with Ulysses Grant in 1843 and earned praise from his superior officers for his gallantry during the war with Mexico (1846–1848). Although born in the North, he married Marie Celeste Mouton, who was the daughter of Alexandre Mouton, governor of Louisiana from 1843 to 1846. When the Civil War began, Gardner was forced

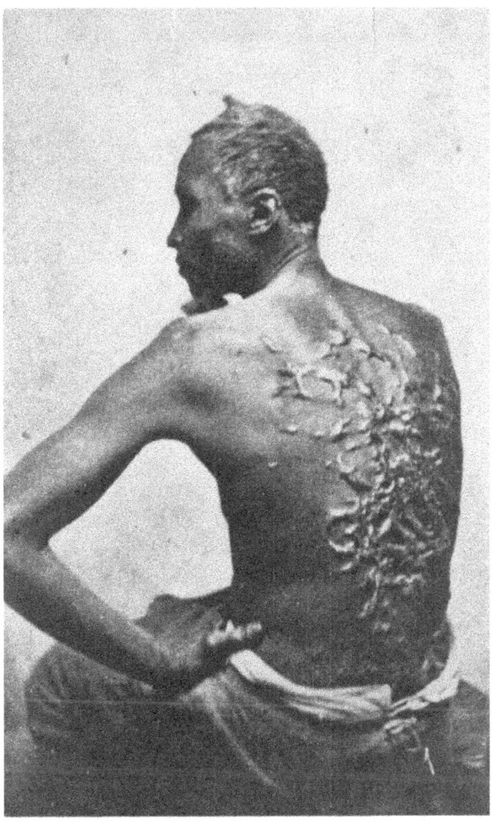

Escaped slave Gordon, also known as "Whipped Peter," showing his scarred back at a medical examination, Baton Rouge, Louisiana. Library of Congress.

to choose between his wife's Louisiana roots and his northern relatives, including his brother who served in the Union army. Gardner resigned from the US Army on April 7, 1861. Gardner commanded a cavalry brigade at Shiloh (April 6–7, 1862) and a brigade of infantry during the fall 1862 invasion of Kentucky. On December 13, 1862, the Confederate army promoted him to major general and ordered him to take command at Port Hudson.[46] The Confederate government ordered Gardner to cooperate with John Pemberton, who, like Gardner, was a northern-born man with a southern wife.

General Frank Gardner, commander of the Confederate Garrison at Port Hudson during the siege. Library of Congress.

Surviving accounts document a variety of Confederate reactions to Gardner's promotion. According to Howard Wright, Gardner immediately impressed the soldiers defending Port Hudson with his "fine, commanding appearance" as he quietly inspected the garrison. Gardner quickly convinced many soldiers that he was "a man of keen observation, a quick and practiced eye, frank and outspoken in all his comments." He addressed every issue "directly and to the point" as he spoke "practically" about every issue confronting the garrison. Gardner demonstrated "more than all" that he was "an able military engineer." According to Wright, most Confederate soldiers liked Gardner from the first moment they met him and the "good will of his men steadily increased." Wright acknowledged that first impressions might seem "trivial," but he explained that officers "will often fail or succeed according to the esteem and confidence he enjoys with his command." The garrison also thought that, by appointing a skilled and high-ranking officer like Gardner to command at Port Hudson, the Confederate government in Richmond was demonstrating their commitment to defending Port Hudson. Corporal John Powers agreed with Wright's assessment, writing in a letter that in General Gardner, "I am proud to say that I believe we have a verry [*sic*] good general and think if he has a chance, he will show himself to be a good one." The *Natchez Daily Courier* referred to Gardner as "a meritorious officer" who was married to daughter of a former Louisiana governor. Some Confederate soldiers were unimpressed with Gardner. Robert Patrick disliked Gardner because the new commander was "a very strict disciplinarian" who canceled all leaves and ended Patrick's frequent trips to his nearby family home near Clinton, Louisiana. Gardner consolidated several depleted regiments into single regiments. According to William Porter, the reorganization caused "great dissatisfaction."[47]

Federals had little nice to say about the new Confederate commander. The *Portland Daily Press* of Maine referred to Gardner as "a brave officer" but one who deserted the Union army to fight "for anarchy and despotism." Lieutenant Jacob Hasbrouck wrote home to his wife that Gardner had been a regular Army officer who deserted to the Confederacy. Erastus Gregory told his brother that Gardner was a thief who served as a paymaster for the Union army until he absconded with the army's payroll and deserted to the Confederacy.[48]

Federal claims that Frank Gardner was a deserter who robbed the government payroll were incorrect. Gardner resigned his commission in the US Army on April 7, 1861, almost a full week before Confederate forces fired on Fort Sumter on April 12, 1861. As part of his resignation, Gardner reported that he had returned all government property in his possession and asked that the army send all future correspondence to him at this father in law's home in Louisiana. At least one newspaper article published in Washington, DC, a short time later confirmed that Gardner resigned without incident on April 7, 1861, and made no mention of theft. On April 14, 1861, Gardner's commanding officer in the US Army, serving at another post many miles from Gardner's last post, accused Gardner of abandoning his post but made no mention of theft. Gardner biographer Michael Dan Jones argued that members of the War Department intentionally slandered Gardner because, while they were somewhat forgiving of southern-born officers who resigned to return to their home states, they were far less tolerant of northerners like Gardner who rejected both their nation and their home states when they resigned their commissions.[49] Jones might be correct, but it is also possible that Gardner's resignation letter initially got lost in the chaos of 1861, giving rise to rumors of malfeasance.

The change of Confederate commanders at Port Hudson took place without any apparent conflict between the garrison's leading officers. Beall remained in Port Hudson and later took command of an infantry brigade. According to Howard Wright, Beall remained popular with the men, who "esteemed and respected" him. Members of the garrison respected Beall as a professional soldier. Perhaps even more importantly, Beall frequently visited the sick and wounded. His kindness earned him the title of "a Christian soldier."[50]

The day after arriving in Port Hudson, Gardner began planning improvements to the defenses. He ordered the heavy artillery to cluster their heaviest guns together where they could deliver concentrated fire. On December 29 Gardner reported that his predecessors had begun fortifying Port Hudson but that "there is yet a great deal of work to do." According to Gardner, the artillery positions were strong, but the supply of ammunition was insufficient. Gardner complimented his predecessors on beginning construction of excellent defensive positions for the infantry, but he believed those positions needed to be both reinforced and expanded. Gardner requested a large supply of "axes, spades, and pickaxes." Gardner noted that the area's difficult terrain made construction difficult in many places, but he promised to build the best defensive works the geography would allow.[51]

General Gardner ordered planters near Natchez, Mississippi, to send slaves equipped with "spades, axes, and shovels," along with two days of rations, to the river boat landing at Natchez, where a steamboat would pick them up and deliver them to Port Hudson. Some Mississippi planters were reluctant to ship their slaves to build fortifications miles away in another state. A coalition of Natchez's citizens demanded Governor Pettus order the construction of "a suitable battery" at Natchez and send "some flying artillery" to protect the area. At least one family of slave owners argued that they should be exempt from the request. James McCutchon explained in a letter to Governor Pettus of Mississippi that he and his family had been forced to flee their sugar plantation near New Orleans, taking only 17 of their 250 slaves to Mississippi. He argued that the government should allow his family to retain all their remaining slaves to plant corn and provide for the family. Despite the protests, at least a few planters sent slaves to Port Hudson. For example, Malcomb Buie sent 133 slaves to Port Hudson, where they worked from February 1 to March 5 on "construction of fortifications" for a fee of $2,616.00.[52]

Southern whites flowed into Union-controlled Baton Rouge. Many white men hoped to avoid Confederate conscript hunters, who would have forced them into the Confederate army. Some of these southerners may have found jobs with the Union army, which employed thousands of southern civilians as teamsters, construction workers, and general laborers. Others joined the ranks of the Union army. It is unclear why men might have fled conscription in one army only to volunteer for service in another, but they may have been more sympathetic to the Union than the Confederacy, and, even if they weren't, the Union army typically offered better food, clothing, and pay. A music teacher from Cadiz, Spain, named Benito Montfort entered Federal lines to avoid Confederate conscription and brought detailed reports of Confederate forces he encountered near Port Hudson. Fredrick Otto, a Baton Rouge merchant, was "a good Union man" with priceless knowledge of the area around Baton Rouge. He served as a volunteer scout for the 3rd Massachusetts Cavalry and even spent time on the front lines at Port Hudson later in the campaign.[53]

Black southerners also flooded into Union-occupied Baton Rouge. William Park reported that, on one day at the end of December, "an unusually large number of darkies came down to the bank." The escaped slaves begged Federal sailors to take them to Federal lines. They explained that the day before Confederate guerillas attacked the escaped slaves, shooting one, and "tied another one by the neck and heels and threw him into the river as an example to deter other darkies from crossing to the Union lines." The *Essex*'s crew transported the escaped slaves across the Mississippi River and helped them continue their trek toward Federal lines. William Smith wrote home to his wife, "the blacks are coming in very fast." According to Smith, the army's commanders "set them to work unloading the vessels and hauling the stuff to camp." Some officers and even a few enlisted men hired former slaves to work as their personal servants. Other former slaves joined the Union army as soldiers. General Halleck believed that each slave or former slave in the South would help either the Union or Confederate war efforts.[54] Halleck was correct. Every former slave who entered Baton Rouge to take a job with the Union army was one fewer slave growing food for the Confederate army or building fortifications for the defenders of Port Hudson. By throwing their weight behind the Union war effort, white and black southerners helped decide the fate of a region that belonged to them just as much as it belonged to the men in gray.

Federal authorities in New Orleans expected General Banks to lead an assault on Port Hudson before the end of 1862, but Banks failed to live up to his promise that "whatever may happen we shall not be idle." Banks complained that his troops lacked the horses and mules that he needed to push north and paused his offensive until he could obtain more draft animals. He also worried that many of the new units under his command were unprepared for combat and ordered his officers to focus on training. Perhaps most importantly, many Federal soldiers were sick. On December 31, 1862, General Banks reported that he had 42,074 officers and men under his command but that only 36,508 were present and ready for duty. Many of the men who were not present for duty were sick. Lawrence Van Alstyne recorded in his diary that many of the men were horribly ill with "measles, scurvy, typhoid fever, and jaundice." Military doctors prescribed citrus fruits, fresh water, and ordered the men to rest.[55] It was good advice, but it was not an instantaneous cure.

Some contemporary and modern critics have suggested that Banks made a huge mistake by failing to attack Port Hudson in December 1862. On June 12, 1863, the *New York Herald* printed an account from John Harris, a Kentuckian visiting Arkansas when the war began who deserted to Federal lines. Harris reported that Port Hudson's defenses were weak in the fall of 1862 but that the Confederacy built "very formidable" works after the Federals approached in the spring, suggesting that the Banks may have missed a golden opportunity by not advancing sooner. Edward Cunningham speculated that if Banks had pressed north as soon as he took command, "he might well have won a notable victory." Lawrence Hewitt was even more direct, arguing "had Banks acted decisively instead of overestimating his opponent and doubting his own troops' capabilities, he might have taken Port Hudson in a matter of days."[56] It is true that the Confederates had no more than about five thousand troops near Port Hudson in December 1862 and that the fortifications guarding the city were far weaker in December 1862 than when Union forces attacked them in full force several months later.

Perhaps the critics are correct, and Banks would have won a great victory in December 1862 if he had pressed forward. However, a winter offensive against Port Hudson would have been difficult. The Confederates near Port Hudson were weaker in the winter of 1862 than in the spring of 1863, but the Federals available for an attack on Port Hudson in 1862 were also far weaker than they were in 1863. Many of the Federals in Louisiana were green troops in desperate need of training. Even the men themselves acknowledged that they were unprepared. William Fowler, a lieutenant in the 173rd New York Infantry, stated that most of his comrades "hardly knew a musket from a pistol" when they arrived in Louisiana.[57] Many of the Federals were fresh off the boats from Boston and New York. They were not acclimated to Louisiana and suffered from serious illnesses. It is unclear what would have happened if Banks had thrown green regiments of unprepared and unacclimated northerners against the Confederate garrison at Port Hudson in the winter of 1862, but it is entirely possible that it would have failed. Perhaps Banks, for all his numerous flaws, understood the obstacles his men faced a little better than his critics.

—4—

I Should Have Resigned Long Ago

FEDERALS GROW IMPATIENT

A daily attack is now looked for upon Port Hudson. . . . We have a very large fleet when they all arrive, they are coming up the river every day from what I can hear Farragut will have a larger fleet to attack Port Hudson then he had when he took New Orleans so you may judge what kind of a fleet it will be. I believe the attack is to be made by land and water since Gen. Banks went up to Baton Rouge last Sunday. He has about 40,000 troops with about 70 pieces of cannon of the best quality. You may look out soon to here of glorious news from our army and navy on the Mississippi. If our grand Army of Virginia dose [*sic*] not do anything we will let them see that we will. Old Farragut is slow but he is sure. If it had not have been for this affair at Port Hudson I should have resigned long ago, but as soon as it is through with I intend to send it in. I will send Pa a copy of it if the admiral will allow me if not I shall write your word when I do it that you may try and get it accepted as I want to see you all very badly.[1]

—LOUIS BOYD, on the Union gunboat *Albatross*

There was a report came here last night that the Yankees had all of their baggage packed up to move. The supposition was that they was coming up here but I do not believe that they are coming with as few men as they have at Baton Rouge. If they do they will be one of the worst whipped set of men that ever was.[2]

—JOHN MORGAN, 4th Louisiana Infantry

ON JANUARY 1, 1863, the Emancipation Proclamation declared "persons held as slaves within any State or designated part of a State, the people whereof shall then be in rebellion against the United States, shall be then, thenceforward, and forever free." The war that began as a fight to preserve the Union enjoyed what Lincoln later called "a new birth of freedom." Lincoln's proclamation, however noble in its impact, was motivated more by the practical need to win a war than a desire to free the enslaved. Lincoln famously wrote, "If I could save the Union without freeing any slave I would do it, and if I could save it by freeing all the slaves I would do it; and if I could save it by freeing some and leaving others alone, I would also do that. What I do about slavery and the colored race, I do because I believe it helps to save this Union."[3]

The Federals who would help decide the fate of Port Hudson expressed mixed emotions about the proclamation. Louis Brooks had apparently never seen a black person before arriving in the South. He wrote home to his friend that "I do not believe they were more than half human" and that he suspected they were "a cross between a man and a monkey, a kind of orangutan baboon." Brooks wrote that if he had known that the war was intended to help the slaves, "I would have never enlisted." William Park wrote in his diary that when his shipmates on the *Essex* heard the news of the proclamation, "the greater part of our crew came out strong, they cursed Old Abe and the abolitionists generally." The men "wished themselves at home and swore that if they had thought that the war was undertaken to free the niggers they never would have joined the service." Park believed that his crew's feelings were consistent with how "the whole western flotilla" felt about the proclamation. It is important to note that Park referred to the "greater part of the crew," suggesting that a significant minority of the crew may have supported the proclamation or been indifferent to it. Private J. Harvey Brown informed his wife that "there is one thing the men in general don't like, that is freeing the niggers." He claimed his comrades believed "the slave here fares better than we do" and better than "the poor class of white people" in the region. Brown had visited plantations where "the niger [*sic*] are all well clothed and fat." He claimed, "many of them even carry a gold watch." Brown reported, "there is a reg't [*sic*] of niggers here" who "treat us as though the ground was not good enough for them to walk on." Charles Dean thought the proclamation was pointless, writing, "Some people think that Lincoln's emancipation is going to do wonders but they are mistaken for nearly all of the places we held now have sent in to congress representatives and are now loyal. The proclamation will not affect them. And where we don't hold we can't free yet, so what is his proclamation going to do?" Erastus

Gregory believed that emancipation was a distraction. He personally had no problem with blacks and was happy to share heaven with people of any color that God found worthy of his almighty grace. However, Gregory was focused on the war and denounced the northern peace advocates, who he felt were stirring up racial animosity to demoralize soldiers and make the war impossible to win. He told his brother, "we have come down here to whip these rebels and crush out their wicked rebellion." Gregory wrote that "after the rebs [*sic*] are completely whipped then I say we shall have time enough to talk about the negro."[4]

The Emancipation Proclamation complicated an already difficult situation for the Federals in Louisiana. Banks had two jobs in Louisiana; govern Union-occupied Louisiana and defeat the Confederate forces in the region. By the end of the first week in January, he was failing at both tasks. His promised offensive had bogged down, almost before it had begun, as the Union advance petered out on the outskirts of Baton Rouge. Banks's military failures should not have surprised anyone who was aware of his poor performance in the Shenandoah Valley. Far more surprisingly, the politician turned general failed to set up an effective government in occupied Louisiana. When Banks failed to win either military or political victories, Union soldiers and civilians began to turn against him.

General Halleck may have been the first major Union leader to question Banks's abilities. On January 4 General Halleck once again urged Banks to advance. Halleck pointed out that Federal forces attacking Vicksburg have "their hands full" and urged Banks to advance on Vicksburg "without waiting to take Port Hudson if it seems advisable to do so." Halleck once again reminded Banks that the reopening of the Mississippi River "must be the main object of all our operations." The next day a subsequent letter from the adjutant general's office formally reorganized Union forces in the Gulf into the 19th Army Corps and placed Banks in command of Union army forces in the region.[5]

Banks replied to Halleck on January 7 with a letter far more focused on politics and economics than fighting. Banks complained that Halleck had failed to explain the "precise nature of the duties" involved in taking command in Louisiana. Banks noted the "multifarious civil business" of the "immense military government" that included "every form of civil administration, the assessment of taxes, fines, punishments, charities, trade, regulation of churches, confiscation estates, and the working of plantations."

Banks claimed that he had no desire to speak ill of his predecessors, but he was adamant that the entire system was in desperate need of reform. Although Halleck urged Banks to advance up the Mississippi immediately, Banks refused, claiming his troops "are not in condition for immediate service" since the infantry was untrained, the artillery was equipped entirely with light field pieces that "would make no impression" on Confederate fortifications, and the cavalry consisted of a mere "four or five weak companies." Banks assured Halleck that he was making "every possible effort" to fix the problems and prepare for an offensive.[6]

Consistent with his messages to Halleck, Banks focused on governing occupied Louisiana. Perhaps drawing on his experience in the textile industry and as a politician, Banks devised plans for regulating the trade in cotton and sugar through New Orleans that he hoped would ensure the loyalty of Louisianans who would profit from the trade while also ensuring that the Federal government got a hefty cut of the revenue. John Palfrey believed that, in contrast to Butler, who ruled "firmly," Banks focused on winning over Louisianans by promoting "social gayety," relaxing restrictions, handing out cash, and helping southerners rebuild. Banks even suggested that slave owners might get their slaves back if the war ended soon, commenting that "if slavery is to be preserved, war must cease."[7]

Regardless of Banks's tepid response to emancipation, former slaves fled the plantations and disrupted Louisiana's slave-based economy. Plantation owners, many of whom were willing to support any government that helped them maintain their wealth and social status, begged Banks to help them. Banks announced that "war is not waged for the overthrow of slavery, but to restore the constitutional relations between the United States and each of the states."[8] Banks forced many former slaves back to the plantations and promised to enforce "conditions of continuous and faithful service, respectful deportment, correct discipline, and perfect subordination on the part of the negroes." Banks announced that his troops would protect the rights of former slaves to work for any employer that wanted them, require employers to pay wages or shares as specified in mutually agreed upon labor contracts, and provide "just treatment," which included prohibitions on physical punishment. Banks also agreed to enforce labor contracts, requiring former slaves to provide "respectful, honest, faithful labor" to former slave masters. Banks threatened to punish any former slave who failed to provide this "respectful, honest, faithful labor" to their employer or who refused to sign a labor contract by arresting them and forcing them to work without pay on public works. In theory, this new system offered some improvements over slavery. However, in practice, the Union military tended to return former slaves to their old masters with little regard for their rights.

Some critics denounced Banks's mistreatment of former slaves. The *New Orleans Tribune*, an African American newspaper, decried the new system as "mock freedom." From Boston, the *Liberator* abolitionist newspaper claimed Banks "re-enslaved" escaped slaves and argued that Banks was worse than Jefferson Davis, who fought to keep slaves in bondage but did not go out of his way to force free people into slavery. Charles Prosper Fauconnet, a French diplomat in New Orleans, informed the French government that the new Union labor policies were "making little progress" because Banks tried to walk a fine line between freedom and slavery, which outraged abolitionists, the former slaves who wanted to be free, and the former masters who wanted their slaves back, leaving Banks with few allies amongst any group. Fauconnet predicted, "this year's harvest will be lost."[9]

Banks's policies placed Federal soldiers into difficult positions. James Dargan believed that "Satan is having a good fling at it now: the fanatical abolitionists of the North, the Radical Slave Holders of the South have drawn the country into a pretty scrape." Captain Nicholas Dederer informed his son that unspecified "authorities" were trying to convince former slaves "to return to their former masters and work for small wages." Instead of fighting the war he volunteered for, he was forced to spend his time caring for "contrabands," which included distributing clothing to the former slaves and playing peacemaker between former slaves and former masters. The worst incident was when he received complaints that an overseer shot a former slave. Dederer was forced to deal with the resulting "chaos." He considered his new role as peacekeeper "annoying" and wished he could focus on military matters.[10]

General Banks attempted to remove black officers. The Native Guards regiments had originally had black officers, and General Butler accepted black officers in black units. However, Banks believed that "the appointment of colored officers is detrimental to the service" and claimed that the presence of black officers "demoralizes both the white troops and the negroes." He began pushing black officers out and replacing them with white officers. Banks also refused to commission any new black men as officers. Banks later threatened to pay black enlisted men and white officers but to withhold pay from all black officers in hopes they would resign. Despite Banks's threats, 2nd Lieutenant John Crowder of the 1st Louisiana Native Guards, a free black man from New Orleans, reassured his mother, "they are bound to pay us." Crowder was correct, Banks backed down, and the black officers received their pay.[11]

Union paymasters failed to pay both white and black men. Chaplain John Moors wrote that the lack of pay meant that sick men were unable to buy luxuries that might have otherwise provided comfort. William Park wrote that they navy failed to pay the boat's enlisted men and officers, causing "dissatisfaction." One officer refused to accept a promotion, reasoning that if the government was unable to pay his current wages, he was remarkably unlikely to ever get the higher pay his new position promised.[12]

The Federals would need all the strength they could muster to confront the increasingly powerful Confederate garrison at Port Hudson. Alabama soldier James Goble believed that Port Hudson's defenses were strong by early 1863. In his diary for January 4, Goble noted, "all of our guns are mounted on a very high bluff along the Miss [*sic*] River." From their perch, the cannons "can play on the enemy boats with ease." Goble believed the Federals "will find it difficult to pass this point as we are in a great bend of the river and the tide runs very swift." Consistent with Gardner's plans to improve the post's defenses, Goble noted that soldiers and "negroes" were hard at work on Port Hudson's defenses. On January 5, Goble reported that "we can hold this point against any force the enemy may bring to beare [*sic*] on it and are ready for them at any moment." Daniel Weaver urged his sister not to worry about rumors that the Union army included "negro regt [*sic*]" because Confederate soldiers would kill any black men that dared take the field. Company K of the 1st Alabama Infantry completed the emplacement for a 30-pounder Parrott rifle and dragged the cannon into place. The men christened their Parrot rifle the "Lady Whitfield," for the wife of their company commander Captain John Whitfield. The gunners stored the cannon's ammunition with the gun while they completed a separate magazine, which took them until March 2 to complete.[13]

While some Confederates focused on the fortifications, others built and deployed improvised explosives. During the Civil War, the devices were known as torpedoes, but today they are usually called mines. James Goble wrote, "there is secret expedition to gou [*sic*] down the river to sink torpedoes to blow up gunboats." He explained the mines he called torpedoes "are made out of the best boiler iron and rived very close together." The mines were "square at the ends" and "filled with powder." They were "fixed with a friction so when the boats strike them, they will explode and blown up everything in contact with them." Goble did not mention, and may not have known, that the Confederacy began using mines to defend the Mississippi River within weeks of the war's outbreak. Mines failed to stop Union advances of 1861, but despite the early failures, Confederates used mines throughout the war.[14]

On January 5, 1863, the *Essex* steamed north from Baton Rouge toward Port Hudson to investigate reports from "darkies" that the Confederates were mounting more heavy artillery at Port Hudson and were "placing torpedoes in the river." On their brief reconnaissance, the *Essex*'s crew saw no torpedoes and no evidence of additional artillery emplacements. The *Essex* sailed to "within easy range" of Port Hudson's artillery, but the rebels did not fire. Park believed it was because they had decided not to fire unless they were guaranteed a hit. The *Essex* began the return trip to Baton Rouge and along the way they spotted a Confederate signal station. Park heard one of the Confederates yell, "hurrah for Jeff Davis!" In response, the *Essex*'s gunner fired a shrapnel shell from one of their 9-inch cannons. It burst amidst the Confederates and according to one observer, "we saw no more of any of them."[15]

On January 18 James Goble and several of his comrades laid in ambush in hopes of destroying the *Essex* with electrically detonated mines. Federal sailors refused to fall into the trap. The gunboat fired shells at Goble and his comrades that forced them to flee and broke the wires running to the mines. From a safe distance, Goble watched the Union sailors deploy small boats and capture the torpedoes. Union sailors cut the torpedo's wires with a cutlass and towed it back on the *Essex*, where the sailors studied the torpedoes and made detailed notes about their construction. Confederates fired small arms at the *Essex*, but the boat's captain refused to return fire, believing "it would be throwing away money" since "each shell costs eleven dollars." The *Essex* returned to Baton Rouge without further incident. Torpedoes remained a constant threat to the Union gunboats, so the *Essex* spent much of its time looking for torpedoes with the help of escaped slaves who were eager to help the Union. When stationary torpedoes proved unreliable, the Confederates dropped torpedoes with impact fuses in the river in hopes that the current would carry them into Union ships. In response, Union sailors built floating shields made of heavy logs and chains, which they fastened to the bank whenever their boats were at anchor.[16]

In addition to preparing for battle, Confederate soldiers also focused on improving their living conditions. F. L. Allen reported that he had plenty of clothing, but, "I need another blanket" and "we need cooking utensils." He also declared, "I need something to eat a gredt [*sic*] deal worss [*sic*] than anything" and urged his brother to "bring your buggy full of hog meet [*sic*] and sausiges [*sic*]." Captain Edward Broughton wrote home that "I have not been able to get any cooking utensils yet, and if I had them, I cannot get much to cook in them." Members of the 1st Alabama Infantry completed "houses" that held twenty-five men each and enjoyed the heat of two fireplaces. In his photographic history of Port Hudson, Lawrence Lee Hewitt identified a photograph that he believed showed of the 1st Alabama's cabins. Hewitt speculated that the 1st Alabama may have invested time in building more substantial cabins than most Confederate soldiers because members of the 1st Alabama believed that they would serve as a long-term garrison for Port Hudson. Hewitt based his speculation on the fact the only references he found to building cabins for barracks concerned the Alabamians and the fact that, with four companies detailed as heavy artillery, members of the 1st Alabama felt confident that they were going to remain at Port Hudson for an extended period.[17]

Illness delayed the Union army's advance. Louis Brooks told his sister that most of the men were sick and called two friends still at home in the North "darn fools for enlisting" when he learned they had joined the army. Lawrence Van Alstyne recorded in his diary that on January 8, 1863, only 200 members of the 128th New York Infantry were healthy enough to drill. James Peck blamed the weather for the illness that forced him and several other members of his regiment to seek treatment in the hospital. He assured his parents that he would be fine and "thair [*sic*] is 6 of our company here and 2 of them I think will die but the rest of us is getting very well." John Moors wrote his wife that the men were "badly demoralized" because the regiment that left home with 930 men just a few weeks before now consisted of only 250 men available for duty. Most of the rest were either sick or detailed to help the sick. William Smith wrote home to his wife that members of his regiment were suffering from "vomiting and diaree [*sic*]" that "was caused by the change of climate."[18] James Peck attended a funeral for a comrade who died in the hospital. The groundwater was so high that the gravediggers struck water after digging only ten inches into the ground. Realizing that they were unlikely to find dryer ground, the grave diggers built a coffin from lumber salvaged from an old house and pushed the coffin under the water. According to Peck, "old soldiers say it was a good burying for a soldier," but Peck seemed unconvinced. He explained it was hard to watch men "shove an [*sic*] man under the water in an old leaky box." Peck predicted "we will get used to such sights before long I sopose [*sic*] and then we will not mind it so much."[19] The Federals expected to suffer from "swamp fever" along the Mississippi River, and many did, but Dr. R. K. Browne, commanding the military's general hospital in New Orleans, reported that most sick Federals suffered from diarrhea because "the troops are uniformly destitute of all notion of cleanliness."[20]

Confederate soldiers also suffered from sickness. G. W. Buntly wrote his brother that seven members of his regiment were diagnosed with smallpox and moved to the camp hospital. On an upbeat note, he noted that at least the disease was "not raging in camp as I expected." Daniel Weaver wrote his sister that, while most of the men "were in fine health," several were "regaining their health," an upbeat acknowledgement that some men had been sick. Port Hudson Confederate hospital's records document the admission of 193 men into the hospital in January 1863. Most men suffered from illnesses including diarrhea, bronchitis, and various fevers. None of the men admitted in January 1863 suffered from wounds, although it appears that several men wounded in 1862 remained in the post hospital.[21]

Confederates who remained healthy focused on improving Port Hudson's fortifications. According to James Harmon, the entire Confederate garrison focused on construction, and the officers canceled virtually all leaves of absence. Jabez Cannon wrote that "spades are trumps" and that the men worked on the ditches every day, including the Sabbath. During the brief breaks when the men were not working on the fortifications, General Gardner conducted drills that sent the men running from their camps to their assigned sections of the defenses to ensure that they were ready to defend Port Hudson at a moment's notice. Robert Patrick recorded in his diary that the men removed oak fence rails that had once protected corn fields and used the timber to reinforce earth works that sat behind six-foot-deep ditches. Patrick did not mention how the farmers felt about the new earthworks that ripped through their cornfields, but he suggested, probably jokingly, that at least the ditches the soldiers dug would ensure that the farmers would never again need to dig drainage ditches. To help the soldiers, Mississippi governor John Pettus ordered planters to provide additional slaves for work on Port Hudson's fortifications and threatened to impress double the number of slaves from any plantation that failed to voluntarily provide the requested number of slaves.[22]

The presence of rapidly improving fortifications may have improved Confederate morale. Captain Edward Broughton wrote home that the men's constant work had produced "very formidable" defenses that he believed would "forever make their knees shake when they hear Port Hudson named . . . should the Yankees be foolhardy enough to come up and attack us." Samuel Thompson wrote a letter home that the men were in good spirts, proud of the fortifications they had built, and ready to defeat the Federals in Louisiana, just as Lee had recently defeated them in Virginia. Robert Patrick observed that, despite the busy pace of work, Port Hudson seemed like an oddly peaceful place where "but for the dark line of entrenchments and an occasional company or regiment out drilling, one would suppose that the Confederacy was at peace with all the world."[23]

Conscription provided an obvious method of enlarging Port Hudson's garrison, but Confederate leaders continued to struggle with balancing the nation's military and civil needs. Rufinia Lawrence, the wife of Theodore Lawrence, who was serving with a Mississippi unit at Port Hudson, wrote to Mississippi governor Pettus to plead for his help. She complained, "I have bin [*sic*] most Shame-fully treated by a Negro man who broke in my house at night he is now in jail at Louisville and will be tried in March for his life." Clearly frightened by the attack, she complained that "thare [*sic*] is no man in this neighbour-hood [*sic*] not enough to protect the wimmen [*sic*] and children from the outrages of the negroes." She begged Pettus to release her husband from duty and allow him to return home where he could protect the family. Pettus did not grant Rufinia's request. The Federals captured Theodore Lawrence at the battle of Champion's Hill (May 16, 1863), and he died at Fort Delaware prison camp on March 15, 1864. Perhaps to keep order on the home front, General Gardner released some soldiers from military service so they could work as overseers on plantations.[24]

On January 3, 1863, Frank Gardner sent a letter to General Richard Taylor, commanding Confederate forces in western Louisiana to ask for help. Gardner explained that the Union had assembled a large force at Baton Rouge. He suggested that cooperation with Taylor's forces "might materially assist in the defense" of Port Hudson. Perhaps to encourage Taylor to cooperate, Gardner pointed out that Union cavalrymen stationed at Baton Rouge crossed the Mississippi River to the west bank, where Taylor was in charge, and gathered supplies for the Union army. Gardner declined to provide too many details on Federal operations or on his ideas for cooperation, "as this letter might fall into the hands of the enemy."[25]

It does not appear that Taylor immediately provided reinforcements, but General Pemberton in Vicksburg was far more eager to support Port Hudson's defenders. Pemberton loaded the 10th Tennessee Infantry onto steamboats and sent them south. According to Private Pat Griffin, when it arrived in Port Hudson, "the boat was minus all its mirrors, knives, forks, spoons, blankets, and rations." The boat's captain reported the theft to the regiment's colonel, Randal McGavock. Rather than punishing the men, McGavock gave the soldiers an opportunity to prove their innocence. McGavock and his officers searched every member of the regiment. Unable to find any of the missing items, McGavock dismissed the men and informed the boat's captain that his men were innocent. Griffin suggested that the story was proof of the "confidence and respect shared" by the soldiers and Colonel McGavock.[26]

Conscription continued to provide Confederates along the Mississippi River with difficult conflicts in early 1863. Major Wailes of the Adams County, Mississippi, militia wrote Governor Pettus a long letter on February 24, complaining that he was receiving contradictory instructions from state and Confederate authorities. He believed that, if he failed to abandon the state militia and report for duty with the Confederacy, the Confederate government would charge him with desertion. He also believed that if he left the state militia and reported for Confederate service, the state of Mississippi might charge him with violating his oath to serve the state. Wailes asked Governor Pettus to intervene before someone arrested him. It is unclear how, or if, the governor's office might have attempted to resolve the conflict. Some men in the ranks encouraged their family members to avoid service. F. L. Allen cautioned his brother, former Confederate soldier William M. Allen, to "bring your discige [*sic*] to show you are not liable to conscript" when he visited Port Hudson. John Walker encouraged family members to stay at home as long and possible and "not to go to war."[27]

General Gardner gave men leave to recruit replacements. Captain Whitfield of the 1st Alabama Infantry published a request for recruits in at least one Alabama newspaper. He pointed out that the conscript law would soon force many men into the army, and he urged men to volunteer for the 1st Alabama rather than be forced into a regiment selected by the army's conscription bureau. He admitted that the regiment was "considerably thinned by disease" and that "our enemy is all around us in immense hordes," which might have given men who valued their lives a moment of pause. However, Whitfield assured potential recruits that the regiment was now at Port Hudson, a location "pleasant and healthy." He even argued, "a better and more agreeable position for a soldier cannot be found in the Confederacy." Whitfield's sales pitch may have resonated with some of the Alabamians who joined the regiment. In early February 1863, 2nd Lieutenant Charles Tuttle and Corporal John Hearn returned to Port Hudson with forty-five new recruits from across south and central Alabama. The Alabamians in Port Hudson welcomed the new recruits, but the new men quickly discovered the hardships of military life. One of the new soldiers, Moses Tarleton of Lowndes County, died a few weeks after arriving in Port Hudson of unspecified causes, and the regiment buried him with military honors, despite his short service. Daniel Weaver of the 45th Alabama Infantry informed his sister that recruiting officers for his regiment returned in late January with large numbers of new recruits who also brought clothing and food to share with the rest of the regiment.[28]

In his diary Lieutenant Richard McClung noted that getting back home to recruit troops was easier said than done. He wrote that the night he left Port Hudson was "dark, muddy" and then, perhaps to emphasize how muddy it was, he wrote "very muddy and raining" later in the same passage. He and the other Confederate recruiting officers went a mile up the river and boarded the "little steamer" *H. W. Baker*. They waited for a day at anchor because they needed the fog to clear. Once underway, the first leg of the journey took the *H. W. Baker* to Bayou Sara, seventeen miles up the Mississippi. The boat was crowded mostly with Confederate officers, but six ladies "running from the Yankees" were also onboard, traveling with children, household goods, and slaves.[29]

On the third day of the voyage, McClung heard the boat's pilot cry out "a gunboat after us." The gunboat "glided noiselessly down" until it was alongside the *H. W. Baker*. McClung later learned that the gunboat was the Union ironclad *Indianola*. A voice from the gunboat yelled, "land that boat damn you or I'll blow you out of the water." The pilot replied, "blow it out and be damned." Despite the pilot's feigned bravado, he aimed the boat toward the shore. The *H. W. Baker*'s crew didn't wait for the gangplank, jumping off as soon as their boat hit the bank. McClung was not far behind, recalling, "I left women screaming, children crying, and Yankees swearing." The Arkansas lieutenant apparently felt no guilt for abandoning the helpless civilians, writing, "I know they would not trouble the ladies and children." In the confusion, McClung lost his coat but managed to retain his sword and knapsack. After spending several days dodging Union patrols, hiding in bushes, and wading through swamps, McClung and two officers from the 16th Arkansas Infantry finally returned to Port Hudson.[30]

A week after returning to Port Hudson, McClung tried once again to return to Arkansas in search of recruits. This time he paid a "negro man" to carry him sixty-five miles northwest in a mule wagon to Natchez, Mississippi. In Natchez, he joined forces with Captain L. W. Matthews of the 15th Arkansas Infantry, and the two men walked twenty-eight miles "over some of the muddiest roads I ever saw" to Trinity, Louisiana. From Trinity, Matthews and McClung rowed across the Mississippi River to Monroe, Louisiana, in a small boat. In Monroe, Matthews and McClung parted ways. McClung paid $200 for a "Spanish pony" and rode the animal to his home in Lafayette County, Arkansas.[31]

McClung's story highlights one often-ignored reason why the Confederacy rallied so few men and so little material to defend Port Hudson. By early 1863 it was incredibly difficult for the Confederates to transport men and supplies through the region. Their few boats were in constant danger of destruction at the hands of Union gunboats. The few roads were often in poor condition. Railroads were rare in the area, and it should not surprise a reader that McClung made no mention of the iron horses that revolutionized transportation in other regions of the country. In 1860 McClung's home state of Arkansas had only 38.5 miles of railroad track, and Louisiana had 334.73 miles. In contrast, New York, Pennsylvania, Massachusetts, Ohio, Indiana, and Illinois each had over 2,000 miles of railroad track.[32]

On January 7, 1863, Gardner reorganized the Port Hudson garrison. General John Gregg's infantry brigade took a position on the right of the line with their right flank on the Mississippi River. Bledsoe's and Hoskins batteries of artillery would provide fire support to Gregg's brigade. Samuel Maxey's infantry brigade occupied the center with artillery support from Boone's, Roberts's, and Fenner's artillery batteries. On the left, Beall's brigade of infantry held the left end of the line with their left flank on the Mississippi River. Beall's men would rely on the artillery batteries of Abbay, Bradford, and Herod. Gardner kept the heavy artillery and cavalry units at Port Hudson separate from the infantry brigades. Several days later, Gardner placed Lieutenant Colonel Marshall Smith, a former US naval officer, in charge of the heavy artillery at Port Hudson.[33]

Gardner sent his cavalry out to gather intelligence in a wide arc that covered the overland approaches from Baton Rouge. The 9th Louisiana Partisan Rangers, under Lieutenant Colonel Wingfield, remained in Port Hudson to act as couriers. Gardner ordered Lieutenant Colonel George Gantt of the 9th Tennessee Cavalry Battalion to establish a camp near Clinton, Louisiana, twenty-two miles east of Port Hudson. Gardner sent Major William Garland, commanding Garland's Mississippi Cavalry Battalion, and T. C. Rhodes's company of Mississippi cavalry, to guard the approaches to Camp Moore, thirty-five miles east of Clinton. Gardner sent Lester's and Herren's companies of Pinson's 1st Mississippi Cavalry to take up a position near Ponchatoula, Louisiana, thirty-five miles southeast of Camp Moore, under the command of Lieutenant Colonel Shields.[34]

Confederate soldiers at Port Hudson suffered as they prepared for a fight. Robert Patrick wrote in his diary that the men were tired of "labor under the greatest difficulties in the world." The weather turned cold, and men barely survived on "very scanty" rations of "inferior quality" that mostly consisted of half rations of rice and peas. A writer for the *Vicksburg Daily Whig* referred to hunger as "our most serious danger." The paper expressed confidence that, despite the massive Union armies on Confederate soil, "these armies we can meet and beat back, but who can fight starvation with hope of success?" The writer worried that, if Port Hudson fell, access to the rich resources of the Red River would evaporate. The unnamed journalist argued, "the army must be fed, or it must disband and retire." A writer for the *Memphis Daily Appeal* argued that that there was "no excuse" for the "shameful" failure to pay the defenders of Port Hudson and claimed the failure rose to the level of "abuse." The newspaper article urged the government to "let them have their just dues" so "they will be enabled to supply themselves with many comforts." While paying the men might have been helpful, it is not clear how many comforts they would have been to afford with their wages. By the end of 1862, inflation was a serious problem in the Confederacy. For example, a pound of bacon that sold for $1.25 in 1860 cost $10.00 in January 1863. Flour went from $1.50 to $3.75 during the same period, and the coffee that so many men craved, which could be bought for $0.50 a pound in 1860, cost $20.00 in early 1863.[35]

The Confederate government was unable to provide enough uniforms for the men and instead planned to give men cash with orders to buy their own clothing under the commutation system. The cash payments, when they arrived, were rarely sufficient to purchase needed clothing, and this became an increasingly pressing problem as inflation destroyed the value of Confederate currency. By the late fall of 1862, the Confederate government conceded that the commutation system had failed and repealed it in favor of depot system that would supply soldiers directly. The shift to depot system was an important change but one that took time to implement, and Confederate soldiers at Port Hudson suffered while they waited for the Confederacy to provide uniforms. While Confederate soldiers waited for the Confederate depots to begin supplying goods, men requested help from southern civilians. In Mississippi, civilians raised money to buy supplies for men at Port Hudson who were isolated from the friends and family members that would have otherwise supplied them with life's necessities. Colonel William Quarles of the 42nd Tennessee Infantry urged the people of Tennessee to provide "blankets, shirts, socks, shoes, and overcoats," which the men desperately needed.[36] A newspaper in Union-governed New Orleans published Quarles's request, perhaps to suggest that the Confederate garrison of Port Hudson was desperate for basic supplies and therefore weak.

According to Howard Wright, the men initially thought that General Gardner would lead them on an offensive to recapture, or at least threaten, the Union forces at Baton Rouge. The men did not blame Gardner for the inaction, believing instead that "a jealous power at the headquarters" that went unnamed refused to go on the offensive and prevented Gardner from attacking, "preferring to let the enemy select his own time and circumstances for attacking." While the idea of a shadowy, unnamed force in the Confederate high command might seem like an odd conspiracy theory, it does have some basis in fact. High ranking officials within the Confederate command structure disagreed about how to defend Port Hudson and the Confederacy as a whole. Pemberton, commanding at Vicksburg, advocated for a passive defense that would rely on constructing the strongest possible fortifications at Vicksburg and Port Hudson. In contrast, General Johnston, in command of the Department of the West that included both Vicksburg and Port Hudson, argued in favor of a mobile defense that would primarily rely on a mobile field army that could come to the aid of any threatened position and counterattack any Union advance. President Davis supported Pemberton and overruled Johnston's proposal for a more offensive-focused approach.[37]

On January 12, 1863, Colonel Charles Fauntleroy inspected the Port Hudson garrison on behalf of General Joseph Johnston. He reported a "lack of discipline and instruction among the troops," a flaw he blamed on "the general inefficiency of the officers of the command." Fauntleroy considered the batteries facing the Mississippi River "very formidable." However, they were rendered "ineffective" by the placement of the magazines in vulnerable positions unlikely to survive an enemy bombardment. Fauntleroy approved of Lieutenant Colonel Smith's promotion to command of the heavy artillery at Port Hudson, noting he had served as an officer in the US Navy and commanded Louisiana troops before coming to Port Hudson. The officers and men of the heavy artillery were "well instructed" in the use of their cannons, suggesting that they might have been better troops than the infantry and cavalrymen at Port Hudson. Fauntleroy reported that the defenses guarding the overland approaches to Port Hudson were already strong and that "the negro force" was working quickly to improve them.[38]

Fauntleroy noted that Port Hudson had about six weeks of supplies, but he also believed Port Hudson's quartermasters were responsible for "the grossest neglect" in caring for supplies. He claimed that local quartermasters left corn in the open, where the weather quickly destroyed it. Port Hudson needed warehouses, but nobody had bothered to build them.

Howard Wright agreed that there were serious supply problems at Port Hudson, but he praised the local officers, including H. C. Miller, who "displayed his energy and capacity" as he tried to build storage facilities. Wright blamed Port Hudson's supply problems on micromanagement from the departmental headquarters, far from Port Hudson. For example, Colonel W. R. Miles sent troops into the countryside around Port Hudson to gather supplies, but officers from departmental headquarters scolded him for daring to acquire provisions outside of official channels. Men became desperate for warm clothing as the weather turned cold. The ground was "frozen hard" and covered with frost that looked "like a young snow." Robert Patrick noted that it was severe weather for soldiers who lacked tents and shoes. Further complicating the supply problems, torrents of freezing rain turned roads "into a smooth sheet of water" that wagons could not cross.[39]

Port Hudson's paymasters failed to receive the money that would allow them to pay the soldiers, much to the "serious detriment" of "the public service." Fauntleroy praised the medical facilities at Port Hudson, which enjoyed "abundant arrangements" of everything needed to care for the men except for ambulances. The post had only three of these to serve the entire command. Fauntleroy praised Surgeon T. R. Barnett, who supervised hospitals at Port Hudson; Jackson, Louisiana; and Clinton, Louisiana. Fauntleroy claimed that Gardner was "embarrassed" by the presence of women and children at Port Hudson, who remained despite recommendations for most civilians to evacuate the area. Fauntleroy urged Gardner to force civilians to leave Port Hudson and use the newly vacant homes for warehouses and hospitals.[40]

Despite the problems the Confederate garrison faced, there is some evidence that men enjoyed good morale. Sarah Morgan, who frequently visited the Confederate camps, wrote in her diary the Confederate defenders "are confident that our fifteen thousand can repulse twice the number." Morgan was incredulous but hopeful. She wrote, "Great God! I say it with all reverence, if we could defeat them! If we could scatter, capture, annihilate them! My heart beats but one prayer, Victory!"[99] H. Steward of the 10th Arkansas Infantry reported, "we have all enjoyed ourselves better than might have been expected within a vast fortification like the one we now occupy." Some men suffered from "chills and diarrhea, but all are improving and in good spirits." Steward believed that the Federal army was advancing on "our impregnable fortress," where "they will receive a warm reception." He used classical imagery in his prediction that "before the ides of March shall have passed, the weapons of the soldiers of liberty will be crossed with the followers of Abraham the first; then will the gallant tenth of old Arkansas remember the battlefield of Shiloh and place another star of victory in the coronet of our native state."[41]

Some Confederate soldiers slipped away to visit civilians in the countryside. On January 30, Sarah Morgan recorded in her diary that several Confederate officers visited her family's home near Port Hudson. After a brief chat, "someone suggested calling the spirits," and they held an impromptu séance. Their "first question, of course, was how long before peace?" The spirits reportedly told them that peace would come in nine months. Next, they turned to questions of romance, and the spirits reportedly told them that Sarah's sister would marry Captain C. E. Fenner, who was also at the séance. Morgan confided, "I do not actually believe in spiritualism," but she admitted, "there is certainly something in it one cannot understand." Morgan's skepticism was wise. Peace did not come in nine months, and Captain Fenner never married Sarah Morgan's sister.[42]

By mid-January sickness and cold killed several men at Port Hudson each day. The Confederate surgeons promptly isolated men as soon as they presented symptoms of smallpox, and Jabez Cannon hoped that the "disease will not spread." According to Robert Patrick, the smallpox outbreak caused "some alarm among the soldiers." Patrick thought the men were overreacting and that there was "very little danger" because "most of the men have been vaccinated." Patrick believed that the men had far more to fear from malnutrition and exposure to the cold weather than from an infectious disease. In a letter dated March 4, F. L. Allen encouraged his brother to "get your school made up for that will keep out of the war, if the shingles won't." He also wished that the war would end.[43]

On February 10, Robert Patrick noted in his diary, "I have been quite unwell lately" and "am now scarcely able to sit up." The doctors were unable to help Patrick, and he condemned them for giving out "a large dose of calomel" (a mercury-based medication) without bothering to diagnose him. When that failed to work, they administered large doses of quinine, blue mass (another mercury-based medication), and "other strong medicines." Patrick suggested that many medicines were poisonous, particularly in the large doses favored by many physicians, and wondered how many men the doctors killed or permanently disabled. Patrick lamented, "I am suffering now from the treatment of ignorant, sap-headed physicians." While it might be easy to dismiss Patrick as an ungrateful patient, he had reasons to complain. Confederate surgeon William Taylor confessed that oftentimes, "diagnosis was rapidly made, usually by intuition." Calomel, which Patrick's doctors gave him in large quantities, was a popular treatment for many illnesses in the mid-nineteenth century, but one that the official manual for Confederate doctors noted was potentially dangerous and that doctors should use only with "wise discretion."[44] Patrick suggested the medical treatment men received often did more harm than good, and he might have been correct.

Cold and sickness combined with homesickness to demoralize some Confederate soldiers. On February 8 William Porter noted in his diary, "am thinking of home and home folks great deal of late." He felt conflicted, believing that he should "be better satisfied here for surely my duty is to serve my country," but he confessed, "I am restless" while "others seem to enjoy the life of a solider with a zeal." He hoped "with the aid of God I will try to struggle through this war," while also admitting, "I do sincerely hope and pray" that the war "may end soon." Robert Patrick grew demoralized as freezing rain drenched Port Hudson. He concluded, "soldiering is an awful business." He believed that "everyone is dreadfully disgusted with it." Patrick confessed that he was tired of it and noted, "from all accounts, the Federal soldiers are as tired of it as we are."[45]

On February 2 Halleck once again urged Banks to attack. Banks claimed that he was unable to advance because his men lacked the horses, mules, and wagons needed to support an offensive. Halleck replied that his sources indicated that Banks could acquire all the animals and wagons he needed from plantations in Louisiana. Halleck agreed to send more cavalry units to Banks but reminded Banks that shipping horses was very expensive and that many of the horses would not survive the trip. Halleck also pointed out that General Grant was operating against Vicksburg and that "the President expects that you will permit no obstacle to prevent you from co-operating with him by some movement up the Mississippi River." Halleck told Banks he would not "excuse any further delay on your part."[46]

Sickness may have slowed the Union advance. Captain Algernon Badger and many of his men suffered from "the fever incidental to the climate." Lieutenant Jacob Hasbrouck wrote home to his wife that many men suffered from "consumption." Like many officers, Hasbrouck tried to visit his men confined to the hospital. Another officer reminded Hasbrouck that if he wanted to see his sick men, he would need to see them quickly. Men who visited the hospital often died swiftly.[47]

The slow pace of the Union advance demoralized some Federal soldiers. Lieutenant Daniel Dewey wrote home, "I must confess that I have not quite as much faith in the ultimate success as I did have; everything seems slow and undetermined, no activity, no life." Brainard Curtis wrote home that "the privates in many cases are mutch [*sic*] beter [*sic*] men & would make mutch [*sic*] better officers." He believed if the enlisted men "could have command I think the war would be brought to a close." William Park wrote that the "Union cause looked worse at this time than it has ever done since the commencement of the war." He believed that "the rebels are getting bolder and more impudent every day." Private Morris Fyfe wrote to his father from Baton Rouge, "we are still here (probably to give the rebels time to complete their fortifications) for I can see no other reason." Colonel Sidney Bean wrote in his diary that, while under Butler "much was accomplished with small means," under General Banks "nothing is accomplished with great means." William Philbrick, a carpenter's mate on the *Monongahela*, wrote that he had no idea when Banks might finally attack Port Hudson. Apparently tired of the delay, Philbrick wrote a friend, "I should much prefer to be at work on some farm."[48]

Other Federals were excited to be on campaign, despite the slow pace. At the age of sixteen, 2nd Lieutenant John Crowder might have been the youngest officer in the Union army. Crowder was born to free black parents in Kentucky in 1846. His father left to participate in the Mexican War and never returned. Crowder's mother brought her young son to New Orleans, where she had friends, and by 1862 Crowder was a well-educated young man who benefited from the mentorship of John Brown, a bishop in the African Methodist Church. When war came, Crowder lied about his age and obtained an officer's commission in the 1st Louisiana Native Guards. Crowder wrote his mother that, while his unit had not yet seen combat, during a recent advance, "the times was stirring for a few days and excitement was at its highest pitch." While others might have felt disappointment to be on guard duty, Crowder told his mother that he took pride in protecting the army's line of retreat.[49]

In his February 12 report, General Banks concluded the works at Port

Hudson were "too strong for a direct attack," particularly "by men who have never fired a gun," a reference to the raw condition of many troops under his command. He feared that attacking the fortifications at Port Hudson, particularly with raw troops, would result in a defeat like the one encountered by the Union forces at Fredericksburg, Virginia (December 11–15, 1862). Instead of a direct attack, Banks planned an indirect assault, beginning with operations he hoped would secure "the control of the water communications and approaches to the Red River." This would cut Port Hudson's garrison off from supplies brought in from the west. Meanwhile, Banks would send forces north from Baton Rouge to cut off supplies to the Port Hudson garrison from the south and east. Banks believed that once he cut off Port Hudson from their supply routes, the Confederate defenders would be forced "to come out of their entrenchments to fight us." Banks requested additional troops, boats, and draft animals from Washington to carry out the plan.[50]

In preparation for the offensive, Banks ordered his officers to drill the men and prepare their equipment for combat. Sergeant John Fleming of the 165th New York Infantry recorded his regiment's training schedule for January and February 1863, which included battalion drills, skirmishing drills, bayonet exercises, and firing blank cartridges. Lieutenant Jacob Hasbrouck wrote home to his wife that he was "very particular" about his men's appearance, requiring them to keep their guns clean and their boots black, earning praise from the army's commanders. Training occasionally became dangerous. Fleming's diary included the comment, "Corporal Brown of Co. D was today accidentally shot, died within half an hour."[51]

While Banks planned the spring campaign, many Federals in Louisiana focused on comfort. Henry Rufus Gardner (of no known relation to the Confederate commander Franklin Gardner) wrote in his diary on February 16, "today is Mardi Gras day and is celebrated by people dressing themselves up and making fools of themselves generally." Union soldiers painted their tents with slogans such as "Get All You Can and Keep What You Can Get," the names of hotels, such as "Hotel DeIreland [*sic*]," and artwork that included the "skull and crossbones, blue eagles, and tombs." Henry Gardner was disappointed when the army ordered men to erase the artwork from their tents. Gardner believed it "was a pity to spoil such beautiful specimens." On February 20 Lieutenant Daniel Dewey wrote home to his sister that he had taken a little lizard that looked like an alligator as a pet, which "sleeps in my vest pocket every night and eats out of my plate." He promised to bring the lizard home after the war, writing, "I have grown so fond of him that I cannot bear the idea of separation."[52]

Theft became a problem for Federal soldiers with time on their hands. William Fowler set up camp with his regiment at Placquemine, a small town a little south of and across the Mississippi River from Baton Rouge. He and his brother officers raided a nearby deserted plantation home and sugar refinery, taking everything of value back to their camp. Fowler built a floor for his tent from three wood doors "from some gentlemanly Secesh" [*sic*]. He made a mattress from sugar cane leaves wrapped in an "India-rubber blanket," which he considered "luxuriousness" and placed on a bedstead taken from a nearby plantation. He also enjoyed the use of two chairs, a table, a wash basin, a stone jug, and tin cups, all taken from nearby homes. Fowler and his comrades feasted on molasses and sweet potatoes. The Federals shared their feast with "poor whites living nearby." According to Fowler, the "poor whites" had refrained from looting the plantation house and associated refinery "out of fear of the owner," but as soon as the Union soldiers invited the civilians to join them in looting the plantation, "their eyes bunged out with joy, and in they went." It is not clear if the "poor whites" were Union supporters or if they were friendly to everyone who provided them with food. However, if nothing else, the shared feast demonstrates that some southern civilians were willing to be friendly to Union soldiers under the right circumstances. Obviously, this conclusion assumes that Fowler's story is accurate and not a postwar embellishment. John Fleming complained in his diary that someone stole his canteen full of whiskey while he was on guard duty. Chaplain John Moors wrote his wife that one of the regiment's officers claimed that he could capture Port Hudson with his regiment alone if he camped the men within five miles of Port Hudson and told them it was off limits, avowing that "within two weeks they would steal the whole of it."[53]

While the Federals floundered, General Gardner went on the offensive. On February 26, 1863, he sent a portion of his garrison to confront Federal troops at Morganza, Louisiana, roughly fifteen miles north of Port Hudson on the west bank of the Mississippi River. Members of the 4th Louisiana Infantry, Miles's Legion, and Fenner's Battery boarded the steamer *Red Chief*. As the boat left Port Hudson, the 4th Louisiana Infantry's band

Colonel William R. Miles
of Miles's Legion Louisiana Infantry
Battalion. Miles was a prisoner of war
on July 9, 1863, at Port Hudson.
Library of Congress.

played the French revolutionary tune "La Marseillaise." The Confederates landed near Hermitage, Louisiana, three miles north of Port Hudson on the west bank of the Mississippi, late on February 26 and marched inland toward Morganza. A thunderstorm broke out, drenching the rebels as they searched for the Federals. The Confederates returned to Port Hudson on February 27, without finding the Union forces.[54]

Gardner also got creative and attempted at least one unconventional offensive. On February 27 Gardner wrote Pemberton a brief note, claiming, "the *Essex* can be bought for 300 bales of cotton" and assuring Pemberton "this is considered reliable." Pemberton replied to Gardner the same day, "Buy her at any price. I will guarantee payment." The plot failed, and the *Essex* remained in Union hands. Several days later, Gardner wrote to Pemberton that Union authorities uncovered the plot and arrested a Union lieutenant on the *Essex* for treason.[55] The details of the plot remain unclear. No reference to the plot appears in available Union sources. The National Archives Court Martial Records list only a single court martial record for a sailor on the *Essex*, and that case was in 1864, the year after Port Hudson fell.

On March 2, Admiral Farragut in New Orleans submitted a report to Secretary of the Navy Gideon Welles, detailing his plans for a spring offensive. Farragut discouraged an attack on Mobile, Alabama, since he doubted "Mobile would be of benefit to us beyond the possession of the forts." He next noted that he was unable to make any impact on Galveston, Texas, until the army could supply enough troops to support naval operations in the area. Finally, Farragut reported that he was fully prepared to run the batteries of Port Hudson, which he considered an urgent mission, considering the recent Confederate attempts to counterattack along the Mississippi River. The presence of strong Confederate batteries at Warrenton, Mississippi, which impeded the passage of the *Queen of the West* on a recent expedition, also concerned Farragut.[56]

Farragut proposed a combined arms offensive against Port Hudson. The Union army would launch a reconnaissance in force against overland defenses to distract the defenders. Meanwhile, the navy would run past the Confederate batteries with the *Hartford, Mississippi, Richmond, Monongahela,* and three gunboats. If the *Brooklyn* arrived in time, it would also make the run. Farragut wanted to take the *Essex* up the river, but he feared that it would "be too heavy a tow to take up against the current." Once past Port Hudson, the navy would destroy all Confederate boats on the Mississippi and Red Rivers; bombard Confederate shore batteries, particularly the dangerous batteries at Warrenton, Mississippi; and support General Grant's operations against Vicksburg. The old sailor was clearly aware of military politics when he assured Welles, "I will only aid and not interfere" with other commanders during the offensive. Farragut told Captain Jenkins, commanding the *Richmond,* "the time has come, there can be no delay." Farragut was adamant that "I must go—army or no army." Banks agreed to Farragut's plan and committed to twelve thousand soldiers to the offensive. Another five thousand soldiers would remain behind in Baton Rouge to guard the city from a Confederate counterattack.[57]

As is so often the case, it is unclear where Farragut received his information on Port Hudson's strength. Union gunboats had patrolled the area for several months, and he might have relied entirely on their reports. However, one Confederate soldier suggested that Farragut might have benefited from espionage. In a postwar account, Thomas Cox of the 6th Mississippi Infantry claimed, "I talked with the Yankee spy who came within the Confederate lines and inspected the situation of our army and guns and then passing down the riverbank escaped to the Federal lines." Cox believed that "from this spy's report Farragut decided to begin the bombardment" and "to make the attempt to pass his fleet by Port Hudson."[58]

The Confederates probably did not know what Farragut was planning, but they did know that a Union offensive was inevitable and prepared to meet the threat. On March 5 General Pemberton in Vicksburg sent additional reinforcements to Port Hudson. General Albert Rust arrived in Port Hudson on March 7 with a brigade of 2,771 troops. Pemberton also sent General Abe Buford and urged Gardner to form a brigade from troops already at Port Hudson for Buford to command. Gardner noted the arrival of Rust's brigade but claimed that he had no troops that could be formed into a brigade for Buford to command.[59]

At least a few of the Confederate soldiers in Port Hudson enjoyed high morale. James Harmon and the 35th Alabama Infantry passed through Clinton, Louisiana, en route to reinforce Port Hudson. As the Alabamians marched toward Port Hudson, "a very handsome girl" called out, "these are the ones to whip the Yankees." She urged the men to "kill a half dozen for me boys." Harmon "could not help smiling at her remarks," but he felt "her patriotic zeal had got a little higher than necessary." In general, Harmon recalled the people of Louisiana he encountered on that march as "very kind and generous" to him and his comrades. The march was difficult as the Alabamians waded creeks up to their waists, finally arriving in Port Hudson on March 8. Harmon was impressed by the fortifications at Port Hudson, which he believed was "almost impregnable." John Morgan, a veteran private in the 4th Louisiana Infantry who was wounded at Shiloh, echoed the confidence of the Alabama officer, telling his sister that if the Union army attacked Port Hudson, "they will be one of the worst whipped set of men that ever was."[60]

Southern journalists amplified and echoed the soldier's confidence. The *Memphis Daily Appeal* published a letter from an unidentified officer in the 1st Alabama Volunteers written the month before. The officer claimed that Port Hudson was "thoroughly fortified and defended by an army of veterans." He described the army as "in splendid trim, well disciplined and all tried men." In contrast to the strength of Confederate forces, the officer claimed that he had learned from Union deserters that the Federal forces in the region were weak. He claimed that many Union officers were resigning because Banks was placing "Yanks on an equal footing with old Abe's free Americans of African descent." The Alabama officer stated that Banks "has about 30,000 men, all niggers and New England men," all of whom were "in a dreadful state of discipline." The officer predicted that the Confederate forces at Port Hudson "will be able to repulse any force the Yankees will be able to bring against us." A newspaper article published in Selma, Alabama, claimed that the only "abolitionists" who would ever get inside Vicksburg and Port Hudson would be prisoners of war. Rumors circulated that the Federal army advancing on Port Hudson was falling apart as men deserted in protest of the recruitment of African American soldiers. The *Vicksburg Daily Whig* republished an article, originally published in the *Port Hudson News*, which praised the Vicksburg garrison's recent repulse of a Federal advance and predicted "what Vicksburg has done Port Hudson will do."[61]

They Yankees were coming, although slowly. On March 8 General Banks and his staff arrived at Baton Rouge. On March 9 a small force of Union cavalry attacked Confederate positions around the Montesano Bridge, near Bayou Sara, about twelve miles north of Port Hudson. Captain J. M. Magruder, commanding the Confederate Bayou Sara picket post, reported that the Federals attacked his force of about fifty men, mortally wounding one man before withdrawing. Members of the 25th Connecticut Infantry, supported by small detachments of cavalry and artillery, occupied nearby Bayou Montesano. Once in place, the Federals built earthworks and constructed a bridge across Bayou Sara.[62]

Private J. Harvey Brown of the 91st New York Infantry wrote his wife that his regiment was preparing to leave Baton Rouge. He expected he and his comrades would march toward Port Hudson. He anticipated that within "24 hours the balls will whistle around my head." He assured his wife, "it

First Lieutenant Sylvester Barrett Shepard of Co. C, 91st New York Infantry Regiment. Shephard was killed at Port Hudson. Library of Congress.

is what I enlisted for and I think I can face the music without flinching." Brown put his faith in God and asked his family to pray for him.[63]

Prussian-born corporal Albert Krause wrote to his family still in Europe that the Union army near Baton Rouge consisted of "25–30 thousand men, and every soldier was reassured by the awareness of our strength." To prepare for the advance, the men were ordered to turn in the large six-person tents they had used up to that point and were issued new shelter tents. Each man received a canvass shelter half to carry on the march. The shelter halves had buttons and buttonholes along the edges so that two or more men could button them together to construct a simple tent. Krause noted the shift from the large garrison tents to the simple shelter tents made the camps look "completely different."[64]

Members of the 16th New Hampshire Infantry had been in Louisiana since December 1862, but they had not encountered the enemy. The men worried that their outdated .69 caliber smoothbore muskets were insufficient for the battles to come. The regiment's officers begged for rifles. Luther Townsend, a 1st Lieutenant in the regiment, reported the men were delighted when the regiment finally received a mix of .57 (probably Enfield) and .58 (probably Springfield) rifles. The new weaponry came with strings attached. The regiment received orders to advance along with the new rifles.[65]

James Peck wrote home on March 8 that the army was about to advance on Port Hudson. He described the army's camps as alive with activity. Men scurried to prepare for action while the music of fifes and drums filled the air. Peck wrote that the Union gunboats at Baton Rouge looked "savage enough to take almost anything." Peck predicted that it would "be a hard fight" but expressed confidence he and his comrades would "hurt them some I think."[66]

On March 9 and 10 James Dargan wrote in his diary that the men were busy drawing rations of hardtack and salted meat, making final preparations for the march, and listening to speeches from the officers. Dargan wrote that on the march he would take a "7lb blanket, 2lb rubber [probably a waterproofed rubber or gum blanket], 6lb shelter tent, 4lb great coat, 60 rounds of ball cartridge, 5lbs canteen, haversack." He did not estimate a weight for his haversack and only complained that it was light because the quartermasters provided very little food. The surgeons examined men who claimed to be sick and determined if they were "playing off" to avoid duty. Dargan admitted his regiment included a few "shirks" but "the noble fellows express scorn and derision" at men who were looking to escape their obligations to the nation. Dargan expressed confidence that he and the rest of the regiment "will do our duty."[67]

Reports of Confederate reinforcements may have slowed the Union advance. General Banks warned Farragut that "the Army of Northern Virginia is moving toward the Mississippi." Banks asked Farragut for a gunboat to thwart the imaginary advance from Virginia. On March 9 Brigadier General George Shepley, the Union military governor of Louisiana, wrote General Weitzel that "a large force" of Confederates were at Camp

Moore, Louisiana, preparing to strike the rear of Banks's forces. Shepley shared inaccurate rumors that Stonewall Jackson was in command of the Confederates at Camp Moore.[68] Perhaps in response to Shepley's letter, Banks kept large garrisons at key points across Louisiana, including Baton Rouge and New Orleans.

On March 10 advancing Federal forces drove in Port Hudson's advanced pickets. Gardner believed that at least 30,000 Federals were advancing on Port Hudson. He was unsure of their exact strength, but he "supposed" it was "a strong raid." Paul de Gournay, commanding Port Hudson's river batteries, estimated "the total weight of metal we could hurl upon an attacking fleet was 770 pounds." De Gournay lamented that the 770 pounds of metal was "much less than a single broadside from some of the ships under Admiral David G. Farragut." A writer for the *Weekly Mississippian* assured readers that the Confederate cavalry was carefully watching the Union forces. The writer predicted that, if the Federal army advanced on Port Hudson, "its reception will be worthy of our people and their cause."[69]

At 9 a.m. on March 11, Farragut arrived at Baton Rouge on board the *Hartford* and began final preparations to run Port Hudson's batteries. Louis Boyd, on the Union gunboat *Albatross*, wrote home to his wife on March 11, "there is a considerable fleet at Baton Rouge." The sailors all expected that they would attack Port Hudson within the next few days. Boyd was optimistic that Union would take Port Hudson with little trouble because the navy had a massive fleet in the river and Banks commanded what he believed was an army of 40,000 troops with seventy cannons. Boyd believed Union leaders would be sure to complete the campaign soon because "the sickly season will soon commence." Boyd told his wife that he was only remaining in the navy because he wanted to participate in the capture of Port Hudson. After that, he promised to resign his commission and come home because "I want to see you all very badly."[70]

On March 12 Farragut and his key aides, including his son Loyall Farragut, attended a grand review of Union forces at Baton Rouge. Twenty-one years later Loyall recalled "they made quite a creditable appearance." Massachusetts artilleryman Henry Aiken informed his mother that the camps near Baton Rouge were filled with troops preparing for an attack on Port Hudson and attending reviews. Aiken knew that his mother wanted him to come home, and he assured her, "I would come home if I could." However, he expected to serve the remainder of his three-year enlistment. Aiken expected that many men would die in the upcoming battles for Vicksburg and Port Hudson and wrote, "if it falls to my lot to be numbered among the dead, mourn for me if it affords you relief, but not to excess." Aiken assured his mother that he had lived a good life while in the army and promised her that, if he died, he would "meet you in heaven with all the rest of the family."[71]

On March 12 Gardner reported to Pemberton, "the enemy appear to be advancing slowly on three roads." He also wrote, "I have three days' corn and thirty days' meat." Gardner ordered men to stack firewood on the west bank of the river, opposite Port Hudson, and to position "headlights with powerful reflectors down near the water's edge." Gardner expected Union ships to attempt passage of Port Hudson's batteries in the dark, but he hoped that lighting bonfires on the riverbank would illuminate the river and allow Confederate gunners to hit Union ships, outlined against the fires.[72]

The Confederate defenders prepared to implement Gardner's defensive plan. Private Pat Griffin of the 10th Tennessee Infantry and many other men spent the evening of March 12 on the riverbank with orders to set fire to a large pyramid of pine knots his regiment had gathered that day if he saw a Union ship in the river during the night. Company K of the 1st Alabama Infantry, serving as heavy artillery, had only one cannon but a full complement of men, so company commander Captain Whitfield split his command into three parts. He kept one part with him to work the company's 30-pounder Parrot cannon. He detached another portion of the company to work as infantry guards for the cannon. Finally, Whitfield gave command of a third detachment to Lieutenant Tuttle and ordered that detachment to serve as "river police" under Major Knox. After the split, members of the garrison began jokingly referring to the company, with its three distinct detachments, as Whitfield's Legion.[73]

—5—

Gorgeous Yet Horrible

THE UNION NAVY BOMBARDS PORT HUDSON

These shells of terror were yet things of beauty as they cut their way athwart the heavens. I see them even now, cleaving their shining, hissing paths, crossing each other in points of bursting brilliancy all gorgeous yet horrible designs thrown across the aerial trestle board of war's master workmen. Even at this day, amid summer night festivals, where fireworks and music rival each other, I startle at the hissing, coruscating meteors shooting upward, for they conjure up to me, as to thousands of comrades, the visions of long days and nights of siege, when these skyscraping curves of terrific beauty flashed overhead; and then there boomed from the armed ships in the great river at our feet the plunging missile, the ponderous cannon-ball.[1]

—GEORGE WATERMAN, Fenner's Louisiana Battery

The whole top of the bluff was alight with flame and shots were crashing through and around us with a rapidity unequal in annals of history. Most of their shots were from rifle cannon as could tell by the peculiar sound they made. I was on deck through the thickest the fight and I only wish I had the power to describe it, tongue and pen is unequal to the task. Those who have never witnessed a battle can form no idea of the grandeur involve in smoke shell and short hissing by you sometimes yes and often so close you can feel the wind of them, expecting every moment for one to strike you.[2]

—LOUIS BOYD, serving on the Union gunboat *Albatross*

Sunrise over Port Hudson

THE SUN ROSE EARLY over Port Hudson on March 13. Jabez Cannon of the 27th Alabama Infantry woke up as the sunlight poured over the riverbanks. He was grateful to enjoy the "beautiful weather" of that spring morning. It was washday for the Alabamians, so they began the day by bathing themselves and their clothes in the river. The soldiers were happy, but according to Cannon, "everybody [was] on the lookout." The soldiers knew that an attack was imminent. Each regiment completed their daily chores under double-strength guard details. Cannon noticed that the army's couriers were "unusually active," a clear sign to veterans like Cannon that a battle was coming. According to Cannon, the men were "in good spirits and eager for the fray."[3]

While infantrymen washed, mounted Confederate scouts arrived in Port Hudson with reports that Federal camps around Baton Rouge were rumbling to life and preparing for an advance. General Gardner informed his officers, "the enemy has at last determined to advance against this place." He expressed his confidence that the "gallant and veteran troops" defending Port Hudson would do their duty with "bravery, endurance, and cheerfulness." He said, "let every man do his duty and we will hold his point in defiance of the numbers they bring against us." Gardner sent all soldiers under arrest back to their units. He ordered all men, except for no more than eight men per company detached as teamsters, cooks, and hospital workers, to "remain continuously in the breastworks." Gardner instructed all men to "have their arms and accouterments at all times within their reach." He ordered ammunition to be stored near the fortifications. He withdrew most infantry pickets and replaced them with fast moving cavalrymen. Gardner ordered each unit in Port Hudson to keep two days of cooked rations constantly on hand and every man to keep his canteen filled with water and his haversack stocked with food. Men gathered water barrels and placed them at strategic locations within the fortifications. Gardner ordered medical officers to prepare teams of litter bearers. Captain J. W. Youngblood, commanding the signal station on the river, unfurled his signal flags and prepared his rockets for flight.[4]

Confederate soldiers took their places, and Gardner reminded his commanders of the battle plan. Gregg's brigade formed on the right flank to the south of Port Hudson, Maxey's brigade occupied the center, and Beall's brigade defended the left flank to the north of Port Hudson. Rust's brigade deployed in front of the works. Gardner ordered Rust to engage the Federal advance a short distance in front of the Confederate breastworks and draw them into the center of the Confederate defenses. As soon as the Federals fully committed to an assault on Port Hudson, Rust's brigade would withdraw behind the defenses, and the full power of the remaining three brigades would attempt to hold their ground. If the garrison successfully stood their ground, and the Federals began to withdraw, Maxey's men would counterattack the Union center as Gregg's and Beall's men launched simultaneous assaults on both Union flanks. Rust's men would remain behind as a reserve and reinforce the other brigades as needed.[5] It was an ambitious plan that demonstrated Gardner's preference for offensive action.

Union Forces Prepare for Action

As the Confederates at Port Hudson prepared for action on the morning of March 13, 1863, Admiral David Farragut inspected his flotilla at Baton Rouge. Farragut's flagship was the screw sloop *Hartford*. Farragut also commanded the screw sloops *Richmond* and *Monongahela*. The *Mississippi* was a unique addition to the Union fleet. She was a sidewheel steamer that served as Commodore Perry's flagship during the 1853 expedition to Japan. Farragut's fleet also included three smaller steam-powered gunboats, the *Albatross*, the *Genesee*, and the *Kineo*. Farragut found his fleet "well arranged and the ships well prepared in every respect." Louis Boyd, a Floridian serving on the *Albatross*, wrote to his wife, "if I have ever caused you any pain or trouble forgive me." He prayed for God to protect her and expressed his "hope to meet again," although he did not specify if he was thinking of an earthly or heavenly meeting.[6]

After confirming that his ships were ready to advance on Port Hudson, Farragut met with General Nathaniel Banks to coordinate their efforts. The primary goal of the Union army's advance on Port Hudson was to create a diversion in support of the navy. Banks had no plans to make a serious assault the Confederate defenses, but according to Assistant Adjutant General Richard Irwin, "we will of course avail ourselves of any advantage that occasion may offer." The Union army began their advance toward Port Hudson on the afternoon of March 13. Grover's Division marched out of Baton Rouge at 4:30 p.m. Companies C, D, and E of the 1st Louisiana Union Cavalry scouted ahead and acted as couriers. The 159th New York Infantry, three companies of the 26th Maine Infantry, and a section of the 2nd Massachusetts Battery formed the core of the advance guard. Emory's Division followed Grover's men later that afternoon. General Christopher Augur planned to follow with his division on March 14.[7]

USS *Mississippi,* 1841–63 (sidewheeler in foreground), in Baton Rouge, Louisiana, the day before she was destroyed in the attack on Port Hudson, March 14, 1863. Courtesy of the Naval History and Heritage Command.

Colonel Chickering of the 41st Massachusetts Infantry remained behind to defend Baton Rouge with about three thousand men. These troops included members of the 41st Massachusetts, 173rd New York, 175th New York, the 3rd Louisiana Native Guards, Mack's 18th New York Light Artillery battery, and F Troop of the Rhode Island Cavalry. The Federal siege train, consisting primarily of the 1st Indiana Heavy Artillery, better known as the Jackass Regiment, prepared to take up defensive positions along the Mississippi River at Baton Rouge.[8]

The Union March Begins

Some Union soldiers enjoyed the first phase of the march toward Port Hudson. William Stevens, a nineteen-year-old corporal, described the start of the march as "a glorious and exciting spectacle." The men were delighted by the "long expected" advance, which they "hailed with eager anticipation." The soldiers expressed their excitement to finally be on the move "in hearty cheers and songs." Mounted officers galloped up and

General C. C. Augur, USA.
Library of Congress.

down the line, and the men "greeted them with continual cheers." The Federals gave their greatest cheers to General Banks. Many years later, Stevens remarked that, at this early stage of the campaign, Banks was still popular with the men. James Dargan wrote in his diary that the road was filled with artillery, cavalry, and "an almost immeasurable host of infantry," all with "colors gaily flying" as they marched to "the martial music of the bands." Dargan described it as "a gorgeous spectacle."[9]

The cheerful blue parade quickly descended into a miserable struggle. This was the first serious march for many of the Federals and their enthusiasm disappeared. William Stevens wrote that, as "the heat grew more oppressive," many men proved unable to keep up and abandoned their units to rest along the roadside. According to Luther Townsend, the entire march became a debacle, where "nothing ever seemed to be done at the time designated," and as a result "our men began to have their confidence shaken in the executive ability of our superior officers." Claudius Rider, a nineteen-year-old fifer, noted in his diary, "our boys have thrown away many of their things," but with apparent pride, Rider wrote that he did not discard anything and kept up with the regiment, despite his fatigue. Some men were hesitant to give up their winter clothing even as they strained under heavy loads, so they cut off the sleeves and skirts of the overcoats, crafting crude vests that would provide some protection against the cold but that weighed far less than full overcoats. Escaped slaves followed the Union columns, quickly picking up anything the soldiers discarded. Union artillery officer Lieutenant William Haskin lamented, "more clothing was thrown away during that short march than would suffice to clothe the whole Confederate garrison of Port Hudson for a year." There was not room for everyone on the road, and many units marched alongside the roads, which snaked through what Corporal George Powers called "dense woods, where the vines and creeping plants wove the forest into an almost impenetrable barrier, which shut out every ray of light." Prussian immigrant Albert Krause of wrote that "the soldiers kicked up so much dust that you couldn't see a man 12–15 paces away." The dust formed a thick coating "especially in our noses and eye sockets" until "we looked like Moors." James Dargan heard an unnamed "genl [*sic*] swearing at the stupidity of his subordinates and they in turn swearing at the men."[10]

The oddest items left along the roadside might have been metal vests. Several companies offered metal vests by 1861 and sold them to soldiers. A review of one model of vest, which was widely quoted in both southern and northern newspapers, claimed, "it can be worn with ease by any officer or soldier during the most active exercise." According to Private Frank Flinn, "many officers had purchased bullet-proof linings for their vests," but on that first march they discovered the misery of carrying "an iron foundry" in the Louisiana heat and left their body armor on the roadside "with the rest of the useless trash." Not every man abandoned his body armor on that first march. Albert Plummer reported that when the men retrieved the body of Lieutenant Colonel James O'Brien after he was killed leading an attack on Port Hudson on May 27, 1863, "the bullet which penetrated his body fell out, it having passed entirely through him and flattened up against a steel vest which he wore into battle."[11]

According to Chaplain John Moors, the men got creative with their loads. Some men "employed a colored brother" to carry their packs. Other men begged Moors to carry their bags on his horse. Moors obliged until his horse was more blanket than animal, and Moors dismounted to avoid straining the miserable creature. Now on foot, the forty-four-year-old minister turned soldier led his horse and carried his pack. He found that he could obtain momentary relief for his shoulders by stooping over and carrying some of the pack's weight on his neck. He considered this "robbing Peter to pay Paul, but poor Paul has so much the harder time that Peter ought to be willing to give him a lift."[12]

The advancing Federals had little to drink or eat along the road north. Union quartermasters provided some coffee and hardtack, but according to James Dargan the men emptied their canteens and were forced to forage for water. With no sources of clean water along the march, men pushed aside the "green scum" that topped "stagnant pools," and "thirsty volunteers" were "glad to drink" the water they would have rejected just hours before. The water was not enough to refresh "exhausted men," who fell to the roadside, unable keep up. Luther Townsend reported that the beef rations were so terrible that the men refused to believe it was beef and decided it must be horseflesh. They began singing a humorous song along the road.

> Old horse, old horse, how came you here?
> You plowed the earth for many a year:
> You've lived along for man's abuse.
> Now salted down for soldier's use.[13]

Hungry men paused to forage. Luther Townsend later recalled that his regiment's ranks were filled with butchers, meat dealers, cooks, and men who claimed that their civilian careers had made them "lawyers enough to know what ought to be done when in an enemy's country." The army had issued orders not to forage, but the orders were "misplaced by the sergeant major." Perhaps with a wink, Townsend explained that because of the lost orders, the men were sadly unaware of the prohibitions on foraging and innocently helped themselves to whatever food they could find along the road.[14]

At about 7:00 p.m., the Federals camped at Green's plantation, roughly eight miles from Baton Rouge. According to a story that circulated among the Union ranks, the plantation belonged to a "Union man." Union officers ordered the men to take only the top rails of fences for firewood, a compromise measure would leave the barriers essentially intact while still providing men with much needed firewood. The policy may have begun as a kindness to the Unionist owner of this specific plantation, but it soon became a standing order in the 19th Corps during the Port Hudson campaign. Corporal Albert Krause wrote that, despite some officers' efforts to protect the homes of loyal civilians, "no house, no home is safe from the soldiers" as the men set up camp, and "for the sake of a couple of boards, the most beautiful homes are ripped down." He admitted "this seems barbaric," but "soldiers do not want to sleep on the ground and get sick." Louisiana civilian Sarah Morgan was unimpressed with Union restraint and loathed the men in blue, who she claimed "stripped all on their road."[15]

The First Shots Are Fired

Early on March 14 the Federals resumed their advance. Members of Wingfield's cavalry and Rust's infantry skirmished with advancing Union troops. Gardner believed the skirmishing "was more benefit to my men than theirs, as it produced immediate cheerfulness and hopes of a fight." While skirmishes broke out, five steamboats loaded with corn arrived in Port Hudson. Gardner estimated the Port Hudson garrison would need 17,000 bushels of corn for the commissary, 20,000 bushels of corn for the quartermaster, and 1,200,000 pounds of fodder each month. He informed General Pemberton "it is impossible to obtain these supplies elsewhere than from Red River." The Confederate supply boats unloaded their cargoes and left Port Hudson just as the Union navy approached Port Hudson from the south.[16]

Farragut's fleet arrived near Profit Island, about six miles south of Port Hudson, early on the morning of March 14. James Goble of the 1st Alabama Infantry was in a small boat, serving as a "coast guard." He heard "the boats come up the river" and "blow their whistles." The first Federals had arrived. At Profit Island, Port Hudson's old nemesis, the *Essex*, joined Farragut's flotilla. Several mortar boats also joined the fleet at Profit Island.[17]

Farragut signaled for the commanders of each boat to meet him on the *Hartford*, where they discussed his plan of attack. Each screw sloop would sail in tandem with a gunboat. The *Mississippi* would bring up the rear as the only boat to pass the batteries alone. According to Bartholomew Diggins, serving on the *Hartford*, "this was the first engagement that the ships were last [lashed] together in pairs." Farragut did not assign a gunboat to the *Mississippi* because he had only three gunboats and because the *Mississippi*'s side wheels would have made it difficult for a gunboat to travel alongside the vessel. The *Essex* and the mortar boats would not attempt to run the batteries. They would remain just south of Port Hudson and bombard Confederate positions. Hopefully they would distract the Confederates from the Union vessels sailing north. The expedition's key goal was "to run the batteries at the least possible damage" and "secure an efficient force" north of Port Hudson to support the army at Vicksburg. The fleet would move as quickly as possible, but the river current flowed swiftly to the south. Even at full throttle, the boats would creep along at no more than two and a half miles an hour, giving Port Hudson's defenders ample time to batter the fleet. Farragut suggested that "the best protection against the enemy's fire is a well-directed fire from our own guns." Once past Port Hudson, the gunboats would travel to the Red River, where they would destroy everything of value to the Confederate war effort on that vital waterway and support the Union forces attacking Vicksburg. After explaining his plans to his officers, Farragut opened the floor to "a free interchange of opinions on the subject," and the officers "conversed freely." The meeting ended after Farragut felt confident that his plans were "well understood" and "concurred in by all." Farragut sent officers back to their ships to make final preparations.[18]

Union sailors readied themselves and their boats for combat. The men fortified boat decks with barricades of hammocks and sails that would not stop a cannon ball but would provide some protection against the bullets and shrapnel that the defenders were sure to unleash. Aboard the *Hartford*, Farragut ordered the men to install a speaking tube from the wheel to the mizzen top, where a pilot could stand tall enough to see above the worst of the smoke and give orders to the helmsmen on the deck. Men spread sand on the decks to ensure a firm footing when the surface became wet with river water and perhaps blood during the fight.[19]

At noon on Saturday, March 14, a teamster informed General Gardner that he had just left the area near Profit Island, six miles south of Port Hudson, where seven Union warships under the command of Farragut were preparing to run Port Hudson's batteries. The teamster described the position of each ship with the vocabulary of man more familiar with wagons than boats. He described the *Hartford* and *Albatross* as "hitched" together to form the "lead-team," the *Richmond* and *Genesee* "hitched" to form the "swing team," while the *Monongahela* and *Kineo* would be the "wheelers." The *Mississippi*, with her large "side-wheels" that made her "as big as a wagon," traveled alone as the very last ship in the line. According to George Waterman, "the grouping of the seven ships of Farragut struck Gen. Gardner very humorously."[20] It is unclear what Gardner found so funny about the groupings. Perhaps Gardner laughed at the teamster's attempt to describe naval tactics in the vocabulary of a wagon master.

The Confederate camps echoed with the long roll calling men to their posts. Members of Port Hudson's garrison rushed to their posts and prepared for action. James Addison Boyd formed in line with the rest of the 1st Mississippi Infantry. For a moment the defenders waited and "*ready* stood each cannoneer." Perhaps to emphasize the point, Boyd underlined the word ready in his poem book. Boyd wrote that, after finding their places among the defenses, the entire garrison waited "for the Yankee fleet to appear."[21]

The Federals opened fire on Port Hudson's defenders. Alabama corporal John Powers saw "seven boats visible" approaching from the south, "formed in line of battle." The Federal "bombardment commenced at 2:00 o'clock p.m." Captain William Parish of the 18th Arkansas Infantry heard "the Yankee thunder" and ordered his men to make final preparations for the fight. At her family home several miles from Port Hudson, Sarah Morgan heard "that dreadful roar" and "silently wondered which of our friends were lying stiff and dead." The Federal fire was initially "very slow" as the Union fleet remained out of range of Confederate artillery for the first part of the engagement. Much of the Federal fire came from mortar boats, which slowly inched closer to the Confederate works until they "threw their shells within the lower part of the breastworks." General Gardner reported that the Federal mortar boats kept up their fire until 6:00 p.m. "without producing any other result than continued cheers from the men." Corporal Powers agreed, claiming the bombardment "did not even scare our boys." Edward McMorries, a veteran who participated in the failed Confederate defense of Island No. 10 (February 28–April 8, 1862), was less cheerful. He suspected that the Union navy only withdrew after they "gained the range of our position" and would soon return. J. H. McNeilly of the 10th Tennessee Infantry reported that the afternoon bombardment terrified less experienced members of the garrison. He wrote that "a big fat fellow" stepped out of his tent as the bombardment began and was so terrified by the bursting shells that he dove into a drainage ditch and laid there so long that McNeilly thought he was dead. The bombardment also frightened the "many negroes in camp" who worked as laborers, cooks, and teamsters for the Confederate army. Most, if not all, of these "negroes" were probably slaves. McNeilly reported that a "negro" began to pray when the bombardment started. When a shell passed a few feet away, he jumped up, exclaiming, "O' Lord I done forgot de res [*sic*]" and bolted for the countryside. He ran into a pole sticking out of a cabin, broke his neck, and died.[22]

While Union ships bombarded the rebels from the river, Federal soldiers approached overland on the afternoon of March 14. Consistent with their prearranged plan, Rust's brigade tried to draw the Union troops toward the center of the Confederate earthworks. Robert Tabor with Company E of the 12th Louisiana Infantry reported, "there was a creek with a bridge over it which was ordered to be torn up." After destroying the bridge, "the company was placed in ambush." Soon, "a company of blue-coats and very fine-looking soldiers, well mounted and equipped," advanced on the Confederate position. One of the Federals noticed the destroyed bridge and said 'the — rebs' [*sic*] have been here." At that moment, Tabor heard the command to fire, and Confederates unleashed a volley. Their gunfire mortally wounded Colonel Clark, a staff officer for General Banks, convinced four Union soldiers to surrender, and startled a horse so badly that it threw its Union rider from the saddle, dragging him by a stirrup to his death. Tabor and his comrades believed "we could whip and drive back the whole Federal army."[23]

Other Union soldiers continued their advance. Members of the 52nd Massachusetts and 91st New York infantry regiments received word of the skirmish, left their knapsacks behind under the care of men too exhausted to march any farther, and advanced toward the Confederate positions. The Federal infantry passed signs of fighting, including wounded men, dead horses, and surgeons treating Colonel Clark's wound. According to Sergeant Edward Whitney of the 52nd Massachusetts, "to most of us it is our first sight of the bloodshed of war." The troops then passed through abandoned Confederate camps, where the Louisianans left behind inscriptions on trees such as, "Yanks, beware! This is a hard road to travel." The Federals pressed ahead despite the warnings and took up positions, where they waited for a Confederate attack that did not come.[24]

The Confederates had hoped to draw the Union troops toward their fortifications, but the Federals did not fall into the trap. Algernon Badger, a captain with the 1st Louisiana Union Cavalry, reported that his company clashed with Confederates, killing one man, "and drove the rest where horses could not follow." Badger was pleased with how his men performed in their first skirmish, telling his father, "there is no white feather about them." Badger was also pleased with his own performance in his first fight. Before going into action, he feared he would "get excited," but he was pleasantly surprised that he was able to keep his cool despite the bullets that "came uncomfortably close to my head." Badger explained, "a man don't notice them after a while if he is attending his business." He believed the Confederates retreated because they "are afraid of our sabers."[25] While some Confederate soldiers were probably scared of the men in blue trying to kill them, the Confederates had planned to retreat in hopes of drawing their Union counterparts into a trap. After briefly waiting for a Confederate counterattack, the Federals withdrew and made camp for the night about two miles to the rear.[26]

The Federal army was there to distract the rebels, not to launch costly assaults against strong positions. Unable to provoke the Federals into an assault on Port Hudson's breastworks, Rust urged Gardner to authorize a daring assault. Rust wanted to attack the Union right flank and rear, while Gardner left the earthworks and attacked the Union front with the remainder of the Confederate garrison. Gardner rejected Rust's suggestion. According to Louisiana infantry officer Howard Wright, the failure to attack "disheartened" the Confederate troops, but they "did not blame Gen. Gardner," who they believed was constrained by departmental officers. Rust's brigade continued to skirmish sporadically with the Federals.[27]

On the evening of March 14, Gardner ordered the 9th Louisiana Partisan Rangers to probe Federal lines. The skirmish with Rust's men proved that the Federals were advancing, but Gardner wanted more details than the infantry could provide. He hoped that the mounted rangers could give him more information. The Louisianans formed their ranks at Plains Store, about four miles east of Port Hudson, and moved forward. They encountered the Federals about half a mile south of Plains Store. The rangers attacked the Union advance guard, fighting until nightfall ended the skirmish.[28]

At 5:00 p.m. on March 14, General Banks received a note from Admiral Farragut announcing that he had changed his plans and now intended to run the Confederate batteries at 8:00 p.m. that evening, instead of "in the gray of morning" on March 15 as previously planned. Farragut was eager to get past Port Hudson's batteries before the rebel gunners could strengthen their positions or bring up reinforcements. The note found Union soldiers still several miles outside of Port Hudson, with little hope of getting their artillery into firing positions on Confederate defenses before Farragut's boats tried to run Port Hudson. Farragut's change of plans meant that the Union army artillery would be unable to distract Port Hudson's gunners. Federal soldiers would be little more than spectators to the navy's work. Aaron Oberly, a surgeon serving on the gunboat *Kineo*, wrote in his diary that, after supper, the ship's officers made final preparations for "a severe engagement." They all dressed in their cleanest clothes, wrote final letters home, placed photographs of loved ones in their pockets, and "all seemed cheery with no forebodings [*sic*] of sorrow."[29]

The Union Fleet Advances

The sun set over Port Hudson at 5:53 p.m. As darkness fell, Farragut signaled for his boats to move into position. At 10:00 p.m. the tugboat *Reliance* came alongside the *Hartford*, and Farragut told the *Reliance* to order the other boats to tighten up their formation. As soon as Farragut was happy that every boat was in the proper position, he led the flotilla north. He ordered Union gunners not to fire until the rebels fired first. The Union fleet sailed north through the darkness.[30]

Most of the garrison was asleep, with only a few sentries to keep watch. James Boyd wrote that he "in sleeping silence lay, unconscious of the pending storm." At 11:00 p.m., Confederate signal crews on the west bank of the Mississippi River spotted Union ships trying to slip past Confederate positions in the darkness and fired signal rockets. Louis Boyd, on the Union gunboat *Albatross*, saw signal rockets from a Confederate signal station fly into the air at 11:40 p.m. Ten minutes later, "the first shot was fired directly opposite to us." According to Louisiana artillerymen George Waterman, the Confederate observation and signal stations carried news of the Federal advance "around the lines with an almost electric impulse." Waterman "saw and felt the magic spell" as men quietly went to their posts. Jabez Cannon was "dreaming sweet dreams of peace and happiness the loved ones at home" when gunfire on the river woke him from his slumber, and "every man was at his post in an instant." Pat Griffin and other members of the 10th Tennessee Infantry set fire to the pyramid of pine knots they had gathered the day before. The wood burst into flames, and "every movement of the fleet was seen by the gunners at the port." At that moment, the *Essex* and the mortar boats opened fire on the Port Hudson from long range. The *Sachem* quickly joined the chorus as well.[31]

As the Union ships moved north, two Confederate supply ships from the Red River were still at Port Hudson's wharf, unloading their cargoes. Daniel Smith listened to the "shrieks of the women." Smith's comment highlights the fact that Port Hudson remained a home for civilians as well as a fortress for soldiers. Smith also heard "the shouts of the officers to their crews." As the boats strained to escape north, "all was confusion." As the supply boats left, General Gardner dashed up to the artillery emplacements. He saw the lights of the supply boats sailing away and yelled to Captain Whitfield "why don't you fire on those boats?" Before Whitfield could answer, Private John Hearn exclaimed, "they are our transports, you infernal thief." Gardner did not respond, either because he did not hear Hearn or because he felt that pretending not to hear Hearn's insubordinate remarks was in everyone's best interests.[32]

Confederate heavy artillerymen prepared to fire on the approaching Union boats. J. Wes Broom of the 49th Tennessee Infantry wrote his sweetheart that "at each battery lay silent men, watching with gleaming eyes." According to George Waterman, "the night was not all overcast," and he suspected that "our enemy must find it hard plowing in the dark against a four-knot current." Most observers believed that the Confederate gunners atop of the Port Hudson bluff were in an ideal firing position since they could plunge their shells down on the vulnerable decks of the Federal ships, but Waterman believed the height also presented a disadvantage, noting that "there was not as good a chance for our balls to ricochet against the armed vessels" as there would have been if the rebels had fired from a lower level. According to Alabama soldier John Powers, every Federal boat "opened their broadsides as rapidly as possible." The Union navy's gunners pounded the Confederate light batteries on the south edge of the defenses, but "strange to say without any harm." As the Federal flotilla moved north, it came within range of Miles's 20-pounder Parrott rifled cannon, which "was beautifully served." The Union fleet finally came within range of Port Hudson's heaviest cannons.[33]

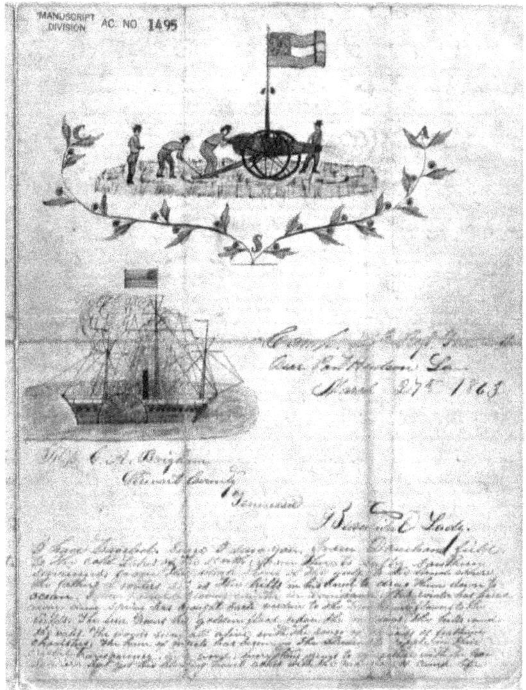

Letter from J. Wes Broom to Miss G. A. Brigham, featuring drawings, 1863. Tennessee State Library and Archives.

The Battle Begins

Flashes of gunfire from cannons on Union boats and from Confederate shore batteries combined with Confederate signal rockets and Confederate bonfires on the west bank to illuminate Federal ships for the benefit of rebel gunners. The Federal ships running the batteries traded fire with the Confederate artillery but did little damage in contrast to the "galling fire" of the mortars. The *Essex* made no effort to get past Port Hudson and, consistent with Farragut's plan, focused on pummeling the Confederate batteries. Howard Wright reported that the Confederate gunners "did not become excited by the deafening roar that reverberated from bank to bank." Union sailors aimed their cannons at the flashes of light produced by the Confederate batteries.[34]

The Battle of Port Hudson, passing the river batteries.

The intense gun battle made an impression on Confederate soldiers, who later described the scene in grandiose terms. Mississippi infantryman James Boyd wrote "*Mars* in all his fury raged" and underlined the word Mars in his account. Acknowledging both the terror and the beauty of the battle, he described the scene as "grand and awful." Edward McMorries, working one of the 1st Alabama's cannons, wrote the "scene now became one of indescribable grandeur." Both the river and the Confederate positions looked "like a solid sheet of electric glare and flame." The "deafening roar drowned the command of officers," and "gunners and squads no longer awaited command but loaded and fired as rapidly as possible." Tennessean J. Wes Broom heard the tempo of the artillery fire increase until it became impossible to determine which flash corresponded with which boom. Private Andre Beauchamp of the 1st Alabama Infantry wrote to his wife that "the air was positively lit up with bombs, it was way beyond anything I ever could conceive." George Waterman estimated that the Federals poured 296 artillery rounds into Port Hudson that night. The "shells of terror were yet things of beauty" that were "gorgeous yet horrible" as they "cut their way through the heavens," flying in, "cleaving their shinning, hissing paths, crossing each other in points of bursting brilliancy." In 1896, more than three decades after that night, Waterman wrote "I see them even now."[35]

In his diary, Louisiana Confederate Robert Patrick described the bombardment as "the grandest scene that I ever beheld." The shells fell in thick clusters with "a tremendous roar" that startled the mules pulling Patrick's supply wagon and sent them careening off the road and into a fence, where they got stuck. Patrick began to free the wagon when he saw "several negroes passing, full speed." He yelled for the fleeing men to help him, but the "negroes were dreadfully frightened" by the bombardment and escaped before Patrick could stop them. A moment later, another "negro" rushed past, and Patrick ordered the man to help him. The man initially refused, but then Patrick drew his pistol and "told him if he didn't help me that I would kill him on the spot." The threatened man reluctantly helped Patrick get the wagon back on the road. Patrick watched other people run past him in the dark. One person tripped over a stump in the darkness and killed himself. Several women had come to Port Hudson to see their husbands serving in the Confederate army. When the bombardment began, they fled, stumbled into a stream, and "a woman and child drowned."[36]

Arkansas infantryman William Parish observed the action from his post in Port Hudson's defenses. He wrote his wife that he heard the Federals before he could see them and continued, "I cannot express the awful noise it seemed as though the whole world was exploding." Union ships came into view, and the Confederate batteries returned fire. Parish watched "the pieces whisking in every direction." He described the battle as "the most beautiful that I ever beheld though there was some terror in it."[37]

Louis Boyd, on the Union gunboat *Albatross*, later wrote his wife that he wished he could accurately describe the battle but that "tongue and pen is unequal to the task." He believed that "those who have never witnessed a battle can form no idea of the grandeur involve in smoke shell and short hissing by you sometimes yes and often so close you can feel the wind of them, expecting every moment for one to strike you." Confederate shells exploded around and even inside the *Albatross*, sending "thousands" of bits of metal through men and machine. The noise was "deafening." A rifle bullet struck a gunner on the *Albatross*, penetrating his arm, ripping through his body, and striking the cannon he was loading as he fell to the deck.[38]

As the first pair of ships in line, the *Hartford* and the *Albatross,* which were lashed together, were in the fleet's best position. The two ships enjoyed the best visibility, cutting through the river ahead of the worst of the gun smoke that drifted over the water, and passed most Confederate artillery positions before Confederate gunners realized the Federals were within range. Despite the advantageous position in line, rebel gunners quickly found the *Hartford*'s range and scored direct hits that cut up her rigging. The *Hartford*'s gunners returned fire, but according to Union sailor Bartholomew Diggins, the *Hartford*'s cannons could not hit the Confederate positions high on the bluff, and the Union fire made no impact. Once the *Hartford* and *Albatross* entered the sharp bend in the river, the swift current that swept around the point pushed her toward the Confederate batteries and sent her crashing into the eastern bank. For a moment, the *Hartford* and the *Albatross* were in great peril. Then *Hartford* pushed her engines to maximum forward speed, while the *Albatross* went into full reverse. The pair of boats turned as if they were on a central pivot, freeing them from the riverbank. The *Hartford* and *Albatross* escaped around the bend, out of range of the Confederate batteries. The lead pair of Federal ships were safe, but as Farragut turned his gaze south, he did not see the rest of the fleet.[39]

The *Richmond* and *Genesee* were next in line behind the *Hartford.* Confederate batteries on the east bank opened fire as Confederate infantrymen on the west bank peppered both the *Richmond* and the *Genesee* with bullets. The *Richmond* returned fire with repeated broadsides. A sailor on the *Richmond* called it "grand and horrific" as the noise grew to a crescendo that "rivaled pandemonium." Just when the pair were almost past the Confederate batteries, a 6-inch solid shot ripped through the *Richmond,* damaging the boilers and disabling the engine. Even with the aid of the *Genesee,* the *Richmond* could not overcome the river's swift current. The two boats floundered as the rebels pummeled the almost stationary target. The Union boats steered toward the eastern bank, just below the gun emplacements manned by the 1st Alabama Infantry, who were working as heavy artillerymen. For a moment the Alabamians thought that the *Richmond* and *Genesee* were about to unload a shore party, and they looked to their muskets stacked nearby, but then they realized that the Federal sailors were trying to get under the bluff, where they hoped Confederate gunners could not hit them.[40]

Perhaps thinking they had found a place of safety, a voice from the *Richmond* called out "now let me see you strike me from those hills, G—d d—n [*sic*] you!" According to Alabamian Edward McMorries, the Union boats had found a spot that was safe from some Confederate artillery, but "the few that could bear upon her were all the more effective from being in such close quarters and in better view." An instant after the voice from the *Richmond* taunted the rebels, Confederate gunners sent a shell crashing through the *Richmond's* forecastle and swept the forward decks with a double charge of grapeshot. A voice from the *Richmond*, perhaps the same one that called out a challenge to the Confederate artillerymen a few moments before, screamed out, "For God's sake don't shoot anymore! We are sinking!" The *Richmond*'s commander made no formal effort to surrender, so the Confederate artillerymen ignored the cry and continued to fire on the floundering *Richmond*. Reluctantly, the sailors on the *Richmond* and *Genesee* gave up all hopes of passing the batteries and retreated, taking additional damage as they sailed south.[41]

While the *Richmond* floundered, Union sailors fought to keep the boat afloat. Confederate artillery fire punctured the already-damaged *Richmond*'s fireroom, sending steam through the ship and threatening the craft with destruction. John Hickman, a second-class fireman on the *Richmond* who by odd coincidence was born in Richmond, Virginia, braved the deadly steam to continue working on the *Richmond*'s engines and keep the boat moving. He worked alongside first-class firemen Matthew McClelland, John Rush, and Joseph Vantine. Somehow, the four firemen managed to keep their boat moving and avoid death by scalding steam. All four men later received the Medal of Honor for their bravery on March 14.[42]

As the *Richmond* and *Genesee* floundered south, the *Monongahela* and *Kineo* advanced northwards, trading fire with the Confederates. Rebel batteries hammered the *Monongahela* at the turn in the river, near the spot where the *Richmond* was badly damaged. According to Aaron Oberly, on the *Kineo*, Confederate shells damaged the steering machinery on both the *Monongahela* and the *Kineo*, making it impossible for either boat to steer as the rebels blasted them with heavy artillery. The *Monongahela* ran aground with so much force that the lighter draft *Kineo* ripped loose, and the two boats that began the fight together were separated. Crews on both boats tried to return fire and repair their steering equipment. Confederate shells disabled three of the *Monongahela*'s cannons and wounded several sailors, but the *Monongahela* eventually freed itself from the riverbank. The pair continued to fight their way north, until a crank pin on the *Monongahela* overheated, making further progress impossible, and the two boats retreated south.[43]

Confederate gunners next focused their fire on the lumbering sidewheel steamer *Mississippi* as she slowed to make the tight turn below Port Hudson's heavy batteries. According to Confederate engineer officer Fredrick Dabney, the "quantity of iron hurled upon her sides was enormous." The *Mississippi*'s crew strained against nearly impossible odds as they tried to work their guns and steer their ship through a narrow, twisting channel in the dark while Confederate gunners poured fire into her from multiple angles. The *Mississippi* ran aground on a sand bar. Tennessee infantryman Pat Griffin wrote that the *Mississippi's* commander raised a white flag, and the Confederates stopped shooting. Griffin claimed that the ship's crew began shooting again after the rebels ceased fire, and in response a Confederate officer ordered the gunners to "give'em [*sic*] red hot shot."[44]

A detachment from the *Mississippi* boarded one of the ship's boats and rowed south in search of assistance from the Union fleet below Port Hudson. They arrived at the *Essex* a few minutes later, and the *Essex*'s officers sent one of their boats south in search of the tugboat *Reliance*, which was supposed to be on standby to help the fleet. The *Essex*'s detachment was unable to find the *Reliance* in time. Unable to free her from the sandbar or to get help, the *Mississippi*'s crew set fire to the ship and rowed for the western bank in the ship's boats. As they came ashore on the west bank, a Confederate cavalry patrol quickly captured many of the *Mississippi*'s sailors. According to William Park, on the *Essex*, members of the *Mississippi*'s crew who got to the *Essex* claimed that most of the *Mississippi*'s wounded "were left in her to burn to death." The claim, documented by Park, that members of the *Mississippi*'s crew were left to "burn to death" was contradicted by the report of Captain Smith of the *Mississippi*. Smith reported that several members of the crew, including Scottish-born sailor Andrew Brinn, remained on the *Mississippi* until they rescued "all the crew" from the *Mississippi*. Brinn later received the Medal of Honor for rescuing his shipmates at great personal risk to himself.[45]

Admiral Farragut's fleet engaging the Confederate batteries at Port Hudson, March 14, 1863. Currer & Ives print, Library of Congress.

As the flames burned off bits of the *Mississippi*, she became lighter, which freed her from the sand bar. The flames then reached her loaded cannons, firing shells into both banks of the river. Confederate soldiers cheered in response to the *Mississippi*'s final salvo. Alabamian Jabez Cannon heard "the old rebel yell" that "went up long and loud" from one end of the line to the other. Confederate soldiers later told Sarah Morgan that they heard Federal sailors, "left by their companions to burn" reply to rebel yells with "shrieks" that "were perfectly appalling." Confederate artillerymen reported that the *Mississippi*'s crew set fire to their own ship, but some infantrymen gave the Confederate artillery credit for setting the *Mississippi* ablaze. In a letter dated March 21, Sergeant David Mullins of the 41st Tennessee Infantry told his brothers that Confederate gunners "threw a hot ball and got it on for they tried to put it out but our men plaid [*sic*] on them so they had to run ashore." The fight was mostly over by a few minutes past midnight, but Union and Confederate artillerymen continued to trade fire at long range. Union ships tried and failed to capture Confederate supply ships that sped away during the engagement. The firing finally ended at about 2:00 a.m.[46]

The Battle Ends

The Union navy achieved some of their objectives on March 14, but blue-clad sailors paid an awful price. The *Hartford* and *Albatross* passed the Confederate batteries with little damage and anchored above Port Hudson. The *Richmond, Monongahela, Genesee,* and *Kineo* regrouped five miles below Port Hudson. Commander Alden on the *Richmond* reported that the decks of his ship presented "a horrible view" and were "covered in blood and brains and particles of human bodies and splinters." About daylight on March 15, the fires on board the *Mississippi* finally reached her magazines. The resulting explosion "scattered her to the four winds of heaven" and littered the river with fragments of what had been a proud warship just a few hours before. Algernon Badger of the 1st Louisiana Union Cavalry lamented that the "noble frigate Mississippi is no more." After watching the remnants of the *Mississippi* drift down the river, General Banks "believed the attempt at a passage was a total failure." Banks blamed Farragut for the defeat, telling his aides that the admiral "had been rash and headstrong and that the whole matter was at his door." Farragut considered the March 14 operation a "disaster."[47]

Many of the Union sailors under Farragut's command may have agreed with Farragut, at least in private. According to Bartholomew Diggins, on the *Hartford,* "all seemed much depressed from the admiral down." In his official report on the bombardment, James Thayer, a gunner on the *Richmond,* provided a dry and businesslike account of the shells fired by the *Richmond*'s cannons. However, in a private letter to a friend, Thayer explained that, while the whole fleet tried to run the batteries, "none succeeded." He described the suffering of friends and comrades, including a shipmate, "A. B.," who was wounded in the leg and suffered a painful amputation, only to die a short time later. He considered A. B.'s story "worst of all" because the sailor's wife had recently written that she was headed to New Orleans to visit A. B. Thayer lamented that A. B.'s wife would soon arrive and learn that her husband had died.[48]

In contrast to the Union losses, Confederate losses were remarkably light. Only a single enlisted man, from the 30th Tennessee Infantry, died. Another nineteen Confederates suffered from wounds during the engagement. With the seeming dismissiveness of veteran who had survived far

Lieutenant Commander Andrew Boyd Cummings of the US Navy. Cummings served on the USS *Richmond* and died of wounds received in battle at Port Hudson, March 18, 1863. Library of Congress.

worse battles, including Shiloh, John Morgan told his sister the brief engagement "was furious for a few minutes."[49]

Confederate soldiers expressed happiness with their performance on March 14. General Gardner estimated Union losses at two hundred men. John Powers considered it "a glorious victory" that had driven back the Federals "in a perfect state of demoralization." Captain Edward Broughton wrote his wife that the Federals "caught a tarter [*sic*] at Port Hudson," which was probably a reference to the feared Tartars of Central Asia. G. W. Buntly told his brother (inaccurately) that the Confederate killed the entire crew of the *Mississippi*. Captain William Parish wrote his wife that the garrison won "a signal victory" and incorrectly reported that they destroyed two Union ships. He marveled at the garrison's light losses and argued that the victory was proof that "God is on our side." Jabez Cannon erroneously believed that Banks had intended to capture Port Hudson on March 14 and that the Confederate garrison "completely foiled" the Union plan. Corporal Joseph Thompson believed that the Federal ships were "met with such a repulse that no attack by land was attempted." J. Wes Broom told his sweetheart that the Confederate victory was "a providential omen of our future success." James Boyd wrote in his poem book, "the storm was o'er [*sic*] our glory won, their loss was great but ours almost none."[50] Louisiana artillerymen mocked Banks as being "like the French king who, with an army of twenty thousand strong, marched up the hill and marched down the hill again" without "even seeing our breastworks." Howard Wright argued that the events of March 14 proved that Union courage and skill could not overcome the Confederate's geographic advantages. Wright believed that "the fight settled one question—that Port Hudson could not be taken by water."[51]

—6—

Tired and Sick of Soldiering

THE SPRING STALEMATE

> You don't know how lonesome it makes me feel to think I can't hear from you more often. Some of the letters get miscarried and I don't get any until I get 2 or 3 at once and there are some, I don't get at all. Dear wife, I am in hope that I will soon be permitted to return home again for I am getting tired and sick of soldiering. For soldiering is hard business.[1]
>
> —HAZEN RUSSELL, 110th New York Infantry

> They have bin throwing some shell in hear every day this week but they do no damage to us. We have taken a good many prisonars [*sic*] since we have bin hear or some of them ar deserters. . . . We can say that we are getting a long tolarby [*sic*] well if we could get enough to eat. We go some meal and meet and sugar and molasas [*sic*]. We don't get as much meal as we want at this time. . . . We have rote about all the news we have at this time. . . . We will close by saing [*sic*] rite soon.[2]
>
> —DAVID MULLINS, 41st Tennessee Infantry

The Union Retreat

With the failure to get most of the Union fleet past Port Hudson, General Banks considered the expedition over. He saw no reason to remain in exposed positions near Port Hudson when the fortified camps of Baton Rouge offered a refuge just a few miles to the south. On the morning of March 15, 1863, Federals began to withdraw south toward Baton Rouge, but sons of Louisiana refused to allow men in blue to depart unmolested. Members of the 9th Louisiana Partisan Rangers punished withdrawing Union soldiers. Federal rear guards briefly tried to stand their ground and blunt the Confederate attacks, but within twenty minutes Union troops gave way and began a fighting withdrawal. Confederate soldiers kept up the pressure, nipping at the heels of the Union retreat. A rainstorm drenched the countryside, and men floundered in the mud. Connecticut soldier Samuel Ellis believed the rain saved many Union lives, because the rain did more to slow the pursuit than the rear guards.[3]

Many Federal soldiers were unhappy. Henry Howe wrote in his diary, "we have accomplished nothing." According to Private Henry Johns, soldiers marched south from Port Hudson "dispirited, angry, fully believing we had suffered a severe defeat, and wondering why our division had been idle." James Peck wrote home he was ready to see a battle and disappointed he did not get into action at Port Hudson before receiving orders to retreat without firing a shot. Rumors spread through the Union ranks that there had been fighting all night and that the entire army was in full retreat. It is not clear if the reports of defeat were exaggerated accounts of the skirmishing that took place or if they were the fabrications of green troops prone to panic. Along the march, Luther Townsend realized with "how little difficulty a panic might be started that would render troops utterly uncontrollable." Albert Krause wrote home that all the soldiers, including himself, agreed that the Union troops could have captured Port Hudson and believed that "our failure was only the fault of cowardice or sluggishness of our highest officers, who don't care how long the war keeps on." According to John Moors, the men were "as sorry and dejected a set of mortals as ever marched up a hill and then marched down again, with stomachs empty, shoes full of mud, feet well parboiled and nearly raw from blisters." Hazen Russell wrote home to his wife "I am in hope that I will soon be permitted to return home again for I am getting tired and sick of soldiering, for soldiering is a hard business."[4]

Some Union soldiers retained reasonably good morale on the retreat. Not long after the march back to Baton Rouge began, new rumors spread through the Union ranks that the *Hartford* and *Albatross* had successfully run the batteries of Port Hudson, fulfilling the expedition's mission. George Powers wrote that in response many men "recovered their accustomed spirits," and, when General Banks rode by men on the march a short time later, "he was heartily cheered." John Hart, commanding the Albatross, acknowledged the Federal losses but noted, "I am proud of my little steamer now since she has taken me through so much danger." New York infantry officer Orton Clark concluded that the army "had accomplished nothing" during the navy's attempt to run past Port Hudson but commented optimistically that, after the return to Baton Rouge, "we felt more like old campaigners than when we started." He even suggested they maintained good order and suffered no losses, remarking, "had we never seen any more service we should have looked back with some pride and satisfaction." Some men remained skeptical of the good news, and Henry Johns wrote that it was "an official lie to cover up a defeat."[5]

According to several accounts, the Union retreat went badly. Some units found themselves in possession of large cattle herds they could not hope to control and abandoned the animals along the retreat. Other Union units had nothing to eat and scavenged for supplies along the march. According to David Strother, a Virginia-born journalist on General Banks's staff, Federal troops "plundered without restraint" on the march, stealing horses, mules, and even robbing houses as they marched south. He claimed the Federals kept up a constant fire on farm animals until "the whole land was covered with blood, guts, horns, hair, and feathers." Confederate horsemen remained on the fringes of the retreat, killing or capturing men in blue who strayed too far into the countryside. James Dargan was astonished to watch Texas Confederates control their "mustangs" with verbal commands that allowed the men and their mounts to work in a partnership that was unlike anything he had ever seen.[6]

Some Federals may have abandoned the Union on the retreat. Texas infantryman Lycurgus Lambert told his parents that southerners who had joined the Union army were deserting the Federals as they retreated. While Lambert's claim might seem like a hopeful rumor, additional evidence supports Lambert's claim. The *Vicksburg Daily Whig* published a report from the *Port Hudson Courier* that Union cavalrymen deserted to the Confederate army at Port Hudson, "well pleased at the idea of becoming sojourners in the land of Dixie." Sergeant John Fleming of the 165th New York Infantry wrote in his diary that he "arrested Olmstead of Co. C attempting to go over to the rebels."[7]

The Confederates Regroup

As the Federals retreated south, some Confederate soldiers in Port Hudson focused on rounding up men and material left behind by their fleeing adversaries. Edward McMorries was delighted to capture of the captain's boat from the destroyed *Mississippi*, which Confederate officers used as a pleasure craft. John Powers rounded up Union "guns, knapsacks, and in fact nearly everything they had." Andre Beauchamp helped guard fifty Union prisoners who were mostly wounded sailors. Beauchamp noted that many of the captured sailors suffered from burns, and one had his leg amputated in Port Hudson's hospital.[8]

Perhaps nothing raised the morale of Confederate soldiers more than ample rations. Alabamian John Powers joked that, during the valley campaign in Virginia, Jackson made "a commissary of Banks," and Powers believed that Gardner was also making "a commissary of Banks," as the men feasted on cattle captured from the retreating Union forces. In recognition of the victory and the ample beef supplies, Gardner increased the men's rations. Edward Broughton of the 7th Texas Infantry was delighted by the capture of weapons, tents, blankets, overcoats, and large numbers of cows and sheep that the Federals abandoned on their retreat. Tennessean David Mullins was less impressed with his rations than some of his comrades, appreciating the meat but complaining to his brother, "we don't get as much meal as we want."[9]

News of the Confederate victory at Port Hudson spread around the Confederacy. Sarah Morgan expressed delight with the Confederate victory and was only disappointed that the Federals were not more "soundly thrashed." The *Charleston Mercury* provided a detailed account of the battle, concluding, "our victory is complete and glorious." The *Vicksburg Daily Whig* celebrated the Port Hudson garrison's devastating fire against the Federal fleet. An article in the *Pointe Coupee Echo*, republished in Memphis, mocked Banks, advising him "to get up a balloon expedition, and even then he would not be sure to drop in upon us unawares." A writer from Port Hudson, identified in the *Memphis Daily Appeal* only as Evelyn, claimed that "the army is in splendid trim and the best of spirits, and anxious for a fight" because the men were "feeling satisfied, healthy, and confident in their ability to defend Port Hudson." Evelyn claimed, "Gen. Gardner is a great favorite" and "the troops have all confidence in him." She concluded the Union was no more likely to open the Mississippi than to "force it to run up stream." The *Memphis Daily Appeal* praised the defenders of Port Hudson, arguing, "if the country is not satisfied with the Port Hudson fight, then it must be unreasonable" since "the result has been as surprising as it had been gratifying." Mississippi soldier Alfred Sandlin missed the March 14 engagement because he was on leave at the time.

When he heard that the Federals had attacked his post, Sandlin rushed back, briefly pausing to tell his wife, "dont [*sic*] be uneasy about me" and promising to write again soon.[10]

Union Forces Prepare for Their Next Move

Some northern newspaper accounts downplayed the Union defeat on March 14. The *New York Herald* pointed out that the Union army did not attack Port Hudson and therefore argued that the "repulse" of the Union fleet, disappointing as it might be for the nation, was "a mere reconnaissance" that meant little. John Hamilton, a British architect working as correspondent and artist for *Harper's Weekly*, informed readers that several Union boats were "repulsed" with "severe" loss but that two vessels achieved their objective of passing Port Hudson. The *Boston Herald* published a letter from an unnamed Massachusetts soldier at Baton Rouge, who wrote, "I take pleasure in informing you that a forward movement has been made towards Port Hudson." He incorrectly stated that the Federals had "succeeded in silencing two of the batteries at Port Hudson." The soldier also predicted that the Union navy would soon cut off Port Hudson from their supplies and starve out the garrison.[11]

The Federals withdrew from Port Hudson, but Confederate commanders knew that they would return. While Confederate soldiers celebrated the victory, the garrison's commanders worked on improving Port Hudson's defenses. On March 15 General Gardner reorganized the Port Hudson garrison. He placed General Abe Buford in command of a new brigade on the right, south of Port Hudson. Beall's brigade remained in the center. Buford's brigade took up a position on the left of Beall's brigade, to the north of town. Rust's brigade formed the garrison's reserve.[12]

In contrast to the reorganized Confederates, the Federals suffered from disorganization. According to Union private Henry Johns, Federal soldiers arrived in Baton Rouge "like scattered sheep, mad at themselves, mad at their generals, and mad at the colonel's horse, which kept on a mad pace." Most men refused to keep up, wandering into Baton Rouge alone or in small groups, "hot, footsore, and tired." Albert Krause told his family that hundreds of slaves followed the Federals to Baton Rouge. Just outside the Union camps, "slave catchers caught two young slaves; the man was ripped to pieces by the dogs." A hastily gathered group of Union soldiers, alerted by the noise, ran out into the countryside "and arrived just in time to save the girl from a similar death." The Federals "took these barbaric men prisoner."[13]

Once safe behind Baton Rouge's defenses, Union soldiers focused on food and shelter. Albert Krause and his comrades built cabins with bunk beds, where "we keep things dry and clean." Claudius Rider wrote that he and his comrades "lived pretty well," enjoying meals of government-issued fresh beef and privately purchased sweet potatoes. William Smith of the 52nd Massachusetts Infantry told his wife he enjoyed plums, peaches, watermelons, and potatoes. James Peck wrote home that a soldier shot a steer but instead of killing the animal as planned, he hit in the shoulder. The enraged beast charged the solider, who took refuge by diving into a tent where several men were playing cards. The tent proved a poor barrier to the crazed animal, which charged in and was about to trample the entire group when another soldier killed the animal with a well-placed shot. The officers sentenced the failed hunter to reduced rations and confinement in the guard tent for endangering his comrades. Peck and several of his comrades taunted the prisoner with questions about hunting techniques as they ate the ill-gotten beef. James Dargan realized that foraging might stiffen southern resistance. He wrote in his diary that many of his comrades happily robbed supplies from southern civilians and concluded, "it is enough to make a southerner fight for his home, and everything he holds dear, to see thus sacrificed to the tender mercies of an ignorant reckless set of vandals."[14]

Some Federals near Baton Rouge focused on fighting dangerous wildlife rather than rebels. Lawrence Van Alstyne described the area around Port Hudson as "headquarters for snakes." Albert Krause wrote his family back in Prussia that he and his comrades killed a nine-foot-long snake and found that it had two young rabbits in its stomach. Sadly, no record survives of how his family reacted to the idea that the land of plenty was home to such fearsome predators. James Peck wrote that the men "take pleasure" in killing alligators and especially snakes, which infested their camps. Private Frank Flinn and other members of the 38th Massachusetts Infantry spent most of their off-duty hours killing alligators, avoiding the "snakes that came out of the water to see us," and swatting "mosquitoes that worried us." Flinn, who also served in the eastern theatre of the war, concluded that "camping in Louisiana is very much more disagreeable than in Virginia."[15]

On the morning of March 16, the 9th Louisiana Partisan Rangers resumed their pursuit of the Federals who retreated to Baton Rouge the night before. The rebels made little impression on the strong defensive works at Baton Rouge where the Federals took refuge. However, the Louisianans captured a large quantity of weapons, equipment, and provisions left behind by the retreating Federals. The rangers were also pleased to find Private Irwin of the partisan rangers resting comfortably in a church along the road to Baton Rouge. The Federals wounded and then captured Irwin the day before. Union surgeons amputated Irwin's wounded leg, which probably saved his life. They then left him behind where his comrades could find him. A writer for the *Memphis Daily Appeal* claimed it was "one of the few instances on record where an act of humanity has been practiced by the enemy."[16]

March 17 found most of the Federal forces safely out of range of Port Hudson's garrison and pointing fingers to explain the defeat. Farragut, on the *Hartford* in the river north of Port Hudson, expressed disappointment that Banks did not stay after March 14 to besiege the Confederate works. Farragut acknowledged that Confederate gunners "gave us a warm reception," but a deserter claimed the Confederates had provisions for only four days and would have been forced to surrender or fight their way out if Banks had besieged them for a week. Farragut believed that Union troops would soon have "to do some hard fighting to make up for" Banks's "hesitation that night." Banks was unsurprisingly just as eager to blame Farragut as Farragut was to blame Banks. Massachusetts infantryman Henry Cross told his family back home, "you talk about my being amid the stirring scenes of war," but it would be more correct that he was at "the stirring scenes of Banks's blunders." Cross believed that the Union could have already captured Port Hudson, but Banks "got frightened and then tries to tell us the object of the expedition was accomplished. Humbug!" Cross wanted Butler back in command so that "we shall have a man, a Department, a Policy."[17]

At least one Union soldier had no idea who to blame. Lieutenant Daniel Dewey of the 25th Connecticut Infantry wrote home expressing confusion about what happened at Port Hudson. Dewey's regiment spent several days in hard marches over difficult ground. They heard gunfire in the distance but saw very little of what they assumed had been a battle for Port Hudson. Rumors abounded that the rebels had destroyed at least one Union ship, but it was "only a rumor" and "we don't know whether it is true or not." In frustration, Dewey asked his mother to mail him a newspaper from Connecticut. He believed that "it is the only way we have of learning about such things, for our leaders let us know as little as possible."[18]

General Banks Shifts His Focus

Realizing that capturing Port Hudson would be difficult, Banks focused on a new plan. On March 17 the Federals began unloading men on the west bank of the Mississippi River, initiating a campaign later known as the 1st Bayou Teche Campaign. Banks eventually sent roughly sixteen thousand men to the Bayou Teche region of central Louisiana with plans to rip the valuable region from the Confederacy and isolate Port Hudson from their supply routes on the Red River. Committees of southern civilians urged General Gardner to send troops to the west bank and defend them from Federals, who "were committing great depredations." However, Gardner "did not feel justified" in sending men to the west bank.[19] Gardner had orders to protect Port Hudson, and he focused entirely on that mission. Defending western Louisiana would be someone else's problem.

Without Gardner's support, defense of western Louisiana fell to the Army of Western Louisiana under the command of General Richard Taylor, a Louisiana sugar planter and the son of former president Zachary Taylor. On April 12 General Weizel and General Emory led 12,000 men up the Teche, while another 4,000 traveled with General Grover on transports, hoping to turn the flank of Confederate positions by sailing up Grand Lake. General Taylor deployed 2,200 men to block their path near Fort Bisland in St. Mary Parish, Louisiana. After two days of fighting, the Confederates withdrew on April 13 in the face of overwhelming manpower. The Federals pursued the rebels, and on April 14 the opposing forces clashed near Franklin, Louisiana, in the Battle of Irish Bend. Aware that he was badly outnumbered, Taylor withdrew rather than commit to a battle he was unlikely to win. Taylor's retreat gave the Federals an important victory. However, some Confederates believed that by resisting the Federals and retreating in good order, Taylor had raised the morale of both Confederate soldiers and civilians.[20]

The remainder of the spring campaign in western Louisiana consisted of small skirmishes and raids but few large battles. Confederate morale remained high, but some Federals were demoralized. Captain Nicholas

Dederer of the 114th New York Infantry was unhappy with his service on the west bank of the Mississippi River. He informed his son that his regiment spent their time rounding up and driving cattle, horses, mules, and sheep. Dederer considered the assignment "humiliating." He wondered aloud if the army's commanders were punishing the men for some perceived failure.[21]

Shortly after the fall of Port Hudson, Louisiana soldier Howard Wright suggested that General Gardner should have taken advantage of a "golden opportunity" to cooperate with General Taylor and defeat Union forces during the Bayou Teche Campaign. Wright argued that if Gardner and Taylor had worked together it might have "altered the aspect of affairs in Louisiana."[22] It is unclear what difference, if any, Gardner might have made by sending troops to western Louisiana. It would have been reckless to leave Port Hudson unguarded, so sending men from Port Hudson across the river would have meant splitting his force, which is rarely a smart move when confronted by larger enemy forces. Even if Gardner and Taylor had thrown caution to the wind and attacked the Federals in western Louisiana with every man under their command, the Union army would have still enjoyed numerical superiority. Outnumbered, in the open, without the benefit of Port Hudson's defenses, a major victory for the Confederacy would have been unlikely, although not impossible. Wright's speculation is interesting, but his comments should be understood as the perspective of a defeated prisoner who clearly wished that the campaign had turned out differently.

While some Federals fought Taylor's men and foraged for supplies on the west bank of the Mississippi, other men in blue remained near Port Hudson. Union gunboats fired on Port Hudson's defenses and tried to prevent Confederates from moving supplies across the river. John Hart, commanding the gunboat *Albatross*, wrote home to his wife, telling her he was safe from Confederate gunfire because he had armored his boat with logs and bales of cotton. As a result of the Federal artillery fire, the Confederates could only use one of their riverboat landings. Unloading was slow, but the Confederates unloaded supply boats by day and night. Goods slowly trickled into Port Hudson. Private John Morgan wrote his sister that he and his comrades were grateful for the corn and meat brought by steamships from the Red River Valley.[23]

Union soldiers probed the countryside near Port Hudson. Captain John

Hart sent parties of sailors ashore from the *Albatross* to gather intelligence and disrupt Confederate supply lines. After conducting their raids, sailors returned to the relative safety provided by the boat's cannons. Hart acknowledged that forays into enemy-held country were dangerous, but he explained that the men enjoyed taking trophies. Hart wrote his wife that he was collecting an arsenal of Confederate guns and planned to give a revolver to their son when he returned home.[24]

Confederates Prepare to Repel Another Attack

General Gardner remained on the offensive and sent detachments outside Port Hudson's defenses. Confederate scouts tried to keep the Federals off balance and provided intelligence about enemy movements. Gardner explained, "my object is not to attack the enemy with my whole force outside, but to interfere with his advance." Gardner promised to send reinforcements to the advanced detachments if "anything can be effected within about nine miles" of Port Hudson's defenses. Gardner instructed his men to keep him updated and always move cautiously with a heavy screen of skirmishers.[25]

At least a few Confederates at Port Hudson were optimistic. Alabama soldier James Goble heard rumors that the Federals were preparing for another expedition north from Baton Rouge. Buoyed by the damage to the Federal fleet earlier in the month, Goble wrote in his diary, "if they want to lose their boats, let them try to pas [*sic*]." In a letter dated March 24, John Morgan told his sister that after the brief action earlier in the month, "everything has become quiet here again." A few days later he (inaccurately) told her that the Union army was leaving Baton Rouge, as they have "given up all hopes of taking this place."[26]

Despite the optimism some men enjoyed, many Confederate soldiers near Port Hudson suffered. On March 26 Captain William Stephens, commanding Company I of the 16th Arkansas Infantry, complained that his men were in a "destitute condition." He requested twenty-three pairs of shoes, twenty-eight pairs of pants, thirty-three over shirts, twelve caps, eight blankets, and seventy pairs of underwear for his men. Captain Lorenzo Swagerty of Company A in the 16th Arkansas Infantry made similar complaints of destitute men and requested clothing for his soldiers. On March 26 southern civilians informed Union officers the Confederate defenders of the Mississippi were sending "extraordinary trains of sick" to hospitals in the interior. Confirming these reports, Gardner discharged men who were too disabled to serve on active duty and released several others to work as overseers. Records for the Port Hudson Confederate hospital verify the reports of southern civilians and document the transfer of sick and wounded men to hospitals in Clinton and Jackson, Louisiana, during March 1863. The Confederates might have sent even more men to interior hospitals, but Port Hudson's garrison had few wagons. Gardner warned Pemberton that, if the Confederacy tried to regroup in the area, "it will be difficult for me to make a move for want of wagon transportation."[27]

Without the transportation needed fight a war of maneuver, Gardner struck a balance. He continued preparations to fight in place, while sending out small offensive groups to keep the enemy off balance and maintain Confederate morale. On March 31 Gardner reported that he had 26,728 men on the roster and 20,388 men present and ready for duty. Gardner ordered the men to construct additional improvements to Port Hudson's defenses. He outlined the construction of four square redoubts within Port Hudson's existing lines that would overlook and command the outer works. It was a good plan, but the rebels were unable to complete it before later attacks made additional construction impossible. According to Howard Wright, "the necessity of obtaining a store of provisions now became more apparent." Forage for draft animals became particularly scarce. Federal attacks along the western banks of the Mississippi River interrupted supply shipments from across the river. Union cavalrymen under General Dudley came up the Pointe Coupee shore and burned a small Confederate gunboat on the False River, west of Port Hudson, destroying desperately needed provisions.[28]

The *Weekly Advertiser* of Montgomery, Alabama, published an account on April 1, 1863, that contradicted other sources, claiming that Port Hudson garrison enjoyed ample provisions. The newspaper reported that the garrison had "five hundred thousand pounds of bacon and sixty bushels of corn." Additional supplies were pouring into the post, which already had enough "to subsist the army for months to come." The unnamed author assured "our noble, uncomplaining, self-sacrificing boys in the army" that they "would never lack for subsistence." While it is unclear where the Alabama newspaper received its information, an account from at least one soldier in Port Hudson corroborated the newspaper's account. Alabama soldier James Goble wrote in his diary that in April the garrison lived off "plenty of fish" and "all kinds of cattle."[29]

While Port Hudson's garrison prepared for another fight, sickness spread through Union camps. Appleton Sturgis, a Maryland-born sailor turned ordnance officer, complained he was suffering from "acclimating fever," which sent him to the hospital for weeks. New York infantryman Orton Clark recalled years later that "the heat of a southern sun now began to manifest itself" and that the weather "was very debilitating." On April 18 John Crowder informed his sister that he had been sick with an unspecified illness that included "a severe cold and a burning fevor [*sic*]" but that he survived thanks to the treatment of a woman in Baton Rouge, who "treated me as if I were her own dear son." Massachusetts infantryman William Smith told his wife he and several of his friends suffered from diarhea [*sic*] but that "diarhea [*sic*] does not affect one here as it does in the north it does not weaken him down as it does there." Like Crowder, Smith recovered with the help of southerners, who "have been very kind to us." Smith was particularly grateful for the former slaves who brought fresh fruits, vegetables, and meat into the Union camps. The supplies helped improve the Federal health and morale. The former slaves explained to Smith that "they are treated much better since the northern men came here."[30] Banks received justifiable criticism for his mistreatment of former slaves, but, at least according to Williams, many of Louisiana's African Americans saw Federal rule as an improvement over Confederate slavery.

Union Forces Prepare for Another Offensive

Union forces built up their strength for the next phase of the war in Louisiana. On April 27, 1863, Captain Pythagoras Holcomb of the 2nd Vermont Artillery formally requested permission from General Banks to raise a "regiment of negro cavalry." Holcomb noted that the Union forces in Louisiana were in desperate need of cavalry and argued that slaves in the region were "generally proficient in the management and care of horses." Many Federal soldiers loathed people of African ancestry, but Holcomb's biases may have run far deeper than most. Before joining the Union army, Holcomb lived in Texas, where he owned fourteen slaves. Holcomb's exact motives for leaving Texas remain unclear, but according to rumors in

Union camps, the Illinois-born artillery officer had lived as a soldier of fortune in South America before settling in Texas and earning a fortune in the Texas cattle business. Holcomb told his Federal comrades, "[S]ome men put prejudice first, and patriotism second." He reportedly mocked southerners who said, "I am as patriotic as the Devil, only don't touch the nigger." Holcomb believed that the war had forced men to choose between their prejudice and their patriotism. Holcomb chose patriotism and proclaimed his hatred for the Confederacy. Holcomb explained, "I have allowed my patriotism to overcome my former prejudices." Several months later, the Union army gave Holcomb a major's commission in the 1st Texas Union Cavalry. Holcomb was an important example of a southerner who wisely chose his patriotism over his prejudice. In the words of Arkansan Guy Lancaster, as southern men, "we are not condemned to honor the slavers and lynchers of our past—we have an array of ancestors from which to choose."[31]

Some Federal soldiers who guarded Baton Rouge found time for leisure. Hazen Russell wrote home to his wife that he was enjoying a life that was "good enough for a solider," feasting on "warm baker's bread and tea and coffee and rice and sugar and beans and potatoes." At night, he slept on what he claimed, probably in an attempt at humor, was "the soft side of a plank," where "I lay thinking of home." Russell was enjoying some comfort but "want to come home so bad I don't know hardly what to do with myself." On April 29 Massachusetts infantryman Henry Cross attended a "negro concert in Academy Hall" in Baton Rouge. Cross considered the show "very comical." He believed that the former masters "feel the loss of their negroes very keenly." One of Cross's comrades saw a white woman washing and mockingly said "fine day for washing." The woman quipped back, "I should think it is to own fifty niggers and can't find one to do a bit of work."[32]

Some Federals got into trouble with local women as they waited to resume the offensive against Port Hudson. African American officer John Crowder of the 1st Louisiana Native Guards told his mother he lost all respect for Captain Lewis and Lieutenant Moss of his regiment. He considered them "dirty low life men" who "seem to think there is not a woman they cannot sleep with." Crowder accused Captain Lewis of approaching a married woman Crowder knew and expressing his interest in her by taking "from his pantaloons his privates and shook them at her." The woman responded by telling her husband and other officers, including Crowder. While Crowder wanted to report Lewis to the army's commanders, Crowder hesitated since Lewis had threatened to report Crowder for lying about his age and getting the underage officer kicked out of the army. As a result, the two men both accepted an uneasy truce.[33]

On April 23, 1863, Sergeant William Aldis sent his wife a letter that contained a poem.

Tis evening, after a long and weary march
Beneath a burning southern sun
I sit me down, my weary limbs to rest
And think of thee and home.
Oh, I am tired and weary, of this toil and strife
Of hunger, thirst and heat
Oft, Oft, I think of home and my wife
As I trudge along with blistered feet.
The days are long and sweltering
The sun enduring hot
At night upon the sod I lie
Little caring if I live or not.
And as I lay upon the dew which grows
With no shelter but the day
I gaze upon that glorious, steady, canopy
And sometimes wish to die.
But then, the thoughts of home and love
Come rushing back to me
I fancy I see the children's happy smile
Then, then I wish I were with thee.
On the day of battle, loud the cannon roared
Amid the glittering throng I rushed
Bayonets glistened, bullets whistled
And every breath seemed hushed.
A fervent prayer above I send
For protection to you and me
Then into the fray I went
For "God and My Country"
Yes I will not yet despair

Nor complain of my hard lot
But strike for my country and my God
While life and strength I've got.
Then after this rebellion's quelled
I will not wish to remain
But with thee and children dear
With Gods [*sic*] will I'll stay at home.[34]

Grierson's Raid

On April 17, 1863, Colonel Benjamin Grierson led 1,700 Union cavalrymen south from La Grange, Tennessee, fifty miles east of Memphis, on a raid into Mississippi. With General Grant's approval, Grierson hoped to distract Confederate troops along the Mississippi River and complicate their efforts to protect the vital waterway. General John Pemberton in Vicksburg sent infantry and cavalry forces to defeat Grierson. At the same time, Confederate cavalry in Louisiana rode north to attack the Federal cavalry. Grierson's men slipped past the Confederate cavalry northwest of Port Hudson, and Gardner sent two regiments of infantry and a section of artillery west with orders to occupy the Tangipahoa and Baton Rouge Road, to block their route into Baton Rouge. While the Confederate infantry and artillery moved west, a company of the 9th Louisiana Partisan Rangers ambushed Grierson's men near Greensburg, Louisiana, about forty-five miles northwest of Port Hudson. The rangers inflicted heavy losses on the Federals but failed to stop their progress as the men in blue continued to push southeast toward Baton Rouge. As soon as General Gardner learned of the ambush, he sent another detachment of artillery and infantry forward, urging them to block Grierson's path. The additional force of rebels tried and failed to intercept Grierson's raiders, and the Union horsemen found refuge in Baton Rouge just ahead of their Confederate pursuers.[35]

In Baton Rouge, Massachusetts infantryman Henry Cross watched Union cavalrymen fill the street, followed by two hundred Confederate prisoners. Behind the prisoners, Cross saw "five hundred niggers, in every conceivable style of plantation dress and undress, each one mounted, and leading from two to three other horses, and many of them armed with shotguns and hunting rifles." Cross believed that these were all escaped slaves who "came of their own accord, taking their masters' horses and guns." Cross took apparent glee in "how they must have cleaned out all the country through which they have passed!"[36]

General Banks publicly congratulated Grierson and claimed that Union now held "the key" to control of the Mississippi River. Banks ordered his remarks read in every Union camp under his command and assured the soldiers the "rebel armies were defeated and demoralized." Some soldiers were skeptical of Banks's claims. Infantryman FrankFlinn sarcastically suggested that someone should tell the rebels that the Union now had the keys, because the Confederates in the region seemed unaware of the important development. Orton Clark was more optimistic, believing that Grierson's raid impressed southern civilians, increasing their respect for the Union army and decreasing their confidence in the Confederate cause.[37]

Confederate Movements

Despite some Union skepticism, Confederate leaders understood the Federals were making rapid advances. In early May, Joseph E. Johnston, commanding the Department of the West, began concentrating Confederate forces along the Mississippi River and ordered General Gardner to reinforce Vicksburg. General Gardner had complained just a short time before that he lacked sufficient wagon transportation to make a major move, but he followed Johnston's orders to the best of his ability. On May 4 Johnston ordered Rust's and Buford's brigades in Port Hudson to reinforce Vicksburg. Gregg's brigade followed on May 5. Maxey's brigade left Port Hudson en route to Vicksburg on May 8, with Miles's Legion following close behind. General Gardner, with his staff, brought up the rear of the forces marching north from Port Hudson. With Gardner's departure, only the heavy artillery and Beall's brigade remained behind to guard Port Hudson. General Beall was once more in command at Port Hudson.[38] It is unclear if the Confederacy intentionally left behind the difficult-to-transport heavy artillery at Port Hudson in hopes of making a last stand, or if the lack of transportation left the Confederacy with little choice. Moving the heavy cannons and supplies at Port Hudson could have been virtually impossible, regardless of what Confederate generals might have preferred.

Word of Confederate departures from Port Hudson spread quickly. General Christopher Auger marched north from Baton Rouge with plans to capture Port Hudson and tighten the noose around Vicksburg. Beall's meager garrison could not hope to hold Port Hudson against the large Union force marching north. Gardner contemplated ordering Beall to evacuate. Howard Wright, serving under Gardner, believed Gardner made the decision to reinforce Port Hudson. However, the official records include an order from Pemberton to Gardner directing Gardner to "return with 2,000 troops to Port Hudson and hold it to the last." Pemberton explained, "President says both places must be held." Pemberton's May 8 message was consistent with the telegraph Davis sent to Pemberton on May 7, stating "to hold both Vicksburg and Port Hudson is necessary to our connection with the Trans-Mississippi." Pemberton's order suggests that Jefferson Davis, and not Gardner, decided to reinforce Port Hudson. In response to his new orders, Gardner ordered Miles's Legion to turn around and return to Port Hudson. Gardner and most of the other troops under his command followed close behind. According to Howard Wright, Gardner's return to Port Hudson was "hailed with every demonstration of delight by the troops there."[39]

Aware that the Federals were approaching, Confederate defenders continued preparations for a siege. Detachments brought supplies, including three hundred cattle, four hundred sheep, and four hundred bushels of corn, to Port Hudson. Gardner mounted the 11th Arkansas Infantry, under Colonel J. L. Logan, on horses and ordered them to "serve outside in harassing the rear of an investing force." James Goble wrote that the men took their places in the breastworks, and all agreed, "we are ready for them."[40]

The Union Navy Advances on Port Hudson Again

On May 8 Union forces probed Port Hudson. Mortar boats anchored four and a half miles below Port Hudson and at 2:00 p.m. they opened fire on the Confederate garrison. Howard Wright believed the mortar boats were trying to "get the range of the river batteries, so as to bombard them during the night." Most of the Federal shells fell on Battery 10, which consisted of one 32-pounder cannon under Lieutenant McDowell, and Battery

11, which consisted of a single Parrot rifle under Lieutenant Kearney. A few Union shells hit Confederate Battery 9, consisting of an 8-inch howitzer under Lieutenant Rodriguez, and Battery 8, which consisted of two rifled 24-pounder cannons, from long range. The mortar boats pounded Port Hudson for two hours but failed to damage the Confederate defenses. Most of the shells fell short and splashed into the river or flew too far, burying themselves in a large ravine behind the river buff.[41]

The Union shells did not inflict any casualties, but Confederate soldiers realized the destructive potential of Union artillery. Howard Wright noted, "the sturdiest trees, when struck, would be riven as if by the lightning and they did not seem to alter the course of the shell or lessen its force." Other shells buried themselves in the soft ground and then exploded, "uprooting the earth like a small volcano and throwing out pieces of roots and other substances which had probably never seen the light of day before." The Confederate garrison constructed excellent fortifications at Port Hudson, but Howard Wright believed that "under such a fire there was no place of shelter, no refuge of safety." He suggested, "one could only remain at his post and tranquilly await his fate, while the air was filed with their rushing and whistling noise, and the fragments of broken shells and clods of up-heavened [*sic*] earth were flying about in every conceivable direction." Wright believed that "no one can get used to a bombardment, though it will not cause a good soldier to flinch." He believed that a heavy bombardment "has the tendency to make a man either a good Christian or a fatalist, according to his early training or latent religious belief."[42]

Beginning on May 8, the Union navy bombarded Port Hudson every day. Howard Wright believed that the Federals mostly struck at night to prevent the rebels from sleeping, but he noted that daytime bombardments were common too. Wright believed that Federal commanders intentionally varied the times and durations of their bombardments "so that we could never know when to expect them." James Goble wrote in his diary that the Union gunboats shelled Port Hudson at long range, beginning on May 8, but their fire was "to no effect." He thought "twas [*sic*] a pritty [*sic*] sight" to "witness the flashing of the morters [*sic*] and the bombs revolving through the air and to see them burst." Richard McClung wrote in his diary, "the prettiest scene I ever beheld was looking at bombs flying over us."[43]

Confederates Strike Back

The Confederates at Port Hudson were not content to suffer as passive defenders and went on the offensive. Lieutenant Colonel de Gournay requested permission to take four heavy cannons down to Troth's Landing, three miles south of Port Hudson, and attack the Federal fleet. Gardner agreed, and on May 9 de Gournay took four cannons to Troth's Landing. The 15th Arkansas Infantry accompanied the gunners as infantry support for the artillery. Paul de Gourney personally commanded one section of the artillery, and Lieutenant L. J. Girard commanded the other. Most of the Union mortar boats had concealed themselves behind trees, but the Confederates could clearly see two mortar boats, along with the *Essex* and the *Richmond.* At 4:00 a.m. on May 10, the Confederate gunners opened fire by the light of a half moon. Federal sailors returned fire. For two and a half hours, rival gunners traded shots.[44]

Richard McClung of the 15th Arkansas Infantry described what he saw in his diary.

> I saw the first ball leave the mouth of the gun. It looked perfectly hot white, perhaps it is the flames in which it was enveloped. Did you ever stand and two artillery batteries play on each other? See the flash—the lurid flames—the volume of smoke whitely and slowly curl upwards and hear the fierce shriek, the hoarse whistle of the ball as it passes you? Did you never hear a charge of grapeshot or canister flying through the air? Which goes as soldiers say, like "a sack of cats." Did you ever see the ground torn up around you almost under you? I have. The firing of a cannon has the effect of a magnet on my feelings, especially at a short distance. Yet I have felt the sound even to bewilderment. I have been stunned by it. By both the first round of the gun and bursting bomb. The Federals replied to our two guns with forty. It was a powerful fleet that we had engaged. I never heard such firing. Fort Henry scarcely equaled it. They discharged broadside after broadside. Mortar after mortar. The air was full of shells and pieces of shell."[45]

Confederate soldiers knew they struck the Federal boats, but "with what effect we could not ascertain." After firing the last of their shells, the Confederates hitched up their cannons and returned to Port Hudson. The rebels concluded that "our weight of metal was not heavy enough to have attacked such vessels as the *Richmond* and *Essex.*" They also believed that they were unable to get into a position that would allow them to "reach the mortar boats with any effect." The Federals, wisely, kept their mortar boats shielded behind more easily defended boats.[46]

While Confederate gunners bombarded Union boats from Troth's Landing, mortar boats farther north bombarded Port Hudson. A Confederate soldier stood on the parapet of Battery 9 as the bombardment began. A shell struck him in the neck, "carrying him, head foremost, through the wooden floor of the battery into the ground beneath, leaving only his feet sticking out." Confederate gunners returned fire. The rebels reported, "damage to the enemy is unknown, but the mortar boats are somewhat injured."[47]

The Union Army Advances on Port Hudson

After completing the Bayou Teche Campaign on the west bank of the Mississippi, Banks considered his next move. General Halleck wanted Grant and Banks to combine forces and act as a single unit before the Confederates concentrated their forces to destroy each army separately. Grant informed Banks that he was tied up trying to capture Vicksburg, that he could not send Banks any reinforcements, and that he would like Banks to move north and help him capture Vicksburg. Banks replied that he could not possibly move toward Vicksburg since he lacked enough transportation to move his entire command that far north. Banks also worried about the potential disaster that might ensue if he got his main force stuck between the Confederate forces at Vicksburg in his front and Port Hudson's garrison in his rear. Taking most of his men north would also leave Baton Rouge and New Orleans vulnerable to a Confederate counterattack. On May 14 Banks ordered his forces to prepare for a new campaign. Their objective was Port Hudson. General Halleck was enraged, but as engineer officer John Palfrey later pointed out, Halleck was far away from the Mississippi River in Washington; in Louisiana, Banks answered to none but God.[48]

Some Union soldiers were more concerned about insects and heat than Confederates. Lawrence Van Alstyne complained in his diary, "mosquitos are the pest of our lives. They hide in our tents, ready to pounce on us the minute we enter, and the only place we are free from them is in the hot sun outside. At night and on cloudy days they give us no peace. Their name is legion." Solon Perkins told his family he was "troubled by mosquitos, lice, fleas, wood ticks, gnats." Louis Brooks described Louisiana as "hot as hell."[49]

As the Union army prepared for a new attack on Port Hudson, some Union soldiers appeared optimistic. On May 14 Federal scouts in Mississippi reported, "Port Hudson is undoubtedly evacuated except by a small garrison and their heavy artillery." A separate report on May 14, from "contrabands," claimed that the Confederates were evacuating ammunition and sending it north toward Port Gibson, Mississippi. On May 19 Charles Wadsworth of the 116th New York Infantry wrote that his regiment would advance on Port Hudson the next day and that he expected the rebels to surrender within a week because "their provisions are very scarce." Colonel Thomas Cahill wrote home that the Confederates at Vicksburg and Port Hudson were cut off and destined to starve to death unless they surrendered soon. Captain Eli Griffin wrote home that "the rebels are nearly cleaned out of Louisiana" and believed Port Hudson was "bound to fall."[50]

The Union navy subjected Port Hudson to a particularly heavy bombardment during the afternoon and evening of May 17. An explosive shell plunged into the dirt near the crest of a parapet where four members of de Gournay's command were sitting. A moment later, the shell exploded, throwing all four men into the air, killing three and wounding the fourth. Flying shrapnel hit two soldiers and ripped off their legs. Artillery fire "tore up the ground" all around Port Hudson. Shells fell on the town's graveyard, disinterring the dead bodies of soldiers and civilians. A Federal shell exploded under the Mississippi River, sending "seventy or eighty" dead fish floating to the surface. Ignoring the danger, rebels quickly rowed out in two boats, gathered fish, and returned "loaded down with their piscatorial burden." At that time, fish sold for "five to fifty dollars apiece according to their size," which made a boatload of fish "a valuable haul." The evening bombardment was deadly, but Howard Wright considered it "beautiful." Each shell "looking like a bright star rising to the zenith in a spasmodic manner, and slowly traversing the dark amphitheater of the sky, steering its strange course among the starts until a flash of light would show that it had burst, sometime before the sound of the explosion reached the ear."

Under the intense bombardment, Confederates quickly "learned to gauge by a tree or post, the flight of the shells, and to foretell where they were going to strike, with remarkable correctness."[51]

On May 20 General Banks received an intelligence report that "Port Hudson will be evacuated on the appearance of troops in the rear." Banks set his army in motion toward Port Hudson, but Confederate defenders were well prepared to observe and report from a series of signal stations. Jean Beaufort, a French-born corporal in the 2nd Louisiana Union Infantry, volunteered to lead a detachment and destroy a Confederate signal station. Seven other men agreed to follow him, and Beaufort's band slipped through Confederate lines. Under Beaufort's leadership, the Union raiders successfully destroyed a Confederate signal station. Beaufort later received the Medal of Honor for his role in the raid.[52]

Confederates Brace for an Attack

Despite the Union efforts to mask their advance, Confederate cavalrymen brought word to General Gardner that General Augur's Union division was approaching Port Hudson on May 20. Aware that the Federals "preferred to overcome the natural obstacles of the woods, rather than the artificial ones in the shape of fortifications," Gardner shifted his forces to counter the new threat. He ordered the 15th Arkansas Infantry, 10th Arkansas Infantry, 18th Arkansas Infantry, 39th Mississippi Infantry, and the dismounted members of Wingfield's 9th Louisiana Partisan Rangers to support Steedman and the 1st Alabama Infantry. Gardner ordered sections of Herrod's and Bradford's batteries of the 1st Mississippi Artillery, along with a section of Watson's Louisiana battery to provide fire support for Steedman's command on the Confederate left. James Goble reported that the Alabamians were in "the most dangerous position" and "waiting for the enemy to attack." According to Howard Wright, "Col. Steedman had the kind of officers under him that he desired, and backed up by the zeal and courage of the line, he felt confident that he was going to hold his new position." However, he expected "that he would have to stand the heaviest shock of battle" Soldiers "hastily" dug rifle pits on the "ridges and spurs of high ground" but left the valleys and gorges untouched, hoping that the fallen timber and steep inclines would prevent the Federals from advancing through them. Union staff officer Richard Irwin later

Left: Captain Daniel Turrentine of Company G, 12th Arkansas Infantry Regiment, in full officer's uniform with musket. Library of Congress.

Right: Major Micajah (Michael) Rodgers Wilson of 1st Arkansas Infantry Battalion. Wilson was wounded at Port Hudson and became a prisoner of war. Library of Congress.

discovered that, while the Federals prepared for another advance, veteran Confederate soldiers skillfully built fortifications that followed the natural lines of the terrain. Their careful placement of these fortifications made it nearly impossible to distinguish ravines from trenches, hills from earthworks, and naturally fallen logs from strategically positioned barriers. The Confederate army continued to use slave labor, offering cash to any planters who would send slaves to Port Hudson.[53]

General Gardner once again reorganized the Port Hudson garrison. Steedman continued to command the Confederate left, north of Port Hudson. Gardner placed General Beall in charge of the Confederate center. Beall commanded a strong infantry force consisting of the 12th Arkansas Infantry, 1st Arkansas Battalion, 16th Arkansas Infantry, 1st Mississippi Infantry, 23rd Arkansas Infantry, and the 49th Alabama Infantry. Sections from Abbay's and Bradford's 1st Mississippi Light Artillery battery, as well as a section of Watson's Louisiana battery, provided artillery support in the Confederate center. Gardner placed Colonel William Miles of Miles's Louisiana Legion in command of the Confederate right wing, with Miles's Legion, the 9th Louisiana Battalion, a provisional battalion drawn from Maxey's brigade, and a detachment of de Gournay's artillerymen, who served as infantry. Sections from Boone's Louisiana Artillery and the Seven Stars Mississippi Artillery supported the infantry.[54]

Early on the morning of May 21, Colonel Ben Johnson of the 15th Arkansas Infantry received orders to lead his regiment north from their position in the Confederate center and report to Colonel Steedman, commanding the Confederate left wing. Steedman instructed Johnson to take up a line on the northeast corner of the Confederate lines. To defend the vital position, Johnson had his own regiment; the 15th Arkansas Infantry, consisting of 293 men; and a section of the 1st Mississippi Artillery, which consisted of two cannons and twenty-five men under the command of Lieutenant Edrington. There were no fortifications, so Johnson ordered the men to begin building defenses. The position they built later became known as Fort Desperate. The entire Confederate garrison at Port Hudson consisted of 5,715 men present and ready for duty that day.[55]

The Battle at Plains Store on May 21, 1863

Early on the morning of May 21, General Augur led his division toward Port Hudson from Baton Rouge. Colonel Grierson's Union cavalry scouted ahead of the infantry. General Augur hoped to secure the crossroads of the Plains Store and Bayou Sara Roads, which would open a path for additional Union units while cutting off possible Confederate supply or evacuation routes to the east. Near the crossroads, the Federals encountered Confederate forces under the command of Colonel Frank Powers.[56]

After a morning of heavy skirmishing, at noon Gardner ordered Colonel W. R. Miles to take four hundred men and a light artillery battery into action to gather intelligence on the Federal advance and relieve the Confederates already in action. Miles sent three companies on the left under Lieutenant Colonel F. B. Brand. Two more companies advanced on the right under Major James Coleman, detouring off the road and through the woods to avoid detection by the Federals. When the troops

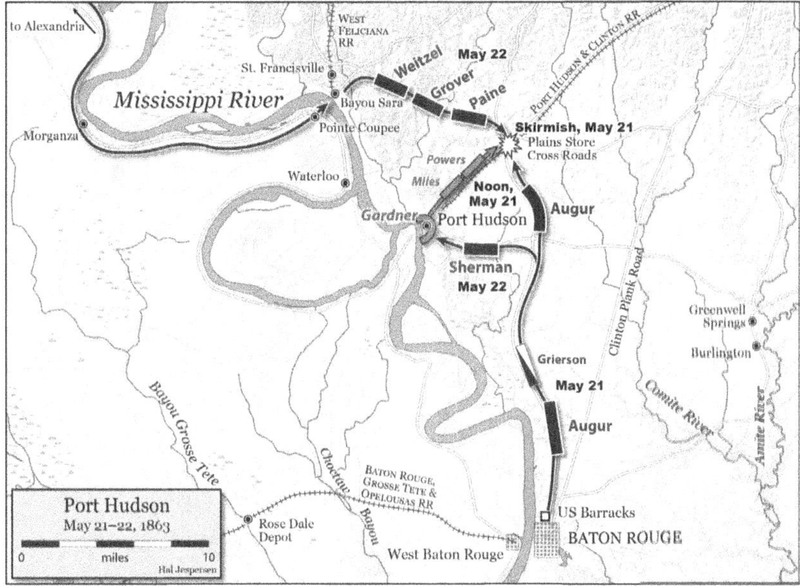

Map 2. The Battle of Plains Store and the Union Encirclement of Port Hudson, May 21 and 22, 1863. Hal Jespersen.

under Coleman emerged from the woods, they saw two Union cannons in an open field, attached by ropes to horses so they could fire and then withdraw in turn. Coleman ordered his men to charge. The Federals were shocked by the unexpected attack. The rebels inflicted heavy casualties on their adversaries, and "with a shout and a hurrah, or boys had possession of the artillery."[57]

General Augur ordered a counterattack. The 49th Massachusetts Infantry and the 116th New York Infantry advanced toward the Confederates. The men in gray responded with "a heavy discharge of musketry." In response, the 49th Massachusetts broke and fled to the rear, passing through the ranks of the 116th New York. Captain Orton Clark of the 116th New York Infantry later remembered that the Confederate gunfire and retreat of panic-stricken men "was sufficient to try the nerve and mettle of a veteran regiment." However, the 116th New York was not a veteran regiment. The New Yorkers were in their first battle, but most of the men stood firm. General Augur ordered the New Yorkers to charge. According to Clark, "the yell which now broke from our throats and echoed through

Left: Sergeant George Lyman Geer of Co. I, 49th Massachusetts Infantry Regiment. Geer was wounded at Port Hudson. Library of Congress.

Right: Colonel William Francis Bartlett of Co. I, 20th Massachusetts Infantry Regiment, 49th Massachusetts Infantry Regiment, and 57th Massachusetts Infantry Regiment. Bartlett was wounded at Yorktown, Port Hudson, and the Wilderness, Virginia. Photograph probably taken after Bartlett was shot in the wrist at Port Hudson in 1863. Library of Congress.

the woods, had in it that which the enemy must have felt to their fingertips." Clark claimed the Confederate retreated immediately in the face of the 116th New York's counterattack.[58]

Confederates claimed that they held out stubbornly but withdrew after a brief fight. They were unable to remove the captured artillery because the Federal artillery horses lay dead, innocent victims of the intense crossfire that echoed through the woods. Federals pursued Coleman's men through the woods. Hearing the gunfire, Colonel Miles sent Lieutenant Harmonson with men to attack the left flank of the Union advance. Harmonson's counterattack prevented the encirclement of Coleman's retreating troops. The Federals withdrew, leaving the Confederacy in control of the battlefield, and the rebels returned to their trenches only after taking the time to load the wounded into ambulances. Colonel Milles reported losing eighty-nine killed, wounded, and missing troops in the fighting that day. The dead included Captain J. B. Turner, Lieutenant Crawford, Lieutenant J. B. Wilson, and Lieutenant Pearson.[59]

Both Union and Confederates soldiers claimed that they won the day. According to Howard Wright, Major Coleman "received deserved praise" and the fight "was looked upon with extreme satisfaction by all our troops in garrison." Captain Orton Clark of the 116th New York Infantry reported that his regiment won "a glorious victory" by "utterly routing the rebels." After the skirmish, the New Yorkers captured seventy Confederate prisoners, most of whom were Frenchmen who loudly argued that they loved the United States and praised the Union in both English and French. Clark took pride in how his regiment performed in their first fight, later arguing that "the character of a regiment is always settled by its first engagement."[60]

The Union Encirclement of Port Hudson

On May 22 the 9th Louisiana Partisan Rangers under Colonel Wingfield skirmished with advance elements of Banks's army, which had just crossed the Mississippi River near Bayou Sara, roughly thirteen miles north of Port Hudson. The attack surprised the Confederates, who had anticipated that the Union army would advance on Port Hudson from the south. As a result, the defenders had not yet constructed any significant fortifications north of town, focusing their efforts on the southern approaches to Port Hudson. The rebels had believed that the very difficult swamps and heavy woods would dissuade the Federals from launching major attacks on the area and blunt the work of any raiders that might probe Confederate lines north of town.[61]

On May 22 Colonel Steedman of the 1st Alabama Infantry led his men to a position roughly half a mile in front of the main works of Port Hudson, on the road leading toward the commissary depot. The 9th Louisiana Partisan Rangers and a section of Watson's Louisiana battery reported to Steedman. Gardner ordered Steedman to oppose any Federal advance on Port Hudson's left, but "without risking a serious engagement." The rangers stayed busy "reconnoitering every possible approach to our defenses." Thorpe Gould, a thirty-year-old captain commanding Company F of the

165 New York Infantry, arrived at Port Hudson after a grueling twenty-mile march. He ordered his men to make camp and surveyed the Confederate lines. He told his friend Ned, "their fortifications present a strong front at the river." The Confederates also enjoyed a position "well protected from land attack," secure behind a line "over four miles in length."[62]

On May 22 and 23, the 9th Louisiana Partisan Rangers fought a series of delaying actions against Union troops, who steadily advanced toward Port Hudson's northern flank. Albert Krause took pride in how he and his comrades pushed the Confederates back at the point of the bayonet. The Prussian born soldier wrote home to his family, still in Europe, that his regiment was "more than 2/3 Germans" and that their successful advance on Port Hudson provided "new proof that the German can fight for freedom." The *Times Picayune* of New Orleans reported that the Confederates "were repulsed with heavy loss, leaving a large number of killed and wounded on the field." As the Union infantry advanced, work crews followed close behind, transforming the "pathless forest" into a network of clearings and roads.[63]

While the Union army approached Port Hudson from the land, the navy prepared to attack the Confederate garrison from the river. Louis Boyd, on the gunboat *Albatross*, wrote his wife on May 22 that he and his shipmates were preparing for action at Bayou Sara, just north of Port Hudson. He told his wife that the tide had turned, that Louisiana civilians who once avoided Federal sailors earlier in the campaign now saluted and welcomed the men in blue. He reported, incorrectly, that the Confederate garrison of Vicksburg had evacuated their works and were on the run. Boyd believed that the Union had Port Hudson "entirely surrounded" with a large army and fleet. He predicted an "immediate attack" by land and water. Boyd believed that Port Hudson would fall within three days.[64]

On May 24 the Federals probed Port Hudson's defenders along the length of the defensive perimeter. Federal gunboats shelled Port Hudson from just outside the range of the Confederate heavy batteries. The crew of the *Essex* picked up a piece of paper floating on a bit of driftwood as it passed by their boat. It read, "Farragut you renegade, what is the good of throwing away so many shells that do not harm, if you want Port Hudson come and take it, you will find plenty of cotton." The letter was signed "Stonewall." In response, the *Essex*'s officers told the crew to be ready for action at a moment's notice.[65]

The area north of Port Hudson was "alive with soldiers" of General Grover's division. As Federal workers constructed roads, Union skirmishers continued to advance "as fast as the nature of the ground would permit." John Hamilton, a correspondent for *Harper's Weekly*, watched as members of the 24th Connecticut and 12th Maine Infantry regiments scouted the woods along the Clinton Road. At about 11:30 a.m., the Federals encountered rebels in rifle pits. Rival infantrymen traded fire, and the reserve companies of the 24th Connecticut Infantry slipped around the rifle pits to flank the rebels. A half hour after the full weight of the men from Connecticut came to bear on the Confederates, the men in gray retreated to their main lines. The Federals pursued the rebels, pausing about eight hundred yards from the Confederate earthworks, where they set up their cannons and began an artillery duel.[66]

At 1:30 p.m. on May 24, Union mortar boats opened fire on Port Hudson once again, and the *Essex* joined the attack a short time later. The first Confederate water battery the Union sailors saw appeared deserted, so the *Essex* focused its fire on the second battery from the south, which the ship's crew called "the citadel." The Confederate garrison returned fire "with great briskness." After firing several rounds, the *Essex* found the mark and knocked a Confederate cannon off its mount. The *Genesee*, *Monongahela*, and *Richmond* joined the *Essex* and bombarded Port Hudson with their heavy artillery. After trading fire with the Confederate batteries for an hour, a Confederate shell struck the *Essex*'s bow, wounding four Union sailors. The *Essex*'s gunners directed their fire at a Confederate officer who exposed himself on the top of the parapet, encouraging his men by waving his sword. After firing several rounds in his direction, the officer disappeared. The Union sailors were unsure if they had hit him, but they did notice that the Confederate gunfire gradually slowed. William Park, serving on the *Essex*, believed that the army could have stormed Port Hudson on May 24, if they had pressed their advantage, but "it seems we must wait a little longer and try it again."[67]

On the evening of May 24, the Federal army came within about four hundred yards of the northeast corner of the Confederate lines. They initially drove in the Confederate work parties building fortifications. Before the Federals could press their advantage, Colonel Ben Johnson sent Captain James Franklin with men from the 15th Arkansas Infantry to drive off the Federals. The Arkansans launched an aggressive assault on the approaching Federals, blunting the Union advance and buying time for the rest of the rebels, who resumed their work building fortifications.[68]

By the evening of May 24, the Union forces completely encircled Port Hudson. The Union army consisted of roughly twenty thousand men, spread along an eight-mile line. General Emory's division occupied the Union right flank, resting against the banks of the Mississippi River north of Port Hudson. General Grover's division was just south of Emory's men. General Augur's division held the line south of General Grover's men. General Sherman's division occupied the Union left flank, south of Port Hudson. General Grierson's cavalrymen remained on the move, trying to protect Union supply lines from Confederate cavalrymen. Union gunboats bobbed in the Mississippi River and prepared for action. On the west bank of the river, Colonel Lewis Benedict commanded the 162nd New York Infantry, the 110th New York, and a section of artillery. The New Yorkers were prepared to intercept any rebels who might try to cross the river, either to reinforce Port Hudson or to escape.[69]

Word of the Union advance spread quickly. Residents of Jackson, Louisiana, roughly fifteen miles northeast of Port Hudson, learned that Port Hudson was besieged on the afternoon of May 24. The Lake Providence Cadets, a company of the 4th Louisiana Infantry, were stationed in Jackson, Louisiana, with orders to defend the town, but their orders provided no directions for how to respond to an emergency. Their commander, Captain Charles Purdy, took it upon himself to lead his men through Union lines and report to Port Hudson. They began their march at nightfall and arrived near Port Hudson at 10:00 p.m. The Federals did not react to the small band of thirty troops marching through their lines in the darkness. The cadets made a far greater impact on the Confederates. A mounted picket raced to Gardner's headquarters, where he claimed the Federals were advancing "in columns of regiments." The incredulous Gardner asked, "was this reported to you, or did you see the columns with your own eyes?" The picket assured Gardner, "I saw them myself." Gardner replied by ordering the garrison to prepare for a night battle. Signal troops fired their rockets, men rushed to their posts, and everyone prepared their weapons for a "fierce night attack."[70]

The Lake Providence Cadets reached Port Hudson's infantry pickets without further incident and explained who they were. Captain Purdy assured members of the garrison that his company was the only unit on the move that night and that the Federals were not preparing for an attack. Purdy explained that he saw a mounted picket and tried to explain himself, but the horseman turned and galloped away before the Purdy could speak. The embarrassed picket tried to explain that he was tired and surprised, but his excuses did nothing to "recover general confidence in his nerve or his reliability."[71] The Lake Providence Cadets were the final unit to join Port Hudson's garrison.

Port Hudson's defenders stood alone. The Federals controlled the Mississippi River near Port Hudson and cut the Confederate garrison off from virtually all contact with the outside world. The boats that had brought supplies to the Confederate garrison would come no more. The rebels would have to survive on the supplies they had stockpiled or on whatever they could scavenge from the bodies of men they killed. A Confederate sailor, identified only as Evan, serving on the steamboat *Drover*, had helped bring men and supplies to Port Hudson that spring, but he never came again after the Federal fleet arrived to stay in late May. As the blue noose tightened around Port Hudson, Evan and the rest of the Confederate supply boats were a hundred miles away, bobbing in the Red River near Alexandria, Louisiana, hoping for happier days and dodging the "Federal pickets between here and home."[72]

The Federals resumed their efforts to squeeze Port Hudson's garrison early on the morning of May 25. According to Lawrence Van Alstyne, Union camps were alive with activity, "roads are being cut through the woods, and everything looks and acts as if business would soon begin." The "generals with their staffs are racing about, and everything is in a whirl." Van Alstyne was confused but explained, "it does no good to ask questions, no one seems to know any more than I do, and I only know what goes on right close by me." Several members of the regiment contemplated the battle they knew was coming and admitted that they were scared. Van Alstyne mocked men who bragged about their courage until they faced danger and then "wilted." Van Alstyne admitted in his diary, "I don't deny that I am coward, but I have so far succeeded in keeping it to myself."[73]

General Neal Dow ordered the 15th New Hampshire Infantry's band to strike up a tune. Lorenzo Frost, the band's veteran leader, suggested that the music might attract Confederate artillery fire. Dow responded, "if you're afraid to play, you'd better go home." Frost ordered the band to gather beside Dow's tent and strike up "Yankee Doodle Dandy." A moment later, "there was a prolonged unearthly screech as a shell from the concealed enemy swept over our heads." The shell landed nearby but did not explode. Dow ordered the band to quit mid-tune, and the band did not play again during the siege. While the story might seem like a postwar joke told by an old enlisted man to poke fun at a general, at least one other Federal solider stated that bands did not play during the siege and that musicians worked as stretcher bearers and orderlies for the medical staff, which provides support for one aspect of the account.[74]

May 25 and 26 saw heavy skirmishing all along the Confederate lines. On the extreme Confederate left, Union troops pushed forward with what Howard Wright called "the aid of engineering skill." The "continual patter of axes in the willow growth that covered this part of the swamp told us that he was working night and day to build roads and bridges." The Confederate heavy artillery blasted Union work crews in a failed attempt to halt their progress. Wingfield's cavalrymen also tried to disrupt the Federal work crews, but they made little impact on Union workers protected by a screen of Federal skirmishers.[75]

Colonel Ben Johnson sent men from Companies A, F, and I of the 15th Arkansas Infantry forward from the northeast corner of the Confederate lines with orders to force the Federals to retreat from their position on a "crest of an abrupt ridge in the edge of the woods." According to Ben Johnson, the men were horribly outnumbered but made up for it with "great gallantry." The Arkansans drove the Federals from their position but paid for the ground with the lives of two men who died immediately and another man who suffered a mortal wound.[76]

Federals also attacked the Confederate right. According to Alabamian John Kennedy, the rebels repulsed the Federals "first with yells, then the artillery opened on them." The Union gunboats opened fire in support of the army. A 150-pound shell, fired by the Union gunboat *Monongahela*, dismounted a Confederate 10-inch Columbiad cannon, and it took several days for the Confederates to bring the big gun back into action. Despite the gunboats' work, Confederate artillery fire repulsed the attacking Union infantrymen.[77]

Confederates fell back, slowly giving way before the overwhelming numerical superiority of the Union army. From his position within Port Hudson's main defenses, James Goble watched Confederate skirmishers in the distance fighting delaying actions, which were designed to buy time for the work crews still improving Port Hudson's fortifications. As the Federals overwhelmed the Confederate skirmishers, survivors fell back into Port Hudson, taking shelter behind the town's fortifications. Goble noted in his diary that his fellow "rebels fight like desperate men, selling their lives dearly." He believed that "many a Fed [*sic*] will bight [*sic*] the dust ere the rebels surrender up Port Hudson."[78]

John Henry of the 31st Massachusetts Infantry rejoined his regiment on May 23. He had been away from his unit, suffering from some unspecified illness in an army hospital. Unlike many other men who died of disease during the campaign, Henry recovered and returned to duty. He rejoined his comrades just in time for an advance on Port Hudson. It is unclear why Henry joined the Union army. His Canadian birth, his job as a skilled mechanic, and his age of forty-four could have all excused him from military service, but Henry joined the regiment in 1861 and pledged to serve for three years. Henry deployed as a skirmisher as the men from Massachusetts entered the woods, which were filled Confederate soldiers. As the skirmish began, a bullet struck Henry in the neck, and he died a moment later. Captain E. P. Nettleton later recalled, "he went into the fight bravely and as I approached him just before he fell, he greeted me warmly."[79]

When not busy fighting, Confederates improved their positions by building barricades and digging ditches. General Gardner ordered that all available tools and "negroes" be sent to the garrison's left flank and placed at the disposal of Lieutenant Dabney, who supervised the work. The rebels placed a field battery on Commissary Hill. In recognition of the shifting threat from the water to the land, the Confederates moved two rifled 24-pounder rifled cannons from their river batteries landward, supporting the Confederate left. Alabamian John Kennedy reported he had never seen so much work done so quickly. Perhaps the looming showdown gave the rebels a burst of motivation. He believed that the Confederate defenders had "slaughtered the Yanks" in the skirmishes leading up to May 26. He noted in his diary, "all seems to smile upon the rebels."[80]

The defenders of Port Hudson "slept on their arms" on the night of May 26. They heard the Federals a short distance away, cutting timber, moving artillery, and preparing for an assault. Colonel Steedman ordered the Confederate troops on the left to remain on the defensive and conserve their strength. Rumors that "negro troops" were in the Federal lines passed through the rebel ranks. Lieutenant Richard McClung of 15th

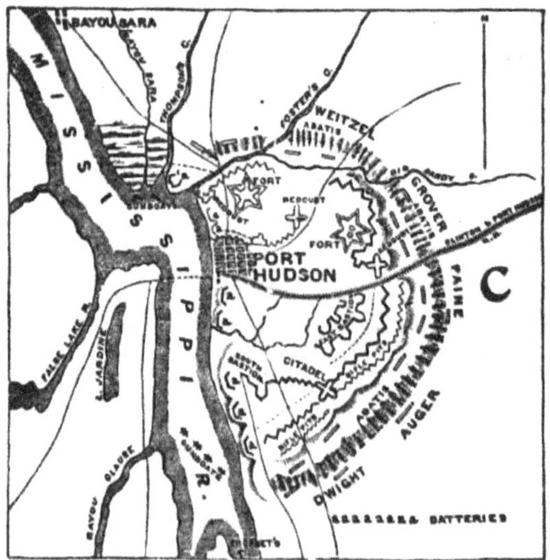

Map 3. The defenses of Port Hudson.
From James Ewer, *The Third Massachusetts Cavalry in the War*, p. 100.

Arkansas Infantry received orders to occupy a picket post half a mile in front of the main Confederate defenses. McClung ordered his men to be "ready at a moment's notice."[81]

Union Officers Plan an Assault

After nightfall on May 26, Union division commanders met on the Bayou Sara Road to contemplate their next move. Almost every officer agreed that they should launch a frontal assault in the morning and capture Port Hudson before nightfall. The officers pointed out that their men were in "high spirts" and "full of confidence in themselves." They also noted that they outnumbered the Confederates at least two to one. Perhaps most importantly, they almost all agreed that they should move quickly, before Johnston could rally forces for an attack on their rear. Banks agreed with the officers who wanted to attack Port Hudson. He ordered the commanders to return to their units and prepare for an attack. The artillery would open fire at first light. The infantry would send skirmishers forward, under cover of the artillery barrage, and try to pick off exposed rebels, paying special attention to officers and artillerymen. The Federals would then launch a frontal assault all along the line, taking "instant advantage of any favorable opportunity." Successful attacks would punch through Confederate positions, and stalled attacks would serve as distractions that would prevent the rebels from concentrating their troops in the most threatened sectors. Banks ordered each division commander to provide his men with whatever ladders, planks, and lumber he felt his men would need to cross the Confederate obstructions.[82]

At least one unnamed Union officer objected to the planned attack. He noted that there was still a great distance between Union and Confederate lines. Federal attackers would advance over unknown terrain that appeared at first glance to be mostly comprised of difficult masses of felled timber, swamps, and broken ground. Confederate defenders would fight from the relative safety of defenses that the Federals had not yet mapped but that appeared formidable. Banks did not specify a time for the attack, which could lead to uncoordinated, piecemeal charges. Banks expected officers to respond quickly to "any favorable opportunity," but coordination would be difficult. Much of the battlefield was obscured by dense woods so it would make it almost impossible for commanders to see what nearby units were doing, particularly after the firing commenced and clouds of smoke obscured the battlefield. At no part of the line could members of one division see another division, even before the firing began. The lack of roads along the Union lines would force couriers to take wide detours or scramble through difficult and unfamiliar terrain as they tried to deliver messages along the line. Banks overruled all objections to his plan and repeated his orders to prepare for an attack in the morning.[83]

Banks could have waited to attack, but he was under intense pressure to move quickly. The War Department in Washington urged Banks to make progress. The northern press condemned Banks for engaging in a lackadaisical advance toward Port Hudson. An article in the *New York Herald* published on April 2 claimed Banks's campaign in Louisiana had "resulted only in failures, losses, and disappointments." According to one rumor, when an unnamed officer at Port Hudson asked Banks why he was determined to launch an assault on the garrison, which was destined to starve, Banks exclaimed, "the people of the north demand blood."[84]

The Union generals ordered their men to prepare for an attack in the morning. Henry Howe wrote in his diary that, when the generals called for volunteers to form advanced storming parties, "all of our officers volunteered except one." The men threw lots to determine who would have the honor of leading the assault. Howe acknowledged that "we are going into a terrible conflict" but stated that "the boys feel gay and happy." As he explained, perhaps with the people of the future in mind, "we came here to fight for country, and why should we falter?" He believed that "the stars and stripes must be planted on their entrenchments."[85]

—7—

It Failed

THE BATTLE OF MAY 27, 1863

Look at a wave rushing up a sloping beach against a line of rocks, and you will see the story of an assaulting column directed against fortifications. At a distance the billow seems irresistible; near at hand the under-current has deprived it of half its force; at last merely a little spray dashes upon the final impediment. Just so slaughter, misdirection, dispersion, and skulking enfeeble the column until only hundreds out of thousands reach the point of hand-to-hand fighting. On reflection it is a wonder that any assault succeeds. The attacking force must do what is very difficult in the open field; it must advance without firing against a line which is firing at it; it must do this in spite of difficulties of ground which inevitably break up its organization; and after long continued slaughter it must scale defenses fringed with bayonets. We were expected that day to charge a mile in face of cannon and musketry, and then to carry earthworks defended by men of our own race. It was right to try the experiment, but it is not surprising that it failed.[1]

—WILLIAM DEFOREST, 12th Connecticut Infantry

Early next morning Gen. Banks obtained a flag of truce for the burial of his dead and removal of his wounded. Col. Locke, by direction of Col. Steedman, met the flag. Several immense openings in the earth were made in front of our regiment each with a capacity of about 100 men. Into these the dead were piled and covered. A brigade of negroes had charged the 39th Mississippi on our left; about half were killed outright on the field, and for the burial of these Gen. Banks never asked a flag of truce. They lay there in the hot sun and putrefied and swelled until the stench became so unbearable to Col. Shelby of the 39th Mississippi, that he asked Gen. Banks to allow him (Shelby) to bury them. Gen. Banks replied that he had no dead there. This ended the greatest battle of Port Hudson during the siege. It taught us that a few men with a determination to stay could hold a fortified position against great odds.[2]

—Edward McMorries, 1st Alabama Infantry

Preparations for Battle

May 27 began as a beautiful day. Charles McGregor later remembered that it was "a very beautiful day." The "face of nature never shown more kindly down." There was "an indescribable freshness and beauty in the tropical green wood where lie thousands all armed and panoplied in glittering steel and the habiliments of war." Orton Clark later remembered that the day "dawned upon us as others had done before and gave no token of what was in store for us." The Confederate garrison "expected a strong attack" to commence at any moment. The men in gray did not wait for long. At 5:30 a.m. the Federals greeted the sun with a heavy bombardment from ship and shore. James Goble described it as "the hottest cannonading" he had ever heard at Port Hudson. Shells crashed into the Confederate center and right, but "there was a prefect calm on the left wing." Colonel Steedman later recalled "the silence was ominous." Confederate gunners initially "replied with spirit" matching the Federals shot for shot, but the rebels could not hope to match the weight or intensity of fire, and, unlike their Union counterparts, they had a very limited amount of ammunition. Confederate artillery fire faded as the gray-clad gunners conserved their precious shells.[3]

While infantrymen enjoyed the pretty weather and listened to artillery fire, members of the Union army's medical department prepared to deal with the results of battle. Dr. John Henry Rauch, a civilian surgeon turned medical director for Union forces in Louisiana, spent the early morning hours of May 27 setting up field hospitals just behind the Union lines. The army did not have enough tents for the numbers of wounded Rauch anticipated, but they had plenty of captured cotton and trees were in abundance, so Rauch told the hospital stewards to pile cotton into improvised beds underneath the shade of magnolia trees. The ambulance drivers hitched their teams and prepared to move. Cooks made soup and prepared to feed it to men who were healthy that morning but who would be horribly wounded before the day ended. Surgeons laid out the grizzly tools of their trade.[4]

Attacks on the Confederate Left

At 6:00 a.m. General Weitzel, on the Union right, ordered his men to attack the Confederate left. Dwight's brigade, under the command of

Map 4. East and west banks of Mississippi River, portions of East and West Baton Rouge parishes, north to Waterloo and south to Baton Rouge. Relief shown by hachures. Entered according to Act of Congress, in the year 1863 by G. W. Tomlinson, Boston, Mass.

Colonel Jacob Van Zandt, took the lead. The 1st Louisiana Union Infantry, composed of white men, some of whom served in the Confederate Army before joining the Union after the fall of New Orleans, formed lines of battle and prepared to advance as part of Dwight's brigade. Members of Company E of the 1st Union Louisiana Infantry "expected a real picnic"

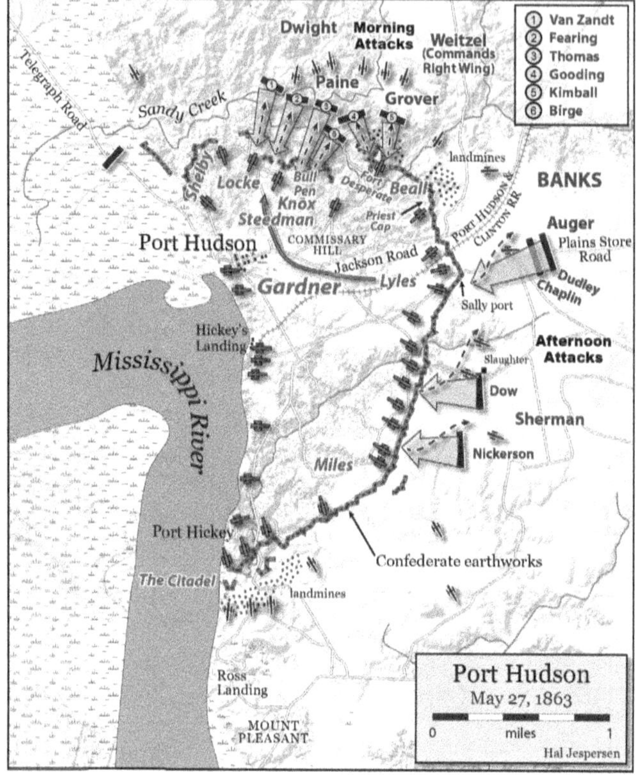

Map 5. The Battle of Port Hudson, May 27, 1863.
Hal Jespersen.

that day. In several skirmishes leading up to the May 27 attack, the rebels had withdrawn from the 1st Louisiana after minimal fighting, convincing many of the Louisianans in blue that Port Hudson's defenders would not fight. Thomas's brigade followed Dwight's brigade as a reserve. Weitzel ordered officers to advance on foot since horses could not cross the difficult ground. Most of the Federal regiments formed in columns to better penetrate the difficult terrain that stood between them and the Confederate positions.[5]

The rebels braced for the attack. Colonel Ben Johnson sent six companies of the 15th Arkansas Infantry to support Colonel Steedman on the Confederate left flank. Colonel Steedman, in command of the Confederate left, ordered six hundred rebels to advance, cross Sandy Creek, and form a line of battle, taking up "a favorable position" about five hundred yards in front of the main Confederate line. The spot Steedman selected was at the edge of a dense woods where the thick brush and forest transitioned into a relatively open space, filled with heavy timber but free from the undergrowth that dominated much of the terrain around Port Hudson. Brush in the area had been cut down "for camping purposes" sometime before. A section of Watson's Louisiana battery under the command of Lieutenant E. A. Toledano covered the road. Confederate infantrymen formed in concealed ambush positions to the right and left of the road. Lieutenant Colonel Locke of the 1st Alabama Infantry commanded the right wing and Major Johnson of the 1st Mississippi Infantry commanded the left wing. Steedman ordered both Locke and Johnson to keep their lines of battle concealed and hold their fire until Steedman gave the order to engage the enemy. The Confederate infantry sent out skirmishers to gather intelligence and harass the advancing Federals.[6]

The Federals advanced into the heavy timber, which was now filled with rebel infantrymen. George Smith, commanding the 1st Louisiana Union Infantry's skirmishers, saw "the grey coats of our enemies appearing among the trees" a moment before the Confederates opened fire. Lieutenant W. W. Wilson of 15th Arkansas Infantry told his men, "take good aim boys," and Lieutenant Richard McClung added, "shoot low and break their legs." Rebels peppered the men in blue with small arms fire. Union infantrymen "pushed forward boldly," filling the air with "yelling and shouting." Federals took cover behind trees and began picking off Confederate artillerymen and artillery horses. Union soldiers in good firing positions kept up a steady fire as their comrades in poor positions passed them loaded rifles. Rank meant little, and, according to Henry Hall of the 75th New York Infantry, "valiant Babcock was among the most active in handling the rifle," even though he was a lieutenant colonel. Steedman wanted to keep his line of battle concealed until he could catch the main Union line, and not just the skirmishers, in an ambush, so he ordered his main line to hold their fire as Confederate skirmishers gradually fell back.[7]

Eventually, Steedman concluded that Union skirmishers were inflicting unacceptable casualties on the Confederate artillery, and he sprung the trap. The concealed Confederate main line unleashed a volley, and "the enemy retreated through the woods in great confusion." John Kennedy, with the 1st Alabama Infantry, reported, "the muskets pop as fast as canes when the fire is in a cane-brake," and "the artillery is deafening; it is one continual roar." Steedman capitalized on his success, throwing skirmishers forward to pursue the fleeing Federals until the Union infantry reformed about half a mile from the main Confederate line and took a stand.[8]

While the Union army regrouped, the Federal gunboats kept up their fire on Port Hudson. The *Essex* tried to shield wooden gunboats with its armor-plated hull, and Confederate gunners tried to shoot around or over it to hit the more vulnerable wooden ships. Union sailors focused their fire on the Confederate citadel. Initially, rebels in the citadel gave as good as they got, but it was not long until the Union navy's firepower proved overwhelming, and the citadel's defenders fled to continue the fight from batteries just to the north. William Park, on the *Essex*, believed that the army could have rushed in at that moment, taking ownership of the abandoned Confederate citadel and capturing Port Hudson. However, no soldiers materialized, so the navy kept firing.[9]

Two hours after the initial skirmish on the Confederate left began, the Federals advanced once again. This time the Union infantry came in greater numbers and with greater force. Confederate troops inflicted heavy losses on the advancing Federals, but the rebels slowly yielded to the overwhelming Union force. For nearly an hour the attacking infantry slowly forced Confederates to fall back toward their fortifications. New York infantryman James Peck believed that "the only thing that saved us was that they fired to high and most of thair [*sic*] grape and canister went over our heads." Federal work crews followed close behind the front line, building roads almost as quickly as the infantry advanced. Gunners from the 1st US Light Artillery and the 2nd Massachusetts Light Artillery rushed up newly built roads and fired on Confederate positions.[10]

Weitzel's brigade used their superior numbers to extend their lines until their line curved around Sandy Creek and threatened the Confederate rear. The Confederates, with a much smaller force, were unable to extend their line and meet the Union advance. At about the same time, a defective friction primer disabled one of the Confederate cannons, and then the artillery ran out of ammunition. Colonel Steedman ordered Lieutenant Toledano withdraw the artillery to the main Confederate line about half a mile north of the mill. In danger of being encircled and deprived of artillery support, Colonel Steedman reluctantly ordered the infantry to withdraw and rendezvous with the artillery forming north of the mill. Lieutenant Richard McClung led his men back as "the balls hailed around us on the way." From his post south of the retreat, Lieutenant Edrington saw the Union infantry advancing and ordered his two gun section of the 1st Mississippi Artillery to open fire, catching the attacking Federals in a deadly flanking fire, which slowed their pursuit. Steedman had worried that the Federals would turn the withdrawal into a route, but "the whole line fell back in perfect order," and the Confederates reformed on their original line.[11]

The Confederate infantry on the left fell back to their defenses on Commissary Hill, in front of the mill. There, they rejoined their artillery, which enjoyed a fresh resupply of ammunition. Colonel Steedman took up a position with the artillery and ordered his men to prepare for a renewed Federal attack. General Beall, commanding the Confederate center, realized that the garrison's left flank was in danger, so he sent reinforcements north and retained only a handful of men to hold the center. For a moment, there was a lull in the fighting. John Kennedy and his comrades in the 1st Alabama Infantry spent the brief pause "laying in our rifle-pit, awaiting the hated foe," as he made a brief note in his diary. He reported that "all are cool and determined." He claimed that, if the Federals advanced, "they will catch it, sure as two and two make four."[12]

Initially pleased with their success forcing Confederates back, Union infantrymen advanced into an area they thought was unoccupied. The men in dirty gray uniforms caught the Federals by surprise, having conspired with their native soil to conceal themselves until they could unleash pain and confusion on their enemies. The rebels greeted the men in blue from a spider's web of carefully concealed foxholes, barriers, entanglements, and sharpshooter's nests that were almost indistinguishable from the natural terrain. The Federals angrily cursed the encounter as a "huge bushwack [*sic*]." Colonel Steedman watched the Confederate infantry pummel the advancing Federals through his telescope. As the Union infantry began to falter, he ordered the Confederate artillery under his command to open fire. William Aldis and the 131st New York Infantry were hit by "a masked battery with grape and canister." The first volley flew over the heads of the New Yorkers, crashing into trees and showering the Federals with splinters that did little harm. Confederate gunners quickly corrected their aim and subsequent rounds inflicted far more damage.[13]

The Union infantry crumbled, destroyed by exhaustion, confusion, and devastating enemy fire. Weitzel ordered Thomas's brigade, held in reserve, to charge through the broken lines of the advance brigades. Men from Connecticut, New York, and Vermont "fell upon the enemy with a rush." According to William Aldis, "the bullets rained down on us a like a furious hailstorm." One of the bullets hit Aldis in the right arm between his wrist and elbow. He tried to bandage himself with a handkerchief, tightening the knot with his left hand and his teeth. As he secured the bandage, "the man on my left, he had the top of his head torn off by grape." Aldis later assured his wife, "by God's mercy I am still alive."[14]

Thomas's brigade got within seventy-five yards of the main Confederate line, where they were "exposed to a murderous fire." Colonel Steedman noticed that a detachment of Union sharpshooters had enfiladed a ditch near a Confederate battery and ordered his brother, Captain S. D. Steedman, to lead a counterattack. As Captain Steedman moved into action, a bullet struck his chest, delivering what the men initially thought was a fatal blow but that ended up causing only a minor wound.[15]

Unable to make their way forward against the artillery fire from Commissary Hill, the Federals split, attacking positions to the east and west of Commissary Hill. For a moment it looked like the Union infantry might penetrate Confederate lines near the area later known as the Bull Pen, west of Commissary Hill, but Steedman called up the 23rd Arkansas Infantry under Colonel O. P. Lyle, and the Arkansans arrived just in time to block the Federals.[16] At about the same time, other Federals assaulted Fort Desperate on the western end of the Confederate left.

Colonel Benjamin Johnson of the 15th Arkansas Infantry defended the fort with fewer than three hundred men and a pair of 12-pounder cannons from the 1st Mississippi Artillery. Union attackers vastly outnumbered the defenders of Fort Desperate, but the rebels stood their ground and prepared to defend themselves. The Federals planted an artillery battery of six cannons roughly four hundred yards away , directly in front of Fort Desperate, and opened fire. A shell from a Union cannon struck one of the two pieces of artillery in Fort Desperate, disabling the cannon, wounding two artillerymen, and killing the section commander, Lieutenant Edrington. Colonel Johnson ordered his men to hold their fire. When the

Federals got within sixty yards of Fort Desperate, Johnson gave the order to fire. The Arkansans opened fire "with a yell" and inflicted heavy losses on the attackers. The Federals staggered back, reformed, and rushed forward again, only to suffer from another "deadly volley." The Union infantry tried to keep moving forward, but "Johnson's backwoods men were making fearful havoc, particularly among the officers," and the Federal lines broke as they retreated. Colonel Steedman believed the "admirable marksmanship" of the Arkansans broke the Union lines.[17]

William Deforest of the 12th Connecticut Infantry did not participate in the initial charge. His company deployed on the flank with orders to throw out skirmishers and pick off Confederate artillerymen. From his vantage point he watched the assault. Several years later he explained that the attack failed because, if you "look at a wave rushing up a sloping beach against a line of rocks," you will "see the history of an assaulting column directed against fortifications." When the wave is still far from the rocks, "the billow seems irresistible." As the water comes closer, "the undercurrent has deprived it of half its force," and when the wave finally reaches the rocks, "merely a little spray dashes upon the final impediment." Deforest explained that, in much the same way, "slaughter, misdirection, dispersion, and skulking enfeeble the column" until the moment of impact, when "only hundreds out of thousands reach the point of hand-to-hand fighting." In an era of muzzle-loading rifles, which were slow to reload, attacking soldiers who hoped to break through enemy lines had to show tremendous restraint by holding their fire against stationary defenders who fired as quickly as they could reload. The Union infantrymen who made that attack charged for a mile into a hailstorm of artillery and small arms fire, only to be greeted by fixed bayonets when they finally got within reach of their opponents. Even after surveying the horrific cost, Deforest believed, "it was right to try the experiment, but it is not surprising that it failed."[18]

Back at their lines, the Federals reformed. After a brief rest, they charged toward Fort Desperate once again. This time the Union infantry got into the ditch at the base of the fort and jumped in. Union artillerymen and sharpshooters swept the Confederate parapet, inflicting heavy losses on the defenders. Arkansans crouched behind the breastworks, lying in wait for any Federals who dared to enter the fort. Every man loaded his gun, and the men with bayonets fixed them to their muzzles. The defenders heard someone in the ditch yell, "are you ready?" A chorus of voices replied "ready." A moment later, a Federal yelled, "charge!" A single officer and four men clambered over the parapet. The rebels gunned them down instantly and tossed their corpses back into the ditch. No other Federals dared cross the parapet. Union officers tried to inspire the men to attack, but they refused.[19]

An uneasy stalemate began between the Union and Confederate soldiers who could hear but not see each other. According to Howard Wright, the rebels taunted the Federals, "why don't you come over?" The Union men dared the Confederates back, "why don't you come out and fight us?" The rebels replied, "if you had had only two to one instead of ten to one, we would do it." In between taunts, the opposing soldiers threw clods of dirt over the parapet. Howard Wright lamented that they did not have any hand grenades, which "could have been used with good effect."[20]

In hopes of breaking the stalemate, a Union colonel whom Deforest did not name in his account ordered Captain Deforest to withdraw his company of the 12th Connecticut Infantry from their skirmishing positions and form a line of battle in preparation for an assault. Deforest recalled that the feeling was "not unlike that in which you take your seat in a dentist's chair." Knowing that his men were watching him, he turned to them "with a smile of simulated gayety" and ordered them to fall into line. His company had spent all morning in combat but "skirmishing is not nearly so trying as charging or line-fighting." Deforest explained that, while skirmishing, "you generally have cover" and you can shoot back at your opponents. This was important because, according to Deforest, "to fire at a person who is firing at you is somehow wonderfully consolatory" and even "sustaining." Perhaps "more than that, it is exciting" and "produces in you the savage but nevertheless natural and unaffected joy of battle." While on the skirmish line, Deforest spent his time "shouting with enthusiasm" and "cheering my men with jokes and laughter." In contrast to the lighthearted danger of skirmishing, Deforest believed that "as to being slaughtered and driven back and scared to death, you cannot make it pleasant under any circumstances."[21]

Just before the men from Connecticut charged forward, a white flag appeared above the fray. Sources disagree about the details. William Deforest claimed that Confederate soldiers raised a white flag, marched out of Port Hudson, and stacked their arms, and that an unidentified

Confederate colonel declared "we have surrendered." For a moment, Deforest believed "Port Hudson was taken." He later claimed that, if the Union high command had acted quickly, they could have marched in and taken possession of Port Hudson that day. While "both armies stood gaping," apparently shocked by the surrender, a mounted Confederate officer who Deforest believed was General Gardner, rode out, placed the surrendering Confederate colonel under arrest, and ordered the Confederate soldiers to return to their positions. Confederate officer Howard Wright told a very different story. He claimed that the Federals were stuck in the ditch, with little hope of safe retreat, and that Union soldiers raised a white flag. Colonel Steedman agreed to a truce, and the Federals trapped in the ditch withdrew, improving their position. According to Howard Wright, this was an improper use of a truce, and he claimed that General Banks denounced his men's improper behavior in later correspondence.[22]

At about 10:00 a.m., Colonel John Nelson ordered the 1st and 3rd Louisiana Native Guards to attack the extreme left of the Confederate flank, across Sandy Creek near the Mississippi River. Colonel W. B. Shelby defended this section of the Confederate line with six companies of the 39th Mississippi Infantry, six field cannons, and long-range support from Confederate water batteries firing 8-inch and 10-inch cannons. The Native Guards took heavy casualties from Confederate fire but pressed ahead for a moment. When the Union attackers got within two hundred yards of the Confederate line, every Confederate cannon in the area opened with antipersonnel canister rounds. In the words of Richard Irwin, it was "more than any men could stand." The Native Guards retreated in confusion and regrouped once they were beyond range of the Confederate forces.[23]

Confederate observers were less impressed with the Native Guards. Howard Wright claimed the "negro" attack "did not amount to a charge" because the Native Guards retreated as soon as the rebels opened fire. John Kennedy of the 1st Alabama Infantry dismissed the Native Guards he and his comrades "repulsed with slaughter." Daniel Smith, also with the 1st Alabama, claimed the "negroes turned and fled, without firing a shot." Walter Turner of the 39th Mississippi Infantry wrote in his diary that "two negro regiments charged us" and "we cut them all to pieces."[24]

After the repulse of the Native Guards, Federal soldiers on the Confederate left realized that it was "wholesale butchery" to remain in place or to advance. Colonel Thomas noted that Weitzel had ordered an attack and not a mass suicide, so he ordered his brigade to withdraw to the relative safety of a ravine. Weitzel ordered Thomas's men to hold their position and maintain pressure on the rebels, if possible. The battle plan called for each Federal division to support the others, and Weitzel hoped for reinforcements or a diversionary attack. Weitzel sent an angry message to Banks, denouncing the lack of support for his attack that forced his men to die alone as they tried to capture Port Hudson single-handedly, despite the battle plan that called for mutually reinforcing attacks. With no apparent way forward, the Federals pulled back a little and began fortifying their line about two hundred yards from the rebels. The centerpiece of the Union position became a log fort atop a little hill they named Fort Babcock, in honor of the 75th New York Infantry's lieutenant colonel, Willoughby Babcock.[25]

About the same time that Weitzel's attack stalled, General Grover sent the 159th New York Infantry to reinforce Weitzel's men. Since the Federals occupied a broad concave arc around the rebel lines, Grover's reinforcements took a wide, curving route. They wisely avoided the worst of the Confederate gunfire by dropping into the ravine that contained Big Sandy Creek. The ravine was "one of the ugliest approaches" the men had ever seen. The ravine was filled with brush, fallen timber, slippery footing, steep inclines, and sharp rocks. It took the reinforcements an hour to move half a mile over the difficult terrain. As men from New York looped around the Confederate defenses, Grover ordered the rest of his division to make a frontal assault on the Confederate positions directly facing them. The 12th Maine Infantry formed in line with the 13th and 25th Connecticut Infantry regiments. The Federals focused their efforts on an exposed angle in the Confederate line, near where the line made a sharp turn to the south.[26]

As the 159th New York emerged from the ravine, they captured a Confederate captain and six skirmishers who had failed to withdraw in time and were cut off from their lines. After a difficult and circuitous path, Grover's reinforcements finally formed their lines and charged the Confederate defenses. Men from New York and Connecticut walked into a horrific crossfire from Confederate rifles. The Federals got within thirty yards of the Confederate line before the rebels forced the men in blue to with withdraw and seek shelter.[27]

Attacks on the Confederate Right

Union attacks against Port Hudson's northern, left flank ended by about noon. General Thomas Sherman waited for guidance from the engineers to select his path of attack in support of the Federal attacks on the Confederate left flank. A frustrated General Banks arrived at Sherman's headquarters, found Sherman eating lunch, and ordered Sherman's division to attack without delay. Sherman complied and led his men forward on horseback. Rebels who had raced north to reinforce their left flank earlier in the day raced south, one step ahead of the Union attack. Confederate defenders watched from their breastworks as Federal troops walked into the open, four hundred yards from their positions.[28]

Captain Thorpe Gould ordered his company of the 165th New York Infantry to form a line of battle with the rest of the regiment. Roughly 1,200 New Yorkers lined up. Gould told his men to prepare for a charge. Soldiers fixed bayonets onto their rifles. Equipped with cold steel, the men from New York walked into their first battle.[29]

Henry Rufus Gardner of the 18th New York Battery took a position near the left center of the Union lines, opposite the Confederate right center. The New Yorkers set up their six field cannons just to the right of the 1st Indiana Heavy Artillery, who were armed with eight 20-pounder Parrotts and four 32-pounder cannons. The gunners from New York and Indiana fired steadily at the Confederate lines. The Confederate artillery directed their minimal counterbattery fire at the 32-pounders and ignored the New Yorkers.[30]

Joseph M. Bailey of the 16th Arkansas Infantry saw "the advancing columns" approach his position. The Arkansans enjoyed an excellent view of the approaching Federals, and there "was not a single obstruction to mar the view." As a veteran soldier who had fought at Wilson's Creek, Pea Ridge, and numerous smaller engagements, Baily admired the "magnificent sight" of soldiers who "came forward with the precision of troops on review; bristling bayonets, glinting in the sunshine; above them, flags fluttering in the breeze," but as a man who wanted to remain alive, Bailey felt sick because "the odds against us looked appalling." The rebels had only one man for every five feet of ditch, with no reserves nearby. To stretch their manpower, every officer in the regiment "stood in line with his men,

View of Indiana artillery, Port Hudson.
Library of Congress.

musket in hand." Most men emptied their cartridge boxes onto the dirt at the top of the trenches, in hopes that by keeping the precious ammunition close at hand, they could reload just a little faster. Bailey later recalled that men dealt with the stress of waiting for the attack in various ways. Some men "were serious and silent," others "joked, danced, or sang short snatches of song." Regardless of how they dealt with the horrible anticipation, "there was an intense earnestness about it all."[31]

The 2nd Battalion of the 165th New York Infantry, better known as Duryee's Zouaves, led the attack. Joseph Bailey heard many men near him lament previous defeats and declare "we would now get even" as they opened fire on the advancing Federals. In contrast to the simple suits of blue worn by most of their comrades, these New Yorkers went into battle in garish uniforms of loose red trousers, dark blue jackets decorated with red trim, matching vests, and red caps, inspired by the legendary light infantrymen of French North Africa. Howard Wright noticed that "the gay colors of the regiment contrasted brilliantly with the green and sombre [*sic*] shades of the trees and field." Wright contemplated the beautiful colors

Matthias Johnston, from *History of the Second Battalion Duryee Zouaves.*

in the abstract for only a moment before returning to the cold realities of the battlefield, where he noted the colorful uniforms were "making a fine mark for our fire."[32]

Confederate riflemen hit their targets, and Federals suffered. Captain Eli Griffin of the 6th Michigan Infantry was leading his men when a Confederate rifle bullet struck his left arm. The bullet tore a hole in Griffin's arm, about two inches above his elbow. Despite the wound and perhaps in shock, Griffin refused to stop, and "we charged on the rebel earthworks."[33]

Smoke obscured the battlefield. A member of the 1st Indiana Heavy Artillery climbed to the top of a tall tree to get a better view of the battery's targets. With the benefit of their lookout, the gunners adjusted their aim and, according to Sergeant Rufus Dooley, "boom goes thirty pounds of iron for the rebels." Quartermasters brought the artillerymen "a bucket of whiskey," which Dooley described as "very acceptable." After a quick drink the men returned to their duty and the "firing goes on." The Indianan's cannons were "very hot" from constant firing, but the blue-clad gunners "kept belting away." Dooley lamented that his battery's fire did little damage because the rebels "burrow deep in the earth."[34]

Writing thirty-one years later, David Hanaburgh of the 128th New York Infantry recalled surging toward the Confederate lines as part of Sherman's command. He wondered if the Confederate defenders thought of themselves as modern Spartans, led by Leonidas, defending their homes against two million Persians. Hanaburgh was sympathetic, at least when he wrote his memoir decades later, to the "misguided citizens of our land" who tried to kill him on May 27, but Hanaburgh argued he and his comrades fought not for Persian despotism but for "broader and loftier views of a nation's welfare." He was proud of "the cool and indomitable courage" he and his comrades displayed in service to "lofty patriotism" as they pressed ahead despite the danger.[35]

The Confederate artillery fired "spherical case, many of them bursting right in their ranks." Men from New York died, but their brothers did not falter as "the gaps were quickly closed up." With a veteran's appreciation for a well-drilled formation, Wright admitted "they came on in splendid style." The neat Union lines disintegrated as the attackers stumbled over felled trees, stumps, and dense underbrush. Thorpe Gould believed that the Confederates had intentionally placed many of the obstructions that hampered the attack and destroyed his company's organization. The Zouaves tried to press forward.[36]

As the Federal infantry came close to the Confederate lines, the Confederate gunners began firing grapeshot, but even those fearsome projectiles could not stop the Federal advance. When the Union infantry got within 150 yards of the Confederate lines, Confederate gunners unleashed double loads of canister shot, and the infantry fired a volley, sweeping the Federal ranks with "a storm of musket balls." Captain Gould later told his friend Ned, "our ranks began to thin in consequence of the dread thunder." Captain Eli Griffin and the 6th Michigan Infantry continued to press forward into "a perfect storm of bullets and grape shot."[37]

According to Howard Wright, the Zouaves "wavered and then halted" as New Yorkers were "mowed down by our deadly fire." After the volley failed to rout the Federals, Confederate defenders began to fire at will, and "an incessant rattle of musketry, intermingled with rapid discharges of canister" filled the air. Zouave officers ran forward and "waved their swords" as they called for their men to follow them. According to Howard

Wright, "they only thereby proved to the men the deadliness of our marksmanship." As quickly as the Union officers tried to rally their men, "they were unerringly dropped by our riflemen." Wright watched as a "showily dressed officer" jumped onto a tree stump, waving his sword with one hand and a US flag in the other as he tried to rally his men. For a moment he lived a charmed life, and it seemed neither shot nor shell could strike him. The officer's luck, like his life, could only last for so long. Confederate gunfire finally found the officer, knocking him off the stump. The Zouaves threw themselves flat, finding shelter behind stumps, logs, and small depressions in the ground, where they began trading shots with the rebels, who refused to give them a moment's peace.[38]

Captain Gould saw "men falling thick and fast" until "I received a ball across my left chest, tearing with it the flesh and just escaping my shoulder." Initially he was unsure of what had happened, and then "I received a spent ball in my right side knocking me down and senseless." As Gould regained his senses, the Federals fell back toward the woods. Gould received another wound to his left foot as he withdrew, but it was "of little consequence," and he made it back to the cover of the woods.[39]

Lieutenant A. M. Trawick and the rest of the 16th Arkansas, positioned near the center of the Confederate lines, received word late in the day to rush north and reinforce the Confederate left in response to what they feared was another Union attack forming to hit the garrison's left flank. Colonel Benjamin Pixlee, commanding the regiment, "unsheathed his sword" and yelled, "Sixteenth, follow me, every devil of you!" The Arkansans followed close behind their colonel, crossing open ground between detached works, and the Federals greeted them with "shot, shell, and bullets that rained through the opening like a hailstorm." Men died as they rushed through the open ground, but the survivors fulfilled the objective and reinforced the Confederate left.[40]

Attacks on the Confederate Center

As soon as General Banks heard the gunfire that confirmed Sherman's men were engaged, he ordered Augur's division in the center to attack. Augur's men were ready. The 21st Maine Infantry formed as skirmishers and took the lead. A storming party, consisting of two hundred volunteers from the 48th Massachusetts followed close behind with cotton bags and bundles of sticks to fill the ditch and create a path for the men who followed. The rest of Edward Chapin's brigade of the 48th Massachusetts, 49th Massachusetts, 116th New York, and the 2nd Louisiana Union Infantry regiments followed the skirmishers as they moved west down the Plains Store Road. Dudley's brigade of Massachusetts and New York men followed in reserve, taking cover in the Osage orange hedges that divided the fields near the road.[41]

J. B. Sutton of the 49th Alabama Infantry was a new, eighteen-year-old recruit in an old regiment. Alongside him in the ranks were veterans who had survived horrific battles such as Shiloh (April 6–7, 1862). According to Sutton, "old soldiers were mad because they were not allowed to fight." Sutton had never seen battle and remarked that "I was not complaining" that the Federals were a safe distance away. Sutton's mood changed as Federals moved into attack formations and the Confederate lines crackled to life with gunfire.[42]

A member of the 116th New York Infantry, identified only as S. J. S., later recalled that the Union artillery briefly fell silent, and the Federal infantry stepped out of the woods into a clearing. Orton Clark, a captain in the same regiment, later explained, "as we waited a painful silence crept over us; but few words were spoken by anyone, and those few were in whispers." Clark explained, "they were awfully solemn moments, such as only those who have experienced them can appreciate." Thoughts turned to home, and "the dear face of a father, mother or wife would present itself, causing more than one eye to grow dim with moisture." Despite the tears, "all seemed and were, calm and determined, ready to do and die" The silence lasted only a moment. S. J. S. reported that, almost as soon as the Union infantry moved into the open, "Port Hudson poured forth a terrible storm of grape and canister." The garrison's fire included "all imaginable missiles and I might say all unimaginable mingled with the death—dealing rifle shots." The "fire of the enemy was thick and fast, and fearfully effective."[43]

John Hamilton, a correspondent for *Harper's Weekly*, watched an "appalling" scene as the Federal infantry marched into "an immense open space" between the cover of the woods and the Confederate defenses. This area had been covered by a dense forest, but according to Hamilton, "the rebels had ingeniously felled the trees, leaving the huge branches to interlace with each other, and forming with the thick brushwood underneath, a barrier all but impassable to anything in human shape." Hamilton explained that it was "so horrible a place." The men were "sinking at every step up to their armpits." Union infantrymen tumbled through the brush and mud, and Confederates were "all the while blazing away at them with grape, shell, and canister." Major Charles Plunkett of the 49th Massachusetts Infantry wrote home to his father that "the bravest thing I ever did in my life was running from one log to another, a distance of three rods, to get to the front of the regiment. How I got through without a scratch is a mystery."[44]

The Federals lost their momentum and organization as their advance slowed to a crawl. Confederate defenders poured small arms and artillery fire into the barely moving Federals. Frederick Deland of the 49th Massachusetts Infantry rallied members of his regiment to gather bundles of sticks dropped by other men and fill a ditch that had slowed the advance. Deland's efforts helped fill the ditch, and the Federals surged forward once again. Private Deland later won the Medal of Honor for his courage that day. Deland's courage might have made the situation even worse. Union infantrymen walked directly into the path of Confederate artillery fire. Gunners operating the two Confederate 24-pounder heavy cannons within range of the attack did not have any antipersonnel rounds, so they improvised by firing assortments of rusty nails, broken chains, and chunks of railroad iron into the attacking Federals. Exploding artillery shells set fire to the brush, turning the battlefield into hellscape of fire, smoke, and death. According to John Hamilton, "it was wholesale slaughter."[45]

Confederate fire devastated the attackers. General Sherman fell off his horse with a severe wound to his leg. Command of the division passed to Brigadier General Neal Dow, but as he was taking command, a Confederate bullet struck Dow and forced him to retreat in search of medical attention. The Federal attackers became confused, and for a brief time it was unclear who, if anyone, was in command. General George Andrews eventually took charge and ordered a retreat when he learned that other Union attacks had failed. Federals near the woods retreated immediately, but men stuck in the open hugged the ground, waiting for darkness to cover their escape. Major Charles Plunkett of the 49th Massachusetts Infantry wrote to his father, "it destroys some of the romance of war to lie three hours in a field, under broiling sun, with shot and shell flying over one, and the cries of the wounded sounding in his ears." Plunkett reported, "when I came off, at the head of my remaining men, Gen. Augur grasped my hand but did not utter a word."[46]

Writing many years later, J. B. Sutton of the 49th Alabama Infantry still remembered his first battle. He began the day as a young novice in the ways of war, but on May 27, 1863, Sutton became a veteran. Sutton explained, "I can never forget the cries of the boys as they scrambled to their feet with the lifeblood streaming from their bodies." On that day, "I began to realize what war really meant."[47]

The Battle Ends

Union attacks on Confederate positions died down in the midafternoon, but occasional small arms fire continued. At about 5:00 p.m., the rebels raised a white flag of truce above their lines. George Smith heard "tremendous cheering" in response to the truce. Confederate and Union soldiers laid down their arms and rushed out to greet each other "as though they had been friends long parted." Since Smith's regiment, the 1st Louisiana Union Infantry, included many Louisianans, some of the men may have been greeting old friends and family members. Officers from each army met and discovered that the truce was a mistake. Soldiers reluctantly returned to their lines and resumed firing at the men they had greeted moments before. Walter Turner of the 39th Mississippi Infantry wrote in his diary, "I never saw so troops so much confused in my life," and confessed he had no idea who had raised the white flag or why. The firing slowly died down a little while after the men returned to their lines. Lieutenant Jacob Hasbrouck of the 156th New York Infantry spent the battle as an ammunition guard, able to hear the "roar of cannon + musketry" in the distance as they hoped "to hear the fort has surrendered." The fight was over, for the moment. Justus Gale of the 8th Vermont Infantry wrote his sister that "I fired nearly 100 rounds . . . and had some good shots at them but whether I killed a man or not I cant [*sic*] say."[48]

The Aftermath of the Battle of May 27

Port Hudson fell quiet on the evening of May 27. The Union army withdrew to the relative safety of new positions just out of range of the Confederate gunfire. The attacks on Port Hudson had failed. The Federals paid a heavy price of 293 killed, 1,545 wounded, and 157 missing. Orton Clark wrote that many wounded men suffered "in great agony" and were only "freed from suffering by death." He believed that "May 27th with its terrible memories, will never be forgotten." Private George Waite wrote a friend back home in Connecticut that the army suffered "considerable loss and it is a wonder that our loss was not greater." A member of the 116th New York Infantry, identified only as S. J. S., gave thanks to the army's medical department for setting up excellent field hospitals, where the wounded "were served with as much iced water, coffee, and soup as they could take." The navy sent surgeons, including Aaron Oberly of the *Kineo*, ashore to help with the army's wounded. Despite the best efforts of dedicated healers, the large numbers of wounded overwhelmed the medical department, and the "the groans of their suffering" disturbed many soldiers. Henry Cross wrote home, "a battle is a horrid thing. You can have no conception of its horrors. I never did before."[49]

The Confederates suffered much less than their adversaries, with only about 225 men killed, wounded, and missing. Thomas Alexander of the 1st Tennessee Heavy Artillery concluded that the battle of May 27 was "the hardest fight I ever was in." Many years later, Joseph Bailey still mourned the loss of Lieutenant Elbert Spain, "one of my warmest personal friends." At daylight on May 28, Baily and his surviving friends lowered Spain's body "unconfined, to its final resting place, to be aroused never again by beat of drum or bugle call."[50]

Unlike the rebels, trapped in Port Hudson, the Federals could at least evacuate their wounded to better hospitals, far from the battlefield. The Union army at Port Hudson sent sick and wounded men to Baton Rouge to recuperate. Captain Gould received initial treatment for his wounds in a field hospital near Port Hudson before being shipped to the Union hospital at Baton Rouge along with several other members of his regiment. After treatment in Baton Rouge, the army moved him again. This time, Gould traveled to the largest Union hospital in the region, at New Orleans. From his hospital bed in New Orleans, Gould lamented that the army would probably declare him too badly wounded for further duty and send him home. Captain Eli Griffin was also evacuated to a New Orleans hospital, where he gave thanks to "the God of Battles," who he believed had saved his life.[51]

A story of one of the men wounded on May 27 might help to illustrate the suffering of the wounded. Major George N. Lewis of the 12th Connecticut Infantry was sheltering behind a tree during the battle when a chunk of grapeshot roughly an inch and a half in diameter and weighing one half of a pound, flying horizontally, struck a tree branch and deflected straight down, breaking Lewis's collarbone, plunged through his shoulder, tearing into his right lung, and lodging under the skin of his back. Miraculously, Lewis did not die on the spot. His men removed him to a field hospital, where surgeon M. D. Benedict of the 75th New York Infantry sliced open Lewis's back and removed the projectile in an operation that caused "considerable primary hemorrhage and of course great prostration." The army evacuated Lewis to St. James's Hospital in New Orleans and later to a hospital in New York. Eventually, Lewis was released to his mother's house in Middletown, Connecticut, where a local physician treated him. Lewis suffered horribly from the wound, which would not heal. Doctors found that, when Lewis closed his nose and mouth, he could blow "air and jets of puss" from both his entrance and exit wounds. Doctors performed several surgeries to remove bone fragments. Somehow, Lewis recovered and returned to active duty in October 1864. He received a military pension in 1865 and, as of a March 1872 report, he was still alive, although no longer able to perform manual labor.[52]

The defeat of May 27 degraded Union morale. In the words of the Union engineer officer John Palfrey, "the result of the day was disastrous." Major Charles Plunkett told his father, "we had one of the most bloody fights on record yesterday, and were unsuccessful." William Park, serving on the *Essex*, believed that the navy did great work but that the Confederate garrison drove the Union army back with loss. Charles McGregor summarized May 27 as "a day of blood, . . . disaster and defeat." Massachusetts infantryman Henry Cross believed that "our men fought like heroes, but the place cannot be carried by assault." He wrote, "it angers us to see the rebel flag gloating so defiantly on their entrenchments." Thorpe Gould of the 165th New York Infantry praised the bravery of his comrades but lamented the losses that gained no ground. J. Harvey Brown told his wife that the thumb of his right hand was blown off in the battle and that, while he expected to recover, he prayed that God would never again let him see a day like May 27.[53]

Some Union soldiers lost faith in General Banks because of the failures of May 27. From a hospital bed in New Orleans, Captain Eli Griffin nursed the hole a Confederate bullet tore through his arm on May 27 and lamented "the terrible slaughter of Port Hudson." Griffin believed that "Banks made a mistake by trying to storm" Port Hudson and should have starved the Confederates out. In his diary entry for June 5, Lieutenant William Fowler described the failed May 27 attack as "outrageous" and claimed, "our officers declare that they will never go into another under______ ______ [*sic*]." It is unclear why Fowler did not mention Banks by name, even though, from the context, he was clearly referring to Banks. Earlier in his diary, Fowler referred to General Banks, but after March 13, he never again mentioned Banks by name. Perhaps Fowler refused to ever write the name Banks again after he apparently turned against the general on May 27. If Fowler was done with Banks, he had company. In a letter home a few days after the battle, James Peck wrote, "the men do not think much of Gen Banks" because of the defeat. Writing in 1894, David Hanaburgh recalled that the men lost confidence in themselves on May 27, and while they later restored their faith in themselves, they never again trusted Banks. According to staff officer Richard Irwin, the Union army began May 27 with high morale, but the men's faith in Banks "never quite returned" after the failed attacks of May 27.[54]

While many men lost faith in General Banks, some Union soldiers remained optimistic. William Smith wrote to his wife that he was sick of the critics in the newspapers. He believed that "Gen. Banks is doing well and if the papers will just hold on, they will have no cause to complain." Smith told his wife that the press "seems to think that unless and army moves as fast as they can write that they are doing nothing." Smith suggested, "if they have nothing better to do than complain, then had better enlist and in that way, they will do more good for their country than they will by finding fault with those that have the command." Smith looked to General Grant's advances against Vicksburg as proof that the overall Union strategy was working and would soon destroy the rebellion. Justus Gale wrote that he and his friends "are all well and in good spirits." Gale acknowledged that "Port Hudson is a verry strongly fortified place" and that the army suffered serious losses on May 27. However, he remained confident that Port Hudson would fall. He told his sister that the Union forces outnumbered the rebels by a huge margin, that they enjoyed the support of navy gunboats, and that Confederates were deserting rather than fight. He therefore concluded that Port Hudson would surrender "if we have to wait and starve them out." He admitted that the siege would be tough but concluded, "I think we can stand it as long as they can." Charles

Lord missed the attacks of May 27 because he was sick in a Baton Rouge hospital, but he wrote his wife, perhaps with a bit of winking bravado, "Port Hudson is a very strong place but it has got to fall when I go up there."[55]

Many Confederate defenders were jubilant. Howard Wright noted with apparent pride, "we had been tried at many points and everywhere we had driven back the foe." James Goble of the 1st Alabama Infantry claimed that the "1st Ala [*sic*] wins all the praise" because they "repulsed the enemy with great slaughter." Mississippian Walter Turner claimed that during a truce a Union officer told them that "their army is weakened" by the failed attack. According to Edward McMorries, the fighting on May 27 "taught us that a few men with a determination to stay could hold a fortified position against great odds."[56]

Confederate newspapers spread word of the victory and praised Port Hudson's garrison. The *Natchez Daily Courier* reported that the Federals broke and fled after the rebels inflicted thousands of casualties and sunk a Federal gunboat. The *Charleston Mercury* congratulated Port Hudson's garrison for the "glorious Confederate victory" and inaccurately claimed that "General Banks's entire staff was captured." In another inaccurate report, the *Montgomery Daily Mail* claimed that General Banks lost an arm during "the brilliant victory at Port Hudson." The *Fayetteville Semi Weekly Observer* in North Carolina reported that the Federals were defeated, suffered three thousand casualties, and that the "negroes" serving in the Union army were "massacred." The *Daily Dispatch* in Richmond predicted "the siege of Port Hudson will be raised."[57]

As the fighting died down, Confederate soldiers left their works to gather up Enfield rifles left behind by the dead, wounded, and retreating Federals. Throughout the rest of the siege, many Confederate infantrymen used a captured rifle for long-range work and kept a smoothbore musket nearby, loaded with an antipersonnel load of buck and ball, as a last-ditch weapon against Federals who got too close. Howard Wright claimed that Confederate soldiers also gathered Federal "canteens partly full of whiskey." Whiskey was a popular beverage with men from both armies, but it is possible that Wright exaggerated reports of captured whiskey as part of a common Confederate myth that Union soldiers were cowards who could only attack when drunk.[58]

The day after New York soldier James Peck retreated from Port Hudson without firing a shot in mid-March, he wrote home, "I have never been in any action as yet I feel as if I would like to see one any way." After participating in the battle of May 27, he felt very differently, writing, "I can say with truth that I never want to see such a sight again and I do not think I will forget it as long as I live." It was "not only dead men but dead horses and broken wagons and dismounted artilery, [*sic*] fallen trees all made up to make a scene of desolation." During the battle, he noted, "we do not fully realise [*sic*] the danger we are so much exposed to, at as it is all excitement. all we think of is to load and fire." While men were "gaining ground on the enemy we feel more confident and work with a will notwithstanding the grape and canister is mowing down our troops like grass." It was only after "the engagement is over and the Regiment is formed in lines again then you can see the difference." Peck reported, "our Regimental line was about 2/3 as long after the 27 of May as it was on the 26 then we could fully realise [*sic*] what we had been trough [*sic*] and have had to sacrifice." Peck told his parents, "I do not think thair [*sic*] is anything so horrible to look on as a battlefield," where "you see death in almost every form and shape." Death presented itself in bewildering varieties, with "some completely mangled up so as no one can tell who they are and others with legs and arms off some shot throug [*sic*] the head some through the bodies, in fact, shot in almost every way." Looking at the wounded might have been worse than viewing the dead because at least the dead were silent, unlike the wounded, who Peck heard "in thair [*sic*] agony whish [*sic*] was awfull [*sic*] to hear, especialy [*sic*] at night when all is still."[59]

Reports of the Native Guards

The performance of the African American Native Guards became a topic of debate almost as soon as the firing stopped. General Banks described the Native Guards as "heroic" men who proved that black men could be "excellent soldiers." Undermining his praise was his inaccurate claim that they made three charges. Other primary sources from both Union and Confederate witnesses confirm that the Native Guards made only a single charge. Northern newspapers, eager to praise the Union experiment with African American soldiers went even farther, claiming that the "Second Regiment of Louisiana Native Guard" left "600 corpses" at Port Hudson. However, the 2nd Native Guards regiment was not at Port Hudson, and the

Lieutenant John W. Ricker, Co. C, 11th Massachusetts Infantry Regiment and Co. A, 48th Massachusetts Infantry Regiment with amputated leg, which was lost at Port Hudson, May 27, 1863. Library of Congress.

1st and 3rd Native Guard regiments, which were at Port Hudson, suffered a total of 112 killed and wounded on May 27. Captain Henry Maglathlin of the 4th Massachusetts Infantry believed that the attacks of May 27 had been "a vast slaughter and little or nothing to compensate, except, perhaps, the proof" that the "colored troops" would fight "with the most determined valor." John Edmond of 161st New York Infantry told his sister that the Native Guards suffered horrifically in the fighting because the rebels gave them "special attention" and that the black men responded by "reciprocating with scalding vengeance." G. S. Buckley, writing for the

Boston Herald, claimed, "the negroes are reported by all parties to have fought well."[60] Buckley was incorrect. Not everyone believed the Native Guards had performed well.

Some Federals were unimpressed with the Native Guards. Union staff officer Wickham Hoffman claimed the Native Guards "turned white from fright" and described their attack as a "useless waste of life." In a bit of a backhanded compliment, Henry Cross of the 48th Massachusetts Infantry wrote home that the "negro troops" had proved they were "equal to any troops, and in many respects, in this climate superior to all." Cross believed that "private soldiers should think nothing, dread nothing, be machines, follow their leaders blindly and fearlessly." As a result, "negroes are the best, foreigners the next, and thinking, independent Yankees the poorest." However, Cross also believed that "Yankees make the by far the best officers." Cross wanted to become an officer and noted, "if I ever get a commission, I hope it will be in a nig. Reg. [*sic*]."[61]

Unsurprisingly, many Confederate soldiers were unimpressed with the Native Guards. John Kennedy, with the 1st Alabama, reported that he and his comrades had "repulsed with slaughter" the attack by the Native Guards and claimed that prisoners from the Native Guards told him that a white regiment behind them forced them to attack. Daniel Smith, also with the 1st Alabama, claimed that the "negroes turned and fled, without firing a shot." New York–born James Goble of the 1st Alabama Infantry believed the "many negroes" who "lie dead on the field of battle unburied" were "a stain on the north that can never be rubbed out." Daniel Smith heard gunfire coming from Federal lines as the Native Guards retreated and speculated that white Federals may have murdered retreating African American soldiers.[62] There is little reason to believe that the Native Guards were forced to attack or that their white comrades intentionally opened fire on them. However, statements by Confederate soldiers do provide insights into what Confederate soldiers thought about the performance of African American troops.

News of the Native Guards at Port Hudson quickly spread across both the Union and Confederacy. The *Natchez Courier* reported that the Native Guards "were massacred." The *Charleston Mercury* claimed that six hundred members of "one negro regiment" were killed and claimed further that Gardner "had given orders to take no negro soldiers prisoners." John Henning Woods, an Alabamian loyal to the Union who was imprisoned for fighting against the Confederacy, heard about the Native Guards at Port Hudson and argued that their courage was proof that slaves wanted and deserved freedom. He urged anyone who doubted the righteousness of the Union cause to "let the battles of Port Hudson tell it."[63]

Both Union and Confederate commentators had reasons to distort the combat record of African American soldiers into a story that supported their preconceived ideologies. As is often but not always the case with emotionally charged topics, the truth may lie somewhere in between extremes. The fact is that the Native Guards failed to achieve their objective, but this was a failure they shared with every other Union unit who attacked Port Hudson on May 27. In terms of combat effectiveness, the Native Guards were therefore little more or less effective than their white counterparts in the assaults of May 27, 1863. John Edmond of the 161st New York Infantry might have summed up the feelings of many soldiers when he told his sister that "none have fought better than the so-called damned niggers."[64]

General Henry Hallock noted the performance of African American troops in Louisiana when he reminded General Grant of the government's policy on using former slaves. He argued that slaves could be "instruments of good or evil" who were "used with much effect against us" by "the enemy" and that the Union must therefore "try to use them with the best possible effect against the rebels." Hallock primarily wanted to use former slaves as "laborers, teamsters, cooks" and other workers. Former slaves in Union army combat units would primarily serve as defensive troops, but Hallock believed that the work of African American servicemen in Louisiana indicated that they might be capable of serving in offensive operations as well. Hallock realized that "many of the officers of your command not only discourage negroes from coming under our protection, but by ill-treatment force them to return to their masters." Hallock reminded Grant that, "whatever may be the individual opinion of an officer," it was the "duty of everyone to cheerfully and honestly endeavor to carry out the measures so adopted." The war had changed. Hallock pointed out that "there is now no possible hope of reconciliation with the rebels." The "north must conquer the slave oligarchy or become slaves themselves."[65] Not every Union officer "cheerfully" accepted former slaves into the army's ranks, but after the battle of May 27, African American soldiers became an increasingly vital component of the Union forces at Port Hudson and across the nation.

— 8 —

Miserable in the Extreme

THE SIEGE OF MAY 28–JUNE 13

> Hot, hotter, hottest 110 in the shade. Landed at 5 AM at Springfield Landing. Infernal heat this torrid sun, the falling out of the men by scores, the suffocating blinding dust, the unquenchable thirst, the nasty water, the lurking guerillas, all conspire together to render our situation miserable in the extreme.[1]
>
> —JAMES DARGAN, 4th Massachusetts Infantry

> Men coming in sick every hour. Gun boats shelling. Constant talk of reinforcements sharpshooters shooting rebels daily they shoot all day and all night tis very dangerous to go from the breast works. Mulatto woman got her breast and arm shot off by the bursting of a shell. Shell bursting in air flying over our house.[2]
>
> —JAMES GOBLE, 1st Alabama Infantry

Pratt's Bombardment

Jubilant rebels did not allow the repulsed Federals to withdraw in peace on May 27. Men in gray conspired to inflict pain on their retreating adversaries. General Gardner ordered Lieutenant Pratt of the 1st Alabama regiment to take command of a 30-pounder Parrott rifle manned by members of the 1st Alabama Infantry and a rifled 24-pounder cannon worked by de Gournay's Louisianans, move to the riverbank, and open fire on the Union fleet at daylight on May 28. The gunners moved their cannons more slowly than expected over roads torn up by the Federal artillery bombardment of May 27.[3]

At 6:00 a.m. Pratt's men opened fired on the *Essex*, a mile away from their position. Union sailors quickly returned fire. Alabamian Daniel Smith later recalled that a Union shell struck a canteen hanging near the

Confederate Parrot rifle and knocked gunner Joe Tunnell to the ground. At first Smith worried that the shell had killed Tunnell, but Tunnell stood up a moment later, brushing the dirt off his face and joking, "well, boys they liked to have got me." Although in good spirts and suffering from only a minor wound, Tunnell was hurt too seriously to continue his work for the day. Lieutenant Pratt took Tunnell's place at the 30-pounder, serving as both gunner and battery commander. A subsequent shell wounded an artilleryman Smith did not name. Minutes later, another Federal shell struck the ground near the battery. This one drove shrapnel into Pratt's hand and hip as the force of the blast threw him to the ground. Pratt refused to leave his post and fought on despite his wound. A shot from the rebel 30-pounder Parrot entered a porthole on the *Essex*. In response, the *Essex*'s crew closed her ports and withdrew out of range without firing another shot that day. The rebels turned their attention to the *Genesee*, striking and partially disabling her with a series of well-placed shots. After firing ninety-nine shells from their two cannons and damaging two Federal warships, the wounded Pratt ordered his gunners to cease fire.[4]

The May 28 Truce

While Pratt's gunners moved into position against the Federal fleet, General Banks sent a message to Gardner at 6:00 a.m. on May 28 requesting a truce so that both armies could remove their dead and wounded. Gardner refused to grant a truce unless Banks would withdraw all his soldiers to at least eight hundred yards away from Confederate positions and order the Federal fleet to sail out of range of the garrison. Banks refused and a series of twelve letters eventually passed between Banks and Gardner. At 3:30 p.m. Gardner gave up his demand for an eight-hundred-yard buffer zone and agreed to a truce that would last until 7:00 p.m. Gardner later accused the Federals of "erecting a battery within easy range of my left" during the truce, which he considered a violation of the truce. Banks fired back that the Confederates were the ones violating the terms of the truce by capturing wounded Federals stuck between the lines rather than returning them to the Union army.[5]

Walter Turner of the 39th Mississippi Infantry claimed in his diary that, while the Union troops "buried all their white men," they "left their negroes to melt in the sun." Turner believed that this callous indifference "shows how much they care for the poor ignorant creatures." He loathed the Federals who "let the bodies of the poor creatures lie and melt in their own blood and to be made prey of both birds and beasts."[6]

While some soldiers cared for the wounded or buried the dead, others met with the men they had been trying to kill hours before. Edward Russell later recalled that, during this truce, "the better part of our natures asserted itself" as Federals and rebels greeted each other warmly, trading coffee for tobacco and exchanging little souvenirs. When the truce was almost over, "we parted as friends, cautioning each other to lie low and so escape each other's bullets." Russell loathed that "men should take each other's lives in cold blood." According to Corporal David Hanaburgh, the truce damaged Union morale worse than the battle. During a battle, the smoke, noise, and the excitement of action obscured the horrors and distracted men from contemplating it. When the Federals visited the battlefield during the truce, "for the first time to the men of our regiment were unfolded the horrors of a battlefield." They saw "bodies torn beyond recognition by the bursting shell," "smitten by musket balls," and "human faces blackening in the hot summer's sun." Some bodies were unrecognizable, others were clearly strangers, but many of the bodies belonged to childhood friends and family members. Writing thirty-one years later, Hanaburgh still vividly remembered the horrific work of "the death angel" he saw on May 28.[7]

During the truce, William Deforest and the 12th Connecticut found a spot in a broad gully under the shade of beech and ash trees. Members of the 8th Vermont and 91st New York infantry regiments lounged along with the men from Connecticut. After a brief rest, Deforest climbed the knoll that protected the Federals from the rebels and peaked over the edge. He saw "a low earthwork" occupied by "sallow, darkly sunburnt men" who wore "dirty reddish homespun, and broad-brimmed wool hats." The Confederates stared back "in grim silence." Deforest looked beyond the Confederate line in front of him and to the left, where "rose the bluff of Port Hudson, crowned with yellow earthworks, dirty tents, ragged shanties, and a forest."[8]

At 7:00 p.m. a Confederate 8-inch Parrot cannon that the Federals nicknamed the Lady Davis fired a shell, declaring an end to the truce. Union infantry officer George Smith watched as the shell burst, throwing dirt and rocks into the air and knocking infantryman Pat Murphy to the ground. Murphy jumped up, yelling, "be jobbers, an 'twas the strongest wind I ever filt [*sic*]."[9]

At 8:00 p.m. the Federals launched "a furious attack" on the Confederate left, probably in hopes that the rebels would not be ready to fight so soon after the conclusion of the truce. The men in blue were wrong. The rebels were prepared, and once again Confederate defenders stood their ground and repulsed another attack. As Union soldiers returned to their lines, "rain fell in torrents," drenching the blue and the gray as both armies settled down for a siege.[10]

Federal Reinforcements

In a May 28 report to General Grant, Banks claimed that his army was successful in several skirmishes against the Confederates on the path to Port Hudson because "outside of his intrenchments he has no power." Banks believed that the May 27 assault failed because the Confederate defenses "are more formidable than have been represented, and his force stronger." According to Banks, the Confederate positions were "impregnable," surrounded by "ravines, woods, valleys, and bayous of the most intricate and labyrinthic character, that make the works themselves almost inaccessible." He lamented, "it takes time even to understand the geography of the position." The defenders "fight with determination" and defeated the Union soldiers, who did "all that could be expected."[11]

The successful Confederate defense of Port Hudson on May 27 and May 28 convinced Banks that he could not capture Port Hudson by a direct attack, so he prepared for a siege. Banks set up a new headquarters to the rear of the center of the Federal position on the Plains Store Road. Banks ordered General Richard Arnold, his chief of artillery, to bring additional heavy artillery and entrenching tools to Port Hudson. Arnold eventually brought forty siege cannons to Port Hudson, including six 8-inch seacoast howitzers on siege carriages, eight 24-pounder cannons, seven 30-pounder Parrott rifled cannons, four 6-inch rifled cannons, four 8-inch mortars, three 10-inch mortars, and four 13-inch mortars. Federal sailors brought four 9-inch Dahlgren cannons ashore and operated them with a mixed team of gunners from the *Richmond* and the *Essex*. The Federals also assembled a force of sixty lighter cannons, including six 6-pounder Sawyer rifles, two 10-pounder Parrott rifles, twelve 20-pounder rifles,

General Andrews's headquarters at Port Hudson.
From James Ewer, *The Third Massachusetts Cavalry in the War.*

twenty-six 12-pounder smoothbore Napoleons, two 12-pounder howitzers, and twelve 3-inch rifles. Banks ordered "all troops that can be spared" from posts across the region to join him at Port Hudson. On June 3 General Banks asked Grant to send ten thousand men to Port Hudson. Grant did not send reinforcements, but troops from across the Deep South did join Banks's forces near Port Hudson. On May 31 Lawrence Van Alstyne recorded in his diary that he saw a pair of "a new style of fighting machine" consisting of "twenty-four rifle barrels, all made to be loaded and fired by one operation of a lever." He joked, "goodbye Johnnies when they get at you." Although he did not name them, the weapons were Billingshurst Requa Batteries, a failed precursor to the modern machine gun. Eight regiments, including the 3rd Massachusetts Cavalry as well as the 114th New York, 4th Massachusetts, 16th New Hampshire, 22nd Maine, 90th New York, 52nd Massachusetts, and 41st Massachusetts infantry regiments, arrived from posts on the Bayou Teche and the Atchafalaya River. The 28th Connecticut Infantry came from Pensacola, Florida.[12]

It was simple for Banks to demand reinforcements but getting to Port Hudson was easier said than done. Joshua Hawkes of the 52nd Massachusetts Infantry wrote home that "the whole reg't [*sic*] is worn down and

Section of Requa Battery, Morris Island, South Carolina, 1863.
From *The history of the Thirty-Ninth Regiment Illinois Volunteer Veteran Infantry, (Yates Phalanx) in the war of the rebellion, 1861–1865* (1889), after p. 362.

unfit for service." Hawkes believed that sending the half-dead regiment to Port Hudson was proof that Banks was desperate. The regiment began the march toward Port Hudson with 650 men, but only 431 reached the objective. The rest broke down with exhaustion, heat stroke, and illness on the road, so the surgeons ordered them to pause for rest. Erastus Gregory and the rest of the 114th New York Infantry joined the besieging army on May 31. He wrote his brother that the area was alive with activity as both Union and Confederate armies threw up defensive works and traded small arms and artillery fire. Gregory believed that "the men are fighting with a will on both sides," but he singled out the Confederates for special praise, writing that the defenders "are fighting like tigers."[13]

James Dargan and the 4th Massachusetts Infantry arrived at Springfield Landing, a few miles south of Port Hudson, on June 1 and prepared to march north. He described the day as "hot, hotter, hottest," with a temperature of 110 degrees in the shade. As the regiment marched north, men cursed "the infernal heat this torrid sun, the falling out of the men by scores, the suffocating blinding dust, the unquenchable thirst, the nasty water, the lurking guerillas, all conspire together to render our situation miserable in the extreme." Many men fell by the roadside, suffering from heatstroke. For some reason Dargan used the French phrase "coup de soliel [*sic*]" ," with each word underlined, to describe what is often called sunburn but that literally translates from French as "struck of the sun." After being "struck of the sun," Dargan finally found a moment of relief in the shade of a tree and took a drink from "the first well that I ever saw in Louisiana." When Dargan finally arrived near Port Hudson, he was one of only sixteen men from his company who had managed to keep up. As reinforcements moved toward Port Hudson, they saw the "legless, armless, eyeless, toothless, and in face almost headless" men who suffered "slaughter at Port Hudson" leaving Port Hudson on their way to rear-echelon hospitals. Many men recoiled in horror from the sight of corpses and didn't "like the notion of us going up to Port Hudson."[14]

To keep the ranks filled with healthy men, the Union constantly cycled sick and wounded between the front lines and the hospitals of Baton Rouge and New Orleans. Charles Lord missed the attacks of May 27 because he was sick in a Baton Rouge hospital. He wrote that Baton Rouge was covered with tents where "the sick ones stay" and "as fast as they get abel [*sic*] they go up on a steamer and as fast as the men get wounded or sick they are set [*sic*] back." Lord wanted his freshly recovered friend to wait for him so that the two men could travel to the front together, but the army sent men to Port Hudson as quickly as the doctors declared them fit for duty, without any interest in the men's personal preferences, and Lord remained in the hospital without his friend.[15]

The Construction of Federal Siege Lines

Banks ordered his growing army to build fortifications. According to infantryman William Stevens, Banks had finally realized that "it is not practical to take the place by assault" and "spades are trumps." The Union navy enjoyed control of the Mississippi River, so the army focused on the land approaches to Port Hudson. The Federal army's lines roughly paralleled the Confederate positions. The Federals rested their northern flank on the banks of the Mississippi River, a little south of Bayou Sara and just west of Thompsons Creek. The Federal lines then looped around the Confederate positions in a concave arc that curved east and then south, straddling Foster's Creek, Big Sandy Creek, and the Clinton Railroad. The

Federal south flank rested against the Mississippi River across from Profit Island. Federal fortifications began with improvised rifle pits but quickly expanded into a network of trenches, rifle pits, protected batteries, bunkers, and earthen forts. The Union army also built several detached fortifications, most notably at the riverboat landing.[16]

Union infantrymen built their own fortifications. George Smith and the 1st Louisiana Union Infantry spent March 28 constructing "very nice breastworks," which were deep enough to allow men to fire while standing up. This was particularly helpful because the Louisianans, like most Civil War soldiers, used muzzle-loading weapons that were difficult to load while sitting or reclining. William Tiemann of the 159th New York Infantry reported that his regiment's trenches were topped with head logs, a double line of logs with a gap between them just large enough to insert the muzzle of a rifle and fire without exposing their heads. According to engineer officer John Palfrey, the Union trenches were "very substantial" positions that were all at least ten feet wide at the bottom and at least eight feet deep. After digging trenches for their own protection, Union soldiers began pushing forward zigzagging trenches toward the Confederate lines.[17]

Former slaves also constructed Union fortifications at Port Hudson. General Daniel Ullmann arrived near Port Hudson with official authorization and all the officers needed to form eighteen regiments of African American enlisted men. The plan was to form all black units into "a distinct command" under the name "Corps d'Afrique." By the end of May, Ullmann had enrolled roughly 1,400 troops into five regiments. The soldiers were unarmed and were put to work improving Union fortifications. The Federals also recruited a separate regiment of black men titled the 1st Louisiana Engineers, which focused exclusively on building and repairing. Charles Prosper Fauconnet, a French diplomat in New Orleans, informed the French government that Ullmann's recruitment of freed slaves from plantations contradicted the Union's official policy, endorsed by Banks, of not removing former slaves under contract to work on plantations. Confusion led to the arrest of Ullmann's recruiting officers by other Union officers, leading to a crisis in which it was unclear who was in charge and which rules applied.[18]

Massachusetts infantryman Henry Cross wrote home that "Banks is trying to sit on two stools," neither fully embracing nor fully rejecting emancipation. Like many northerners, Cross saw black men as valuable, although racially inferior, allies in the war. He believed that "the black man needs open encouragement and invitation which he don't get." In another letter, Cross told his family, "we have a negro regiment" camped nearby and "they do almost all the work on the fortifications."[19]

Private Henry Johns wrote home that the "stalwart negroes," who he described as "great, lusty, fellows who put our muscles to shame," did most of the hard labor required to build fortifications. Johns told his family back home, "never fear that soldiers will be objecting to negro enlistments" because after "one hour's digging in Louisiana clay under a Louisiana sun, we are forever pledged to do all we can filled up our ranks with the despised and long neglected race."[20]

Former slaves also helped the Union army as civilian workers. Many officers enjoyed the services of former slaves. Some black workers were on the government payroll, and others were paid directly by the officers they served. Lieutenant Colonel Willoughby Babcock of the 75th New York Infantry hired a young former slave named Daniel as a "body servant" when Babcock was stationed at Pensacola, Florida. Babcock brought Daniel to Louisiana with him and frequently mentioned "my faithful Daniel" in his letters. Willoughby's letters indicate that Daniel spent most of his time cleaning and cooking for Willoughby.[21]

The Improvement of Confederate Defenses

Like their Union counterparts, the rebels improved their defenses after the attacks of May 27. General Gardner divided the Port Hudson lines into three zones and assigned an engineer officer to supervise work on fortifications in each area. Lieutenant Stork took charge of the river batteries and the Confederate right flank. Lieutenant James Freret supervised work on the defenses in the Confederate center. Captain Fred Dabney, Port Hudson's chief engineer officer, focused his attention on the Confederate left flank while also supervising Freret and Stork. The Confederate engineers supervised the construction of loopholes at the top of the fortifications. In some places the men build loopholes with sandbags and in others with loose dirt. The small holes provided some protection for

North side views from Port Hudson, showing Confederate artillery after the surrender of Port Hudson in July of 1863. Library of Congress.

the Confederate infantry, but "bullets would frequently come through these little openings, ending the earthly career of many a brave fellow." Colonel Johnson ordered his men to construct an additional line of rifle pits behind and slightly above the main defenses at Fort Desperate. His plan was to keep sixty men in the secondary position where they could fire over the heads of their comrades at any Union attackers. Walter Turner of the 39th Mississippi Infantry wrote in his diary on June 2 that, when his regiment first arrived in Port Hudson, "we had nothing but rifle pits," but after working hard to improve their positions, he believed that "we are now very well fortified." To protect themselves from Union artillery fire, Joseph Bailey and the 16th Arkansas Infantry dug holes at right angles within their trenches, which were about four feet deep and six to thirty feet long. The men took turns keeping watch and whenever a sentry saw the fire of a Union cannon, he would yell "lie down" and everyman would dive into a hole. Soon, "our clothing took on the color of the yellow reddish clay of the ditches."[22] There is little evidence that the Confederates ever intentionally produced camouflage uniforms, but Federal observers often noted that it was almost impossible to see the rebels, who blended in with the ground. Most Confederate uniforms were produced in shades of gray, brown, and butternut. When coated with the local dirt, such uniforms might have been as effective at concealing their wearers as intentional camouflage.

Heat and Sickness at Port Hudson

The heat was intense, particularly for northern men unaccustomed to a Louisiana spring. On May 31 Irish-born Charles Kennedy of the 156th New York Infantry wrote home to his wife that "the weather is awfully hot—perfectly melting and we suffer a good deal." Perhaps because of the heat, Kennedy wrote, "we nearly have all got a kind of ground itch which keeps us scratching nearly all our time." It was so bad that "it is scratch when you eat, scratch when you drill, scratch everywhere and all the time." Men were unable to sleep, constantly waking in the middle of the night only to discover "half the camp engaged in the same pleasant occupation" of scratching. Lieutenant Solon Perkins of the 3rd Massachusetts Cavalry told his family, "we are made nearly crazy at times by the prickly heat, it is torture." Appleton Sturgis, an ordnance officer serving on General Paine's staff, wrote that, on a single sortie into the countryside in pursuit of Confederate guerillas, "we lost 200 men by sunstroke." New York infantryman Orton Clark complained about the heat and the water, which "was warm, unpalatable, being obtained from a swamp." To protect themselves from the sun, members of the 49th Massachusetts Infantry began wearing straw hats, until the broad brimmed headwear attracted Confederate sharpshooter fire for some unknown reason and the soldiers returned to their dark blue issued caps.[23]

Joshua Hawkes of the 52nd Massachusetts Infantry wrote home that some men wore a "head covering" but that most men had abandoned the havelocks that were initially common in the new regiments. To fight the heat, "usually I have green leaves in my cap when on the march, and I wet my head often." Hawkes complained, "the caps are not fit for this climate and season" because they were "small" and "do not protect the face at all." During the day, the heat shone down into the Union trenches, which provided protection from Confederate gunfire but none from the sun's heat. Some men hung blankets over their trenches to provide shade, but the blankets that blocked the sun also limited the flow of air, and most men decided that the shade was not worth the lack of ventilation. During the night the air cooled somewhat, providing men with a welcome relief.[24]

Confederate soldiers built similar sunshades. According to Edward McMorries, the sun beat down relentlessly, so men began building "shebangs" [*sic*], which he described as three-foot-high sunshades made of blankets held in place by ropes and stakes. The men kept the shelters low because the Federals often shot anyone who stood up. McMorries lamented the death of Newton Soles, a sixteen-year-old soldier "inclined to be a little thoughtless," who was killed by a Union bullet when Soles failed to keep his head down while constructing a sun shade. Joseph Bailey reported that not long after the siege began, the Federal artillery fire shredded every blanket or tent they pitched as sunshades, leaving the men with no protection from the relentless sun.[25]

The heat made men sick and lowered their morale. Shortly before the May 27 attack, Louis Boyd on the gunboat *Albatross* had expressed optimism, convinced that victory was only a few days away, but his May 31 letter revealed that his mood had changed. He missed his wife and wanted to hold his eight-month-old son, who he had never seen but thought about constantly. Like many men, Boyd was sick, telling his wife, "I have been unwell for the last week." Boyd clearly felt he had suffered enough. He explained, "if ever I wanted to get out of any place in my life it is this southern country." Several days later, Boyd scolded his wife for writing that she would rather be dead than go on living alone. He reminded her that she was a mother and promised to come home soon.[26]

Miserable men sought comfort wherever they could find it. In his diary, Lieutenant William Fowler of the 173rd New York Infantry described alcohol as "the bane of our regiment." He believed that "if that could be banished from officers and soldiers, it would be a priceless blessing." While condemning their drinking, Fowler also noted that life in the Union camps was hard. The "water is very poor," the men had "no covering whatever," and the "effluvia from half-buried horses and offal is sickening." As a result, "many a poor fellow is carried off every day on a stretcher."[27]

As the Federals settled into a siege, some men came to grips with their own mortality. On May 31 Solon Perkins listed the friends and comrades who had died in the campaign and told his family, "I had a strong feeling once, that I should fall in this campaign." Despite his premonition of death, "I think I may come out alive." Private George Waite wrote a friend back home on the eve of a planned attack in early June, "this letter will not come home to you until after this fight is over, but I write because I may not come back." Justus Gale used the phrases "if we should get home" and "if I am so lucky as to live through this war" in an otherwise upbeat letter to his sister.[28]

Cavalry Skirmishes

While the infantry and artillery focused on siegecraft, the Union and Confederate cavalry remained on the move. Lieutenant Solon Perkins was officially assigned to the 3rd Massachusetts Cavalry, but the army gave him a detached company and ordered him to scout behind Confederate lines. Perkins had learned to speak French and Spanish during his prewar career with New England mercantile firms in Argentina and Chile, only returning to the United States after Chilean officials ordered his removal from their country, possibly because Perkins was spying for the United States government. Perkins fought so many small engagements in Louisiana that he told his parents and siblings, "I cannot recount to you the many skirmishes we have had." In one of the small battles, he wrote, "I was wounded in the right hand rather severely," and in another he had a horse shot out from under him. Despite his wound, he put his arm in a sling and remained on duty. In another engagement, he suffered a minor wound to his knee and had two more horses shot out from under him but remained on active duty with his regiment. Perkins told his family, "I do not seek death, but I do sometimes think that the brave soldier who dies on the battlefield is far better off than he who lives years in civil life." Perkins told his family in Massachusetts back at home, "you people at home know nothing of what our brave soldiers are suffering, that you may rest quietly at home free from Confederate attack." He felt that he had "grown much older than when you last saw me" because "cavalry work is hot, quick as a flash." He had "not slept inside of a tent in six weeks" and rested only "in the heat, rain, and mud, on the ground." Perkins and his troopers lived exclusively on hard bread and a little coffee. He longed for "butter, soft bread, pickles, and canned meats."[29]

On May 29 Colonel John Logan, commanding the Confederate cavalry just outside Port Hudson, informed General Joseph Johnston that he had been unable to contact Port Hudson since May 24 and concluded that the garrison was completely cut off from the rest of the Confederacy. Logan believed that, if the defenders of Port Hudson tried to escape, they would suffer "very great loss" at the hands of the much larger Union army surrounding them. Logan assured Johnston that he remained outside Port Hudson, doing everything he could to distract the Federals from Port Hudson by raiding Union flanks and disrupting their supply lines. Logan believed that, if Johnston could send eight thousand troops to attack the Federals near Port Hudson, the Union army would be forced to retreat.[30]

Some of Port Hudson's defenders hoped that a relief army would come to save them, but a relief expedition became less likely with each passing day. Thomas Alexander of the 1st Tennessee Heavy Artillery wrote in his diary on May 30 that he "took a musket and went to the Biffle [*sic*] Pitts [*sic*]." This suggests that Confederate officers may have been reassigning artillerymen to the trenches to reinforce the thinning infantry ranks. According to James Goble, men who slipped out of Port Hudson to bring reinforcements never returned. Confederates who remained in Port Hudson assumed that anyone who tried to slip away suffered death, capture, or joined the hated foe. Unable to obtain reinforcements, General Gardner ordered men to spread out into skirmish formations within Port Hudson's defenses. If the Federals attacked a section of the line, the men would immediately rush to the sound of the guns and reinforce the threatened sector without waiting for orders. New York–born Goble wrote in his diary, "with the stern, determined, courage southern men only are capable of the enemy can be repulsed with great slaughter."[31]

Battle of Clinton, Louisiana, on June 3

While the artillery and infantry focused on the siege, the cavalry of both armies fought for control of the countryside. Confederate cavalry under Colonel John Logan harassed Union supply routes. General Banks realized that Logan's cavalry posed a threat to his operations and ordered Colonel Benjamin Grierson to find and destroy Confederate cavalrymen in the region. On June 3 Grierson received word that Logan's Confederate cavalry was camped near Clinton, Louisiana, roughly twenty-five miles northeast of Port Hudson. In response, Grierson led 1,200 Union cavalry and artillerymen, toward Clinton. Alphonso Curl, serving as a 1st Lieutenant with the consolidated 11th and 17th Arkansas Mounted Infantry, heard "boots and saddles" at 3:00 p.m. The men instantly realized that Federals were attacking. Curl and his comrades rushed from their camps north of Clinton toward the western edge of town.[32]

Confederate forces ambushed the Federals as the men in blue crossed the Comite River, a mile west of Clinton. Despite the ambush, the Federals pushed across a bridge spanning the Comite. Grierson ordered a section of 2-pounder cannons and a section of Nims's Battery to provide fire support. The 7th Illinois Cavalry ran out of ammunition for their Smith carbines and were forced to withdraw.[33] The Confederates took advantage of the withdrawal to attempt a double flanking maneuver, which badly damaged the Union forces. Grierson ordered his artillery to fire canister into the attacking men in gray and buy time for his troopers to withdraw. The Confederates in the center surged forward, while their comrades on the flanks tried to encircle the Federals. Rebels tried to capture the Union artillery, but Union gunners withdrew their cannons one step ahead of the attackers. The Confederate lines briefly became tangled as they moved forward, and the Confederate forces stopped to reorganize before pushing the Federals back once again.[34]

Grierson ordered his men to retreat toward the Union army besieging Port Hudson. Confederates pursued the retreating troopers. Grierson's command lost eight killed, twenty-eight wounded, and fifteen men missing during the fight at Clinton. The day's most notable casualty might have been Lieutenant Solon Perkins, who was shot in the heat of the battle and died soon after. According to James Ewer, a bugler with the 3rd Massachusetts Cavalry, Perkins's death demoralized the men like Ewer who had grown to admire Perkins's "skill and daring" in numerous previous skirmishes. The War Department posthumously promoted Perkins to major, in recognition of his "gallant and meritorious service at the battle of Clinton, Louisiana."[35]

The Confederates won the Battle of Clinton, but the sources disagree on the details. Colonel Logan informed General Joseph Johnston that his forces defeated the Federals at Clinton. Logan reported that his command suffered twenty casualties and repulsed an enemy force of two thousand men after a three-hour battle. Logan estimated that the Union lost twenty killed, fifty wounded, and reported that his men captured forty Union prisoners. While the Confederate cavalrymen initially hoped that the battle would open a path to Port Hudson, the Union army blocked the road to Port Hudson. Grierson's report provided a slightly different account. He acknowledged his command was forced to withdraw but he claimed that his command lost only eight killed, twenty-eight wounded, and fifteen missing. He believed that the Confederates suffered twenty or thirty killed, more than sixty wounded, and that the Union captured twenty Confederate prisoners. Arkansas trooper Alphonso Curl described the encounter as "one of those small, red-hot engagements, something more than a skirmish, but not of sufficient importance to be called a battle, of which there were thousands during the war."[36]

The Siege Continued

According to Captain William Deforest, "if you want to know how a hero feels in the trenches get behind a tree not quite big enough to cover you and let two or three persons throw stones at you." He explained that "like everything else in the way of fighting it is frankly uncomfortable and nothing makes ones put up with it but a sense of right and duty and honor." He pointed out that his description was "not the poetical view of battle" written by men he mocked for running "like an assistant company cook" at the sounds of gunfire. Instead of listening to his more romantic rivals, Deforest urged people to "take the word of one who has fought often enough to know the truth, and respectably well enough to dare tell it."[37]

Henry Rufus Gardner wrote home that the Confederates "have a rifled piece which moves on a track and which they move as soon as we get their range." The Union artillerymen were unable to silence the elusive rebel gun, and "the boys are beginning to be impatient for a decision of this question." Gardner also complained "out loss in officers has been large." He blamed the officers for being "too anxious to exhibit their gold lace," which presented "a fair target for the enemy's sharp-shooters."[38]

George Hughes Hepworth claimed that a particular Confederate sharpshooter tormented Federals by climbing forty feet up into a cypress tree, covering himself in moss, and firing at them with "a double-barreled shotgun of English make" that fired bullets "double the size of those made for the Enfield rifle." Hepworth claimed that the sharpshooter "disabled men standing more than three quarters of a mile off." Hepworth's claim must be treated with skepticism because shotguns are almost never accurate beyond a hundred yards, and even the most accurate rifles of the Civil War era could barely, if ever, hit targets at three quarters of a mile.[39] However, Hepworth's account, written during the war, does provide insights into how men in the Union lines around Port Hudson viewed the dangers they faced and how they discussed those dangers.

George Thomson of the 38th Massachusetts Infantry wrote home that a Confederate sharpshooter had killed Lieutenant Colonel Rodman with a single shot to the chest, which killed him instantly. Thomson seemed to struggle with his words to explain the "very severe loss" he felt. Thomson told his mother that Rodman was "the most perfect gentlemen I ever saw" and underlined the word gentlemen, perhaps to emphasize it. Thompson explained that the regiment had "come together more like a band of brothers than anything else and we all looked to Col. Rodman as we would an elder brother."[40]

Erastus Gregory of the 114th New York Infantry wrote home that the Confederate sharpshooters and gunners inflicted few casualties on his regiment but acknowledged that the siege was dangerous. He wrote that, when an unexpected boom from the artillery startled a member of his company, the man's foot slipped, and he fell "so his gun went off the ball passed through his foot." The New Yorkers took their unnamed comrade to the field hospital. Surgeons amputated the unnamed man's foot in hopes of saving his life. During the operation, "he sudenly [*sic*] passed into eternity."[41]

William Tiemann and the rest of the 159th New York Infantry occupied trenches within two hundred yards of the Confederate lines. A crew from the 1st Indiana Battery operated artillery just behind the 159th New York Infantry's trenches. When the New Yorkers were unable to silence a Confederate sharpshooter perched high in a tree behind the Confederate lines, the Indiana gunners fired a single shell that ripped up the tree by the roots and ended the sniper's reign of terror. At night, Tiemann and his comrades lay in their trench watching "the bombs as they flew through the air like revolving stars," and the Confederate artillery responded with shells that arced in opposing trajectories toward the Federal lines. When the fuses of Confederate shells sailed toward the New Yorkers, the men dove for cover. Every artillery projectile "made a horrible sound" but "nothing compared from the unearthly shriek caused by the bars of railroad iron" that the rebels occasionally fired from what was rumored to be a heavy cannon mounted on a railroad car and constantly moved.[42]

The Union cut off Port Hudson's garrison from outside supplies, so the men in gray conserved what they had while trying to capture supplies from their adversaries. The defenders of Port Hudson benefitted from a large shipment of gunpowder, which was enroute to Confederates west of the Mississippi when the siege began. Unable to ship the gunpowder across the river, which was now blockaded by Federal gunboats, and in desperate need of supplies, Port Hudson's defenders kept the gunpowder for themselves. While the gunpowder was helpful, it did not come with projectiles, and the garrison quickly ran short of anything to shoot with the gunpowder. Rebels became scavengers, picking up anything the Federals fired into Port Hudson, from bullets to unexploded shells, and firing them back at their original owners. On the Confederate right, south of Port Hudson, the Federal artillery set up an 8-inch howitzer to launch enfilading rounds into the rebel lines. According to Alabamian Daniel Smith, the howitzer caused "amusement as well as annoyance" among the rebels, who nicknamed the cannon "Bounding Bet" because of the odd trajectory that caused shells to skip and bounce into Confederate lines. Whenever the men saw a puff of smoke that indicated Bounding Bet had fired, they dove for cover. When a shell failed to explode, adventurous rebels opened it up to discover that it contained "480 copper balls of less than half an inch in diameter."[43]

Scavenging may have helped alleviate but did not fully relieve the Confederate ammunition shortage. Aware of the serious shortages, Confederate officers ordered most of their men to avoid firing, unless they were directly attacked. Officers selected a few of the best marksmen from each unit and gave them permission to fire at their discretion. The Confederate artillery could not fire a gun without drawing the counterbattery fire of a dozen Union cannons. Daniel Smith later recalled that a cannon he helped crew was repeatedly put out of action by Union artillery fire that cut the cannon's wooden wheels out from under it. After several days of horrific shelling, the rebels withdrew their cannons from the outer line of Port Hudson's defenses and brought them up only when the Federals charged the lines.[44] The Confederates may have limited their artillery fire to conserve their precious ammunition as well.

Unlike the Federals, who only had to contend with batteries on land, the rebels suffered at the hands of artillery based on the land and the water. On June 6 at 2:30 p.m., General Banks signaled Admiral Farragut that a bombardment by Farragut's mortar boats the night before had "seriously inconvenienced the enemy." Banks reported that the navy's fire had killed cattle, wounded Confederate soldiers, and rendered a Confederate camp unlivable. The terse Farragut responded at 4:00 p.m., "I am glad to know I hurt him." This brief exchange, preserved in the official records, is just one of many examples of how the Union army and navy worked together at Port Hudson, coordinating their fire from ship and shore to bombard Port Hudson from multiple reinforcing angles, as each service sought to destroy anything out of sight or reach of their comrades. Alabama infantryman James Goble noted that the Union army and navy fired in overlapping arcs from multiple directions and suggested, "they are in great danger of killing their own men."[45]

During this early phase of the siege, Union soldiers enjoyed luxuries unimaginable to their adversaries. William Stevens reported that he and his comrades lived off ample supplies of hardtack. When men became tired of the monotonous, although filling, rations, they purchased "gingerbread of the sutler" and shared the treat with "talk of Christmas cheer." He also reported that every soldier carried coffee in his haversack and that, when the men had nothing else to do, they made coffee. Stevens called coffee "the cup that cheers, but not does not inebriate." Coffee, more than bread or water, was "the staff of life" for Union soldiers.[46]

Luxuries were nearly universal in the Union army's camps, but men believed that the danger was not always shared fairly. According to Private Henry Johns of the 49th Massachusetts Infantry, General Banks made a distinction between the units that enlisted for nine months and the three-year units like the 49th Massachusetts. Johns claimed that "the best of the food and the heaviest of the work go to the nine months' men" because the army wanted to "get what you can out of the nine-monthlings and save the three years' troops for subsequent labors." Members of the 50th Massachusetts Infantry carried smoothbore muskets, which were effective at short range but, unlike the rifles carried by many other regiments, were unable to hit long-range targets. William Stevens recalled that, when the regiment formed, the men demanded, "give us rifles or give us corn brooms," but the men decided to "thank their stars" for the old-fashioned weaponry at Port Hudson. According to Stevens, regiments armed with rifles occupied trenches and picket posts within the danger zone of Confederate sharpshooters, but the 50th Massachusetts, with their more antiquated weaponry, enjoyed a more leisurely position guarding the artillery, camped in the woods out of range of most Confederates.[47]

Union sailors continued to bombard on Port Hudson's batteries, regardless of their enlistment status. Confederate gunners replied with just enough shells to demonstrate their defiance. Some Union sailors became indifferent to the danger, drinking coffee and eating meals on their boats' open decks while Confederate shells passed overhead and only diving for cover when shells nearly hit them. William Park, on the *Essex,* wrote in his diary that the Union sailors' indifference to Confederate gunfire was "laughable." He thought that "it must have puzzled them rebels not a little to see our meal presented in the heaviest of the fire and it must have hurt their pride" to realize how little Union sailors feared their artillery. John Hart, commanding the *Albatross,* wrote that he was proud of what his crew had accomplished during the campaign. He explained, "I want to see the old flag on those cliffs," and claimed his men were just as eager for victory as he was. Hart looked forward to what he believed was an inevitable Confederate surrender and made plans for the aftermath. He told his wife that he recently learned that his old friend and classmate at the naval academy, Marshall Smith, was a Confederate colonel in Port Hudson. Hart felt no animosity for his old friend and told his wife that he looked forward to a friendly reunion with Smith as soon as Port Hudson surrendered.[48]

The siege wore down the Federals. According to Lieutenant Luther Townsend of the 16th New Hampshire Infantry, "daily and hourly our boys sickened and died." As the sun rose "every morning they were found dead in their blankets." On more than one occasion, Townsend saw a man walking to his post only to "stagger and sink to the ground where they had been standing, as dead as if shot in their tracks." He recalled one funeral where men buried a recently deceased comrade and before they could return to camp a member of the burial detail fell dead. The remaining men dug a second grave, buried the new casualty, and returned to camp with little surprise or comment. John Whitehead of the 28th Connecticut Infantry told his wife that his regiment was wasting away as men succumbed to disease and heatstroke, and noted that even the men who remained on duty were so sick that some could "just crawl about." Proper medical care might have helped, but Whitehead believed the surgeons often did more harm than good. He even claimed that the regimental surgeon was a drunk who killed one of Whitehead's friends with an overdose of wolfsbane, a dangerous herbal medication. Albert Plummer believed that men suffered from "rheumatism, malaria, and kindred ailments" because the men lived in defensive positions, which were "much of the time half full of water."[49]

Erastus Gregory of the 114th New York Infantry wrote to his brother with a uniquely illuminating explanation of what he was doing at Port Hudson and why he was doing it.

> I suppose you have an idea of what takes place in a fight like this but your ideas fall short of the reality) [*sic*] when I get home I will try and tell you so you will know something about it but I have not time to write it. But I tell you it is nothing that anyone would crave after) [*sic*] to see a regiment of brave boys go proudly into the field where shot and shell fly thickly around them perhaps before the first round is fired a piece of shell or musket ball hits a man on the head and he is carried from the field in an expiring condition another perhaps has his leg or arm shot off by a cannon ball or grape shot while another is shot in the breast in such a manner that you can see right inside of him) [*sic*] . . . I tell you it is not very often that one word of complaint is heard from these brave men so eager are they to save their country from ruin) [*sic*] yet strange to say we have men in the north that do us a great deal of harm by their cowardly cries of peace . . . when there is no peace it dampens the faith of many an unthinking soldier and at the same time gives great courage to the traitors or rebels but I would say to such men as they are go on say all and do all you can we have taken the job to put down this unholy rebellion and with the help of almighty God we will see that it is done and done handsomely too if it takes ten long years. . . . For my part I dare not come home and tell my neighbor that I gave in (to have peace on any terms) after the rebels had killed over two hundred thousand of the brave boys. I dare not come home and take my old gray headed father & mother by the hand & tell them their gray hairs must go down in sorrow to the grave because I had given in my voice to have peace on any terms, and therefore give the rebels all they demanded in the first place) [*sic*] I dare not come home where my wife and children are and take them by the hand and pat the little children on the head and tell them that I had brought a curse upon them and their children for generation and generations to come by giving in my voice towards having a peace which would be more ruinous than defeat itself) [*sic*] I dare come home and look my brothers & sisters in the face and take them by the hand and tell them I had signed away their peace the remainder of their lives (by giving in my cowardly voice for peace and back out at

> this critical juncture after more than two hundred and fifty thousand of our brave and noble young men had been buried beneath the Southern sod) [*sic*] I dare not do it I say. No I had rather brave the storm of iron and lead a spell longer.[50]

Union Camps Outside Port Hudson

The Union fortifications were uncomfortable places to live, but the Union army's superior numbers of men allowed units to rotate into and out of the front lines. When not actively manning the fortifications, many Federals camped in the groves of magnolia trees that covered the countryside outside Port Hudson. Lieutenant Colonel Willoughby Babcock of the 75th New York Infantry wrote home that he lived in a "bough hut" surrounded by trees and foliage "as bright and green as ever you saw." When William Tiemann of the 159th New York wrote his memoirs almost thirty years later, he still remembered how "the beauty and fragrance" of the flowering trees "helped to ameliorate our condition." Edward Bacon of the 6th Michigan Infantry visited the army's headquarters and described it as an extravagant place where "genteel negro waiters" served food from silver trays and poured liquor into "finely cut glasses." On another occasion Bacon dined with General Dwight at his headquarters and enjoyed "a real feast" of "cooked chicken, mutton, and fresh beef, excellent soft bread, ice water, and the best coffee," which was all served by "two gentlemanly waiters." After dinner the officers drank "old wines and brandies," which Bacon believed had been stolen from either planters or the army's hospital department. Bacon enjoyed his meal but felt guilty about filling his belly while his men suffered on rotten food and bad water.[51]

Former Slaves Near Port Hudson

On June 10 Private Henry Johns wrote home that he and several of his comrades visited a plantation outside Port Hudson, where the matriarch, who boasted of her husband's status as a Confederate soldier, traded military rations for chickens and milk. Johns was surprised to see that the plantation was worked by forty slaves who the plantation's matriarch claimed "will not leave her" because they were "so attached to her." The matriarch "did not fear the Yankees but stood in mortal terror of the black

General Weitzel's headquarters before Port Hudson.
Library of Congress.

Unidentified soldiers in camp during the siege of Port Hudson.
Library of Congress.

troops," who she believed would happily rape and murder her if white men did not stand by with guns to keep the peace. Johns thought such fears were absurd and believed "the negro is docile race," who he described as far "too glad that they are free to harbor thoughts of vengeance." He informed his family that "slavery in Louisiana is dead" and predicted that "if the masters will not attempt to revive it, they can live at peace with their negroes; but any attempt to re-enslave men who have felt the inspiration of May 27th will arouse a fiend before whose ravages the horrors of St. Domingo will sink into insignificance." He did not acknowledge the seeming contradiction between his claim that "the negro is a docile race" and his warnings that those same people could become fiends capable of "horrors." A short time later, Johns visited the same plantation to discover that the Union quartermasters had seized all the lady's livestock and that "her servants had caught the inspiration of freedom to join the damned Yankees." Johns wryly noted, "some assert that negroes are not human; certainly, they have a strange knack of doing what human beings do when placed in similar circumstances."[52]

Questions of slavery and abolition led to at least one family quarrel. In an apparent reference to his southern wife's accusations that he was no longer a true southerner, Louis Boyd told her that she was being unfair. Boyd assured his wife that he was still a proud son of the South and that his feelings for the South had not changed since he left home. Boyd denounced the abolitionists, explaining, "I am for the Union Constitution and enforcement of the laws." He urged his wife to reconsider her insults and be proud of him as he risked his life in the pursuit of duty.[53]

Confederate Raiders

Confederate raiders outside Port Hudson tortured the Federals. According to Massachusetts infantryman William Stevens, the road from Baton Rouge to Port Hudson was "considered open and under Federal control." However, "the trip is surrounded with many obstacles and bands of guerrillas infest the woods and are ready to waylay a solitary horseman, and take his equipment, horse and all, consequently the baggage trains go well protected but are often delayed." Union soldiers grew hungry when their supplies failed to arrive on time. Stevens lamented that soldiers occasionally resorted to licking the crumbs out of the bottom of hard tack crates when supplies briefly ran low.[54]

John Hart, commander of the USS *Albatross*, which was stationed just north of Port Hudson, tried to keep Confederate raiders at bay by sending counter-raiding parties ashore and by firing shells as at anyone in gray who came within range of his boat. The Confederates were not intimidated and frequently taunted Union sailors. In a letter to his wife, Hart quoted one exchange as an example of the conversations. It began when a sailor on the *Albatross* saw a Confederate soldier approach the shore. The sailor yelled "you d- [*sic*] Rebel beggar are you pretty nearly played out over yonder?" The Confederate replied, "go to —— [*sic*] you infernal Yankee, I'll make hog's meat of you any how [*sic*]." At that moment the *Albatross*'s crew fired one of their cannons but missed the Confederate, who taunted, "Bah! Do you call that firing, somebody aught [*sic*] to give you a hundred lashes for that!" Apparently unwilling to push his luck, the Confederate retreated behind the levee just as the *Albatross* fired another shot, which missed the now departed Confederate. According to Hart, such encounters were common.[55]

The City of Port Hudson

Port Hudson remained a dangerous home for civilians as well as soldiers. Eliza Goble—married to James Goble, who was serving in the 1st Alabama Infantry—moved from Alabama to Port Hudson so she could be close to her husband during the siege. James Goble complained in his diary that "grape and canister fall all around our house ladies and children in the house very much frightened." Staff at Confederate hospitals that were near civilian homes and military headquarters "climb the highest trees to put up their flag," probably in hopes that Union artillerymen would direct their fire away from the hospitals. James Goble wrote that he was sitting in a house with "ladies sewing when 3 rifled shells came whizzing over" and "burst on the opposite side of the house." Understandably, "we then thought it time to leave." Goble was unharmed, but that day "many were killed." Several days later, Goble reported, "a little boy in town was playing with a bomb shell." It exploded, "cutting his foot off shattering his mothers [*sic*] leg." The mother died, and the surgeons removed what was left of the boy's foot. Goble also reported that he saw "a mulatto woman get her breast and arm shot off by the bursting of a shell," and Goble, wisely, remarked, "it is very dangerous to go home from the breastworks." Goble seemed to suggest that the Federals intentionally made war on civilians, but he admitted that "Gens [*sic*] headquarters not more than 50ft from our house," which indicates that Port Hudson's civilians lived near legitimate military targets. Artillery fire damaged buildings, and on June 3 Goble reported, "Genls [*sic*] are now quartered in tents." Probably in a reference to "The Star Spangled Banner," James Goble wrote in his diary, "bombs bursting in air the fires red glair [*sic*] gave proof through the night ruen [*sic*] and death was there." Rumors circulated through the Confederate camps that the Federals were intentionally setting fires in hopes of burning southern soldiers and civilians to death. On one occasion, a Union artillery shell set a house on fire five hundred yards away from the house Goble shared with his wife. Goble and his wife were looking at the fire when another shell passed over their heads, barely missing them, and Goble concluded that the "yank army is very destructive to rebel property." Smoke drifted over the town as Confederates burned five hundred bales of cotton, probably to prevent its capture by the Federals. Smoke hung over Port Hudson, coating everything in grit and ash. Goble also wrote that, while Confederate soldiers were brave men, happy to "stand and to be killed," the prospect of being "shot as it were in cold blood" as they were pounded by artillery caused him to cry, "o my God how long will mortal man have to endure such wanton cruelty." As a result of the intense artillery fire, some women took shelter in the Confederate army's bunkers.[56]

As the siege tightened, some Confederate soldiers grew understandably more cautious. Prentiss Ingraham later recalled that General Beall was inspecting the lines when he heard "the ping of the Berdan [*sic*] rifles" of Union sharpshooters and bowed his head to avoid the gunfire. The Confederates on the line thought Beall was bowing in courtesy, and they replied by tipping their caps. A moment later they realized the real reason for Beall's bow, and everyone chuckled at the misunderstanding. Beall made all future inspections of the front line under cover of darkness.[57]

Union and Confederate soldiers both commented on the men's ability to sleep despite the noise of constant gunfire. Confederate artillery officer Paul de Gournay claimed the men "got used to the deafening roar, and it did not hinder them from sleeping." Harris Beecher, an assistant surgeon with the 114th New York Infantry, explained that people quickly become "accustomed to situations the most unnatural." Within a few days of arriving at the front, "every man in the regiment could lie down at night, and sleep as sweetly as in his own bed at home," despite the constant artillery fire just over their heads. James Goble provided a very different perspective, writing that he did not sleep because "the land is hideous with doleful sounds, causing women and children to shriek with deaths [*sic*] dreadful fear."[58]

Disease

Disease swept through Union camps and killed far more men than gunfire. Captain Henry Maglathlin of the 4th Massachusetts Infantry described efforts to avoid sickness as "a warfare with which bravery cannot cope." Without access to clean clothes or bathing facilities, men soon suffered from infestations of lice and fleas, which spread disease. William Tiemann called the pests "gray backs" and considered them a more persistent enemy than the rebel army. The 16th New Hampshire arrived in Port Hudson having already suffered horribly from malaria. It got worse outside Port Hudson, where 221 men eventually died of disease. The survivors were so few and so weak that Banks removed them from the front lines and assigned them to guard the ammunition depot. Henry Johns wrote home that the army was losing fifty men every day to disease and sunstroke. His own regiment had lost eighty men to battle and seventy-five to illness since coming to Port Hudson.[59]

John Hart, commander of the USS *Albatross*, which was stationed just north of Port Hudson, was one of many men who contracted yellow fever. On June 11, 1863, Charles Washburn on the *Albatross* reported, "at 4:15 p.m. the Capt (Hart) shot himself in his own room with a pistol killing himself instantly." Newspapers elaborated, explaining that Hart "shot himself through the head with a revolver, while suffering from an intermittent fever." It is unclear if Hart shot himself with the same captured Confederate revolver he was saving as present for his son. Hart was a devoted Mason and had often expressed a desire for a Masonic funeral. Theodore Dubois, the executive officer and new commander of the *Albatross*, sent sailors ashore under a flag of truce to make contact with Confederates and request permission to bury Hart with Masonic honors. Although the Union sailors were apparently unaware, they were within a few miles of the Feliciana Lodge, the oldest Masonic Lodge in Louisiana. The lodge's leader was Captain W. W. Leake, who also commanded a Confederate a cavalry unit in the area. Leake agreed to allow the sailors to bury Hart in the graveyard of the Grace Episcopal Church Cemetery with full Masonic honors. Local people still have an annual reenactment to celebrate Hart's 1863 funeral as "the Day the War Stopped."[60]

The Union military enlisted black men largely because they believed that former slaves, particularly those who had lived in Louisiana, were better equipped to survive the diseases that plagued the area than northern white men. Initial reports conducted by the Union army in Louisiana tended to support this idea, with one study finding that, while 11 percent of troops from Maine suffered from "intermittent or remittent fever" along the Gulf of Mexico, less than 1 percent of black troops from Louisiana suffered from the same illnesses. Reports from other Union surgeons refuted the belief that blacks were less susceptible to "malarial fevers" and found that up to 35 percent of African Americans in Louisiana suffered from "intermittent or remittent fever."[61] It is unclear what genetic protections from local illnesses, if any, people of African ancestry might have enjoyed.

The Confederate defenders, most of whom came from the southern states of Louisiana, Alabama, Mississippi, and Arkansas, were more accustomed to a southern spring than their northern counterparts, but they too fell ill during the siege. The men grew tired from the constant work improving fortifications. With little shelter to protect them from the weather, men baked in the sun and shivered in the rain as they became sick. Joseph Bailey remembered the "swarms of mosquitos" that tortured him and his comrades until "often our faces in the morning looked like a patient just broken out with measles." In a desperate bid to keep the pests at bay, some men burned rags near their heads all night. James Goble wrote in his diary that "hospitals are full of sick and wounded and men with limbs cut off." He explained, "men are worn out with hunger and fatigued from over exurtion [*sic*]. Rebels who remained at their posts "are nearly all sick lying in the ditches exposed to the sun and the Feds [*sic*] bullets." Daniel Smith estimated that roughly one-third of the Confederate defenders were so sick that they could not report for duty by June 3, 1863. Common illnesses included conditions the men described as "camp fever, diarrhea, and chills." Confederate doctors treated malaria patients with quinine until they ran out of the precious medication. Next, the doctors prescribed ipecac, which did little to help the sick and ran out soon after the quinine. In desperation, the Confederate medical department gave the sick homebrewed teas made from local plants. Many sick Confederates chose to remain near their posts with their friends rather than die among strangers in the poorly equipped garrison hospitals. Colonel Ben Johnson, commanding the defense of Fort Desperate, reported that, while Federal gunfire killed and wounded some men, "my sick list, notwithstanding every effort of mine to prevent it, was quite large." Johnson wrote that many of the men "I compelled to remain and report for duty, were so worn down with ague and fever, and dysentery, as scarcely to be called soldiers or be of any service to me." The men were sick and tired, but "they could fight, and so I kept them."[62]

Confederate Morale

Some Confederate soldiers remained confident despite the grinding misery of the siege. Walter Turner wrote in his diary that the men kept their heads down as the Federals fired but remained confident that their breastworks would protect them from Federal fire, which was more noise than danger. James Goble wrote in his diary with apparent pride that the garrison "have held the place against five times their own number." By his arithmetic, "20 thousand Feds [*sic*]" had charged Port Hudson thirteen times and been soundly defeated each time. Goble's apparent pride was mixed with a touch of sorrow as he also noted the men who had won against overwhelming odds "are most all worn out with constant fighting and fatigue." The New York–born infantryman serving in the Confederate army believed "southerners are the bravest people in the world," and he felt they had proved it by holding Port Hudson against overwhelming odds. The men continued to "work on with a desperate resolve intending to hold the place to the last."[63]

Not every Confederate soldier was content to die in the ditches. On June 8 General Beall formally complained that General Gardner had assigned eighty men to his brigade who "cannot be trusted" because they were likely to desert. Gardner had ordered Beall to "put them where they can be watched" and have them "shot down in case they desert." Beall formally complained that the eighty men were more trouble than they were worth, that his lines were stretched thin, and that he could not spare men to guard the eighty men who "cannot be trusted." He asked Gardner to place them in the guardhouse. James Goble wrote in his diary that the Confederates executed a former postmaster for "showing a yank officer how to get inside our breastworks."[64]

A trickle of Confederate deserters slipped out of Port Hudson and surrendered to the Union army. Lawrence Van Alstyne recorded in his diary that Confederate deserters "sneak out during the night and hide in the bushes until daylight and then come in." The deserters all claimed that they were hungry, that there was little food in Port Hudson, and that the garrison would surrender soon. Union soldiers greeted the deserters with food and then sent them to the river, where Union boats transported them to prisoner of war camps. Other Confederates took the oath of allegiance and avoided the horrors of prison camps. Erastus Gregory wrote that one of the Confederate deserters reported that two Confederate regiments in Port Hudson had laid down their arms and refused to fight anymore. Henry Johns wrote home that Union soldiers always greeted the deserters with "great kindness" because, while they might be "scaly patriots," the Federals knew that each Confederate deserter was "one less rifle to march up against." John Harris, a Kentuckian visiting Arkansas when the war began, deserted to Federal lines. After telling the Federals everything he knew, Harris took the oath of allegiance and returned home to Kentucky. Union staff officer Wickham Hoffman claimed that most Confederate deserters at Port Hudson were from Louisiana. In contrast, the Arkansas men, who he called "Wrackensackers" [*sic*] for some unknown reason, and the Texans rarely deserted. Walter Turner of the 39th Mississippi Infantry wrote in his diary that a trickle of Union deserters, both white and black, surrendered to the rebels and provided information about the Union army's plans.[65]

According to Alabama soldier James Goble, the Federals squeezed the garrison until Confederate Port Hudson consisted of an area only five miles long and two miles wide, and he declared that there "is not a place within the whole enclosure but wat [*sic*] has felt the dreadful effects of the murdering missiles of death." Despite the intense artillery fire, Goble continued to live in a house with his wife and five other people. Their house was "in the center of the left wing," a mile from the Union lines and within range of Federal artillery. Goble believed that he and his wife only survived because "a guardian angel" protected their house.[66]

Truces

Men often made informal truces without official approval. According to Harris Beecher, the men traded copies of the New York *Tribune* for copies of the Port Hudson *Gazette.* Soldiers also traded Union hardtack for Confederate "hoecake," which was probably cornbread. The oddest exchange might have been the exchange of Federal tobacco for Confederate wooden canteens. Men unwilling to trust that the truce was real and expose themselves fastened trade goods to the tips of their bayonets and passed them over the line while keeping their bodies concealed from gunfire. Erastus Gregory enjoyed truces because he regretted that the country was torn apart. He had no "hatred" for the Confederate soldiers as people. He wrote, "I only hate their actions." Gregory told his brother, "all I want is to bring them to terms that is bring them to an unconditional surrender and then with as much joy as the father experienced at the return of the prodigal I will receive them back and call them brothers again." Gregory hated northern men who supported the peace movement, which he felt betrayed the army. Rufus Dooley wrote that truces provided him with rare moments of peace, when he could relax and look at the sun "shining in at the doors and windows of our dwelling." Dooley's next comment suggests that his mind might not have been quiet even when guns were briefly silent. Dooley told his mother that "the old saying is a calm always precedes a storm."[67]

Confederate soldiers wrote that they also enjoyed the frequent truces. According to a 1927 memoir by Joseph Bailey, truces were common during the siege. He reported that sharpshooters took breaks so that men could reposition themselves in safety. He even claimed that men often met between the lines to trade Confederate sugar for Union coffee and tobacco. As the men traded, Federals teased the rebels about their lack of rations and promised to feed them bacon, bread, and coffee after they captured Port Hudson. Bailey shared stories of truces "to show there was very little hatred or unkind feeling existing among the men in the fighting line." Bailey's claims that "there was very little hatred" must be treated with skepticism. Bailey himself reported in his same memoir that his comrades proclaimed "we would now get even" for past defeats when they opened fire on the Federals. Perhaps Bailey's comments in 1927 were more about healing old wounds than accurately reporting history. Bailey's claim might also demonstrate that human emotions are complicated enough to allow men to murder each other one day and happily trade jokes with the survivors the next day. James Goble noted in his diary that, during the truces, "everything seems to be quiet." The "gentle breeze seems to clear the dreadful screams of the past day and to look on sweet nature one would think that peace indeed had come at last." He contrasted "how nature looks on with a sweet smile" and the "birds warble out their songs of praise" with "the devastation of man" that waves "the cruel hand of war," which "sweeps over us like a storm." Goble believed the truces allowed men to slip into an "honorable delusion" that was always broken by "the murderous guns" that fired with "fury."[68]

The Assault of June 11

After two weeks of digging in, the Union army prepared for an assault once again. General Banks ordered the army to begin by filling bags with cotton and gathering bundles of brush, which were placed near the mortar batteries. These would be used to fill ditches and provide paths over obstructions. General Franklin Nickerson would detail two hundred men to carry the bags of cotton. Another one hundred men would follow close behind "to pick up those which may be dropped," suggesting that Banks expected up to 50 percent casualties among the first wave of two hundred. Members of the African American 1st Louisiana Engineers would carry the brush bundles. A detachment of one hundred combat engineers would then follow to clear a path and build a road for the artillery. Once a path was open, fifty men from the 6th Michigan Infantry under the command of Captain Stark would attempt to make a quick dash through the Confederate lines and capture General Gardner's headquarters. Colonel Clark would detail another two hundred men of the 6th Michigan Infantry to conduct an unspecified "important and decisive movement." The 128th New York Infantry would support the 6th Michigan. Except for the specially selected men in the storming parties, "the nine-months troops of the command will lead the advance in the attack."[69]

Rumors had already circulated through the Union camps that Banks viewed the nine-month men as disposable. Banks's direct order to put the nine-month men in the lead of the June 11 attack suggests that the rumor

Captain Jedediah Randall of Co. K,
26th Connecticut Infantry Regiment.
Randall died after being wounded at
Port Hudson. Library of Congress.

might have been true. George Waite served in the 26th Connecticut Infantry, which was one of the nine-month regiments that Banks may have considered disposable. He wrote home to a friend on June 10, on the eve of the battle, that "there will probably be a great loss of life." Waite worried that he might die in the morning.[70]

The night of June 10 was "warm, cloudy, and dark." About midnight orders came down the line that sent men into action. Skirmishers advanced out of the breastworks to forward positions and waited for the order to attack. Erastus Gregory and the 114th New York Infantry moved forward to clear brush and prepare the way for the attack. When the New Yorkers came within "a few rods" of the Confederate lines, the rebels charged the work party. Gregory admitted that "of course we dropped everything" and ran back to the Union lines. He was surprised to report that the regiment suffered only three or four wounded men, one of whom wounded himself when fell on his axe in his haste to retreat. Gregory acknowledged, "we are having a terrible fight," but he remained confident that God would protect the army and ensure its victory.[71] Late on the night of June 10, the Union artillery launched a heavy bombardment. The cannon fire did little damage, but it did alert the Confederates that an attack might be coming. Rebels prepared to defend themselves.[72]

At 3:00 a.m. on June 11, Union skirmishers finally received orders to advance. They moved forward cautiously, but the caution meant little. The rebels detected the Federal advance almost instantly and opened fire with what George Carpenter of the 8th Vermont Infantry called "a leaden hail." The Confederate defenders drove the men in blue back with "a vigorous onslaught upon them in front and flank." George Carpenter lamented that the attack failed. The Confederate artillery refused to fire or expose themselves, relying on the Confederate infantry to drive the Union infantry back and keep them from making any significant improvements to their position. Walter Turner of the 39th Mississippi Infantry reported that his regiment took twenty-seven prisoners in the brief fighting on June 11. James Goble recorded in his diary that, by the end of the day, "many thousands of Feds [*sic*] lye [*sic*] bleaching on the soil of Port Hudson."[73]

Union Confidence

Many Union soldiers and observers remained confident that Port Hudson would fall, eventually. On June 13 Henry Rufus Gardner wrote home that "three weeks ago today the forces under Banks and Auger [*sic*] invested this place" with promises Port Hudson would fall "easy prey," but he lamented "the rag still floats, and rebellion nearly holds his own." Despite his obvious frustration, Gardner reported "the commanding general's intentions to save life at the expense of time, which however wearisome to those engaged, may be the best in the end." The Union artillery was "firing slowly all the time," and Gardner believed they were making progress, having "dismounted or broken every gun on the parapet." Rufus Dooley took apparent pride in the work done by his battery's heavy artillery, telling his mother what was left of the Confederate artillery "cannot fire more than one shot from a place if they do they are sure to get their goods impacted." A writer for the *New York Herald* provided a detailed examination of Banks's history of command and concluded that, while Banks had suffered from some failures in Louisiana and had not won any "great battles," he "done all that occasion required" to besiege Port Hudson and, in a less than enthusiastic endorsement, predicted that "he will probably take it."[74]

Union Preparations for Another Attack

General Nathaniel Banks announced plans for another attack. Banks informed Admiral Farragut that he planned to begin a "vigorous bombardment" of Port Hudson at 11:15 a.m. on June 13. Banks asked Farragut to help the army by "throwing as many shells as you can into the place during that time, commencing and ceasing fire with us." After pausing the bombardment, Banks would send "a summons to surrender." If the rebels refused to surrender, Banks would launch an attack on June 14. Farragut agreed to help Banks but wryly noted, "there is but little use in the demand for surrender." Farragut was confident that Gardner would not surrender. Captain Henry Maglathlin wrote that Union generals were desperate. Unable to combat the outbreaks of disease that were killing the men, the generals concluded that "whatever was to be done must be done soon."[75]

Union soldiers prepared for the attack. Federals constructed a series of advanced fortifications. In the middle of the night, they rolled bales of cotton to within about a hundred yards of the Confederate lines. They then assembled them into forts large enough to house two or three regiments and piled sandbags against the exterior of the bales. The Confederates bombarded the new Union forts, but their shells made little impact, and the Union soldiers inside remained reasonably safe. The Union army also distributed hand grenades. According to infantryman James Dargan, on June 12 "we were drilled in the use of hand grenades by Genl [*sic*] Paine."[76]

In retrospect, it is easy to say that Banks should have waited, that starvation would have soon forced the Confederates to surrender, and that another assault was a needless sacrifice. However, Banks was under tremendous pressure to act decisively. Rumors that a Confederate army was marching to relieve Port Hudson circulated through the Union camps.[77]

Grant's army was besieging the larger Confederate garrison at Vicksburg and needed help distracting Confederates in Mississippi. Sickness made the Union forces near Port Hudson weaker with each passing day. Starving out Port Hudson would only work if starvation weakened the defenders more quickly than illness and demoralization weakened the besiegers. In June 1863 that was not a sure bet.

The planned Union attack would strike Confederate fortifications that were much stronger than they had been just a few weeks before. According to Daniel Smith, by June 13 the rebels had conspired with their native soil to craft remarkably strong fortifications. Union engineer officer John Palfrey later described Port Hudson's defenses as "impregnable." The Confederate line began on the southern edge of Port Hudson, along the river, where a strong fortification known as the Citadel guarded the rebel right flank from behind a series of ravines, rifle pits, trenches, and detached works. The Confederate lines of trenches and obstructions then looped north toward an angle that was protected by "a strong detached redan." The rebel line then ran north for a about a mile to the Plains Road near the Priest Gap. North of Priest Gap, the rebels did not have a continuous line because they did not need one. According to Palfrey, "the space was too difficult for approach," and the Confederates defended the area with a maze of rifle pits, ravines, and small forts in a line that curved northwest until it butted against the riverbank north of town. All the Confederate defenses were "well fitted to the ground, the inequalities of which were well turned to account." The rebel works were more organic than artificial, growing from the southern soil in irregular shapes that complimented the natural obstacles "with no sharply defined lines," which made them "harder to reconnoiter and comprehend." Men in gray burrowed into the ground, taking shelter in shallow holes and emerging only to fire from concealed positions.[78]

By June 13 the Confederates had improved their firepower as well as their defensive positions. Most Confederate infantrymen began the siege with smoothbore muskets, which could fire devastating loads of buckshot at point blank range but were almost worthless beyond a hundred yards. After the failed Union attacks of May 27, the rebels gathered abandoned Union rifles and soon almost every Confederate infantryman had two weapons: a captured rifle for sniping at long range and a smoothbore, which they kept ready for attackers who got too close. During lulls in the fighting, Confederate soldiers sorted through earthworks to collect the bullets fired at them by the Federals. The infantry kept the best-preserved bullets for their own rifles and sent the rest to the artillery. According to Daniel Smith, "it was but the work of a few minutes to pick up enough to charge a 12-pounder gun."[79]

At 3:00 a.m. on June 13, Union forces "commenced a heavy skirmishing" along the entire line of Confederate defenders. At 11:00 a.m. the Union navy's mortar boats opened fire on the rebels. Union infantry formed into a line of battle near Slaughter's Field and began to advance on the Confederate lines. They quickly retreated when the Confederate artillery opened fire on the Union infantry.[80]

At 1:00 p.m. Union fire tapered off, and General Banks sent a demand for surrender to General Gardner. Banks stated, "respect for the usages of war, and a desire to avoid unnecessary sacrifice of life, impose on me the necessity of formally demanding the surrender of the garrison of Port Hudson." Banks complimented his adversaries, admitting, "I am not unconscious in making this demand that the garrison is capable of continuing a vigorous and gallant defense." In a vague admission of Union failures, Banks suggested recent events "exhibit in the commander and garrison a spirt of constancy and courage, that in a different cause, would be universally regarded as heroism." Banks then shifted from flattery to threats, claiming that he had learned from deserters, prisoners of war, and Gardner's private dispatches, which the Federals had captured, that the garrison was suffering horribly. Banks claimed to have an overwhelming superiority in artillery and infantry, which "no ordinary fortress can successfully resist." Banks ended with a warning, claiming that, if the siege continued, Gardner would "place the protection of life beyond the control of the commanders of the respective forces." Historian Edward Cunningham suggested that Banks was threatening to "massacre the Port Hudson garrison if the place were taken by storm."[81] Cunningham's interpretation is a harsh reading of the demand for surrender, but Cunningham may have been correct.

Alabama soldier Crawford Jackson was in Gardner's headquarters when Gardner received Banks's demand for surrender. Jackson reported that Gardner "broke out in a fit of laughter" when he read the message. Gardner sent orders to his commanders to prepare for a fight. Gardner's official reply to Banks was devoid of laughter but clear. He informed Banks, "my duty requires me to defend this position, and, therefore, I decline to surrender."[82]

It does not appear that the Federals were surprised by Gardner's refusal to surrender. When General Cuvier Grover learned that Gardner refused to surrender, Grover replied, "Old Gardner"—who Grover served with in the US Army before the Civil War—"always was as obstinate as a mule." General Weitzel replied, "well, we know what is to come next." Banks replied to Gardner's refusal to surrender by opening fire on the Port Hudson garrison with every cannon at his disposal. Howard Wright later recalled that "the mortar boats rained a perfect torrent of shells upon us" and that the land batteries "poured forth their volleys of destructive missiles, rending the very air with their deafening roar." Alabamian Daniel Smith noted that the Union gunboats fired with "unusual rapidity."[83]

The Confederates took shelter and prepared for an infantry assault. As the rebels sought shelter from the bombardment, Daniel Smith witnessed "a singular phenomenon." As the Union cannons roared, "an immense wave at least six feet in height, rushed up the river, and at the same time the Confederate Battery No. 6 caved into the river, one gun being lost." The Confederates debated if the wave caused the bluff to cave in or if the cave in caused the wave, but all agreed that it was a mysterious event. The Confederate artillery did not respond to the bombardment. Colonel Edward Bacon of the 6th Michigan Infantry heard "some declare that the Confederate artillery is mostly silenced and disabled by our fire, and that nothing is wanting but a general assault to carry our army in the fort at once, and that delay will bring a relieving army upon our rear."[84]

While men in the ranks speculated on what might happen next, Union generals finalized a complex battle plan that would require a precise sequence of complex movements early on June 14:

2:45 a.m., Augur's artillery would bombard the Confederate right.
2:45 a.m., Confederate deserters would guide two of General Dwight's regiments to a rumored entrance to Port Hudson on the extreme left of the Confederate positions near the river.
3:00 a.m., multiple batteries would bombard the Priest Gap near the Confederate center.
3:15 a.m., Augur's infantry would feign an attack on the Confederate center just south of the Plains Store Road.
3:30 a.m., General Grover's infantry would launch the army's primary attack on the Priest Gap north of the Plains Store Road.[85]

Each of General Grover's two assault columns would consist of three hundred skirmishers, followed by seventy engineers carrying tools, followed by a three-hundred-man storming party carrying bags stuffed with cotton to fill ditches, followed by thirty-four men carrying preassembled lumber to build bridges over the ditches for the artillery. After the bridges were completed, the artillery would cross them and set up, while the main assault columns of two thousand men each would advance close behind the artillery in lines of battle. Many of the attackers carried hand grenades. James Peck of the 173rd New York described each of the three hand grenades he carried as "a shell weighing 5 pounds," shaped like an "egg with a small hole in one end" with "a cap to explode the shell" and "card board [*sic*] in the shape of a feather to guide it." Although he did not name it, Peck probably described Ketchum grenades, which were used at Port Hudson.[86]

Each Union grenadier would sling their rifle, carry one to three grenades, and advance as a skirmisher after throwing their grenade(s).[87] While the Federal artillery and infantry focused on the Confederates in Port Hudson, the Union cavalry would form a screen to protect the Union rear from harassing Confederate cavalry and block the Telegraph Road north toward Bayou Sara, which the Federals believed was the Confederate's planned escape route if Port Hudson fell. The Union council of war finalized their plans at 11:30 p.m. on June 13. At midnight, the Union boats bobbing near Port Hudson received a message from General Banks, asking them to fire "as rapidly as possible for two hours." The sailors complied and opened a horrific barrage on Port Hudson. Union staff officers wrote and distributed the army's orders, which did not arrive in many units until 1:00 a.m. on June 14. This gave most Union soldiers less than two hours to prepare for battle.[88]

According to Major (later Colonel) Edward Bacon of the 6th Michigan Infantry, General William Dwight planned to support the June 14 assault with a daring raid. On the evening of June 13, Dwight ordered Bacon to report to his headquarters. After offering Bacon a stiff drink, Dwight introduced Bacon to two Confederate deserters and shared a crudely drawn map of Port Hudson's defenses. Dwight ordered Bacon to take fifty men and do anything he could to disguise the men to look like Confederates. The group would approach Port Hudson's water battery, known as the Citadel, on the extreme south end of the Confederate lines.

The two deserters would lead Bacon's command through the predawn darkness toward a set of secret steps cut into the fort, which the men could use to slip into the Citadel unnoticed. Dwight told Bacon that, after he got inside the Citadel, he should find General Gardner's headquarters and take him prisoner. Incredulous, Bacon asked how he was supposed to find Gardner's headquarters. Dwight replied that Bacon should "make a prisoner of the first man you meet, and holding your revolver to his head, extort the information from him." Dwight told Bacon that, if the first prisoner did not know or would not reveal the location of Gardner's headquarters, Bacon should take additional prisoners until someone eventually revealed Gardner's location. Dwight told Bacon that after capturing Gardner he should fire a signal rocket to request reinforcements and hold Gardner until help arrived. Dwight assured Bacon that Grierson's cavalry would charge through the Citadel and relieve Bacon of his prisoner before the rebels could recapture their commander. Bacon was incredulous but dared not protest. He enjoyed a luxurious dinner with General Dwight and his staff before returning to his regiment.[89]

Union soldiers prepared for combat. Private George Powers and the rest of the 38th Massachusetts Infantry were roused from slumber a little before midnight and given orders to prepare for battle. The men packed their blankets, which they would leave in camp during the battle. Camp cooks served hot cups of coffee, giving the men a much-appreciated boost of caffeine, and they filled their canteens with water and their haversacks with food in the darkness. With their preparations complete, members of the 38th Massachusetts Infantry began to move forward to their staging positions. Powers later recalled that he and his comrades "expected a short, sharp fight." General Paine expected the men to "be inside the words within half an hour." To prevent the attack from bogging down, Paine ordered the men to leave the wounded on the field until the battle was over. The 48th Massachusetts Infantry spent June 13 clearing brush and building new battery positions. Just as they were about to set up camp for the night, they received orders to advance and prepare for an attack the next day. The regiment began the march with 500 men, but when they arrived near the front line, they had only 175 enlisted men and four captains. Everyone else had fallen out, suffering from illness or exhaustion. John Barnard of the 52nd Massachusetts Infantry drank coffee in the darkness and prepared for combat. After filling their bellies with hot coffee, the men moved into assault positions. Barnard told his cousin Mary, "I never felt the want of sight at night as I did that march, I could not distinguish my file leader although at the distance of twenty inches from me." Barnard "stumbled over stumps, ran against trees, fell over roots." Barnard was disoriented by his inability to see and by his constant stumbling. He worried that he might be responsible "for some disaster to the men with me" if he was unable to perform his duty. The 13th Connecticut Infantry, in Birge's Brigade of Grover's Division, did not begin moving into position until nearly 3:00 a.m. Captain Homer Sprague, commanding Company H of the 13th Connecticut Infantry, led his company to "the places assigned them for the bloody drama." Some units got lost in the dark maze of ravines, woods, and underbrush that stood between them and their designated staging locations. Once in position, the infantrymen enjoyed cups of hot coffee. Chaplain John Moors of the 52nd Massachusetts Infantry told his wife that he heard a captain tell the men of his company to prepare for battle and told them to remember "a dead brave man is better than a living coward."[90]

Confederate soldiers braced for the attack. Walter Turner of the 39th Mississippi Infantry wrote in his diary that, when he went on guard duty at about 2:00 a.m., he could hear the enemy's infantrymen and artillery moving. Beginning at about 3:30 a.m., he could hear Union officers giving commands. Turner predicted that at first light the Federals would launch "one of the most desperate attacks that has ever occurred at Port Hudson." Colonel Ben Johnson, commanding the defense of Fort Desperate, anticipated the Federals to attack on June 14. He ordered every man he could find to take a spot in the ditches and load his gun.[91]

Many Union soldiers were unhappy with the battle plan. Some disliked initiating a battle on Sunday, a day they felt should be reserved for church and rest, not for killing. Connecticut infantry officer Homer Sprague noted that "Sunday attacks are seldom successful" and considered the entire plan an "ill-advised calculation." Union infantryman John Barnard wondered aloud if God would punish men who worked on Sunday. Harris Beecher, an assistant surgeon with the 114th New York Infantry, heard men grumble that Port Hudson was "impregnable" simply because of its natural position on high ground, behind nearly impassible terrain. A member of the 53rd Massachusetts Infantry who had toured the Union lines told his comrades that Banks had selected a terrible place for an attack because, while there were some brush and stumps that could provide cover near most of the Confederate works, the area near the Priest Gap was the most barren part of the line and completely devoid of anything that might provide cover or concealment. According to Henry Willis, an adjutant with the regiment, the men accepted the news stoically, writing "their last brief messages home," and "had a good sleep in spite of the dreadful prospect before them."[92]

Massachusetts infantryman James Dargan listened to General Banks give the men an "oratical [*sic*] display," which Dargan did not quote. After Banks was done, General Paine gave "a short harangue," which Dargan also did quote. Paine predicted, "we will scale the works, and grasp the enemy, and destroy his hold upon this place and contribute in conjunction with Grant to open the Mississippi." He told the men that "the eyes of nations are upon us and our effort tomorrow." Paine believed "the pen of the historian" would record that they acted not from malice but from a desire to correct "a noble foe." He predicted that "the 14th of June" would be remembered by the nation "as among her proudest victories."[93]

— 9 —

A Hell of a Fellow Long Enough

THE BATTLE OF JUNE 14, 1863

I started out this morning with the determination to be a h—— of a fellow! I've been a h—— of a fellow long enough.[1]

—NICHOLAS DAY, 131st New York Infantry

The fight lasted 3 or 4 hours. The enemy used hand grenades when they got up near enough to throw them over the works. But our boys caught them as they were coming over and threw them back at the enemy, killing a great many. The first Mississippi was charged 3 times and Miles Legion twice. Our loss is very small in comparison to that of the enemy. The dead of the enemy are lying 3 deep all over the battlefield. We have taken up 100 prisoners, they got so near the works when they made the charge they could not get back without running a great risk. Therefore, they gave themselves up as prisoners.[2]

—WALTER TURNER, 39th Mississippi Infantry

The Bombardment

The "sun rose beautiful and bright" over Port Hudson on the morning of June 14, 1863. Alabama soldier Crawford Jackson watched General Gardner emerge from his bedroom at first light. Gardner wondered aloud what Banks was up to that day. A moment later, as if to answer Gardner's question, a cannon fired from the Union army's lines. According to Jackson, the single cannon announced that "a battle had begun."[3]

General Halbert Paine prepared to lead the primary Union advance against the south section of the Priest Gap, deploying the 4th Wisconsin Infantry and the 8th New Hampshire in the front as skirmishers. The 4th Massachusetts Infantry would follow with improvised hand grenades, made from 6-pounder cannon shells. The 38th and 53rd Massachusetts

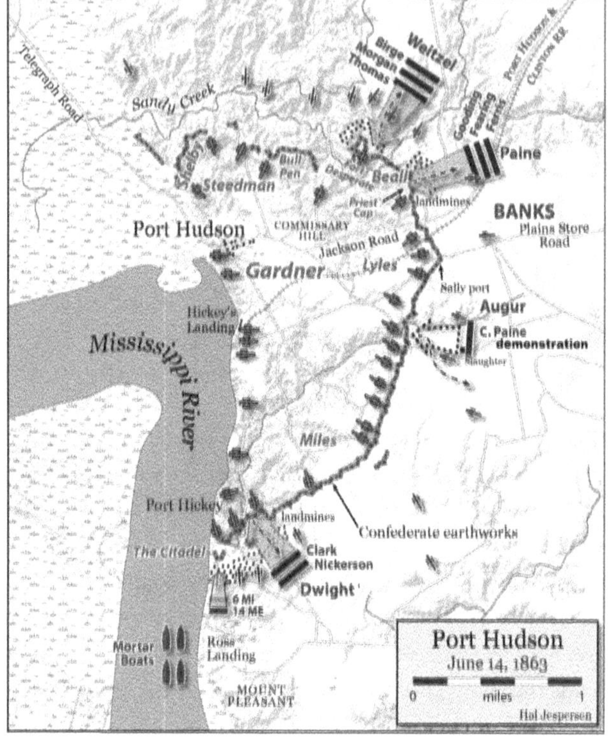

Map 6. The Battle of Port Hudson, June 14, 1863.
Hal Jespersen.

Infantry regiments formed in line of battle behind the grenadiers. The 31st Massachusetts Infantry also formed in line of battle but carried cotton bags to fill the ditches. Behind the main assault column, members of Gooding's, Fearing's, and Ingram's (commanded by Ferris) brigades followed in support. The artillery, under the command of Ormand F. Nims, prepared to follow the infantry. James Hosmer of the 52nd Massachusetts Infantry walked forward with his comrades in the predawn darkness. In his diary he described the path he took toward the front as decorated with "Rembrandt pictures, a bright blaze under a tree, the faces and arms of soldiers aglow about it, the wheel of an army wagon, or the brass of a cannon, lit up, then the gloom of the wood, and the night shutting down about it."[4]

Some Union soldiers felt foreboding. David Hanaburgh later remembered "a depressed felling pervaded the minds of the men, which found expression on the part of some in words, because an assault was to be made on the sabbath." Charles McGregor wrote that the Confederates to their front were "ominously silent." James Dargan believed the men in gray would "reserve their fire for more noble game." Harris Beecher heard men predict that the rebels would not be surprised by the attack, and they "pledged to each other mutual acts of assistance and protection when the trial should come."[5] The men would need all the help they could get in the attack.

Private George Powers and the rest of the 38th Massachusetts Infantry crossed a bridge covered with cotton to deaden the sound, deployed as skirmishers in an open field, and laid down. The Union artillery opened fire, throwing shells over the heads of Union skirmishers. Most of the gunfire struck the rebel lines, but some shells fell short and injured men in blue. The first Union casualties of the battle of June 14 may have been victims of friendly fire, maimed by their own artillerymen before the Confederates even opened fire. General Paine walked up and down the line telling each group of men he passed that the attack was about to begin.[6]

Captain Homer Sprague, commanding Company H of the 13th Connecticut Infantry, led his company to advanced positions to prepare for the attack. As the company laid down, "a large number of wounded were brought past, and a hospital was established on the slope." Men from Connecticut "looked on in silence" at the "rough performance of the surgeons" and listened to the "groaning sufferers," none of which was "calculated to whet the appetite for battle."[7]

Chaplain John Moors of the 52nd Massachusetts Infantry reported to a field hospital and began helping the wounded, as he typically did during battles. Moors had little medical training. However, he could bring water, and during previous battles he dressed wounds, reasoning that bandages tied by an amateur were better than nothing. Almost as soon as Moors arrived at the hospital, wounded soldiers poured into the field hospital. Moors later wrote than on June 14, "I saw more horrible sights than ever before."[8]

Captain Sprague turned his attention to the ground his men were assigned to cross. He believed that "it is impossible to convey in words any adequate idea the difficulties, natural and artificial, presented by the ground between us and the enemy." The ground was "in clear view and point-blank range of the enemy." It was filled with "a tangled mass of felled trees, vines, and brambles," which would slow the advance but do nothing to shield the men from Confederate defenders, who "fired from safe cover," revealing their lines with "incessant puffs of smoke."[9]

Despite the Union attempts to confuse their adversaries with feint attacks and diversionary bombardments, Colonel Steedman of the 1st Alabama Infantry noticed the massing Federal forces near the Priest Gap as the sun came up. Confederate soldiers opened fire on the Union infantry. Federal gunners on ship and shore continued their general bombardment against the entire Confederate line. Homer Sprague noted that the attack was supposed to be "a surprise" but that the clamor of gunfire from the Confederate lines proved that "the enemy comprehended the movement." Walter Turner of the 39th Mississippi Infantry wrote in his diary, "I have never heard such firing."[10]

Some Union soldiers moved forward with the help of whiskey. According to Private Henry Johns, the surgeons sent liquor to the men assembling for battle. Almost every man enjoyed a drink. Most refused to get drunk, but a few took advantage of the opportunity for overindulgence. Johns claimed, "the Second Louisiana were nearly all drunk." According to James Dargan, "a decotation [*sic*] of whiskey and some other substance is offered to us, about all accept." Henry Maglathlin later recalled that the men were ordered to remain silent as they prepared for action, in hopes that they would catch the rebels by surprise. However, the men "who had been plentifully supplied with whiskey, could not be restrained from shouting as they went." Maglathlin moved forward convinced that the Confederates now knew exactly when and where the attack would come.[11]

Henry Willis, with the 53rd Massachusetts Infantry, watched "the bursting of the shells in the air and the dense clouds of smoke from the artillery gave a fearful aspect to the scene." The men from Massachusetts watched the bombardment as Confederate gunfire began to strike members of the regiment. A bit of rebel lead hit Captain Stratton, commanding Company C, entering his head near his ear and exiting under his left eye. Willis watched him walk off the field "with characteristic pluck," leaning on the arm of a surgeon.[12]

Henry Willis, with the 53rd Massachusetts Infantry, heard General Paine order the advance. The 38th and 53rd Massachusetts advanced as skirmishers and began to cross five hundred yards of open ground between the Union and Confederate breastworks. Men from Massachusetts rushed forward toward the Confederate lines. Union infantryman, deployed in lines of battle, followed close behind the skirmishers.[13]

Joseph Bailey of the 16th Arkansas Infantry heard the "loud huzzas" of the northern men, and the men in gray replied with "the old familiar rebel yell, gathering volume as it swept down our line." Private George Powers and the rest of the 38th Massachusetts Infantry rushed forward with a shout. The rebels greeted the New Englander's war cry with "a volley of musketry," and "the cries of wounded men told us what to expect." Despite the horrific cries, "not one hesitated," and men in blue pressed forward. Powers heard General Paine yell above the sounds of gunfire, "forward 38th, forward 53rd." Men from Massachusetts rushed forward through hills, ravines, and prickly brush. Federal units lost all organization as men fell to the ground dead and wounded, but the survivors pushed forward.[14]

Massachusetts infantryman James Hosmer claimed in his diary, "I felt no sensation of fear, nor do I think those about me did." He "thanked God that Sunday morning that I was in perfect strength in every limb for that day's most solemn service." This was not a conventional service "rendered in a peaceful temple" but a far different ritual that took place "amid grime of powder and sweat of blood." However unconventional the service might have been, Hosmer considered it a religious service destined to "bring about for him the acceptable things."[15]

Appleton Sturgis, an ordnance officer serving on General Paine's staff, was near General Paine as the Federals began to take fire. Within moments of coming within range of Confederate lines, multiple bullets struck Sturgis. The first bullet was a spent ball that bruised but did not seriously injure Sturgis. Three more bullets struck Sturgis's sword, cutting the weapon into pieces without wounding Sturgis. Another bullet grazed Sturgis, tearing one of his pockets open without hurting him. A final bullet hit Sturgis in the thigh, knocking him to the ground and ending his advance. Sturgis noticed that he was less than two hundred yards from Federal lines, and he began crawling to the rear in search of safety while his comrades pressed forward.[16]

The Union infantry attack hit the 1st Mississippi, 49th Alabama, and 15th Arkansas Infantry at almost the same moment. Only 165 men were available to defend Fort Desperate, the vital position at the northeast corner of the Confederate line. According to Howard Wright, the rebels ducked down into their trenches, allowing the storm of Union gunfire to pass overhead, and lay "waiting for them with the ball and the bayonet." Men in blue pressed forward as they absorbed what Henry Willis of the 53rd Massachusetts Infantry described as "a most galling front and enfilading fire." The Federals flung hand grenades toward the Confederate lines just before making their final rush, but the percussion impact grenades failed to detonate when they hit the soft earth of the Confederate defenses. Initially surprised by the grenades, quick-thinking rebels spread blankets to catch additional Federal grenades, which they hurled back at the men in blue. New Yorker James Peck lamented that the grenades "did not explode to our satisfaction." Despite the failure of most of their grenades, the Federals kept advancing.[17]

As the Union infantry came within a few feet of the parapet, Confederate soldiers fired blasts of buckshot at point blank range that killed some attackers and wounded many others. The Federals had more men than the rebels had bullets, and a handful of Union infantrymen kept running forward. As Federals crossed the crest of the Confederate earthworks, rebels in the reserve line of rifle pits at Fort Desperate fired a volley into the Federals and "swept them off the parapet as if they were chaff caught by a sudden gust of wind." A few members of the 4th Wisconsin, 8th New Hampshire, and 38th Massachusetts Infantry regiments somehow survived and captured a small section of the Confederate line. Members of the 53rd Massachusetts Infantry paused for a moment, but the promised reinforcements did not arrive, and men from Massachusetts were unable to continue the charge. They laid in the bottom of the ditches and hoped for reinforcements. Some men tried to build breastworks with the bags of cotton they brought to fill in ditches.[18]

A bullet struck General Paine's leg and knocked him to the ground. Private George Powers suddenly realized that he could no longer hear the voice of General Paine, which had pushed the men forward. Powers later claimed, "whatever chance of success there may have been at the outset, the fall of Gen. Paine destroyed it." Appleton Sturgis, serving on Paine's staff, agreed, telling his mother that, despite everything that went wrong in that attack, "if Paine had not been wounded, we should have taken the place."[19]

John Whitehead and the 28th Connecticut Infantry brought up the rear, which protected them from the first volleys of Confederate gunfire.

However, it did not protect them from the sight of those volleys. Whitehead saw "many come back alone, some with only one finger gone, some two, some the hand all tore to pieces." The wounds he saw were mostly wounds to the hands and arms because men shot in the legs could not walk to the rear, and most of the men who were shot in the head or body never walked again. Despite the miserable sight of shattered bodies headed to the rear, Whitehead and his comrades pushed forward into the sounds of gunfire.[20]

James Dargan of the 4th Massachusetts Infantry wrote that "we have begun to meet the wounded and to see the dead, they are numerous, we shudder." Dargan believed the plan failed almost as soon as it began. Confederate obstructions made it impossible for Federal grenadiers to effectively throw their bombs. The bundles of sticks and cotton Federals carried were not nearly large or numerous enough to fill the ditches. Confederate bullets killed and wounded men until "the earth is fairly covered with frames writhing in blue uniforms." Dargan wrote that "the yelling, screaming, groaning, shouting, swearing of wounded excited and dying men" filled his ears. He had never thought much about the phrase "bite the dust," but it suddenly made perfect sense to him as he and his comrades flopped to the earth, pressing their faces into the ground where "the dust is deep."[21]

Homer Sprague and the 13th Connecticut Infantry formed a line of battle and prepared to attack as Sprague found General Weitzel sitting on a fallen tree. Rumors circulated among the troops that the Union army had captured a portion of the Confederate line, and Sprague asked Weitzel if it was true. Weitzel responded "with a despondent look" that "no, we've not got a foothold inside." Sprague then pressed, asking, "why can't we go in at once?" Weitzel replied that "we can go in if the officers and men will only do their duty." At that moment, a messenger from General Banks arrived and ordered Weitzel to send his men forward and "force an entrance at once into the rebel works at all hazards." This attack would hit the northern end of the Priest Gap. Sprague was disappointed when Weitzel ordered the men to advance but did not lead them, choosing instead to remain seated on the fallen tree, a choice which "discouraged" and "astonished" the men forming in line of battle.[22]

Union reserves advanced through Confederate artillery and small arms fire and toward "the indescribable din." Their path was littered with unexploded hand grenades, muskets, cartridge boxes, and "pools of blood" left by the dead and wounded men who remained where they fell. As the company came into a clearing, Colonel Richard Holcomb, who previously served in the 13th Connecticut but was then in command of the 1st Louisiana Union Infantry, gave a rousing speech that sounded "like the growl and roar of a lion." Holcomb yelled, "All I ask of you is to follow me! Will you follow me?" Fifty members of the 1st Louisiana shouted "Yes! Yes!" but "the majority sat sullen and cowed." Clearly unsatisfied with the Louisianans' response, Holcomb turned to the members his old regiment, the 13th Connecticut, and yelled "there's the glorious old 13th Connecticut! I know they'll follow me! Thirteenth, I'll lead you!" Captain Sprague responded, "the 13th Connecticut will follow Colonel Holcomb anywhere." Soldiers from Connecticut gave "a rousing cheer" in response to Sprague's claim. John B. Whitehead and the 28th Connecticut Infantry were nearby, but it does not appear that they joined the "rousing cheer." They advanced until they got with "15 or 20 rods" (roughly eighty to a hundred and ten yards) of the Confederate position, where they took cover behind a small embankment, unable to advance any farther.[23]

The Federals attacking the northern end of the Priest Gap faced even more difficult terrain than their comrades to the south. Roughly parallel irregular gorges cut by Sandy Creek and its tributaries stretched from the Union to the Confederate positions on the north end of the Priest Gap. The gorges grew steeper and deeper as they moved to the Confederate lines. Within a few feet of the Confederate positions, the smaller stream and its ravine twisted sharply to the north, creating a natural ditch that protected the Confederates. Rebel positions towered over the main ravine, and Confederate defenders were well situated to sweep the ravine with multiple interlocking fields of fire. A smaller ravine trailed south toward the scene of the attack Paine led. That ravine was already filled with the dead, the dying, and the desperately trapped. Weitzel therefore ordered his men to focus on crossing the main ravine, which was exposed but was at least not already stuffed with the broken remnants of a failed attack.[24] Perhaps Weitzel hoped that his men could force their way through the main ravine and capture a section of Confederate line while the rebels focused on slaughtering the remnants of Paine's command.

Weitzel's men bore to the right from the Jackson Road. As with Paine's command, Weitzel's troops advanced with a line of skirmishers in the lead, followed by grenadiers, followed a short distance behind by men deployed in lines of battle. The artillery trailed behind. The Federal skirmishers tried to conceal themselves, hiding behind whatever vegetation they could find, until they crossed the main ravine and popped up between twenty and fifty yards from the Confederate lines. The rebels greeted the men in blue with a horrific blast of fire. Undeterred, the surviving Federals charged.[25]

Colonel Holcomb swung his sword, yelled "forward!" and led the Union infantry north of the Priest Gap in a charge toward the rebel lines. The Federals surged forward. Unable to maintain anything resembling a formation over the difficult ground, the already mixed-up units lost all pretense of organization, becoming "a mob rather than an army." Almost as quickly as the charge began, Colonel Holcomb dropped dead with a bullet to his head. Confederates picked off numerous other officers. The attack failed. Many men died, others fled, and most dove for cover. The most advanced members of the 13th Connecticut Infantry huddled in a ravine, thirty yards from the Confederate lines. The time was 10:00 a.m.[26]

As Weitzel's men attacked the northern end of the Priest Gap, the Confederates launched a counterattack against the Union breakthrough that had come from the south. The rebels enjoyed almost instant success, retaking their original line and forcing the Federal survivors to choose among surrender, retreat, or a scramble for cover. As many Federals retreated, the men in gray picked up unexploded grenades and flung them back at the fleeing Union infantry. Many years later, Alabama soldier Daniel Smith noted that the grenades, which did not detonate when thrown uphill onto the soft earth of the Confederate positions, did explode when he and his comrades threw them back from the elevated positions atop the Confederate breastworks, striking human bodies that were firmer than soft ground, "carrying death to their former owners." Company K of the 1st Alabama Infantry, acting as gunners for the 24-pounder cannon nicknamed Virginia, fired exploding shells into the retreating Federals from a flanking position nearby. James Goble believed that several of the Federals who penetrated Confederate breastworks "got faint hearted" when they saw from their elevated position that they were nearly alone and that several hundred of their comrades were lying dead on the field.[27]

Diversionary Attack on the Confederate Center

In an effort to distract the rebels from defending the Priest Gap, General Augur ordered his troops to feign an attack on the Confederate center. Augur's infantrymen attacked briskly and in good order. The feint did

The tunnel under the "Citadel" dug by Union forces with a view to blowing it up, June 1863. Library of Congress.

little to distract the rebels, who opened fire on the attacking Federals. Realizing that the Confederates were not distracted from the main Union attacks, Augur ordered his men to fall back. The Federals reported that they suffered little loss. However, Thomas Alexander of the 1st Tennessee Heavy Artillery claimed in his diary that "our artillery played on them" and that the Federal "loss very heavy." In his diary, John Chamberlin of the 75th New York Infantry described the "horrors" of wounds inflicted on his comrades in that attack by loads of Confederate buckshot.[28]

Fighting on the Confederate Right Flank and the Citadel

General Dwight had hoped to send Major Edward Bacon of the 6th Michigan Infantry and fifty men on a daring predawn raid to capture General Gardner and open a path into Port Hudson for Grierson's cavalrymen. Bacon was unable to locate the promised path. Grierson simply refused to acknowledge or support what he saw as a foolish plan. Dwight's plan therefore failed before it even began.[29]

With the failure of the unconventional raid, Dwight reverted to a more conventional approach. Shortly after sunrise, Dwight ordered the 15th

South view from Port Hudson, showing the damaged interior of Port Hudson after the siege in July 1863. Library of Congress.

New Hampshire and the 26th Connecticut Infantry regiments to form lines of battle and march to within seven hundred yards of the Confederate lines. Charles McGregor saw mounted officers ride up and down the line as they ordered the men to advance. The infantrymen obeyed and moved forward, emerging from the wood as the Confederate artillery opened "with tremendous power." McGregor heard someone order the double quick just as they stepped to within rifle range and the Confederate line burst in "one unbroken sheet of flame." The brigade's center crashed into the smoldering ruins of the Slaughter House as Confederate fire ripped holes in what was left of the Union line. McGregor called it "the very vortex of hell." Men near the Slaughter House gave up the advance and dove for cover. Charles McGregor heard "the enemy send up a great shout of victory." The infantry fight lasted less than two hours, but the artillery bombardment and snipping continued all day.[30]

The Stalemate

Many Union soldiers clung to the ground in no man's land near the Priest Gap. Massachusetts soldier Henry Willis later wrote that Union soldiers in no man's land felt stuck, "scarcely daring to move." Federals worried that any movement they made would draw Confederate gunfire. According to

Colonel Steedman, the area in front of the Confederate works "was blue with their uniforms, and the weeds and bushes still further forward were strewn with them." A few mudholes in the ravines contained the only water available to the men stuck between the lines. Nicholas Fox of the 28th Connecticut repeatedly crossed the open field to deliver water to stranded men, later earning a medal of honor for his efforts. Union troops fired back whenever they dared risk a shot.[31]

Appleton Sturgis lay bleeding less than two hundred yards from Federal lines. He began crawling to the rear, either because he did not think his wounded leg would support him or because he did not dare stand up and give the rebels another clear shot at him. As he slowly crept to the rear, a bullet struck him in the back of the head. Sturgis did not know if it was a spent ball, a glancing shot, or if his cap had provided just enough padding to keep the bullet outside his brain. Sturgis did know that he was alive, although with "a severe pain and a big lump" on his head. A moment later he fainted. He awoke later to find that "I was covered with dirt and dust by the shots that fell around me." Sturgis remained completely still, afraid to move. He later told his mother, "I never expected to get off the field alive." Sturgis did not tell his mother how he escaped the battlefield. Perhaps he did not know. He did know that he awoke again in a field hospital, where he wrote his mother a letter to tell her that he was still alive and expected to make a full recovery.[32]

According to Walter Turner of the 39th Mississippi Infantry, roughly a hundred Union soldiers realized that they were hopelessly stuck between the lines. They had no chance of breaking through the Confederate positions and feared they would be shot down if they abandoned the cover of no man's land and retreated. Unable to advance or retreat, they surrendered to the Mississippians.[33]

Lieutenant A. M. Trawick of the 16th Arkansas had been firing all day, until "my face and hands were covered with powder." Colonel Pixlee approached Trawick and said, "Lieut. Trawick, you are tired, let me get in there and shoot a few Yankees," explaining that "my carbine is much longer ranged than your musket." Trawick pointed out that the Federals were keeping up a steady fire and that it was therefore too dangerous for the colonel. Trawick refused to relinquish his firing position unless Pixlee ordered Trawick to step aside. The colonel gave the command, and Trawick made himself comfortable a short distance behind the line and began reading from his pocket New Testament. Ten minutes later, Trawick "heard something as thrown against a tree." He looked up and saw Pixlee fall, with a wound to his head. The colonel died without speaking another word. Another soldier, N. C. Berry, eulogized Pixlee: "no braver or truer man, no better soldier, ever died beneath the stars and bars."[34]

Captain Sprague of the 13th Connecticut Infantry later remembered that "the sunshine was now burning like fire." Stuck thirty yards from Confederate sharpshooters, the Federals traded rifle shots with men clothed in dirty gray that made them nearly indistinguishable from their native soil. General Banks repeatedly sent messengers with orders that the Union infantry should "enter the works at all hazards." In response to the cries from the rear to go forwards, the men at the front urged everyone to go back. An officer of the 159th New York called out, "if General Banks wants to go in there, let him go in and be d— [*sic*]!" Colonel Nicholas Day of the 131st New York Infantry said, "I started out this morning with the determination to be a h— [*sic*] of a fellow! I've been a h— [*sic*] of a fellow long enough. If anybody else wants to be a h— [*sic*] of a fellow, I've got no objections! But it's too d— [*sic*] risky!" Day was not the only man who felt he had been a hell of a fellow long enough. Union officers in no man's land refused to renew the attack, but Banks kept sending messengers to scream at them with orders to move forward.[35]

As a member of the 52nd Massachusetts Infantry's color guard, James Hosmer was under strict orders "not to fire, except when the colors are especially threatened." He kept his weapon loaded and ready to fire but noted, "I can only be shot at without returning the discharge."[36] It is unclear why Hosmer obeyed the order to hold fire while ignoring orders from the army's commander to advance. Rules, like men, became tangled in the hellscape between the lines. Each man made decisions that might seem incomprehensible to those that were not in that horrific place.

Union stretcher-bearers tried to rescue the wounded, but the Confederates fired at anyone who dared move within range of their guns. Massachusetts soldier George Powers watched "two colored men" somehow avoid rebel gunfire long enough to get to a wounded Union soldier, but the Confederates wounded both men with rifle fire before they could retrieve the wounded man. One of the "colored men" lay motionless, but the other tried to escape. The Confederate shot him a second time, and when he moved again, they sent a third bullet crashing into his body.

Several Federals tried to rescue General Paine, who was unable to walk on his wounded leg, but Confederate sharpshooters struck down each man who tried to save the general until General Paine "begged them to make no further efforts to get to him." Henry Rufus Gardner wrote home that Paine suffered because he "was too brave." Captain Washburn, who was also wounded and stuck in no man's land, was able to throw a canteen of water to Paine, and the precious liquid probably saved Paine's life. With nothing better to do, Washburn pulled out his last cigar and smoked it. Later he joked that if he had brought a half a dozen cigars, he would have had a fine day. Colonel John Kimball asked General Grover to propose a truce for the removal of the wounded, but Grover replied with "disdain," and there was no truce.[37]

John Barnard of the 52nd Massachusetts Infantry and his comrades "lay flat on our backs or sides" as they suffered under the "full heat of the sun." If the men dared move, "we were reminded of where we were by the sharp crack of the rebel rifle." Several Confederate bullets "passed close to my face as I lay on my back." While he lay almost motionless and unharmed, bullets crashed into a comrade just a few feet away. Barnard dared not move to help him and tried to say still in hopes that he would not be wounded next.[38]

Other Federals refused to stay still and took their chances, choosing to make mad dashes for the safety of the rear. James Dargan laid on the ground until a Confederate bullet grazed his scalp, causing a minor wound that came within an inch of killing him. Unwilling to remain within range of Confederate gunfire, he abandoned his weapon and fled to the rear. Dargan knew that retreating was dangerous but believed that "I could not be any worse that I was." With the satisfaction of a man who survived the run, he wrote in his diary later that day, "I made excellent time getting out." According to Henry Johns, "the most unpleasant part of the 14th of June was the fierce heat." It was "one of our sultriest days, a day, too, without a cloud." The sun "scorched us and we had to shade the barrels of our guns to keep them from becoming too hot to handle." Johns laid in the miserable heat until "I thought I would go crazy." Johns crafted an awning from his gun, ramrod, and jacket. Confederate sharpshooters responded with a stream of bullets, and he disassembled the improvised shade. At about noon, Johns decided that "a living dog is better than a dead lion," and he resolved to make a run for it in search of shade. Before beginning his sprint, he pulled out a half pint of whiskey, which he had purchased several days before, and gulped it down. Johns initially ran in a zigzag as the bullets whipped past until he grew so exhausted that he could barely move and ran straight for the Union lines. Somehow the bullets all missed him, and he collapsed in the shade just inside the Union positions, where he fell asleep.[39]

The Confederate infantry could have inflicted even more pain on the stranded men in blue, but their ammunition was running low. Confederate officers ordered most of the men to hold their fire, while only a few designated sharpshooters from each unit were allowed to snipe at the Federals. Joseph Bailey believed that the Federals made a horrible mistake by trying to flee one at a time and inadvertently giving Confederate sharpshooters time to focus on one target at a time. By the end of the day, Bailey's shoulder was bruised from constantly firing his rifle.[40]

As night fell, more Union soldiers escaped under the cover of darkness. The rebels could not see the men in blue slipping away, but they could hear something moving in the darkness and fired into the void. John Barnard escaped, but it was "heartbreaking" to realize that many men were unable to escape and to "hear their cries for water." James Goble could hear the cries of the wounded for water from his sick bed behind the lines in Port Hudson. As sick as he was, he was luckier than most of his comrades and adversaries. He might have been the only soldier in Port Hudson who enjoyed a bed in a house and the comfort of wife who was eager to nurse him back to health.[41] Most of the sick and wounded at Port Hudson suffered horribly, without a personal nurse.

Private C. Hamilton, serving in Company H of the 3rd Corps Afrique, was working as a stretcher-bearer, removing the wounded from the field, when a bullet struck him. The projectile hit him in the upper left back of his thigh, near the "gluteal fold," fracturing his thigh bone and exiting the front of his leg near his femoral artery. Comrades took him to the regimental hospital as he suffered "excessive pain in the limb." Hamilton bled profusely. To slow the bleeding a surgeon inserted a finger into the wound and pressed on an artery. The surgeon then sliced into Hamilton's flesh, exploring the wound and attempting to remove splinters of shattered bone. Several surgeons quickly consulted on the wound and concluded that only an amputation at the hip could save Hamilton's life. They administered chloroform as an anesthetic. The surgeons removed

Hamilton's leg at the upper thigh, leaving a flap of skin to cover the exposed flesh. Hamilton "bore the operation remarkably well." Hospital orderlies bandaged his wound and tried to make him comfortable. After he regained consciousness, Hamilton reported that he felt much better and thanked the surgeons for their work. After forty-eight hours he appeared to be making a full recovery and he reported that he was "very hopeful." Hamilton then took a turn for the worse, slowly slipping away until he died four days after the operation.[42]

William Aldis died of wounds received at Port Hudson on June 14, 1863. Aldis received a wound to his right arm on May 27 but remained on duty. It is unclear if Aldis finally succumbed to that wound or if he died from another wound suffered on June 14. His wife, Sarah Aldis, died on May 20, 1864, in New York, of "congestive fever." The Aldis children became orphans and disappeared from the historical records. It is unclear what happened to them or if they ever read their father's letters home.[43]

At a Union field hospital, James Dargan received a bandage for his wound and had a "copious draught of brandy poured into me to counteract my sinking spirits and declining strength." Unlike many of the wounded, Dargan could walk, so he did not wait for a stretcher and wandered to a rear hospital, where he saw "such dreadful scenes!" that included "amputation of limbs, of hope of life; by butchers, botchers and pseudo surgeons." Dargan claimed, "the froth on the fast-ebbing blood beneath that table is a foot high." He watched the stretcher-bearers sort the wounded into groups based on the seriousness of their wounds. Doctors examined wounds with "useless probing, cutting, and gouging." Dargan smelled "the confounded scent of chloroform" and watched the "amazed look" of men who awoke from surgery to discover that that they were now missing an arm or leg. He wrote, "Oh! Rather than fall into the clutches of the experimentalists I would prefer to die the death of a hero!" Determined to escape the surgeons, he walked away from "this horrid place, while yet I am able to walk." He walked until he could walk no more and then he crawled, finally resting in a tent his regiment set aside for their wounded.[44] Dargan ended his diary entry for June 14 with a poem:

> Come to the bridal chamber, Death!
> Come to the mother, when she feels
> For the first time, her first born's breath;

Come when the blessed seals
Which close the pestilence are broke,
And crowded cities wail its stroke;
Come in consumption's ghastly form,
The earthquake shock, the ocean storm;
Come when the heart beats high and warm,
With banquet song and dance and wine,
And thou art terrible: the tear,
The groan, the kneel, the fall, the tear,
And all we know, our dreams, our fear
Of agony, are thine.
But to the Hero—when his sword
Had won the battle for the free,
Thy voice sounds like a prophet's word,
And in its hollow tones are heard
The thanks of millions to be.
We tell thy door without a sigh;
For thou art Freedom's now, and fame's
One of the few, the immortal names,
That were not born to die.[45]

The Aftermath

The battle of June 14 improved the morale of at least some Confederates. Once again, the Federals tried and failed to capture Port Hudson. Walter Turner wrote in his diary, "our loss is very small in comparison to that of the enemy." James Goble claimed in his diary that the Confederates stood "like heroes" and drove the Federals back at every point." He mocked Banks for claiming in his demand for surrender that he had "overwhelming numbers and is bound to take Port Hudson." Goble recalled Gardner's taunt for Banks to "come and take it" and pointed out that Banks had failed to "come and take it" as Gardner dared. Sarah Morgan wished that she was a man "to have the blessed privilege of fighting." She wanted to be "on the breastworks, or perchance on the water batteries." Morgan loathed that she "was unfortunately born a woman" and could therefore take no part in the glory of Port Hudson's defense. Unable to fight, she turned to prayer and offered herself "on the altar of my country to mosquitos" if God would continue to protect Port Hudson. Howard Wright reported that, despite the overwhelming numbers, firepower, and courage of the Union troops, the Confederate defenders had repelled every attack, and the Federals had left "heaps of their slain upon the field." Wright believed that after the fighting on June 14, Confederate soldiers became convinced it was "an impossibility to take Port Hudson."[46]

Confederate newspapers spread word of the Union defeat at Port Hudson. The *Daily Dispatch* of Richmond, Virginia, reported that the defenders of Port Hudson "repulsed the enemy twenty-seven times" and were "in fine spirits." The *Memphis Daily Appeal* praised General Gardner as "a great commander" and his men as "brave boys." Confederate surgeon David Fentress wrote home to his wife from his posting at an Arkansas hospital that "the almost annihilation of Banks at Port Hudson" was "so much good news."[47] By this time, Port Hudson's garrison was completely cut off from the rest of the Confederacy, so it is unclear where Confederate newspapers received their information. It is possible that their articles were based on a mix of Union sources and creative writing.

In the aftermath of defeat, Union soldiers and sailors tried to assess blame. According to Henry Willis, members of the 53rd Massachusetts Infantry believed that the June 14 attack failed because, while General Grover's men, including the 53rd Massachusetts Infantry, did their part, the promised diversionary attacks by General Weitzel's forces (including men from New York, Vermont, and Connecticut) never materialized. James Hardenbergh of the 133rd New York Infantry believed that "we would have taken it" in the last charge on Port Hudson if we had been supported by other regmt [*sic*] but masachusetts [*sic*] troops are not worth their salt." William Park, onboard the *Essex*, believed that every attack failed because the army attacked piecemeal and failed to concentrate their strength against a single point. He also believed that many Union officers refused to lead their units and abandoned their men. Staff officer Richard Irwin summarized the battle of June 14 as "a bloody repulse" that "may be even termed a disaster." In retrospect, Irwin believed that the Union bombardment, which preceded the infantry attack, was to blame for the day's failures. He believed the Confederates were asleep when the artillery woke them just in time to prepare for the attack that might have otherwise caught them by surprise. Irwin also argued that one more push by the Union infantry would have broken the wavering Confederate lines.[48] Suggesting that the infantry should have pushed a little harder is an interesting criticism from a staff officer who did not participate in the attack.

At least some Union enlisted men who participated in the attack disagreed with Irwin's argument that one more push could have punched through the Confederate lines. Corporal David Hanaburgh of the 128th New York Infantry, who participated in the attack, agreed with Irwin that the pre-attack bombardment was a mistake that served only to alert the rebels. However, he disagreed that infantrymen like himself could have won the day if they had been a little more aggressive, arguing that the army's commanders were entirely to blame because they laid aside every lesson of warfare when they refused to launch a surprise attack "for the sake of some perceived theory of honors, or a worse theory of an attempt to strike terror to the heart of the foe by mere noise." Lieutenant Luther Townsend of the 16th New Hampshire Infantry was blunter, writing, "no one familiar with the events of that and the previous Sunday assaults can blame the disheartened men."[49]

Men disagreed about blame, but all available sources acknowledged the horrific Union losses. The Federals lost over seven hundred men in the attack, eighty-six of them were among the roughly 280 members of the 53rd Massachusetts Infantry who went into action. Writing in 1893 with the benefit of three decades of hindsight, Chaplain John Moors of the 52nd Massachusetts Infantry concluded that June 14 was the greatest disaster the 19th Corps ever suffered. Colonel Richard Irwin reported that the Union forces lost 216 killed, 1,401 wounded, and 188 men missing in the day's fighting. Irwin believed that the reality was even worse than the numbers suggested, noting that many of the wounded were unlikely to ever recover, that most of the missing were dead, and that many of the men taken out of action by death or disabling wounds were among the best leaders in the army. Appleton Sturgis, on General Paine's staff, wrote his mother from a hospital bed that she should not believe the official reports of the army's losses. He was adamant that the army's report "will not [the words "will not" are underlined in the original document] be a correct one for we have lost too heavily for it to be acknowledged."[50]

The failed attacks of June 14 demoralized many Union soldiers. In his diary, John Chamberlin described the battle as "a terrible slaughter without any good results." Lieutenant Luther Townsend described the men as "discouraged, worn out, almost dazed with grief and disappointment." In his memoir, Harris Beecher, an assistant surgeon with the 114th New York Infantry, recalled the members of his regiment that died on June 14 and lamented, "it hardly seemed possible that the cause of American liberty could require such noble sacrifices." Beecher believed that the attacks of June 14 were "a decided defeat, and had been productive of such frightful carnage, that it cast over the whole army a spirt of gloom and despondency." John Barnard wrote his cousin a detailed account of the horrors of June 14, concluding, "I have seen enough of war and when we think of the loss of life that is likely to be before Port Hudson is taken, it makes our hearts sick." James Hosmer thought that, after the attack, whippoorwills changed their song to "whipped you well!" He knew it was bizarre but, "I will never believe the bullfrogs that night croaked anything but "rebs, rebs!" Hosmer even thought that the owls "hooted out from the treetops 'what can you do-o-o?' [*sic*]." He claimed that, in response, a storm gathered and "behind the black clouds shook the lighting, like the menacing finger of an almighty power threatening to doom this obstinate stronghold." Captain Orton Clark wrote that the failure "again depressed our spirits" and "lead us to question if our commander in chief knew aught of his profession."[51]

Captain Sprague and the survivors of the 13th Connecticut Infantry reformed in the dark of night:

> And now came the fearfully depressing realization that all these efforts, all this heroism, and all this appalling carnage, had failed. Yonder still floated the rebel flag. Their batteries still dammed the great river. From their bands inside, we could hear their jubilant secession music. We were defeated! With bitter anguish we thought of this, and then of the unavailing slaughter of our near and dear friends. Two thousand men, young, gallant, brave, the flower of our army, had fallen. . . . In the gloomy hospital, or still under the rebel fire on the scorched field, they were sleeping their last sleep or writhing in agony! And all in vain! No, not in vain! For home, country, honor, freedom, civilization, they had indeed poured out their blood like water. On our right lay the bleeding form of Col. Paine. Besprinkling the garments of our soldiers were the brains of the gifted Holcomb.

The thirsty earth drank the life-blood of our loved Strikland, and McManus, and Carey, and Cramm, and Burns, and Merwin ; and how many more! . . . In the dense thicket, in the deep gully, in the tangled ravine, in the open field, on the hostile ramparts, wherever the mimic lightning blazed, or the hissing bolt flew, or the huge shell thundered in showers of death, they cheerfully gave their lives. Many a heroic deed of that eventful day will forever remain untold. Many a manly form sleeps in an unknown grave beneath those crimsoned battlements. But, thank God! each patriot name, each self-sacrificing soul, forgotten here, yet "liveth evermore!" And, long as the Mississippi shall roll its mighty volume to the sea the memory of Port Hudson shall kindle the loftiest emotions of every lover of the human race.[52]

—10—

We Lay in the Ditches

THE SIEGE OF JUNE 15, 1863-JULY 9, 1863

> We lay in the ditches, in the mud and water in the sunshine, in the blood of fallen comrades. . . . It was here that I was bespattered with the blood and brains of my comrades—stepped across their bodies to give orders—lay on the very boards at night on which they had fallen and tinged them gory red. I had more chills during this siege. We eat all the meat and bread in the Fort. Prepared an old railroad engine to grind corn and peas on—eat all the beef, all the mules—all the dogs and all the rats around us.[1]
>
> —RICHARD McCLUNG, 15th Arkansas Infantry

> It is 7 months over since you were mustered into the U.S. Service, the time is passing away & I am continuing the weeks of thinking that will not be a great while now before you will be at home. Marion received a letter from Malcom Tuesday he was then in the Hospital & did not know where all of the company was. She is anticipating going to Greenfield the 11th of July to see the 52nd mustered out of service. I think it will be an interesting time. Sad to many yet joyful to those whose loved ones are spared.[2]
>
> —CAROLINE SMITH to her husband, William Smith, of the 52nd Massachusetts Infantry

The Morning of June 15

On the morning of June 15, the Confederate cavalrymen outside Port Hudson refused to give the Union army time to recover from their defeat on June 14. On June 15 Colonel Logan's Confederate cavalry dashed down the Clinton Road. Gray-clad troopers caught the 14th New York Cavalry by surprise. After a brief skirmish, the Confederates defeated their adversaries, routing the Union troopers, who fled from the field. With the Union guards out of the way, rebels captured nearly a hundred Union hospital patients and numerous supply wagons. Grierson's Union cavalry mounted up and launched a counterattack against Logan's men. The Confederate cavalrymen decided to quit while they were ahead and retreated, taking Union supplies and prisoners with them into the interior of Louisiana. The Federals held the ground, but the rebels retained the initiative.[3]

On the morning of June 15, General Banks issued General Orders Number 49. Ignoring the failures of the day before, Banks congratulated his troops on "the steady advance made upon the enemy's works." He claimed he was "confident of an immediate and triumphant issue of the contest." Banks even predicted, "once more advance and they are ours!" He requested a thousand men to volunteer for a storming party. Probably aware that most men would be reluctant to volunteer, Banks offered to give medals, furloughs, and official recognition to any man who stepped forward.[4]

Some Union soldiers did not appreciate the proclamation from their army's commander. Joshua Hawkes wrote home, "it seems to me time to put an end to assaults, they do not pay." Lawrence Van Alstyne wrote in his diary, "I believe it must be a joke." He asked himself, "if the whole 19th Army Corps together can't get in, how can a thousand men expect to do it?" Lieutenant Luther Townsend was shocked that the rebels did not counterattack. He believed the Confederate garrison could have easily driven the Federals from the field if they attacked on June 15. Townsend believed there was no reason to think that another Union attack would be any more successful than the failed assaults of May 27 or June 14 and condemned Banks as "foolhardy." John Barnard refused to volunteer for the storming party because "I have no confidence in the Gens." James Peck mocked the men who volunteered for the attack, pointing out that Banks promised them a furlough after the attack, which Peck believed most of the volunteers would not live long enough to enjoy. Peck confirmed that he would attack if ordered but declared, "I will not volunteer to charge a place when almost certain death stares me in the face." Union engineer officer John Palfrey claimed that General Banks did not consult the engineers before developing his plan for a new attack and that, after learning about the new plan, all the engineers predicted the attack "would be unsuccessful." Palfrey pled with members of Banks's staff to reconsider the planned assault.[5]

Despite the horrors of the failed June 14 attack and the understandable cynicism of many Union soldiers, men volunteered for the assault column. Colonel Henry Birge of the 13th Connecticut Infantry immediately volunteered to lead the assault party and, "although the whole project was disapproved by many of the best officers and men in the corps," Birge enjoyed the respect of so many men that within days 80 officers and 956 men volunteered for the assault. Members of some units were more eager to join than others. In several regiments, only a single man volunteered for the storming party, but the entire 1st and 3rd Louisiana Native Guards volunteered for the assignment, and the colonels of those regiments allowed only the best men to join the detachment.[6]

Colonel Henry Birge took overall command of the assault party, which he then split into two battalions, with Lieutenant Colonel Van Petten of the 160th New York Infantry in command of one battalion and Lieutenant Colonel Bickmore of the 14th Maine Infantry in command of the second. Captain Duncan Walker joined the party as an adjutant general, and Lieutenant Edmund Russell became the detachment's signal officer. With their organization in place and their ranks filled, the men made their wills, left their units, and gathered in a grove of trees behind the navy's shore battery to begin training for the attack. Sergeant John Fleming of the 165th New York Infantry noted in his diary that he volunteered for the assault column, which he considered good duty since "the stormers have no duty to perform, we are well treated" and the men enjoyed "whiskey rations."[7]

Banks punished men who he believed were cowards. When William Park of the *Essex* visited the navy's shore battery outside Port Hudson, he noticed that unspecified regiments of white men were hard at work while black regiments lounged in the shade. Park thought this was odd because the army almost always made black men do the bulk of the hard labor. A soldier told Park that "the white regiment were their [*sic*] for punishments for their cowardly conduct on the 14th." The soldier also said that "to make their punishment more degrading, Banks sent the nigger regiments that behaved so well down to look at them." Park thought it was a "first rate plan" and only objected to the fact that the enlisted men, and not officers, were forced to do hard labor. Park believed the officers "are a great deal more to blame."[8]

On the morning of June 15, General Banks sent a courier under a flag of truce to Port Hudson. The courier carried a request for permission to provide the Confederates with medical supplies, if Gardner promised to share the supplies with Union prisoners. Gardner gratefully accepted Banks's offer and suggested a truce so that the Federals could remove their wounded, trapped between the lines. Banks sent in medical supplies but ignored Gardner's suggestion of a truce. Despite the lack of a formal truce, men of both armies tried to comfort the wounded. A group of rebels slipped out of their lines and tried to take water to wounded Federals. Union sharpshooters fired at the rebels as soon as they exposed themselves, and the Confederates returned to their lines without delivering any water. Another group of Confederate soldiers found a "stalwart negro suffering the most excruciating agony" from five wounds and horrific thirst. They brought him back to Confederate lines, using a blanket as a stretcher, and comforted him until he died shortly after they delivered him to the post hospital.[9]

There is some disagreement in the sources about which side initiated the truce on June 16. According to Howard Wright, on June 16, "the effluvia from the decomposing bodies" had become "very offensive." General Beall then sent a flag of truce to the Union commander directly across from his position asking permission to deliver the Union dead to their army for burial. The Federals accepted the offer, and Beall's command delivered 160 dead Federals along with one horribly wounded man who had somehow survived. Arkansas Confederate Joseph Bailey wrote in 1927 that Gardner must have asked for the truce because Gardner "would willingly have allowed the removal of all dead and wounded," but Banks may have felt it would be humiliating to ask a second time [he asked for a truce after the May 27 attack] for such a favor. Bailey's speculative comments might say more about how he felt about General Gardner and General Banks in 1927 than about what happened in 1863. According to Union staff officer Richard Irwin, "it was not until the evening of the 16th that Banks could bring himself to ask for a suspension of hostilities for the relief of the suffering and the burial of the slain," which suggests that Irwin believed that Banks initiated the request. New York infantryman Harris Beecher claimed in his memoir that "for three days after the assault, General Banks refused to accept of a truce for the burial of the dead and care of the wounded" and only agreed to the truce after "the indignation of the army compelled him to accede to the humane requests of the rebels." Beecher believed that the Banks's "cruelty seems to admit of no justification." Alabama infantryman James Goble's diary entry for June 16 also includes a claim that Banks refused to agree to a truce because he was "cruel," although Goble believed that Banks hoped that the stench of dead bodies would demoralize Confederate soldiers. It is tempting to see Goble's diary, written during the war, as more trustworthy, but Goble was a lowly private who was sick at the time and would not have enjoyed any firsthand knowledge of Banks or his motives.[10]

Battlefields were never pleasant, but two days of Louisiana heat made the battlefield of June 14 particularly horrific. James Peck told his parents that "we had to tie clothes over our faces to stand the smell. It was awful." Some of the men had wounds filled with flies." He wrote, "Mother it was awful to see the dead with thair [*sic*] eyes wide open covered in blood." John B. Whitehead told his wife that helped bury men who "were covered with maggots and smelt so we couldn't stand by them." All the wounded who were able to crawl away had already left, but the ones that could not escape had lain "in that boiling sun and died by inches." Whitehead found two wounded men "crazy, with their ears full of maggots." Arkansas Infantryman Joseph helped bury the dead and comfort the wounded Federals who were somehow still alive in no man's land. In 1927 Bailey still vividly remembered "those who survived were in a horrible condition, fly blown, and wounds full of maggots."[11]

Despite the revolting work, the truce provided an opportunity for rest and conversation. During the truce, one "middle-aged Johnnie" told New York soldier Lawrence Van Alstyne that the Federals "were not at all like they had been told, and there were some who believed we had horns on our heads and had feet like cattle." The rebel explained that "now that they know better, they don't want to fight us, and will only do so when obligated to." Louisiana infantryman Howard Wright expressed gratitude to the generous Union soldiers who demonstrated kindness to their opponents during the truce "making presents of tobacco, coffee, and newspapers." The rebels replied with gifts of sugar and molasses. In contrast to other sources that suggest these were trades, Wright referred to the exchanges as "presents" and suggests that the Federals were carried "the courtesies of war to an unusual extent." When not busy exchanging luxuries, both Union and Confederate soldiers improved their fortifications, and rival work crews chatted about their work "as amicably and jovially as if the siege was only a joke and the contending parties were the best of friends."[12]

Improving Fortifications

While the Union storming party prepared to launch another attack, most Union soldiers focused on siegecraft. The engineers thought the attack was doomed to fail but worked tirelessly to try and prove themselves wrong. The Federals drove their works forward with "zig-zag ditches." When Confederate sharpshooters made it difficult for men in blue to push forward, Union soldiers rolled cotton bales and barrels filled with dirt in front of their approach trenches. From their advanced positions, they Federals could hear but not see that the Confederates were also hard at work improving their positions. Engineer officer John Palfrey was delighted to report that, while Confederate rifle bullets occasionally penetrated the Federals' dirt filled barriers, "their force was spent" by the barriers and did not hurt the workers they struck. Palfrey believed that the work of "negro soldiers directed by white officers left nothing to be desired." In an odd bit of appreciation mixed with bigoted language, Henry Cross wrote home that "the niggers have done nine-tenths of all this immense and superhuman labor."[13]

Confederate defenders struck back at the blue lines that crept toward them. According to Richard Irwin, rebels set the cotton on fire during raids in the dead of night or by firing "blazing arrows" into the bales. Irwin's claim that Confederates fired "blazing arrows" must be treated with great skepticism since Irwin was a staff officer who appears to have spent little time on the front lines, and because no surviving eyewitness testimony of "blazing arrows" at Port Hudson appears to exist. Considering the bizarre nature of "blazing arrows," it seems unlikely that only Irwin would mention the presence of Confederate archers firing "blazing arrows" if the Confederates ever fired such projectiles. A more reasonable description comes from John Moors, who spent a great deal of time at the front and reported that "they throw back cartridges, to which they attach burning saltpeter paper, evidently with the intention to set our cotton on fire." The statement is far more likely to be accurate because, while there is little evidence that any Confederate soldier at Port Hudson used a bow and flaming arrows, Confederate soldiers did have cartridges and paper. Corporal Skelton of the 1st Mississippi Infantry won acclaim from General Gardner on June 25 when he dodged Union sharpshooter fire and set fire to Federal cotton bales with bit of flaming wood before returning to his unit somehow unharmed. John Palfrey reported that Confederates set fires by firing incendiary bullets into cotton bales, which is also possible. Improvised incendiary bullets, crafted from bullets combined with cotton saturated with turpentine, were used by Confederate soldiers at Vicksburg, and rebels at Port Hudson could have crafted similar bullets. Confederates carried improvised explosives on their nighttime trench raids, "occasionally pitching a bomb within the sleeping camp" of unwary Federals. When not trying to set the Federals on fire, the Confederates set fires within their own lines, burning houses in Port Hudson to provide better fields of fire against the approaching Union lines.[14]

Struggling with how to proceed against pyromaniac rebels, Union engineer John Palfrey argued that they should stop using cotton bales, which were flammable, to shield their work and only use sandbags or barrels filled with dirt. Colonel Edward Prince was not content with Palfrey's simple solution and took inspiration from the Middle Ages. He suggested the construction of siege towers. Each tower would be composed of two layers of sugar barrels, filled with dirt, which would support a floor for a team of sharpshooters, who would enjoy the protection of sandbags. Prince won approval for his plan, and the men got to work. After a night of hard labor, the men in gray awoke to see the improvised gun platforms towering above their lines, ripping the height advantage away from them.[15]

The Confederate sharpshooters were not deterred by siege towers and continued to hammer away at the Federals, who fought back just as ferociously. In response to Confederate sharpshooters who fired at any Union gunner who dared expose his face, Union artillerymen constructed iron shutters , backed by cotton, which covered the cannon sights, leaving only a tiny hole just big enough for a gunner to aim but very difficult for even the best Confederate sharpshooters to hit. Members of the 1st Indiana Heavy Artillery went on the offensive. The battery's heavy cannons were less than ideal tools for targeting single sharpshooters, so Sergeant Rufus Dooley distributed rifles to a team of his artillerymen, who slipped into no man's land and tried to pick off Confederate soldiers. According to Corporal David Hanaburgh of the 128th New York Infantry, a red-shirted Confederate sharpshooter his comrades nicknamed "Arkansas Joe" tormented the New Yorkers from a treetop sniping post until one of the Federals knocked him out of the tree with a well-placed rifle bullet. James Hardenbergh wrote home that the siege lines were "rather a bad position

Ruins of a defensive installation or battery, Port Hudson.
Library of Congress.

for a timmid [*sic*] person for a man no sooner shows his head above the riffle pitts [*sic*] than he gets a ball through it from some neighborly reb [*sic*] and vice versa."[16]

Confederate soldiers went low as the Federals went high. Colonel Ben Johnson, commanding the Confederate defenders of Fort Desperate, ordered his men to dig tunnels under the breastworks, which allowed men to move from the upper defenses on the top of the parapet to the outer ditch, which was lower but much closer to the Union lines, without exposing themselves. Captain L. J. Girard of the Confederate ordnance department created improvised landmines by attaching friction primers and trigger wires to the vent holes of 13-inch cannon shells. He then slipped out of the Confederate defenses and buried the mines just outside the most threatened sectors, leaving trigger wires trailing back to Confederate lines, which allowed the defenders to set off the mines at their leisure. Lieutenant Dabney directed the placement of sharpened wooden stakes between the 1st Mississippi Infantry's front line and their secondary positions where the Mississippians could retreat if needed. The Confederates stretched wire among the stakes about a foot and a half high to trip advancing infantry and also buried landmines among the stakes. According to Howard Wright, the Confederate defenders primarily planted the obstructions to prevent surprise attacks during the night and were confident that they could hold their positions with nothing but bayonets, if they could see their enemy coming.[17]

Private Frank Flinn of the 38th Massachusetts Infantry provided one the most detailed descriptions of life in the Union trenches in the final stages of the siege.

> We will now go into the ravine and know what sights and sounds it is our business to be familiar with. First, we must creep out of the ravine, through the tops of prostrated trees, whose boughs catch our clothing; then up by the charred trunk, the feet slipping in the mud. Your head now comes in range of riflemen in the trees over there. A few steps more and we come within full range from the parapet; but do not stop to look. Stoop as low as you can and run. The stumps will shelter you, pitted with the striking of balls against it, as if it had the smallpox when a sapling. When you have caught your breath, run for a trunk; it is an ugly one to get over, for it is breast high, and one's whole body has to come into the enemy's view. Once over this, and the road is smoother. We soon gain the cover of the woods and are comparatively safe.
>
> Down through a little gully and we enter the beginning of the sap, at the end of the military road. Behind the angle, just back there, is the station of the ambulance men. They wait there, day and night, with stretchers ready. Three or four a day out of the brigade and working party are carried out. The ambulance corps: but music, we never hear it now, not even the drum and fife. It is too stern a time for that. We pass out into the sap. Here is the most dangerous point of all, just at the entrance. You can see how the rebel parapet commanded it. We are going considerable nearer to it, but we shall be better sheltered. T [*sic*] is just in front, with an old shot pierced building behind it, and white sandbags laying on top of the tawny slope. That old building might be a ruinous mill, those bags might be grist, laid out there along the wall until the miller was ready for it, but every day or two, there is a sharp-eyed Mississippian with his rifle pointed through some chink. The trench goes under a large trunk, stretching from bank to bank, and from here we are tolerably safe. Only tolerable;

for one of our boys was hit in the face by a glancing ball, and another was mortally wounded by a fragment from one of our shells, which flew back into our lines from over the rebel parapet, where the shell exploded.

Climb a steep pitch now, and we reach the station of Co. The sap is here about six feet wide, and four feet deep, dug out of the hard soil, the dirt being thrown out on the side toward the enemy, forming a banking rising about five feet from the surface, and therefore about nine feet about the bottom of the trench. Here, now, are our boys, the few that are left, barely twenty. Along the top of the ridge of earth, logs are placed into the underside of which, notches are cut at intervals of three or four feet, leaving between the earth below and the timber above a loophole four or five inches in diameter for the men to fire through.

Let us climb up and take a view of the world through the hole. Carefully laying your body up against the steeply sloping bank, resting the feet on the edge of the sap. By all means take care that the top of your head does not project above the narrow timber. Your face is at the hole now. From the outside, a grove runs along the top of the thick bank; then comes the open air; and opposite to you, within call easily enough, is the deadly ridge; the two or three tents behind it, the old, ruinous chimneys, the one or two shattered buildings, so near you can plainly see threads, and bricks and splinters.

Try one more look. Can you see anyone? No head, I'll warrant; for though they are brave enough, they are not often careless. The most you will be likely to see will be a hand for a moment with a ramrod, as the charge is pushed home, or a glimpse of butternut, as a fellow jumps past some interval at the sandbags. You duck your head now as the balls whistle over. It is a nervous sound, but you would soon get over that here. They go with one hundred different sounds.[18]

Captain Orton Clark and the rest of the 116th New York Infantry spent most of their time rotating through alternating shifts supporting the artillery batteries and occupying advanced rifle pits. Clark later revealed that, while it might seem strange, the men always preferred time in the exposed rifle pits, rather than in the relative safety of artillery positions. He explained that, when the men entered the rifle pits, they would "watch as intently as a cat does a mouse." The New Yorkers fired on any "Johnnie" who "dared to show so much as his top-knot." Clark took apparent pride at the work of his men, claiming, "Port Hudson had made excellent marksmen of most of us." Sharpshooting "was no easy task, but there was excitement about it, and very few were found who did not prefer it to the support of the batteries."[19]

An unidentified Union soldier wrote to "friend Charley" from under a tree near the front lines. He wrote, "We are thundering away at the gates of this tough hole yet; these fellows hang on like green death." He seemed frustrated that, rather than surrender, Confederate soldiers were all willing to risk "a huge shell droppings in their bed at night." Before ending his letter, the unidentified author complained, "this is written under a tree with the flies terrible and plenty and the thermometer less than 120 degrees in the shade."[20] The writer did not seem to consider that, across the lines, Confederate soldiers may have expressed frustration with Union men who held on, enduring danger, heat, and flies rather than simply going home.

Confederate soldiers jokingly taunted the Federals with questions of when the thousand men were coming to get them. Union soldiers wondered how the rebels knew about the assault column, but the rebels would not reveal how they knew about the planned storming party. New York infantryman Lawrence Van Alstyne sarcastically suggested in his diary that perhaps "Banks has sent them word, as he has done of every move yet." In his diary, John Chamberlin wrote that "the rebels say we might as well try to storm Hell as their intrenchments [sic] ." Perhaps reluctantly, Chamberlin confessed, "I think there is some truth in what they say."[21]

The Union mortar boat fire, which had pounded Port Hudson for weeks, dramatically decreased beginning on June 18. Howard Wright did not know why the fire slacked, but he suspected that Confederate deserters had told the Union forces that the shells inflicted little damage on the Confederate garrison, which enjoyed the protection of excellent earthworks, and had made "Port Hudson valuable as an almost inexhaustible iron mine." William Park, serving on the *Essex,* provided a more plausible explanation, writing in his diary that the fleet received a request from General Banks to end the bombardment by the mortar boats because Banks was afraid that their shells might hit the Union army's lines, which were getting very close to Port Hudson. Banks later asked the fleet to provide fire support for the army, but only on specific targets and for limited periods of time. The men on the *Essex* grumbled that Banks's request was foolish and that the navy should be free to bombard Port Hudson whenever they felt they could do so safely. However, the sailors deferred to Banks and only fired when someone from the army requested their help. From the deck of the gunboat *Albatross*, Louis Boyd wondered aloud how it was possible for the battered and starved rebels to still resist the Union's overwhelming power.[22]

Federal artillery and small arms fire continued to slowly wear down the Confederate army. Lieutenant Richard McClung wrote in his diary, "it was here that I was bespattered with the blood and brains of my comrades." He "stepped across their bodies to give orders." At night he laid on ground where men had died, turning the earth "gory red."[23] While McClung's description of ground colored "gory red" by blood must be treated skeptically, McClung was there, and his choice of words provide important insights into how it felt to participate in the battles for Port Hudson.

The Expiration of Federal Enlistments

The expiration of enlistments for nine-month men caused conflicts within the Union forces. Many Union soldiers who enlisted in nine-month regiments believed that their terms expired in mid- to late June and wanted to go home. General Banks argued that the terms of enlistment had not expired and ordered the men to remain on duty. Private Henry Johns of the 49th Massachusetts Infantry was "sick of hearing the cry 'time's out' as if the country's claims on us expired with the 19th of June." When some members of the 4th Massachusetts Infantry refused to extend their nine-month enlistments or remain on duty, Johns felt that "the honor of Massachusetts is somewhat stained." Johns believed that men like himself who wanted to go home "have the letter of the law on our side" but that, more importantly for Johns, "patriotism demands our continued service." John Barnard of the 52nd Massachusetts Infantry, another nine-month regiment, believed that "the government have not done honorable by the nine months men," but he still supported the men who wanted to extend their enlistments by one month, which would send them home on August 11 instead of July 11 as originally planned. In a similar vein, George Waite of the 26th Connecticut Infantry wrote home, "as soon as we take this place if we take it we shall come home what of us does not get killed." James Peck of the 173rd New York told his parents that, while he was suffering from hunger and exposure, "I must not find fault for it was all my own doing." He explained, "I am not sorry that I enlisted." However, he admitted, "I would like to be home for a little while."[24]

Rufus Dooley of the 1st Indiana Heavy Artillery was not in a nine-month unit and expressed disdain for the "nine months men" in a letter to his mother. He complained that much of the army was composed "of nine months men which were never made to fight and never will fight." Dooley also made a distinction between "eastern men" from "Mass–Conn–Vermont," who "will not do for soldiers," and suggested that the army would be more successful if it had "a few more such regiments as the Wisconsin and Michigan and the works would not have been in the hands of the rebels" for so long.[25]

A rare example of a preserved exchange between a nine-month man and his family discussing enlistments provides insights into the difficult decisions faced by soldiers and their families. On May 14, 1863, Caroline Smith wrote her husband, William Smith of the 52nd Massachusetts Infantry, expressing sorrow for women she knew who were made widows by the war. She expressed her eagerness to see William return home as soon as his nine-month enlistment term expired. Perhaps Caroline worried that, if William extended his enlistment, he too would die, and she would be forced to raise their daughter alone. William Smith responded on June 9 that, while he missed his family and wanted to return home as soon as possible, "if the government see fit to keep us here . . . they can do it." He assured his wife, "I think I am good for it for my health is good." He asked her to "give my love to all and much for yourself and [his daughter] Hattie."[26] John Whitehead of the 28th Connecticut Infantry told his wife that he would not renew his nine-month enlistment because "I am not down hearted or discouraged but am looking for a time when I shall see you all again." True to his word, Whitehead left Port Hudson when his enlistment expired, returned home to his family, and lived until 1898.[27]

Living Conditions in the Siege Lines

Regardless of their enlistment status, Federals continued to search for comfort outside Port Hudson. Some officers lived on an elevated platform made of fence rails, protected by a roof made from two shelter tents. Private Henry Johns pondered in his diary that, when he and his comrades returned home, they would offer great hospitalities to their guests as they gave up their beds and enjoyed "what we would now consider luxurious accommodations, a pillow on a carpeted floor." Johns wondered how long it would be before soldiers would be "reconciled to the efficiency of feather beds." Union soldiers enjoyed some access to the river, which gave them opportunities for bathing and doing laundry. Lawrence Van Alstyne washed his shirt until it shrunk and the buttons fell off. William Smith thanked his wife for sending him tea. However, while he appreciated the gift, he told her not to worry about sending more because "I have plenty of it," and he was even able to save the tea she sent "for a time of need." Smith told his wife not to worry about him, even if he ran out of tea, because "I am as tough as a bear." Justus Gale of the thanked his sister for the "little papers of cayene [*sic*]."[28]

Sutlers filled the Union camps with luxuries. Justus Gale purchased pickles from sutlers to go with meals of "melted sugar and crackers." James Dargan stole enough pickled onions from sutlers to feed his entire company. He explained that he felt justified stealing from the sutlers, who he believed were "daylight robbers and plunderers." Dargan's comrades thanked him "with a rousing cheer." Dargan's company was nicknamed "the faithful thieves." Henry Johns noted in his diary that the sutlers provided Union soldiers with "tobacco, gingerbread, cheese, and other articles considered superfluous" by the government.[29]

Luxuries provided brief comfort for soldiers still on an active campaign with no end in sight and poor-quality government rations. Henry Johns noted in his diary that men were particularly eager to purchase luxuries because the climate spoiled much of the food supplied by the government. The army provided the men with fresh beef, but "in less than two hours the meat was so fly blown that we could not use it." For the first time in the history of the regiment, members of the 49th Massachusetts Infantry were forced to eat "wormy bread" in the final stages of the fight for Port Hudson. Hungry men learned to knock the worms out of their bread before eating. William Whitney wrote home that his rations were "rotten and poor," which caused many men to get "somewhat scurveyish [*sic*]." He complained that he was unable to enjoy even his poor rations because flies were so numerous that he did not "have undisputed ownership of the dish" as he fought bugs for possession of his food.[30]

Port Hudson's Confederate defenders enjoyed few of the luxuries that sustained the Federals and a trickle of Confederate soldiers deserted. Union infantryman Lawrence Van Alstyne noted in his diary entry for June 18 that "another squad of deserters came in this morning." He believed that desertion "must weaken the enemy faster than our fighting has done." All the deserters told "of hard times and short rations." Another group of Confederate deserters surrendered to Van Alstyne's regiment and said that "there were others that would come if they were sure of good, fair treatment." The deserters had told their comrades remaining in Port Hudson that, if the Federals treated them well, they would place a green bush in a particular point in the Union lines as a sign that it was safe to desert. Louisiana infantryman Howard Wright stated that during the siege roughly a hundred and fifty men who "could not reconcile themselves so easily to the hardships and dangers of the siege" deserted in search of "the better provided commissariat of the enemy." Wright described the men as "almost entirely foreigners of a low class, or ignorant conscripts from Western Louisiana" who lacked "patriotism." Wright claimed that Port Hudson's defenders did not miss the deserters.[31]

Confederate Resilience

While some Confederate defenders gave up the fight, most remained defiant. Port Hudson's garrison continued to hold their formidable defenses, despite the Federal pressure. Not content to stay in the relative safety of fortified positions, men in gray remained on the offensive and launched trench raids against Union besiegers. Confederate raiders operated in small groups and attacked in the dark of night. The raiders expressed no hopes of punching through Union lines or breaking the siege. Their goal was to drive in Union pickets, gather intelligence, and capture supplies before returning to their own lines. Perhaps most importantly, Confederate trench raids kept Union soldiers off balance and reminded them that the men in gray were dangerous and unpredictable adversaries.[32]

Outside Port Hudson's lines, Confederate forces fought the Federals for control of Louisiana. General Kirby Smith, headquartered west of the Mississippi River, ordered General Richard Taylor to cross the Mississippi River and relieve pressure on Vicksburg and Port Hudson. The rebels tried and failed to cut Union supply lines at the Battle of Milken's Bend (June 7, 1863), roughly thirty miles north of Vicksburg. Taylor next turned south, looking for a weak point between New Orleans and Port Hudson, where only a few Union soldiers protected supply depots in scattered garrisons. Taylor believed that, if he struck a strong blow, he could cut Banks's forces off from New Orleans and that he might even be able to recapture New Orleans, which he hoped would rise in rebellion against the Federals if a Confederate army appeared near the city.[33] It was an ambitious plan, but Taylor was a daring commander.

Taylor's forces advanced on the Federals while Confederate raiders already near Port Hudson kept the pressure on their enemies. Early on the morning of June 18, Confederate cavalrymen stormed into Plaquemine, Louisiana, roughly thirty miles south of Port Hudson. They surprised the Federals and captured Lieutenant C. H. Witham, along with twenty-two members of the 28th Maine Infantry. Captain Albert Stearns, serving as the provost marshal of the parish, escaped with thirteen members of the 131st New York Infantry. In the brief skirmish before the New Yorkers fled, the Federals killed one Confederate and wounded two more rebels. The Confederates then opened fire on the *Sykes*, *Anglo-American*, and *Belfast*, three steamboats lying in the bayou, and wounded two sailors. The sailors surrendered, and the Confederate cavalrymen burned all three boats. Three hours later, the Union gunboat *Winona*, commanded by Captain Weaver, arrived at Plaquemine from Baton Rouge. The sailors fired shells into the Confederate cavalry, forcing them to retreat. Rumors circulated through Union ranks that the Confederates who attacked Plaquemine were the advance guard of Richard Taylor's army on their way to break the siege and relieve Port Hudson.[34]

Union soldiers and sailors worried that Confederate raiders might take them prisoner at any moment. Louis Boyd, on the Union gunboat *Albatross* complained to his wife that he was "really tired of laying up" on the ship. He would have left the boat, but "we cannot go on shore or at least not out of sight of the ship for fear of the rebel Guerillas" who "are very plentiful in this neighborhood." He claimed the rebels captured sixteen men from another gunboat. Boyd wanted to go home, not to a Confederate prison camp, and he remained on the *Albatross*. Lawrence Van Alstyne noted in his diary that Federals on foraging expeditions were sometimes grabbed by Confederate guerillas who constantly hovered just outside the Union lines.[35]

At sunrise on June 23, Major Sherod Hunter and 325 Confederate cavalrymen attacked the Union supply depot at Brashear City (later renamed Morgan City), roughly eighty miles south of Port Hudson. Taken by surprise, the Federal garrison and their supporting gunboats offered only "feeble resistance." The fighting, although "severe," was of only "short duration," and the Union surrendered the town. The rebels lost only 3 men killed and 18 wounded. The Federals suffered 46 killed and 40 wounded. The Confederates captured roughly 1,300 Union prisoners, 2,000 "negroes," eleven 24-pounder and 32-pounder siege cannons, 2,400 Enfield and Burnside rifles, over two hundred wagons, and "immense quantities of quartermaster's commissary, and ordnance stores."[36]

On the same day, in an apparently unrelated incident, Rufus Dooley wrote that Confederate cavalrymen ambushed a Union foraging party, killing or wounding most of the foragers. Justus Gale heard of the raid on Brashear City and lamented the loss of the personal baggage and knapsacks his regiment had left in the depot for safekeeping. The loss of the depot was a serious problem for soldiers like James Peck, who wrote that all of his clothing wore out and the army failed to provide replacements. Peck was reduced to a shirt, underwear, and socks. He joked that, in his all-white clothing, "I look more like a ghost that like one of Uncle Sams [*sic*] soldiers."[37]

Union morale fell. Rufus Dooley remained somewhat optimistic, expressing his confidence that the Federals would eventually capture Port Hudson. He acknowledged that "there has been already more lives lost than should have been" since "there is but few men in it and their rations is three ears of corn per day." He believed the Union attacks failed because they were not properly coordinated and because each unit worked alone. Dooley did not name anyone he felt was at fault, and it is unclear who, if anyone specific, he felt deserved the blame. James Dargan wrote in his diary on June 21, "here we are today with a beleaguered fortress and a series of forts before us, as defiant, stubborn, and vigilant as ever." Dargan saw no sign that the rebels were planning to surrender. He worried that a Confederate relief army was coming to strike the Union rear and "scatter us." Dargan and his comrades were "scared to death" by worries that Banks would soon order them to attack Port Hudson again. Colonel Thomas Cahill wrote home from his post in New Orleans that "the siege of Port Hudson drags its slow length along." He predicted that "Banks must either take it or leave it" before his next letter arrived in his wife's hand.

Cahill's wife in New Haven, Connecticut, wrote to her husband, "we hear very discouraging accounts from Port Hudson," and recommended, "if you are ordered up I hope you will form some excuse or other and not go." Perhaps to prevent bad news from spreading from the army into civilian life, General Banks forbade men from mailing letters.[38]

Beginning on June 26, the Federals redoubled their efforts to grind their way into Port Hudson. Union artillery batteries on ship and shore pummeled the Confederate fortifications. Every day, the Union cannons blasted holes in the Confederate parapets while the infantry pushed their advanced positions closer to the rebel lines. Every night the Confederate defenders repaired the holes in the darkness but were unable to push the Federals back. Thomas Alexander of the 1st Tennessee Heavy Artillery called the June 26 bombardment the "hardest sheeling [*sic*] I ever seen by land or water." Four of Alexander's comrades died that day, and several more were wounded on that one day alone.[39]

The Federal artillery fire made Confederates miserable, but it did not force them to surrender. On June 26 Louis Boyd wrote that he was "sick and tired" waiting for Port Hudson to surrender. Boyd wrote that Banks had lost thousands of men in failed assaults and fired countless artillery shells, but Port Hudson's defenders remained defiant. From his perch on the deck of the *Albatross*, he viewed Port Hudson's interconnected lines of forts, rifle pits, and water batteries, all perched on the tall bluff that was the most "naturally fortified place" he had ever seen. Boyd noted that, even after enduring the horrible siege and endless bombardment, "I do not think there are a stronger place in the whole southern Confederacy than Port Hudson." However, "the Black Republicans says it must be taken and I suppose it will be" with the help of "their negro brothers." In a previous letter, the Florida-born Boyd had defended himself from his wife's accusation that he was not a true southerner. Perhaps he referred to the "Black Republicans" and "their negro brothers" in an effort to distance himself from the political cause his wife disdained, or perhaps this was an honest expression of his feelings. Regardless of the motives that may have impacted his word choice, Boyd committed to "wait patiently" for the rebels to starve and looked forward to resigning his commission after the surrender so he could return home to his family.[40]

Confederate defenders continued to send trench raids against the slowly advancing Union siege lines. After dark on June 26, Colonel David

Provence of the 16th Arkansas Infantry sent thirty volunteers under Lieutenant McKennon to raid the Union lines and destroy their progress on battery 16. For some unknown reason, Lieutenant Bartlett, commanding a detachment of the 21st Maine Infantry, ordered his men to hold their fire. Perhaps he thought the mysterious figures in the dark were a work crew returning from a forward position. The Arkansans took Bartlett and five of his men prisoners, captured a stack of unfired muskets, and destroyed the battery. A single son of Maine injured a rebel by knocking him off a parapet, reasoning that, while Bartlett had ordered the men not to fire, he had said nothing about a well-placed punch. Another Federal ignored his orders not to shoot and fired a single shot, which missed but alerted Major Merry, who arrived with another detachment of the 21st Maine and drove the Confederate raiders back. The rebels retreated with their prisoners and newly captured firearms. According to Howard Wright, the Arkansans forced their prisoners to carry empty sandbags back to the rebel lines.[41] By that point in the siege, sandbags might have been more precious to the Confederate army than firearms.

Late on June 26, Captain Robert Pryne of the 4th Louisiana Infantry slipped into the Confederate lines, bringing dispatches from General Johnston and news of the world. Pryne had escaped Port Hudson by floating down the river on an improvised raft made of canteens several weeks before. He returned by slipping across the river once again. Up until Pryne's arrival, many members of the Confederate garrison had believed that a Confederate army would soon arrive to raise the siege. Pryne brought the disappointing news that the Confederacy would not send a relief army and that, aside from small numbers of raiders and guerillas, the defenders of Port Hudson would fight General Banks's army alone. Perhaps even more troubling, Pryne reported that Federal forces had engaged in "rascality" and pillaged the Mississippi countryside.[42]

Several Confederate accounts claim that the Confederate defenders were not depressed by Pryne's news. Howard Wright claimed that the news "did not by any means discourage" members of the garrison. Instead, "the effect was to instill even a deeper spirt of resistance into the soldiers' hearts." The men "felt a greater pride in the success of their own fighting, and never for a moment despaired of holding the place so long as the provisions and ammunition held out." They did realize that they could not hold out long after they ate the last of their rations and responded favorably when Gardner suggested that they might have to cut their way out. Paul de Gournay heard "a jolly major, whose foible was an inordinate love for the game of poker exclaim we have staked too heavily already not to see the game out." Walter Turner wrote in his diary that Pryne's news of Federal abuses only reaffirmed his belief that God would ensure the victory of the righteous Confederacy over the "rougish [*sic*] hounds" who ravaged the homes of Mississippi soldiers like himself who were serving at Port Hudson.[43]

A Confederate relief army was not coming to Port Hudson, but small Confederate units remained on the offensive. On June 27 Confederate cavalrymen under the command of General Thomas Green approached Fort Butler, an earthwork fortification helping the Federals control the junction of the Lafourche and Mississippi Rivers, near Donaldsonville, roughly halfway between New Orleans and Port Hudson. A Union small garrison consisting of a hundred-man detachment from the 28th Maine Infantry and another hundred convalescents from various units, only thirty of whom were healthy enough to fight, prepared to defend the fort. Several of the convalescents manned the fort's cannons. The gunboat *Princess Royal* was anchored nearby, prepared to provide fire support.[44]

Just before dawn on June 28, General Green ordered Colonel Joseph Phillips to lead the 3rd Texas Cavalry of the Arizona Brigade in an attack on Fort Butler. Captain Augustin Thompson of the 28th Maine Infantry "heard a terrific yell from 600 Texas Rangers" as the rebels charged forward. The Federals in Fort Butler and onboard the *Princess Royal* opened "a perfect storm of fire on the attackers." For a moment it looked as though the Texans might capture the fort, but they got stuck in a ditch just outside the fort's walls. Union artillery found their range and, according to Captain Thompson, within minutes, the "Texans lay dead in a heap." After three hours of fighting, the surviving Texans in the ditch surrendered. The Confederate attack on Fort Butler failed, but General Richard Taylor posted artillery batteries on the west bank of the Mississippi River to contest Union control of the river. Harris Beecher, in the works near Port Hudson with the 114th New York Infantry, believed Taylor's artillery enjoyed a "complete blockade of the Mississippi," which cut off the besieging forces from their supplies. Beecher reported that many of the men were "filled with serious forebodings for the future."[45]

Late on the evening of June 28, Confederate cavalrymen captured a wagon train en route to the Federal supply depot at Springfield Landing. In response, Banks ordered Grierson's cavalry and infantrymen of Weitzel's brigade to leave Port Hudson and recapture the wagons. Harris Beecher and other members of the 114th New York Infantry felt "great relief" to leave Port Hudson and "breathe the fresh air out in open fields." The New Yorkers moved slowly, frequently halting to "feast upon green corn, blackberries, and fruits." Beecher believed "no one can describe the exquisite enjoyment there is in eating vegetables, after living for a long time upon a steady diet of salt meat and hard tack." After several days of wandering the Louisiana countryside and filling their bellies, the Federals gave up on catching the elusive Confederate cavalry and returned to Port Hudson.[46]

Federals began to wonder aloud if they were now the besiegers or the besieged. John Palfrey noted in his private journal that Confederate guerillas often cut Union telegraph lines, making it impossible for the Federals across Louisiana and Mississippi to coordinate their attacks. The Confederate raiders repeatedly captured sections of the roads connecting Port Hudson to the rest of the world, forcing the Union army to suffer from a lack of supplies. Perhaps most importantly, the raids demoralized Union soldiers.[47]

Confederate raiders inflicted pain on the Federals and may have slowed but could not prevent the advance toward Port Hudson. By June 30 the Union sharpshooters occupied positions barely thirty yards from the Confederate lines. Federal infantrymen and artillerymen fired constantly, even when the Confederates remained safely hidden from view. A detachment of artillerymen from de Gournay's command arrived on the Confederate right with 12-pounder and 24-pounder artillery shells that had been modified into hand grenades. It was hard to throw the large grenades, but the Confederates constructed a wooden gutter that allowed them to roll grenades down the parapet into the Union lines.[48]

The noise was horrific as the Federals crept closer to Port Hudson. John Moors told his wife it was "like living in a perpetual thunderstorm." Rufus Dooley wrote his mother that he and many other members of his unit were "a little deaf from the roaring of the thirty-pounders," a reference to the heavy artillery his unit operated. Dooley believed that his suffering was worth it because by June 27 "the rebel parapet look like the ruins of some ancient city all tore to atoms." In another letter, Dooley wrote his mother that "we are no [*sic*] near their works that pieces of our own shell [*sic*] fly back here when they burst." Not content to blast the rebels from nearly point-blank range, Union engineers kept working until "they are now making a road for the artillery to get into the forte [*sic*]." He predicted, "I think our men shurely [*sic*] will take possession" of Port Hudson.[49]

At 6:00 p.m. on June 30, the Federals assaulted the Confederate right while the rebels ate a meager supper. The Federals captured a section of the outer ditch and attacked the main parapet. According to Howard Wright, "the first six men who got inside paid their lives as the entrance fee." Confederate reinforcements counterattacked the breakthrough and forced the Federals to retreat. Tennessee artilleryman Thomas Alexander noted that, while he and his comrades repulsed the attack, they suffered four killed and seven wounded in the fight. The Confederates reclaimed their ground but could not replace the men they lost as the garrison continued to wither away. Confederate engineers decided that the Federals were destined to capture a section of the line, so they began construction of fallback positions where they could retreat if the Federals broke through.[50]

William Park watched the fight from the deck of the *Essex*. He wrote in his diary that he saw Union and Confederate infantrymen fire at each other from barely twenty yards away. The lines were so close that the Federals threw hand grenades directly from their rifle pits into the Confederate trenches. The rebels replied by lighting short fuses on heavy artillery shells and rolling them down the bluff into the Union lines.[51] Forbidden from firing unless given a specific fire mission by the Union army, Park and his comrades sat on the deck of their boat, spectators to the horror.

Confederate engineers detected signs that the Federals were digging a mine under Fort Desperate. In response, Lieutenant Dabney ordered the construction of a fallback position behind the fort. He also asked Captain Girard to supervise the digging of a counter gallery in hopes of blowing up the Union mine from underneath. The rebels worked as silently as possible. They could hear the Federals digging, and the Confederates hoped that the Union engineers could not hear them dig too.[52]

The siege continued to wear down the Confederate garrison physically, but some rebels remained confident. Walter Turner wrote in his diary on June 28 that "the enemy admis [*sic*] the loss of 15,000 in front of Port Hudson." In the Louisiana countryside, "our cavalry is disturbing and harrowing the flanks of the enemy daily." General Taylor's troops conducted a counteroffensive from across the Mississippi River, capturing Federal supply depots. Rebels passed around letters taken from captured and dead Federals that complained of horrific losses and corpses left to rot in the sun. On the evening of June 30, Logan's Confederate cavalry captured Union general Neal Dow, who was recuperating from a wound in a house behind the lines.[53]

Confederate Hunger

On June 29 the Confederates ate the last of their beef. On July 1 the men killed and butchered a wounded mule as an experiment. According to a report in the regimental history files for the 1st Alabama Infantry, when General Gardner asked the men if they would prefer to eat mule meat rather than surrender, the Alabamians replied "yes! give us dog, if necessary!" Howard Wright claimed that "all those who partook of it spoke highly of the dish." Wright described mule meat as "a darker color than beef, of a finer grain, quite tender and juicy" with "a flavor between that of beef and venison." The army also issued some horsemeat, which Howard Wright said "was very good eating, but not equal to a mule." By July 4 mule meat was a regular part of Confederate rations in Port Hudson, and almost every soldier ate the unconventional meat. Corn supplies were almost gone by July 4, and the men had little to eat other than mule meat, peas, sugar, and molasses. Soldiers also killed and ate rats, which Wright claimed were "quite a luxury" and even better than chicken. Joseph Bailey ate rats, as well as mule and horsemeat. He thought the unusual meats might have tasted good if they were properly fried in grease, but the men had no grease, so they "usually boiled and put over live coals to barbecue" whatever meat they were issued. Men grew weak from malnutrition and hunger. The animals the Confederates ate may have provided precious few nutrients. James Goble wrote in his diary that a courier tied up his horse and was killed before he could return to the animal. Four days later, soldiers finally realized why the horse was left unattended and turned him loose. Goble claimed that the animal, which was already thin before his rider tied him up, was so thin that it was possible to see through him "like a lantern." Goble did not reveal if the men ate the horse. B. W. Ratcliff recalled many years later that "when I look back to these times, I wonder how any of us lived." Ratcliff remembered that he and his comrades survived "on not a mouthful of bread for twelve days" and that "we had but little chance to sleep because the mosquitos tried to eat us up."[54]

Howard Wright believed the peas were "the most indigestible and unwholesome articles that were ever given to soldiers to eat." To stretch their supplies, the Confederate commissary began feeding the dreaded peas to their horses and mules. It probably seemed like a great idea initially, but according to Howard Wright the peas "killed a great many of these animals." The animals that died from eating peas were eaten, along with any other draft animals that died of starvation or artillery fire. George H. Julian claimed that even mule meat eventually ran out and that the men lived entirely on peas for the last eight days of the siege. Walter Turner complained in his diary that "the peas are kept in a church that is just riddled with cannon balls, and the glasses [*sic*] are shattered all through the peas, which makes them quite dangerous for a man to eat." Still Turner remained defiant: "if we can hold our line, am willing to live on it."[55]

In a postwar account, Prentiss Ingraham made light of the men's misery at Port Hudson. He claimed that the men used ramrods as spears to hunt rats, which they called "house squirrels"; tricked officers into eating a puppy they claimed was a lamb; and pulled molasses into strands of candy until their fingers became hopelessly sticky. On another occasion, a Union soldier yelled out across the line to ask the rebels if they were hungry. In reply, a Confederate soldier held up a mule's jawbone above the breastworks, picked clean of meat, and said, "no, got plenty." The rebels then recalled the biblical story of how Samson killed a thousand Philistines with the jawbone of a mule and searched their testaments for some clue of how the trick was performed. Ingraham lamented that the search was fruitless and noted that the chaplains steered the men toward other passages.[56] Ingraham's account, written almost forty years after the siege, is interesting but might say more about the postwar novelist's sense of humor than his wartime experiences.

According to both Union and Confederate sources, hunger squeezed some rebels out of Port Hudson and into the open arms of the Union army. James Goble of the 1st Alabama Infantry wrote in his diary on June 28, "men desert daily for they are starving." Goble was not ready to surrender but he did suffer horribly, and the next day he wondered, "how long can such cruel misery be endured heaven only knows." On June 30 Henry

View of Captain Mac's battery, 18th New York Battery, Port Hudson. Library of Congress.

Gardner of the 18th New York Battery wrote his brother that "deserters have been coming out very fast lately, giving as a reason that they could not stand mule meat." Gardner was initially skeptical that anyone would eat mule meat, but he eventually became convinced because "30 came out yesterday & all tell the same story." A Confederate telegraph operator deserted to Union lines, and "in searching him, his journal was found to confirm" that the garrison was living off mule meat. William Smith of the 52nd Massachusetts Infantry listened to Confederate deserters complain about their hunger, but, with the skeptical weariness of a veteran nearing the end of his enlistment, he told his wife "how much dependence we can place upon there [*sic*] reports I cannot tell." Charles Kennedy of the 156th New York Infantry wrote home to his wife on June 29 that the Confederates were "almost out of provisions and that hunger will soon force them to surrender." Kennedy confessed, "I hope it is so, it will save a great deal of bloodshed."[57]

Many of the Confederates could not live on the meager rations and sought medical care. Paul de Gournay claimed that "the worst feature was the want of medicine." As the men grew weak from malnutrition, exposure, and fatigue, he said, "our hospitals were getting full." The garrison gradually wasted away, and, according to de Gournay, "our ranks grew thinner and thinner every day." Records for the Confederate general hospital at Port Hudson confirm de Gournay's comments, revealing a long list of patients suffering from a variety of problems during the final stages of the siege.[58]

Confederate soldiers supplemented their rations with beer and tobacco. Rebels turned sugar and molasses into "a weak description of beer." Soldiers kept barrels full of the beer-like liquid near the front lines and preferred it to the "miserable water," which was the only other available beverage. When tobacco ran out, men grew desperate for the precious plant and began smoking sumac leaves. Howard Wright considered it "a tolerably good substitute for tobacco." Prentiss Ingraham disagreed, claiming the tobacco substitutes made "their mouths and throats sore, thus adding to their misery."[59]

Union Morale and Mutiny

Union soldiers had food, but some of the men were on the verge of open rebellion. General Banks blamed the army's morale problems on "the nine-months men whose terms had expired or were about to expire." They were "dissatisfied with their situation and unwilling to enter upon duty involving danger." Banks reported that "great embarrassment and trouble was caused" by the nine-month men. The situation went from bad to worse when the 4th Massachusetts Infantry broke out "in open mutiny." James Dargan of the 4th Massachusetts Infantry wrote in his diary on June 28, "the regt [*sic*] refuse to do duty." The army took the regiment's flags and gave them one day to return to duty. Banks threatened to send anyone who would not repent and return to duty to the Dry Tortugas for the remainder of the war. The 91st New York Infantry guarded the mutineers and urged them "apparently in good faith, to return to duty."[60] On June 30 about a hundred members of the 4th Massachusetts declared their intention to "stand firm and will not surrender what they consider their rights." Guards marched the "obstinate" men to General Grover's headquarters, where the rebelling officers and NCOs suffered the "humiliating exercise of having their sidearms taken and their insignia torn from their persons by no gentle hands and a dull pair of scissors." Adding to the humiliation, "the three-year loaders gather around and taunt" the mutineers with "innuendos and nick names." A band played the "Rogue's March," and the men were marched off to an unspecified location.[61]

Some Union soldiers who did not rebel still expressed anger with the way General Banks handled the men with expired enlistments. According to New York Captain Orton Clark, many men expressed "dissatisfaction" with General Banks because he "did not at once discharge them and send them home." James Dargan of the 4th Massachusetts Infantry did not rebel, but he believed that Banks committed an act of "military tyranny" against his regiment because about twenty-five other regiments were at the end of their enlistment contracts and were on the verge of refusing to extend their service. According to Dargan, Banks hoped that by crushing the first mutineers, he could prevent further disobedience. Dargan believed that the mutineers were right and that Banks treated them unfairly. He explained that, before the men were soldiers, they were citizens. As citizens they signed enlistment contracts of their own free will. The mutineers had fulfilled their contractual obligations, and the enlistment contracts had expired. In his opinion, the government had no right to force free men to serve one day longer than their contracts dictated. Dargan wrote in his diary that he wanted to join the mutineers but that he was in the hospital dealing with a head wound he suffered on June 14, which made it physically impossible for him to participate in the rebellion. Rumors circulated through Union ranks that the 4th Massachusetts had "refused duty all together" and that General Banks punished them harshly.[62] It is unclear if General Banks's harsh punishments prevented a widespread mutiny, or if his punishments might have done more harm than good to an army in which most men were dedicated patriots determined to do whatever their nation asked. However, it is clear that, for whatever reason, most Union soldiers did not rebel and remained at their posts for the duration of the siege.

While Federals focused on the military situation, at least one was far more concerned with personal matters. Union sailor Louis Boyd wrote to his wife on July 1 that he was mostly thinking of home. In an unusually frank comment on sexual matters, Boyd complained that "I have experienced many times what it is to be alone in the midnight hour." Boyd had never seen his young son, born after he left home to join the navy, but based on his wife's letters he believed the child was "perfectly splendid and I don't think we could occupy our time better than manufacturing another." The homesick soldier wrote, "if I ever get home, I shall have to participate two and three times a night to make up for lost time." He asked his wife to "let me know your opinion in your mind and if you are ready to cooperate with me in the good work."[63] It is unclear how Boyd's wife responded to the sailor's plan.

Raid on Springfield Landing

At daylight on July 2, Confederate cavalry under Colonel Logan attacked the Union supply depot at Springfield Landing. The 162nd New York Infantry and a detachment of the 16th New Hampshire Infantry were on guard duty. Union staff officer Richard Irwin believed that the Union pickets were "careless," which allowed Confederate raiders to surprise and rout the depot's guards. Colonel Logan reported to General Johnston that he captured the landing, "burned their commissary and quartermaster's stores, destroyed 100 wagons, killed and wounded 140, captured 35 prisoners." After the war, Luther Townsend, who served in the 16th New Hampshire Infantry, accused Logan of spreading a "Confederate falsehood" and claimed that, while the rebels surprised the depot guards, the Confederates did "little damage," retreating in the face of stiffening Union resistance almost as quickly as they arrived. When the *Essex* arrived a short time later, Union sailors discovered that "all the fun was over." Union soldiers had already repulsed the Confederates.[64] While the Federal accounts seem to suggest that the Confederate attack had failed, the attack did inflict some damage and helped the rebels maintain the initiative.

The Final Days of the Siege

On July 2 Alabama infantryman James Goble wrote in his diary that "the garrison at P. H. die very fast." Union artillery shells killed and wounded Confederate soldiers. The weather was "intensely hot." Men died of hunger and malnutrition. Well-equipped medical facilities might have saved some of the sick and wounded, but Port Hudson's hospitals had few supplies left, and men died from a lack of medical care. Goble believed that the men were brave but explained, "they cannot live forever on two peas a day." On July 3 he wrote in his diary, "everybody sick and dying," which he followed with an oddly optimistic request—"may God soon send relief"—suggesting that Goble still held out hope for victory, despite reports that no relief was coming.[65]

On July 3 the Confederates completed their countermine near Fort Desperate. They filled their tunnels with gunpowder and set off the charge shortly after midnight. According to Howard Wright, "a black column rose high up in the air, and a mass of earth was thrown in every direction." Union shovels, picks, and masses of dirt rained down from the explosion. The Union engineers could not believe that the rebels had built a counter tunnel and concluded that the explosion must have been caused by the premature explosion of their own gunpowder.[66]

On July 4 rumors circulated through the Confederate camps that the Federals would launch an attack in honor of Independence Day. No attack came, and the rebels passed the day in relative quiet, listening to Union soldiers laugh and joke as they tried to celebrate the holiday. Confederate sharpshooters did not take the day off, firing occasional shots at their opponents. Marcus Hanna of the 50th Massachusetts Infantry repeatedly exposed himself to enemy fire on the holiday to deliver water to his comrades in advanced rifle pits. He later received the Medal of Honor for his work that day. New York infantryman John Chamberlin wrote in his diary that "we are in no condition to celebrate" because "we should have been in Port Hudson today but is very difficult to tell when we shall get in." James Hardenbergh remained confident that "we will surely get in a few days" but "this has been rather a dull fourth of July to me for we have had no chance to raise our heads to see what was going on with our neighbours [*sic*].[67]

On July 4 Charles Kennedy wrote home that he had decided to join the storming party, which was still training for a final attack. Recently promoted to 2nd lieutenant, Kennedy explained to his wife that he offered to join the dangerous detachment in hopes of motivating the enlisted men to join. He realized that the assignment would be dangerous, and he had every hope of surviving, but "if I should fall on the field of battle, it will be a create consolation to you to know that it was while trying to do my duty in the cause of liberty and humanity." He thanked "God that you were given to me to make me a happier man than I ever deserved to be." Kennedy urged his wife to raise his sons to be "honorable men" and his daughter to be "a pride and comfort" to the family.[68]

On July 4 Union sailor William Park celebrated the holiday by listening to a twenty-one-gun salute fired in unison at noon by every Union boat near Port Hudson. Park worried that Banks and the army were in trouble. He believed that "if this next attack should prove a failure, he will be forced to raise the siege, for the rebels is [*sic*] swarming along the banks of the river, and has cut off most of his supplies from New Orleans." Park listed several recent Confederate attacks on Union supply lines and, with a sailor's pride, he suggested that the gunboats were the only thing that had kept the Confederates at bay and prevented the army from starving.[69]

On July 5, 1863, General Banks sent a demand for surrender to the General Gardner. Alabamian James Goble heard grumbling in the ranks and believed the men were "on the edge of mutiny." Men claimed that they would "lay down arms if no relief arrives." The July 5 entry in Goble's diary does not include a deadline for the relief, and it is unclear how much longer the men might wait for the reinforcements to come. However, Goble was dismissive of the threats of potential mutineers, still believing the men "will never give up the place as long as they can get a mouthful to eat." Goble also claimed that the demand for surrender came with provisions from Banks for the Union prisoners, but that "rebel officers get the most of it and laugh at Banks for sending" provisions.[70]

Union sailor Louis Boyd expressed frustration when the rebels did not surrender. In his June 26 letter, Boyd committed to "wait patiently" for the Confederate surrender he believed was inevitable. Boyd's patience had clearly expired by his July 5 letter home. For "six weeks" the sailors heard daily reports from the army's officers that they could capture Port Hudson anytime and that the rebels would surrender "tomorrow," but tomorrow kept coming and the rebels remained defiant until "we have become disgusted with Banks and his whole army." Boyd believed Banks "is getting his army crippled." Despite the army's supposed strength, the sailors dared not go ashore for fear they would be captured by Confederate guerillas, who the army seemed powerless to stop. The sailors were "cooped up on an old boat" with "nothing to look at but the banks of old Port Hudson which I am heartily tired of seeing." Boyd wanted to go home and told his wife that he worried "you have forsaken me for some other." The only reason Boyd did not immediately resign his commission was because he did not believe the navy would accept his resignation until Port Hudson surrendered.[71]

Union sailors preparing to engage the Confederates at Battery 10 during the siege in May and June of 1863, Port Hudson. View of Union naval nine-inch Dahlgren gun battery, commanded by Lieutenant Commander Edward Terry, looking north-northwest. Library of Congress.

Rufus Dooley noted that July 5, 1863, was the two-year anniversary his departure from Indiana to enlist in the Union army. He told his mother in a letter, "little did I think when I left home that this year would find me in Louisiana." Dooley was not alone. It is unlikely that any of the thousands of men who fought at Port Hudson could have possibly predicted in 1861 that they would encounter some of the defining challenges of their lives at a small riverboat town most of them had probably never heard of. Dooley told his mother, "there is cool breeze blowing today and I can almost imagine myself at the old meeting house instead of in front of Port Hudson with many heavy guns bearing on us."[72]

William Park left the *Essex* on the morning of July 5 to take his turn serving with the navy's shore battery. After a taking a long and difficult path that looped around Port Hudson, he arrived at the battery roughly five hundred yards from the Confederate lines, near the tracks of the Port Hudson and Clinton Railroad. Park found that the Union artillery was almost entirely silent. The men believed that most of the Confederate artillery was disabled, and the Union crews lounged under canvas shades or in crude huts. Perhaps in honor of the new arrival, the naval battery rumbled to life and fired a few rounds toward what was left of Port Hudson.

The Confederate artillery did not reply, but gray-clad sharpshooters did. Park wrote in his diary that "their first shot came close to my ear with its peculiar ping, which I did not half like." Unsure of how to respond, Park "looked around at the rest of the guns [*sic*] crew to see if they were dodging, but they all stood round the guns and seemed to take it as a matter of course." Perhaps because he valued his comrades' respect more than his own life, Park reported, "I had to brace my nerves and look as disconcerned [*sic*] as possible." As a veteran of the navy's gunboats, Park "had got used to the big shot passing, but the rifle bullets was some thing [*sic*] I had not been used to." After firing a few rounds, the sailors ceased fire, the Confederates returned the favor, and Park survived with both his life and dignity intact.[73]

On July 6 Confederate soldiers traded newspapers with the Federals. The rebels rejoiced when they read stories that Confederate cavalry were raiding through Union-occupied Arkansas and Tennessee. They were also delighted to read that General Lee's army had invaded Pennsylvania.[74] Although they did not realize it, Lee's invasion ended with the Confederate defeat at the Battle of Gettysburg (July 1–3, 1863), and by the time the Port Hudson garrison read the newspapers on July 6, Lee's men were retreating to Virginia in defeat.

Union Losses

By the end of June, the Union forces near Port Hudson were wasting away. A month of fighting had killed four thousand federal troops. Another four thousand were sick or wounded in the hospitals and unlikely to return to service anytime soon, if ever. During the siege, roughly three thousand Union reinforcements had arrived at Port Hudson, but by the end of June, the Federals in Louisiana had no more reserves in the state, and no more reinforcements were likely to arrive in the foreseeable future. The effective strength of the Union besiegers had never exceeded seventeen thousand men. By the end of June, no more than twelve thousand Union soldiers were available for service, and only about eight thousand were actively besieging Port Hudson. The remainder were mostly cavalrymen guarding the supply routes. Joshua Hawkes wrote home that the army's true casualties were unknown since "many slight wounds were dressed up by surgeons without the hospitals," suggesting that the army underreported the losses. The horrific heat and constant rains sapped the strength from even the toughest Union soldiers, and many could do little more than conserve their energy as they dodged Confederate sharpshooter bullets. Samuel Ellis spent most of his time trying to stay cool. When not on duty, the men stripped down to their underwear and rested while "our comical colored boy, Adam, squatted down on the ground in front of us keeping the flies off."[75]

Inadequate medical care became an increasingly serious issue for the Federals. New York assistant surgeon Harris Beecher reported that brigades withered into regiments and regiments into companies. The army no longer had enough transportation to remove all the sick and wounded who needed treatment in permanent hospitals. The field hospitals "were filled with disease and death." Men suffered from "fevers, scurvy, and that scourge of all scourges, chronic diarrhea." Chaplain John Moors spent most of his time helping men in the hospital. Three times a day, he rolled over each of the roughly twenty patients in his assigned section, most of whom rested on a "rubber blanket" that laid on the ground. He adjusted the knapsacks that the men used for pillows and tried to comfort them. Moors then fetched "gruel" and fed the men. Most of the wounded suffered from infestations of "inhabitants." Moors tried and mostly failed to keep the unwanted "inhabitants" off his clothes. The Union navy sent surgeons ashore to provide medical care for their sick and wounded brothers in the army. The navy also evacuated some soldiers to hospitals in Baton Rouge and New Orleans.[76]

James Dargan was one of the lucky soldiers in need of medical care who was transported to a permanent hospital, but the trip was uncomfortable. It began with a wagon ride over difficult roads, which were so bumpy that even the sickest men begged for an opportunity to walk. Dargan made the best of his "bed of cotton, not of roses," which smelled of "dirt, . . . contrabands, and Teutons"—probably references to the escaped slaves and immigrant soldiers from Germany who Dargan suggested had distinctive smells. After arriving at the boat docks of Springfield Landing, patients were preparing to board transport boats for the next phase of their journey when Confederate cavalry attacked. While some Federals panicked and tried to board the transport boats only to be shoved off by sailors, black Union soldiers fired on the Confederate raiders, "emptying many a saddle." Dargan took a rifle from a soldier wounded in the skirmish and shot a Confederate in the leg as the rebel tried to set fire to supply crates. A moment later, Dargan saw "a little drummer boy kill an officer by a shot in his head." A Union gunboat opened fire, which forced the Confederates to retreat. As the Confederates melted back into the countryside, the wounded resumed their journey, arriving at Baton Rouge the next day.[77]

At least a few Federals believed that some men were avoiding duty by feigning illness in the army hospitals. Dr. R. K. Browne, commanding the army's general hospital in New Orleans, claimed "the hospital is sought by the men as a refuge from camp duty." John Barnard of the 52nd Massachusetts Infantry informed his cousin that "large numbers of men" sought only to escape their duty and reported to the hospital anytime they felt discomfort. General Banks ordered officers who were recuperating in the hospitals to either return to duty or resign their commissions. In response, army doctors declared some soldiers too sick to return to duty and authorized medical discharges.[78]

Animals may have suffered worse than men. Artillery horses suffered for lack of exercise as they waited near static batteries, and animals pulling supply wagons suffered from overwork. It might have been possible to help both groups of animals by swapping horses that needed exercise with horses that needed a rest, but it does not appear that an exchange program was ever authorized. All animals suffered in the heat and from swarms of bugs. Initially, the Union army enjoyed ample forage for their animals, but supplies quickly ran low as the Confederate cavalry cut supply lines and General Taylor sent artillery batteries to fire on Union riverboat traffic.[79]

Union Morale

Union soldiers and sailors became increasingly demoralized in the final stages of the siege. Lawrence Van Alstyne stated in his diary, "I don't care who has Port Hudson; I don't want it. I wouldn't turn by my hand over for the whole Confederacy." John Whitehead told his wife stories of the sickness, heatstroke, and wounded men filling the camps outside Port Hudson who were driven to madness by the bugs that filled their rotting sores. He asked her to show his letters to anyone thinking about enlisting. Whitehead acknowledged he was placing himself and his family in danger by openly opposing the authorities, but he considered it worth the risk if it would spare anyone from the misery he had experienced and witnessed. Eli Griffin complained in a letter to his wife that the senior officers of his regiment were all drunk and lazy men who stayed as far away from the front lines as they could. Griffin concluded, "I am completely disgusted with everything." In his diary entry for July 6, Henry Johns worried that "the assaults have failed," that disease disabled so many men that less than ten thousand Union troops were healthy enough to fight, that Confederate raiders constantly smashed unwary Federals across Louisiana, that at any moment a Confederate uprising might threaten Union control of New Orleans, and that Johnston was gathering a Confederate army that would "compel the abandonment of the siege within a week." Johns believed that the Union army "must get into Port Hudson" very soon. John Moors loathed the noise and the sickness and the heat and the hunger and concluded, "everything makes us miserable"[80]

James Hardenbergh of the 133rd New York Infantry lamented, "our regiment has suffered a good deal." When the regiment arrived in Port Hudson they had 728 men, but by July 7 they had "lost two Hundred killed and as many more wounded." Hardenbergh believed that Port Hudson would fall within a few days but declared that, as soon as the siege ended, "I'm agoing [*sic*] to try and get a furlough for a month."[81]

Harris Beecher, with the 114th New York Infantry, later recalled that his regiment increasingly "wore an air of solemnity, not a joyous laugh was heard, not a smile was seen, no a man was disposed to engage in any game ore [*sic*] sport." The men sat alone, "their faces bearing the impress of sadness." The men struggled with the loss of their comrades for "not a particle of advantage." The worst part was that the men "were tormented with the shouts of the victors, which the breeze wafted over from the rebel works."[82]

A Union officer, identified only as Frank, suffered from survivor's guilt. He wrote after the death of a friend, "I cant [*sic*] help feeling . . . as if I were responsible for his death for if it hadn't been for me he would never have come here in this accursed Dept."[83] While Frank's note is brief and vague, it does provide a rare glimpse of the often ignored mental health problems that plagued Union and Confederate soldiers. It is unclear how many seemingly healthy men at Port Hudson might have struggled with feelings of depression, grief, and guilt.

Lieutenant Colonel Willoughby Babcock of the 75th New York Infantry wrote home that "affairs at Port Hudson are badly managed." He believed that "the most intimate and influential friends of Banks are mere adventurers, not in the service of the government except as Gen. Banks employs them." Babcock suggested that officers who Banks did trust "have not the confidence of those who know them best." Amongst the rank and file of the army, "Banks himself is very unpopular with all except Massachusetts troops." Massachusetts was Banks's home state, where he enjoyed a prewar political career. Apart from these men, Babcock wrote, "I do not think he has the confidence of anybody."[84] If Babcock's claims were accurate, Banks and the army he commanded was in serious danger of collapse.

Despite the hardships, at least one Union soldier remained optimistic. Justus Gale of the 8th Vermont Infantry told his sister that men were dying of "chronic dierhea [*sic*]" and that an officer "was unfit for duty, got the blue some I guess with the rest." A few days after lamenting the misery of Port Hudson, Gale explained in another letter, "I dont [*sic*] wish to have you think that I am complaining." He argued, "most of the complaints we hear or you hear at home about food and hard times are made by those who thought they were coming out here to have a good easy time out of it." Gale, like many soldiers, took apparent pride in his ability to endure hardships. He believed the complainers "were never weaned til [*sic*] they come out here—but I guess they will get weaned before they get home again."[85]

Confederate Losses

Like their adversaries in blue, the Confederates suffered horrible losses as the campaign dragged on. On May 19 Gardner reported that the Port Hudson garrison consisted of 5,715 men present for duty. On June 30 Gardner reported that only 4,098 Confederate soldiers were present for duty. On July 9 Confederate staff officer C. M. Jackson reported that only 2,500 Confederates were present for duty. It is unclear what might explain the difference between the reports on June 30 and July 9. Perhaps the Confederates were wasting away at an astonishing rate in the first week of July, or there might have been some discrepancies between accounting methods, possibly both. Union artillery fire damaged or disabled most of the Confederate artillery. The Confederate cannons that remained operational rested on damaged carriages that were more patches and repairs than original equipment. Some carriages became so badly damaged that

Quaker gun mounted on bluff of Port Hudson.
Library of Congress.

Cannon and artillery in the battery at Port Hudson after the siege.
Library of Congress.

they were beyond repair, so rebels mounted these cannons on blocks, placed them in camouflaged positions, loaded them with improvised antipersonnel rounds made of scrap metal, and kept them ready for emergency service. To distract and confuse their adversaries, the Confederates painted logs to look like cannons and placed them in visible locations.[86] With the concealment of real guns and the prominent display of fake guns, any Federals participating in future attacks might have been blasted by artillery they did not see while trying to capture logs they thought were cannons.

Walter Turner wrote in his diary that he was the sickest he had ever been in his life. He was not alone, writing, "our men are getting sick very fast, indeed all most the whole command is either sick or wounded." On June 19 his company had only twenty-seven men left, and all twenty-seven reported that they were sick. On June 24 the nineteen-year-old Turner wrote that he was sick of the war and just wanted to go home to his mother. On June 25 he rattled off a list of casualties before writing, "another man was killed." He was "leaning on his gun with his hands, and his chin was resting on his hands and I suppose he must have cocked his gun with his foot." The gun "went off and shot both hands off and the whole part of his face from his chin up."[87] Although Turner did not use the word, the unnamed soldier might have intentionally committed suicide.

—11—

The First Time I Felt Sorry for the Brave Fellows

THE SURRENDER

At eight o'clock we marched in, and I should day went three-quarters of a mile, when we found the Rebs in line. We marched along their front and halted, faced to the left, and stood facing each other, some twenty feet apart. Both lines were at order arms. The officers held a short confab, and then took their respective places, as if on parade. Our regiment was directly opposite of Miles Legion, or what is left of it. The commanding general gave the order ground arms. This was the first time I felt sorry for the brave fellows. If their cause is not just, they have been true to it, and it must be like death itself for a brave fighter to lay his arms down before his enemy. However, I did not see any sign of tears.[1]

—LAWRENCE VAN ALSTYNE, 128th New York Infantry

At seven o'clock on the morning of the 9th our line was formed in the field back of the railroad depot, near the landing, every man not too sick to be confined in the hospital being in the ranks. As Gen. Gardner rode along the line, with his staff, he was enthusiastically cheered by the men who had served so faithfully under him, and whose affection and confidence he had permanently gained during days and weeks of trial. The enemy's column, marching down the road to the landing, approached the right of our line, preceded by Gen. Andrews and staff, to whom Gen. Gardner tendered his sword, briefly surrendering his command. With a few complimentary words it was returned, when the order was given along our line to ground arms, which was obeyed, and our men stood in line before us, when they hoisted their flag upon the bluff, fired a salute, and the ceremony was over. It was now announced to our men that they would be paroled—news that was received by them with great satisfaction—particularly as they had made up their minds to a term of imprisonment.[2]

—HOWARD WRIGHT, 30th Louisiana Infantry

The Surrender of Vicksburg

On July 7, 1863, men fighting for Port Hudson learned that Vicksburg, Mississippi, had surrendered to Union forces. According to New York soldier Lawrence Van Alstyne, the men "shouted themselves hoarse" in celebration. The Confederates sent over a messenger, under flag of truce, to learn why the Federals were so happy, and the Union soldiers happily shared the news. Van Alstyne noted, perhaps with a bit of tongue in cheek humor, "they didn't seem as glad as we are." According to Louisiana infantry officer Howard Wright, many Confederates refused to believe that Vicksburg had fallen. They suspected that the Federals were lying to them. Some Confederates did not believe that the fall of Vicksburg, even if true, required Port Hudson to surrender. Confederate diehards believed that Port Hudson's garrison had a duty to defend their position as long as possible, regardless of what anyone else did.[3]

The Decision to Surrender Port Hudson

News of Vicksburg's surrender found Port Hudson's defenders stretched to the breaking point. Early on July 7, 1863, General Beall informed General Gardner that the Union positions opposite the 1st Mississippi Infantry "are very strong and extensive." As a result, Beall believed the Federals could "throw a force of men inside our works without our being able to drive him back, unless heavy reinforcements are brought from other points of the line." Beall realized that sending reinforcements to his sector from other parts of the line would "leave said points unguarded, and to permit the enemy to come over there also." Beall also reported, "there is more discontent among the men within the last few days that I have discovered before," and stated, "I very much fear that the officers are at the bottom of it." Beall told Gardner, "if you have an directions to give me in reference to use of the troops in case the enemy get over the works, I should like to have them." He expected the Union assault to come soon. Walter Turner of the 39th Mississippi Infantry wrote in his diary that Colonel Steedman visited his position and told the men to be "very vigilant" because he expected the Federals to crawl up to their lines in the darkness.[4]

In response to news of the Vicksburg surrender and General Beall's dire report, General Gardner called a council of war at his headquarters. The garrison had fought well, holding out far longer, with far less, than anyone had anticipated. When the siege began, the garrison expected that they would be relieved, but little help had arrived, and no army of relief was coming to break the siege. Officers estimated that the garrison's provisions could keep them alive for no more than ten days, at which time the rebels would be forced to surrender. If the Federals became impatient, the siege might end even sooner. The garrison had successfully repelled every Union assault, but the Federals had improved their positions since the June 14 assault, and the Confederates were wasting away from hunger, illness, and exhaustion. The Federals occupied several positions within twenty yards of the Confederate lines. Union work crews were tunneling under Confederate lines, and despite their best efforts, the Confederate engineers could not be sure that they had located every Union tunnel. Confederate officers expected that at any moment the Federals might ignite gunpowder in mines deep under the Confederate positions, unleash a blast of heavy artillery, launch a human wave attack with overwhelming numbers of infantry, and capture Port Hudson.[5]

With Vicksburg in Union hands, Gardner did not feel that continued resistance, which could not last longer than a few more days, was worth additional deaths. At 9:00 a.m. on July 8, Gardner sent colonels G. W. Steedman, W. R. Miles, and M. J. Smith into Union lines with orders to negotiate Port Hudson's surrender. Word of the plan quickly spread to the enlisted men. Walter Turner wrote in his diary on July 8, "oh how awful to think that I am or soon will be a prisoner and at the mercy of the Federals and away from home."[6]

Confederate colonels fought for generous terms, arguing that, if the Federals did not treat them fairly, they would return to their ditches, where they could happily hold out for another month and make the Union pay an even more horrific price for Port Hudson. After initially refusing to offer any terms at all, the Federals agreed to parole all Confederate enlisted men. All Confederate officers would become prisoners of war, but the Federals promised that the officers could retain their personal property while in captivity. It was a tough bargain, but the men in gray conceded that it was fair, and the Federals wrote out the surrender document. The officers who prepared to sign knew that they were about to march into the horrors of a prison camp, but their hard bargaining ensured that their men could go home. Apparently that was good enough for the officers, who seemed more focused on their men than on themselves.

Just before signing, Colonel Miles exclaimed that he had one more demand. Union General Charles Stone scoffed that Miles was pressing his luck. Miles unapologetically demanded rations, since the men "must have a square meal tonight." Stone burst out laughing, pointing out that Miles had just claimed that the Confederate garrison had ample rations for another month. Miles admitted that he had done everything he could to win the best possible terms for his men, but having won good terms, "the truth may as well come out." Stone laughed and agreed, "provisions you shall have, and that speedily."[7]

The Confederate colonels returned to Port Hudson late on July 8 and announced that they had agreed to the unconditional surrender of Port Hudson at 7:00 a.m. on July 9.[8] General Frank Gardner issued General Orders No. 61 to the garrison.

General Orders No. 61
Headquarters, Port Hudson, July 8, 1863

I. Nobly have the troops performed their duty in the defense of this position, continued from 21st of May to the present day. The cheerfulness, bravery and zeal displayed by the troops during the hardships and suffering of this long siege has never been surpassed, and every man can feel the proud satisfaction that he has done his part in this heroic defense of Port Hudson. The place is surrendered at the last moment it is proper to hold it, and after a most gallant defense in several severe attacks in all which the enemy have been signally repulsed. Let all continue, during the duties that still remain to be performed, to show that cheerful obedience which has distinguished them as soldiers up to this time.

II. The troops will be paraded at 6'Oclock am tomorrow for surrender in line of battle in the same order as they are now at the breastworks, with the heavy artillery on the right edge of the prairie in rear of the railroad depot; the left extending towards the town of Port Hudson. All officers and men will be in their places under arms.

By Command of
Maj. Gen. Frank Gardner.[9]

News of the impending surrender spread quickly. The official ceremony would take place in the morning, but the fighting was already over. According to Howard Wright, Union and Confederate soldiers who had been busy trying to kill each other just hours ago poured out of their positions and "met each other in the most cordial and fraternal spirit." They visited each other's fortifications and admired the handiwork of their rivals. New York infantryman James Peck examined the Confederate defenses, confirmed that Confederate positions were very strong, and concluded, "if we had taken the place by storm, we would have lost a great many men." The Federals gave the rebels tobacco and other luxuries. In exchange, the Union soldiers asked for souvenirs of the siege. At least one Union surgeon visited Port Hudson, bringing a large quantity of quinine. Shortly after dark on July 8, Union commissary wagons visited Port Hudson, and early on the morning of July 9, the rebels "enjoyed the first good meal they had partaken of for a long time." Paul de Gournay was not surprised by Union kindness to the defeated rebels, explaining years later that "it is only the coward or the savage who will trample upon the vanquished foe." Henry Gardner chatted with Confederate prisoners, reporting that "some say if they are paroled they won't catch them again in the army, while others express a determination to go in again as soon as possible."[10]

Some Confederate soldiers refused to surrender. Joe Daniel, his brother Dock Daniel, and their friend Charlie Graham were all committed never to surrender and prepared to escape. When Colonel Johnson discovered that the men planned to escape rather than surrender, he told them that escape was impossible and urged them to surrender with the rest of the garrison. The three men politely refused to take the colonel's advice and prepared to hide in Lake Solitaire. They hoped to hide with most of their bodies below the water, concealing their faces in the willows of the lake, until the surrender was over and the Federals abandoned their siege lines. The Daniel brothers and Graham hoped that they could then emerge from concealment and slip through the Federal lines in the darkness. As the men looked for hiding places in the lake, they were soon surrounded by other rebels with the same idea. Other men decided to swim across the Mississippi and join Confederate forces on the west bank. After several days of hiding from Federal pickets, fighting the terrain, bugs, hunger, and illness along the way, the brothers and their friend eventually picked their way through the countryside and joined Logan's cavalrymen, still harassing Union forces outside Port Hudson. The men continued their service in the Confederate army after time to recuperate from their difficult escape. Two unspecified lieutenants in the 18th Arkansas Infantry escaped Federal captivity by jumping overboard while being transported to a prisoner of war camp.[11]

The Buried Treasure of Port Hudson

While many Confederates plotted their escape or feasted on Federal rations, at least three Confederate soldiers buried something valuable. During the siege, Sergeant John Bryant served as the chief quartermaster for Miles's Legion. Bryant later wrote that, when he learned of Gardner's plans to surrender, he consulted with Colonel Miles, commanding the legion. Based on the "advice" but evidently not the orders of Miles, Bryant "concluded to make the effort to save the books, papers, vouchers, and etc." Bryant did not specific what he meant by "etc." It is unlikely that the "etc." included any precious metals or treasure in the conventional sense, but whatever Bryant sought to save was clearly more valuable to hungry, tired men than leisure or a feast. Bryant ordered Private Erasmus Greaves and Private Richard Leonard to help him bury the precious goods. Bryant later testified that they "selected a safe place had a good strong box made." The three men filed the box and buried it "dark on the night previous to the surrender." After the surrender and Bryant's parole, he reported, "I visited the place where the box had been buried in company with Erasmus Greaves and found that it had been discovered and the box removed by the Federals."[12]

The mysterious package that Bryant and his comrades buried was valuable enough to interest Confederate authorities. The files of Confederate judge George Bond include written testimony from John Bryant, as well as Major James Coleman, Erasmus Greaves, and Richard Leonard. Coleman did not claim to have any direct knowledge of Bryant's burial of valuables but testified that Bryant served "with ability and faithfully." Erasmus Greaves agreed with Bryant's testimony and added that, after discovering that the box was missing, "particles" of the buried goods "were found near the spot." Richard Leonard also agreed with Bryant and Greaves, adding that "every effort was used" to protect the goods.[13] The

Surrender of Port Hudson, July 9, 1863.
Library of Congress.

files for Judge Bond provide no indication of what he or other authorities concluded about the disappearance of the mysterious box. Unless other documents come to light, it may never be known who took the valuables, what the mysterious "etc." might have included, or what other Confederates at Port Hudson with access to valuables might have been doing on the night of July 8, while most men enjoyed food and relaxation.

The Surrender

At 6:00 a.m. on Thursday July 9, 1863, the Confederate garrison lined up in the field behind the railroad depot, near the river landing. General Gardner rode along the line with his staff, and, according to Howard Wright, Gardner "was enthusiastically cheered by the men who had served so faithfully under him, and whose affection and confidence he had permanently gained during the days and weeks of trial." Reflecting on the siege several weeks later, Howard Wright told the *Daily True Delta Sun* that the defenders of Port Hudson had displayed "Spartan courage" with General Gardner as their own "Leonidas at their head" in a battle where they were prepared "to repeat the story of Thermopylae." Colonel de Gournay believed "the marks of respect and sympathy the defenders of Port Hudson received at the hands of Banks's victorious army was a soothing balm that took away much of the bitterness of defeat."[14]

A Union column marched down the road, with General George Andrews in the lead. In his diary, John Chamberlin described the surrendering Confederate soldiers as "a rusting looking crew," a possible reference to the rust-like, dirty brown color of filthy uniforms and bodies. Lawrence Van Alstyne and the rest of the 128th New York Infantry lined up directly across from "what is left of" Miles's Legion. Looking across at the rebels at the surrender was "the first time I felt sorry for the brave fellows." The New Yorker believed "if their cause is not just, they have been true to it." As a veteran, he realized that "it must be like death itself for a brave fighter to lay down his arms before his enemy." Despite the sadness, Van Alstyne "did not see any sign of tears."[15]

According to Howard Wright, General Gardner offered General Andrews his sword, and Andrews returned the sword "with a few complimentary words." Paul de Gournay's account is slightly different than Wright's. According to de Gournay, General Gardner offered his sword to Andrews, and Andrews replied, "I return your sword with my compliment to the gallant commander of such gallant men and their conduct that would be heroic for another cause." The comment about causes was a direct quote from General Banks's first demand for the surrender of Port Hudson. Perhaps that stung a little. Perhaps Andrews wanted it to. According to de Gournay, Andrews's comment "was properly rebuked by General Gardner's words, as he returned his sword to the scabbard with an emphatic clang." Gardner snapped, "This is neither the time nor place to discuss the cause." Both Wright and de Gournay's accounts agreed that after the exchange between Gardner and Andrews, the Federals raised the United States flag over Port Hudson, fired a salute, and the brief ceremony concluded.[16]

After collecting Confederate guns and ammunition, the men of both armies broke ranks. Lawrence Van Alstyne found a Confederate soldier he had traded with across the lines with during the siege, and they enjoyed a friendly conversation. He described "the rebs [*sic*]" as "mostly large, fine-looking men" who were dressed just as poorly as their Union counterparts. Only the color of their rags distinguished members of the two armies. The rebels wore fragments of gray, and the Federals wore clothing that had once been blue but was now the color "of the ground on which we have slept so long." Van Alstyne complimented the rebels for treating prisoners well and giving the prisoners the same rations as Confederate soldiers.[17]

After the surrender, Orton Clark visited the Confederate works and chatted with his former enemies. Initially he doubted Confederate stories that they had lived on nothing but mule meat for several days, but after watching them devour Union hardtack "so greedily," he decided that the stories must be true. Only horrifically hungry men would eat something as terrible as hardtack "so greedily." The New Yorkers "could not but admire the endurance and pluck manifested so often by the men." Clark claimed the enlisted men he met were sick of fighting, claimed to be entirely ignorant of the war's causes, and promised to never fight again. In contrast, he found the Confederate officers "aloof" and filled with "a surly desire to renew the conflict as soon as they were able."[18]

Shortly after the surrender, Bartholomew Diggins went ashore with many of his shipmates from the *Hartford.* He said Port Hudson was in "a deplorable condition." Confederate soldiers and civilians were "lank and hungry looking." He believed that "there was nothing living within the fort that had not been eaten, except human beings." Diggins wrote, "their bravery and indurance [*sic*] won the admiration and respect of our side." As a result, "we emmediately [*sic*] gave them all our provisions except enough to take us to New Orleans."[19]

Unwilling to walk when they could ride, William Park and other crewmen on the navy's shore battery mounted the battery's horses and mules for the short trip into Port Hudson. Other than a few officers, those sailors might have been the only mounted men in Port Hudson that day. Park was shocked to examine the Confederate fortifications, which were "neither more nor less than a line of rifle pits with a ditch about three feet wide on the outside." Park seemed astonished that the rebels had needed little more than simple ditches to keep the Union at bay for so long. Park wrote that the rebels "looked well and seemed to be growing fat on the mule meat." After the surrender ceremony, Park walked among the Confederate prisoners and chatted with them. They had surrendered, and they were "all tired of the war" but remained proudly defiant. They taunted the Federals, telling them that, if Banks had attacked again, they "would have gobbled him up and the whole of his nine-month nutmegs, as they call the nine months men." Confederate soldiers pointed out that there were no nine-month men in their army. Every man enlisted for the duration, and most believed they would fight until they died or achieved victory. Rebels inaccurately claimed that "the whole garrison" had fought in the battles of Fort Donelson or Shiloh and "had been prisoners before." Park had little time to rest in Port Hudson. The naval gunners onshore received orders to return to their ships. Port Hudson had surrendered, but the Confederate guerillas had not. They were still raiding Union supply lines, and the gunboats sailed away to counter their attacks.[20]

The Confederate enlisted men learned that they would be paroled, which made them very happy. James Goble wrote that "all the boys seem to enjoy the change of masters." For the first time since before the siege began "they can get plenty to eat and a chance to go home." These were "privileges the Rebel Govt [*sic*] never lets them have." It took the Federals several days to process the paroles, and conflict simmered between the rebel prisoners and their guards. Walter Turner wrote in his diary that "all the great buck negroes are walking around the posts as big as life." In response, "there have been several negroes knocked down for their impudence." Turner did not reveal what consequences, if any, Confederate prisoners suffered for attacking their guards.[21]

Confederate officers learned that they would be sent to northern prison camps, which made them very unhappy. The Federals imprisoned Confederate officers in some of the few surviving buildings near the riverbank. A double line of guards sought to prevent any escapes. Joseph Bailey was desperate to avoid the horrors of a northern prison camp. When he saw a Union teamster prepare to drive his wagon away late at night, Bailey seized his opportunity, slipping into the back of the wagon, where he found that Captain William Poynor of his regiment was already aboard, clearly planning on the same method of escape. Without saying a word, the two Arkansas officers concealed themselves until the wagon passed through both lines of Federal guards. Once past the guards, Bailey and Poynor jumped out of the wagon, joining a crowd of Union soldiers enjoying some welcomed leisure in Port Hudson. In the dark, their dirty uniforms were indistinguishable from Federal uniforms. The escapees tried to act inconspicuously, using the intimate knowledge of the terrain they obtained during the siege as they gradually wandered through the Federals until they slipped outside Port Hudson's now abandoned defenses. After a long

Captain John M. Kean of Co. A, 12th Louisiana Heavy Artillery Battery. Kean was a prisoner of war on July 9, 1863, at Port Hudson. He died of pneumonia on November 21, 1863, at Johnson's Island. Library of Congress.

and difficult journey across the countryside, Bailey eventually made it to Little Rock, Arkansas. Bailey never rejoined his regiment, choosing instead to support the Confederacy as a guerilla behind Union lines in Arkansas and Missouri until the end of the war. Union general Godfrey Weitzel personally asked General Banks to make an exception and parole Colonel Fredrick Brand of Miles's Legion, who Weitzel described as "an old friend" and a "sick" man. Banks complied with Weitzel's request, and Brand went home while most of his brother officers went to prison camps.

J. B. Sutton later recalled, "we laid down our arms and were marched off to prison—not whipped, but overpowered."[22]

At least one Confederate officer accepted his captivity stoically. Lieutenant Alfred Sandlin of the 1st Mississippi Infantry later wrote home to his family from the notorious prison camp at Johnson's Island, Ohio, where hundreds of Confederate prisoners died of exposure and illness. Sandlin told his young children to give thanks to God who watched over them and who kept him safe in battles where many men died. He urged his children to treat others as they would like to be treated, to never tell lies, and to be obedient to their mother. Sandlin acknowledged that he might never see them again in this life, but he believed that if they followed his advice, they would enjoy a happy eternity together.[23]

On July 12, New York–born James Goble, who had served as an enlisted man in the 1st Alabama Infantry during the siege, and his Maine-born wife Emma, who lived in Port Hudson to support her husband, visited General Banks. They explained that, while James had fought for the Confederacy, both James and Emma were northerners. The couple wanted to go home to reunite with their northern family, and they asked General Banks to help them. Banks agreed to send them to New York, and the couple left Port Hudson on a Federal transport ship. In his diary, James revealed that he visited his family in New York and shared stories of his time in the Confederate army. It is unclear if James's family was angry with him for serving in the Confederate army. The diary makes no mention of how they felt. Perhaps they were just happy that he was alive. James and Emma Goble eventually made their home in Chelsea, Massachusetts. James wrote his last diary entry on August 13, 1863. It says simply "went to work."[24]

Howard Wright went into captivity, where he wrote one of the most detailed and thorough accounts of the battles for Port Hudson. The *Daily True Delta* of New Orleans published Wright's account in a series of articles from August 2–August 16, 1863. Edited versions of Wright's accounts later appeared in book form.[25] Wright's accounts are unique because Wright was born and raised in New York, although he enjoyed extended visits in the South during his childhood to visit family members. When war came, Wright supported the Confederacy and explained to his South Carolina–born mother that "if slavery is right in the estimation of the South, she is right in upholding it." After the surrender of Port Hudson, Wright spent a year at the Johnson's Island prisoner of war camp. Wright was exchanged in 1864 and rejoined the Confederate army. On April 14, 1865, at West Point,

Georgia, an artillery shell struck Wright in the chest, killing him instantly. Paul de Gournay, Wright's friend and his brother-in-arms at Port Hudson, eulogized Wright as someone who embodied "every manly virtue."[26]

Losses

On July 9 Confederate staff officer C. M. Jackson reported that, during the siege, the Confederates at Port Hudson lost "200 killed and between 300 and 400 wounded." He also noted "200 have died from sickness." Union surgeon J. R. Barnett reported that 176 Confederate soldiers died in action at the siege of Port Hudson and that 447 were wounded. He listed fighting at Plains Store, near Port Hudson, separately and reported 12 dead and 36 wounded in the fighting there. Barnett did not list deaths caused by disease. In a postwar account, John Graves of the 15th Arkansas Infantry claimed, "they simply starved us out; however, not until we had eaten all the mules we had." He pointed out that "our loss was heavy, but not so heavy as the enemy's." At least 10,000 Union soldiers and sailors died at Port Hudson. Roughly half from disease and another half from battle.[27]

On July 15 the Nineteenth Corps reported that had paroled 5,935 Confederate "enlisted men" and kept 405 Confederate officers in captivity. According to historian Edward Cunningham, the 5,935 also included civilian employees of the Confederate government. However, the official report does not mention civilians and only refers to the 5,935 parolees as "enlisted men." Assistant surgeon Harris Beecher of the 114th New York Infantry believed "the number of killed and wounded during the investment and siege can never be ascertained." However, he was confident "the mortality from all causes had been appalling."[28]

Captain Orton Clark toured the remnants of the town of Port Hudson shortly after the siege ended. He concluded that it was a small and insignificant place that "probably never would have been heard of outside its immediate vicinity" except for the fact that it was the place where the Confederacy made their last stand on the Mississippi River.[29]

Aftermath at Port Hudson

With the fall of Port Hudson's Confederate garrison, both Union and Confederate forces turned their attention to new battlefields. Some Confederate soldiers who served at Port Hudson later joined the partisan rangers in the region, and others were transferred to the Army of Tennessee and participated in the battles for Atlanta and Nashville. Many of the Federals who fought at Port Hudson participated in the Red River Campaign of 1864. The Union retained a small garrison at Port Hudson until the end of the Civil War. Most of the garrison consisted of African Americans, probably because Union leaders believed that people of African ancestry were less susceptible to Louisiana's diseases than white troops. Life at Port Hudson was relatively peaceful after July 1863, consisting mostly of trying to stay healthy while launching occasional forays into the countryside to combat rebel guerrillas and civil unrest.[30]

With few Confederates near Port Hudson, Union soldiers turned on each other. On February 10, 1865, First Lieutenant Henry M. Kidder of the 1st Arkansas Union Cavalry was charged with "conduct unbecoming an officer" at Port Hudson. According to a witness, when a member of the 81st Colored Infantry on guard duty ordered Kidder to halt, Kidder "did refuse to halt and did use profane and blasphemous language." Apparently, the incident did not hurt Kidder's career. On March 15, 1865, Kidder requested and received a promotion to major in the 5th US Colored Infantry.[31]

Conclusion

LET THE BATTLES OF PORT HUDSON TELL IT

> Let the battles of Port Hudson tell it.—Let them have their liberties. The rebel armies became demoralized and disheartened, and desolved [*sic*] before our invincible hosts, like rotten banks before the rolling flood. The executive abilities of Mr. Lincoln, put to silence and confusion the boasted plans of Jeff. Davis. The Davis conspiracy was "playing out" [*sic*] The rebel leaders found themselves suddenly in a very dependant [*sic*] condition. They neither had bread for their clamoring subjects nor men to fill recruit their depleted ranks.[1]
>
> —JOHN HENNING WOODS, former Confederate soldier awaiting execution for supporting the Union

CHARLES PROSPER FAUCONNET, a French diplomat serving in New Orleans during the Civil War, was skeptical that the fall of Port Hudson and Vicksburg would "deliver a mortal blow to the Confederacy" as many Union officials claimed. He predicted that the war would not end but that it would change from a war of battles to a war of "pillaging, seizures, and devastation." Fauconnet believed that Confederate "guerrillas and flying batteries will appear at every unguarded point along the unguarded extensive course," where they would "thoroughly harass steamboats" and render Union shipping "if not impossible, then at least excessively difficult and perilous."[2]

Milton Chambers, a twenty-two-year-old farmer serving in the 29th Iowa Infantry stationed at Helena, Arkansas, during the siege of Port Hudson, disagreed with the distinguished Fauconnet. Chambers wrote to his brother that, with the fall of Vicksburg and Port Hudson, the Mississippi "is ours." He believed that the fall of Port Hudson was bringing Confederate soldiers "to their minds," and they were "coming in here almost every day and giving themselves up and say they are tired of it and will not fight any longer." Chambers heard rumors that Sterling Price was gathering a

Confederate army for a counterattack along the Mississippi River. With apparent confidence, Chambers wrote "let him come!" punctuating his taunt with an exclamation point.[3]

The farmer was right, and the diplomat was wrong. Port Hudson was not the end of the war, but it was one of the war's most important turning points. Confederates tried and failed to challenge Union control of the Mississippi River after Port Hudson, but their efforts had little impact on the Union war effort or on the eventual outcome of the war. Port Hudson was a vital turning point, and one that should never be forgotten. The fall of Port Hudson, in combination with Confederate defeats at Vicksburg and Gettysburg, improved Union morale and convinced many people across the nation that the Confederacy was destined to fall.[4]

In a recent interview, historian Larry Daniel stated that the Confederacy failed in the western theatre because "the rivers ran in the wrong direction."[5] In Virginia, the Potomac, Rappahannock, York, and James Rivers ran mostly east to west and provided Confederates with barriers to Union attacks. In the west, the Mississippi River cut through the Confederacy from north to south in an ideal path for Union forces. Numerous rivers, including the Cumberland, Tennessee, Arkansas, Yazoo, and Red Rivers, connected with the Mississippi River, giving Union forces highways from the Mississippi River into the Confederate heartland. The Confederacy tried and failed to defend the Mississippi River, losing something close to sixty-five thousand men and huge quantities of supplies along the way. It was a horrific loss, but the Confederacy had little choice but to try to defend at least some of the Mississippi River that ran through the heart of the Confederacy.

It is easy to wonder what might have happened if every Confederate force had held out as long and fought as well as the defenders of Port Hudson. Would the Union have continued to advance if every Confederate garrison had held out for forty-eight days of continuous fighting like the defenders of Port Hudson? Could the Union have sustained a war in which they suffered ten casualties for every Confederate loss on every campaign, as they did at Port Hudson? How would Union voters and Union soldiers have reacted to a war in which every victory was as slow and painful as the eventual capture of Port Hudson?

Writing from an Atlanta prison cell where he was awaiting execution for supporting the Union while serving in the Confederate army, John

Henning Woods wrote that we should "let the battles of Port Hudson tell it." Henning believed that a nation committed to freeing slaves was fundamentally stronger than a nation committed to the preservation of slavery. He pointed out that the former slaves who rallied to the Union after the Emancipation Proclamation made the Union stronger. Their blood and sweat made the Union armies invincible and ensured their success in the Port Hudson campaign.[6]

It is tempting to say that, if every Confederate force had performed as well as the defenders of Port Hudson, the war might have turned out very differently. Perhaps northerners might have lost the will to fight. The presidential election of 1864 was hotly contested, even in a war where Port Hudson was the exception to the rule. A few more forty-eight-day sieges might have sent Union voters into the arms of a presidential candidate who promised peace. Lincoln might have lost reelection in 1864, and his successor might have granted the Confederacy their independence. That is possible. However, it is also unlikely.

Port Hudson demonstrated the insignificance of Confederate resistance. At Port Hudson, the Confederacy had almost every possible advantage they could ever hope to enjoy, and it did not matter. Despite horrendous suffering and enormous obstacles, the Union did not retreat, they did not surrender, they did not even bother to change commanders. While a few men mutinied rather than extend their enlistments, most Union soldiers and sailors remained loyal to the cause. The unstoppable blue machine pounded the defenders of Port Hudson until even the most determined rebel waved the white flag or disappeared into the night in hopes that the next fight would be a little different. At Port Hudson, the Federals proved, once again, that they would pay any price for victory. A year after the fall of Port Hudson, General William Tecumseh Sherman, who helped the Union capture Vicksburg a few miles north of Port Hudson, wrote, "let us give those southern fellows all the fighting they want, and when they are tired we can tell them we are just warming to the work." Proving his sincere willingness to sacrifice men on the altar of victory, Sherman explained a few weeks later that he regarded "the death and mangling of a couple thousand men as a small affair, a kind of morning dash—and it may be well that we become so hardened."[7]

The Confederate defenders at Port Hudson delayed but could not change the outcome. They could not defeat armies of dedicated northerners, loyal

Overall view of cemetery entrance gate, looking into cemetery. View to east. Port Hudson National Cemetery, East Baton Rouge Parish, Louisiana. Library of Congress.

southerners, and former slaves led by highly skilled professional officers with an abundance of resources who were "just warming to the work" and who considered piles of dead bodies "a morning dash." It is possible that another Port Hudson–like siege or two would have shifted the balance in favor of the men in gray and changed the world in unexpected ways. Perhaps Union soldiers and voters were not as dedicated as they appear from a modern vantage point. However, it is far more likely that Union forces would have kept coming after each subsequent bloodbath, just like they did after they captured Port Hudson.

Port Hudson Today

The river that once brought life and then brought death no longer brings anything to Port Hudson. The river shifted west, cutting a new channel on its path to the sea. The town of Port Hudson died, and today there is no longer a town in its location. Tourists in sport utility vehicles have replaced sailors on riverboats on the ground that was once a bustling town. Port Hudson is home to the Port Hudson Historic Site, which is part of the Louisiana State Park System. The park, consisting of a museum, artillery displays, and six miles of hiking trails, preserves a section of the northern part of the battlefield, including Fort Desperate.[8] A few miles south of the Port Hudson Historic Site sits Port Hudson National Cemetery. In 1866 Congress established the cemetery on the site of an existing graveyard. Since 1866 additional burials have joined the original inhabitants. Today the cemetery is home to roughly ten thousand veterans, many of whom died during the battles for Port Hudson.[9]

Half a century after he fought at Port Hudson, Samuel Ellis lamented how quickly the years had passed. He knew that life's evening sun was setting low, and he worried that soon nobody would be left to tell the stories of Port Hudson. Today, every member of Port Hudson's miserable conglomeration has gone the way we must all go. They are gone, but we remain, and now we tell the tale of Port Hudson.

> Now fifty years have gone,
> How soon they pass away,
> Since we did wear the army blue;
> And now we wear the gray,
> For time has turned our hair to gray,
> To show us near the end,
> And soon will none be left to
> Tell the tale of Port Hudson.[10]
>
> —Samuel Ellis, 25th Connecticut Infantry

Appendix: Orders of Battle

Union Naval Forces Near Port Hudson on March 14, 1863[1]

Ships That Attempted to Run Past Port Hudson on March 14, 1863

Hartford, Screw Sloop, 2,900 Ton Displacement
Armament: Twenty 9-inch Dahlgren Smoothbores; Twenty 20-pounder Rifles; One 12-pounder

Albatross, Three-Masted Schooner Rigged Screw Steamer, 378 Ton Displacement
Armament: One-inch Dahlgren Smoothbore; Two 32-pounder Smoothbores

Richmond, Steam Sloop, 2,604 Ton Displacement
Armament: One 80-pounder Rifle; Twenty 9-inch Smoothbores; One 30-pounder Rifle

Genessee, Sidewheel Gunboat, 803 Ton Displacement
Armament: One 10-inch Dahlgren Smoothbore; One 100-pounder Parrott Rifle; Six 24-pounder Howitzers

Monongahela, Screw Sloop of War, 2,078 Ton Displacement
Armament: One 200-pounder Parrot Rifle; Two 11-inch Smoothbores; Two 24-pounder Smoothbores; Two 12-pounder Smoothbores

Kineo, Sidewheel Steamer, 507 Ton Displacement
Armament: One 11-inch Dahlgren Smoothbore; One 20-pounder Parrott Rifle; Two 24-pounder Howitzers

Mississippi, Sidewheel Steamer, 3,220 Ton Displacement
Armament: Two 10" Smoothbores; Eight 8" Smoothbores

Ships That Supported the Attempt to Run Past Port Hudson on March 14, 1863

Essex, Ironclad Steamer, 614 Ton Displacement
Armament: One 32-pounder (Probably Smoothbore); Three 9" Smoothbores; One 10-inch Smoothbore

Reliance, Tugboat, Details Unclear

Six Mortar Boats

Unspecified Boat Names, Commanders, and Displacements
Armament: Each Carried a Single 13-inch Mortar; Some May Have Also Carried a Howitzer

Sachem, Screw Steamer Gunboat, 197 Ton Displacement
Armament: One 20-pounder Rifle; Four 30-pounders (Probably Smoothbores)

Port Hudson's Garrison Defending the Overland Approaches on May 24, 1863[2]

Garrison Commander: Major General Franklin Gardner

Left Wing: Colonel Isaiah G. W. Steedman

INFANTRY

15th Arkansas Infantry: Colonel Benjamin Johnson
10th Arkansas Infantry Regiment: Lieutenant Colonel E. L. Vaughan
1st Alabama Infantry: Lieutenant Colonel M. B. Locke and Major S. L. Knox
18th Arkansas Infantry: Colonel J. C. Parish
39th Mississippi Infantry: Colonel W. D. Shelby

CAVALRY (DISMOUNTED)

Winfield's Cavalry (Dismounted): Captain O. P. Amacker (during Wingfield's illness)
Artillery
Herod's Mississippi Battery
Section From Bradford's Mississippi Battery
Section from Watson's Louisiana Battery

Center Wing: Brigadier General William Beall

INFANTRY

12th Arkansas Infantry: Colonel T. J. Read
1st Arkansas Infantry Battalion: Lieutenant Colonel Batt Jones
16th Arkansas Infantry: Colonel David Provence
1st Mississippi Infantry: Lieutenant Colonel A. S. Hamilton
23rd Arkansas Infantry Regiment: Colonel O.P. Lyles
49th Alabama: Major Thomas Street

ARTILLERY

Two sections from Watson's Louisiana Battery
Section From Bradford's Mississippi Battery

Right Wing: Colonel William Miles

INFANTRY

Miles's Louisiana Legion: Lieutenant Frederick Brand
9th Louisiana Infantry Battalion: Captain T. B. Chinn

Detachment from Maxey's Brigade: Captain S. A. Whiteside

Detachment from de Gournay's Louisiana Artillery (Acting as Infantry): Major Anderson Merchant

ARTILLERY

Boone's Louisiana Battery

Two sections of Robert's Mississippi Battery

Confederate Heavy Artillery Batteries at Port Hudson on March 27, 1863[3]

No. 1: Captain Whitfield
- Four 62-pounder Parrot Rifles

No. 2: Lieutenant Harman
- One 42-pounder Smoothbore
- Two 24-pounder Rifle

No. 3: Captain Riley
- One 32-pounder Rifle
- One 42-pounder Smoothbore

No. 4: Captain Seawell [*sic*]
- One 8-inch Columbiad
- One 10-inch Columbiad

No. 5: Captain Ramsey
- One 10-inch Columbiad
- One 42-pounder Smoothbore
- One 32-pounder Smoothbore

No. 6: Captain Kean
- One 24-pounder Rifle
- One 24-pounder Smoothbore

No. 7: Hot Shot Battery: Captain Sparkman
- Two 24-pounder Smoothbores

No. 8: Captain Coffin
- Two 24-pounder Rifles

No. 9: Captain Le Bisque
- One 8-inch Shell Gun
- One 32-pounder Smoothbore

Confederate Cavalry Operating Near Port Hudson on March 31, 1863[4]

9th Louisiana Battalion: Colonel J. H. Wingfield

Mississippi Battalion: Major W. H. Garland
- Captain T. C. Rhodes's Mississippi Company Attached to Garland's Command

Herren's Company: Lieutenant Colonel Miller

Lester's Company: Lieutenant Colonel Miller
Lewis's Infantry Company: Commander Unlisted
Norman's Company: Commander Unlisted
Stuart's Company: Commander Unlisted
9th Tennessee Battalion: Lieutenant Colonel George Gantt
Bryan's Company: Lieutenant Colonel George Gantt
Cage's Company: Lieutenant Colonel George Gantt
Daigre's Company: Lieutenant Colonel George Gantt
Stockdale's Company: Lieutenant Colonel George Gantt
Terrell's Company: Lieutenant Colonel George Gantt
Willbourn's Mississippi Battalion: Lieutenant Colonel George Gantt

Confederate Organizations Paroled at Port Hudson[5]

1st Alabama: Colonel I. G. W. Steedman
49th Alabama: Major T. A. Street
Maury (Tennessee) Artillery: No Commander Listed
1st [8th] Arkansas Battalion: Lieutenant Colonel B. Jones
10th Arkansas: Major C. M. Cargile
11th and 17th Arkansas (detachment): No Commander Listed
12th Arkansas: Colonel T. J. Reid Jr.
14th Arkansas: Lieutenant Colonel Pleasant Fowler
15th Arkansas: Colonel Ben. W. Johnson
16th Arkansas: Colonel David Provence
18th Arkansas: Lieutenant Colonel W. N. Parish
23rd Arkansas: Colonel O. P. Lyles
4th Louisiana (detachment): Captain Chas. T. Whitman
9th Louisiana Battalion (Infantry): Captain T. B. R. Chinn
9th Louisiana Battalion (Partisan Rangers): Major J. De Baun
12th Louisiana Heavy Artillery Battalion: Lieutenant Colonel P. F. de Gournay
30th Louisiana (detachment): Captain T. K. Porter
Miles' (Louisiana) Legion: Colonel W. R. Miles
Boone's (Louisiana) battery: Captain S. M. Thomas
Watson (Louisiana) battery: Lieutenant E. A. Toledano
1st Mississippi: Lieutenant Colonel A. S. Hamilton
39th Mississippi: Colonel W. B. Shelby
Claiborne (Mississippi) Light Infantry: Captain A. J. Lewis
1st Mississippi Light Artillery (three batteries): No Commander Listed
English's (Mississippi) battery: Lieutenant P. J. Noland
Seven Stars (Mississippi) Artillery: Lieutenant F. G. W. Coleman
1st Tennessee Heavy Artillery: Company G, Captain James A. Fisher
1st Tennessee Light Artillery: Company B, Lieutenant Oswald Tilghman
Improvised Tennessee Battalion: Captain S. A. Whiteside

Organization of the Troops in the Department of the Gulf (Nineteenth Army Corps), Major General Nathaniel P. Banks, US Army, Commanding, May 31, 1863[6]

First Division: Major General Christopher C. Augur
First Brigade: Colonel Charles Paine
2nd Louisiana: Lieutenant Colonel Charles Everett
21st Maine: Colonel Elijah D. Johnson
48th Massachusetts: Colonel Eben F. Stone
49th Massachusetts: Major Charles T. Plinkett
116th New York: Captain John Higgins.
Second Brigade: Brigadier General Godfrey Weitzel
12th Connecticut: Lieutenant Colonel Frank H. Peck
75th New York: Colonel Robert B. Merritt
114th New York: Colonel Elisha B. Smith
160th New York: Lieutenant Colonel Jon B. Van Petten
8th Vermont: Lieutenant Colonel Charles Dillingham
Third Brigade: Colonel Nathan Dudley
30th Massachusetts: Lieutenant Colonel William W. Bullock
50th Massachusetts: Colonel Carlos P. Messer
161st New York: Colonel Gabriel T. Harrower
174th New York: Major George Keating

ARTILLERY

1st Indiana Heavy (seven companies): Colonel John A. Keith
1st Maine Battery: Lieutenant John E. Morton
6th Massachusetts Battery: Lieutenant John F. Phelps
12th Massachusetts Battery (one section): Lieutenant Edwin M. Chamberlin
18th New York Battery: Captain Albert G. Mack
1st United States, Battery A: Captain Edmund C. Bainbridge
5th United States, Battery G: Lieutenant Jacob B. Rawles

MISCELLANEOUS.

1st Louisiana Engineers, Corps d'Afrique: Colonel Justin Hodge
1st Louisiana Native Guards: Lieutenant Colonel Chauncey J. Bassett
3rd Louisiana Native Guards: Colonel John A. Nelson
4th Louisiana Native Guards: Colonel Charles W. Drew
1st Louisiana Cavalry: Major Haral Robinson
2nd Rhode Island Cavalry: Lieutenant Colonel Augustus W. Corliss

Second Division: Brigadier General William Dwight
First Brigade: Colonel Thomas Clark
26th Connecticut: Lieutenant Colonel J. Selden
6th Michigan: Lieutenant Colonel E. Bacon

15th New Hampshire: Colonel John W. Kingman
128th New York: Colonel James Smith
162nd New York: Lieutenant Colonel Justus W. Blanchard
Third Brigade: Brigadier General Frank S. Nickerson
14th Maine: Colonel Thomas W. Porter
24th Maine: Colonel George M. Atwood
28th Maine (detachment consisting of companies A, D, E, and parts of F, H, and I):
Colonel Ephraim W. Woodman
165th New York: Captain Felix Angus
175th New York: Major John Gray
177th New York: Colonel Ira W. Ainsworth

ARTILLERY

1st Indiana Heavy (one company): Captain William Roy
21st New York Battery: Captain James Barnes
1st Vermont Battery: Captain George T. Hebard

Third Division: Brigadier General Halbert Paine
First Brigade: Colonel Timothy Ingram
4th Massachusetts: Colonel Henry Walker
16th New Hampshire: Colonel James Pike
110th New York: Colonel Clinton H. Sage
Second Brigade: Colonel Hawkes Fearing Jr.
8th New Hampshire: Captain William M. Barrett
133rd New York: Colonel Leonard D. H. Currie
173rd New York: Captain George W. Rogers
4th Wisconsin: Colonel Sidney A. Bean
Third Brigade: Colonel Oliver Gooding
31st Massachusetts (seven companies): Lieutenant Colonel W. S. B. Hopkins
38th Massachusetts: Major James P. Richardson
53rd Massachusetts: Colonel John W. Kimball
156th New York: Lieutenant Colonel Jacob Sharpe

ARTILLERY

4th Massachusetts Battery: Lieutenant Fred. W. Reinhard
1st United States, Battery F: Captain Richard C. Dureya
2nd Vermont Battery: Captain Pythagoras E. Holcomb

Fourth Division: Brigadier Cuvier Grover
First Brigade: Colonel Joseph Morgan
1st Louisiana: Colonel Richard E. Holcomb
22nd Maine: Colonel Simon G. Jerrard

90th New York: Major Nelson Shaurman
91st New York: Colonel Jacob Van Zandt
131st New York: Lieutenant Colonel Nicholas W. Day
Second Brigade: Colonel William Kimball
24th Connecticut: Colonel Samuel M. Mansfield
12th Maine: Lieutenant Colonel Edward Ilsley
41st Massachusetts: Lieutenant Colonel Lorenzo D. Sargent
52nd Massachusetts: Colonel Halbert S. Greenleaf
Third Brigade: Colonel Henry Birge
13th Connecticut: Captain Appolos Comstock
25th Connecticut: Lieutenant Colonel Mason C. Weld
26th Maine: Colonel Nathaniel H. Hubbard
159th New York: Lieutenant Colonel Charles A. Burt

ARTILLERY

2nd Massachusetts Battery: Captain Ormand F. Nims
1st United States, Battery L: Captain Henry W. Closson
2nd United States, Battery C: Lieutenant Theodore Bradley

CAVALRY

14th Illinois: Lieutenant Colonel Reuben Loomis
7th Illinois: Colonel Edward Prince
1st Louisiana: No Commander Listed
2nd Massachusetts Battalion: No Commander Listed
14th New York (detachment): No Commander Listed
Corps D'Afrique: Brigadier General Daniel Ullmann
6th Infantry: No Commander Listed
7th Infantry: No Commander Listed
8th Infantry: No Commander Listed
9th Infantry: No Commander Listed
10th Infantry: No Commander Listed

Defenses of New Orleans: Brigadier General William H. Emory
23rd Connecticut: Colonel Charles E. L. Holmes
1st Indiana Heavy Artillery, Company I: Captain Richard Campbell
1st Louisiana Native Guards Artillery:
Company B: Captain Loren Rygaard
1st Louisiana Native Guards (detachment): No Commander Listed
2nd Louisiana Native Guards (detachment): Lieutenant Colonel Alfred G. Hall
12th Maine, Company D: Captain Elisha Winter
13th Maine: Colonel Henry Rust Jr.
12th Massachusetts Battery: Captain Jacob Miler
13th Massachusetts Battery: Captain C. H. J. Hamlen

31st Massachusetts (three companies): Major Robert Bache
14th New York Cavalry (three companies): Captain John Ennis
25th New York Battery: Captain John A. Grow
26th New York Battery: Lieutenant George W. Fox
176th New York: Colonel Charles C. Nott
1st Texas Cavalry (three companies): Colonel Edmund J. Davis
4th Wisconsin, Company G: Captain James Keefe
Second Brigade, Second Division: Colonel Thomas Cahill
9th Connecticut: Lieutenant Colonel Richard Fitz Gibbons
28th Maine (four companies): Major Joseph D. Bullen
26th Massachusetts: Colonel Alpha B. Farr
42nd Massachusetts: Lieutenant Colonel Joseph Stedman
47th Massachusetts: Colonel Lucius B. Marsh

District of Key West and Tortugas: Brigadier General Daniel Woodbury
47th Pennsylvania (five companies): Colonel Tilghman H. Good, Key West
47th Pennsylvania (five companies): Lieutenant Colonel George W. Alexander, Tortugas
District of Pensacola: Colonel Isaac Dryer
15th Maine: Lieutenant Colonel Benjamin B. Murray Jr.
7th Vermont: Lieutenant Colonel David B. Peck
2nd US Artillery, Battery H: Captain Frank H. Larned
2nd US Artillery, Battery K: Captain Harvey A. Alen

Ship Island:
2nd Louisiana Native Guards (seven companies): Colonel Nathan W. Daniels

Notes

Introduction

1. J. R. Hamilton, "Port Hudson," *Harper's Weekly*, August 8, 1863, 498.

2. Flinn, *Campaigning with Banks*, 26.

3. See, for example, McPherson, *Battle Cry of Freedom*, which mentions Vicksburg 163 times and Port Hudson only 18 times; and Glatthaar, *The American Civil War*, which mentions Vicksburg 50 times and Port Hudson only 13 times.

4. De Gournay, "Defending Port Hudson," in *Battles and Leaders of the Civil War*, vol. 5, p. 393.

5. Accounts published during the war: Rufus Dooley Letters, Indiana Historical Society; William Park Civil War Journal, Newberry Library; William M. Allen Correspondence, Louisiana State University; and J. R. Hamilton, "Port Hudson," *Harper's Weekly*, August 8, 1863, 498; accounts of the siege published after the war: Goodloe, *Confederate Echoes and Some Rebel Relics*; Smith, *Company K, First Alabama Regiment*; Powers, *The Story of the Thirty Eighth Regiment of Massachusetts Volunteers*; Dawson, *Sarah Morgan: A Confederate Girl's Diary*; and Smith, *Leaves from a Soldier's Diary: The Personal Record of Lieutenant George G. Smith, Co. C., 1st Louisiana Regiment Infantry Volunteers.*

6. Cunningham, *The Port Hudson Campaign*, xi, xii.

7. Edmonds, *The Guns of Port Hudson*, vol. 1, xvi, xvii.

8. Hewitt, *Port Hudson, Confederate Bastion*, 179.

9. Hollandsworth, *The Louisiana Native Guards*, 64; Dobak, *Freedom by the Sword*, 499.

10. Technology of warfare: Catton, *America Goes to War*, 14; Hacker, ed., *Astride Two Worlds*, viii; Rutherford, *America's Buried History*, 44–57.

11. Woods, "Memoir of John Henning Woods," VTU.

1. Prepared for Anything

1. At the time of the Port Hudson campaign, her name was Sarah Morgan, but she later married and published her diary under the name Sarah Morgan Dawson. Therefore, she appears as Sarah Morgan in the text and as Dawson in the citations. Dawson, *A Confederate Girl's Diary*, 16.

2. Skipwith, *East Feliciana, Louisiana, Past and Present*, 10.

3. Landry, "Interview with Louis Love," *Slave Narratives of Louisianans Living in Texas*, 54.

4. Railroads: Reed, *Louisiana's Transportation Revolution—the Railroads 1830–1850*, 259; mileage listed in "Preliminary Report on the Eighth Census, Table No. 38 Railroads of the United States," 224; steamboats: Skipwith, *East Feliciana, Louisiana, Past and Present*, 10.

5. Port Hudson incorporation: Thompson, *The Story of Louisiana*, 316; commercial importance: Cunningham, *The Port Hudson Campaign*, 6; prewar merchants: Skipwith, *East Feliciana, Louisiana, Past and Present*, 10.

6. Port Hudson in 1860: F. L. Richardson, "Siege of Port Hudson," *Times Democrat of New Orleans*, April 26, 1906; population of Louisiana: United States Census of Louisiana for 1860, 194; description of Port Hudson: Cunningham, *The Port Hudson Campaign*, 8; and Skipwith, *East Feliciana, Louisiana, Past and Present*, 10.

7. "The Militia," *Natchez (MS) Daily Courier*, August 27, 1862.

8. Anaconda Plan: Foote, *The Civil War: A Narrative—Fort Sumter to Perryville*, 111; Union navy on the Atlantic Coast: McPherson, *War on the Waters*, 7.

9. Capture of New Orleans: Hearn, *The Capture of New Orleans*, 188; Morgan: Dawson, *A Confederate Girl's Diary*, 16; McHatton: Ripley, *From Flag to Flag*, 17.

10. Butler: OR, ser. 1, vol. 15, p. 555; 1st Louisiana Infantry and Smith: Smith, *Leaves from a Soldier's Diary*, 24, 147; 2nd Louisiana Union Infantry: Hunter, "Politics of Resentment," 195; Badger: Algernon Badger, Compiled Service Records of Volunteer Union Soldiers Who Served in Organizations from the State of Massachusetts, NARA; and Algernon Badger, Numerical Index to Pensions, 1860–1934, NARA; Louisiana regiments: Dyer, *Compendium of the War of the Rebellion*, 1213–14.

11. Confederate government in Opelousas, LA: OR, ser. 1, vol. 53, p. 806; Love: Landry, "Interview with Louis Love," *Slave Narratives of Louisianans Living in Texas*, 54; Morgan: Dawson, *A Confederate Girl's Diary*, 18.

12. Capture of Baton Rouge: ORN, ser. 1, vol. 17, pp. 474–75; McHatton: Ripley, *From Flag to Flag*, 21; Morgan: Dawson, *A Confederate Girl's Diary*, 23.

13. "Army Operations," *Appleton's Annual Cyclopaedia and Register of Important Events—1871*, p. 172.

14. OR, ser. 1, vol. 15, p. 771.

15. Dawson, *A Confederate Girl's Diary*, 24.

16. A. G. Carter to Daniel Ruggles, July 13, 1862, Louisiana and Lower Mississippi Valley Collection, LSU.

17. Van Dorn to hold Port Hudson and recapture Baton Rouge: OR, ser. 1, vol. 53, p. 334; and Love, *Wisconsin in the War of the Rebellion*, 536.

18. Van Dorn sends troops south with Breckenridge: OR, ser. 1, vol. 53, p. 334; disease among Confederate troops: Foote, *The Civil War: A Narrative—Fort Sumter to Perryville*, 578.

19. Read: C. W. Read, "Reminiscences of the Confederate States Navy," *SHSP*,

1876, p. 361; *Arkansas* sailing to Baton Rouge: Foote, *The Civil War: A Narrative—Fort Sumter to Perryville*, 578.

20. Harmon, "Memoir of J. W. Harmon," 12, TSLA.

21. C. W. Read, "Reminiscences of the Confederate States Navy," *SHSP*, 1876, p. 361.

22. Breckenridge ordering assault on Baton Rouge: Foote, *The Civil War: A Narrative—Fort Sumter to Perryville*, 580; Confederate advance: Harmon, "Memoir of J. W. Harmon," 13, TSLA; Dixon: Dixon, "William Y. Dixon Diary," William Y. Dixon Papers, LSU.

23. Initial Union retreat: Harmon, "Memoir of J. W. Harmon," 13, TSLA; Thomas Williams's death and Union gunboats covering retreat: Foote, *The Civil War: A Narrative—Fort Sumter to Perryville*, 580; Harmon: Harmon, "Memoir of J. W. Harmon," 13, TSLA; Dixon: Dixon, "William Y. Dixon Diary," William Y. Dixon Papers, LSU.

24. Foote, *The Civil War: A Narrative—Fort Sumter to Perryville*, 580.

25. Confederate withdrawal: Foote, *The Civil War: A Narrative—Fort Sumter to Perryville*, 580–81; destruction of the *Arkansas*: C. W. Read, "Reminiscences of the Confederate States Navy," *SHSP*, 1876, p. 361; death of A. H. Todd: Tucker, *Civil War Naval Encyclopedia*, vol. 1, p. 56; Stubblefield: Stubblefield, "Diary of William J. Stubblefield," entry dated August 5, 1862, MSUK.

26. USS *Sumter* running aground: *ORN*, ser. 1, vol. 17, p. 159; Confederate militia boarding and looting the *Sumter*: "The Militia," *Natchez (MS) Daily Courier*, August 27, 1862; captured goods go to Port Hudson: "Heroic Deed of Lieutenant Mumford," *CV* 10, no. 8 (August 1902): 365.

27. OR, ser. 1, vol. 27, p. 549.

28. "The Militia," *Natchez (MS) Daily Courier*, August 27, 1862.

29. Stubblefield, "Diary of William J. Stubblefield," entry dated August 5, 1862, MSUK.

30. Aldis enlistment records: William H. Aldis, New York Civil War Muster Roll Abstracts, NYSA; New York state draft: New York, Militia Law of the State of New York, April 23, 1862, p. 64; Aldis: William Aldis to his wife, October 29, 1862, Aldis Collection, NYHS; enlistment to avoid draft: McPherson, *For Cause and Comrades*, 102.

31. Butler to Stanton: OR, ser. 1, vol. 27, p. 549; Union authorizing recruitment of black soldiers: Dobak, *Freedom by the Sword*, 10.

32. Native Guards: Hollandsworth, *The Louisiana Native Guards*, 2; Butler on Native Guards for Union: OR, ser. 1, vol. 27, p. 549; Halleck authorizing Native Guard service: OR, ser. 1, vol. 27, p. 557.

33. Glatthaar, "The Civil War Through the Eyes of Sixteen-Year-Old Black Officer," 202.

34. Cross: Bryant, "A Yankee Soldier Looks at the Negro," 135; Peck: James

Peck to Mother and Father, June 8, 1863, NYSMM; Aldis: William Aldis to his wife, February 24, 1863, Aldis Collection, NYHS; Illinois soldier: Dobak, *Freedom by the Sword*, 15.

35. Aiken: Henry Aiken to Mother and Father, February 15, 1863, Henry T. Aiken Papers, UTBC; Park: Park, "Diary of William Park," entry dated January 30, 1863, NLSC. I used scans of Park's original diary when researching this book. An edited version of Park's diary is also available in Katherine Jeffrey, ed., *Two Civil Wars: The Curious Shared Journal of a Baton Rouge Schoolgirl and a Union Sailor on the USS* Essex (Baton Rouge: Louisiana State Univ. Press, 2016).

36. Aldis: William H. Aldis, New York Civil War Muster Roll Abstracts, NYSA; Perkins: Solon Perkins to his parents, brother, and sisters, March 17, 1863, Civil War Letters Collection, NYHS.

37. Ruggles: "A Guide to the Daniel Ruggles Papers, 1846–1909," UTBC; Breckenridge's orders: OR, ser. 1, vol. 15, p. 800; Nocquet: OR, ser. 1, vol. 15, p. 801; and Kundahl, *Confederate Engineer*, 265.

38. Port Hudson daily rations: OR, ser. 1, vol. 15, p. 800; Breckenridge orders preparations: OR, ser. 1, vol. 15, p. 800; Breckenridge confidence in Port Hudson: OR, ser. 1, vol. 15, p. 81.

2. We Are Obliged to Stay and Fight

1. Samuel Thompson to Wife, December 25, 1862, Samuel J. and Margaret Starnes Thompson Collection, BCAS.

2. Henry Aiken to Mother, November 1, 1862, Henry T. Aiken Papers, UTBC.

3. Brown, *Spencer Kellogg Brown: His Life in Kansas and His Death as a Spy*, 290.

4. Brown, "Orville Chester Brown Collection Finding Aid," KSHS , accessed April 25, 2020, https://www.kshs.org/p/orville-chester-brown-collection/13995; Ward, *Public Executions in Richmond*, 86.

5. Spencer Brown's ferryboat raid: Brown, *Spencer Kellogg Brown: His Life in Kansas and His Death as a Spy*, 290; Union supporters in the South: Sutherland, *Guerrillas, Unionists, and Violence on the Confederate Home Front*, 155.

6. "The Execution of Spencer Kellogg," *New York Times*, October 4, 1863; "Execution of a Spy at Camp Lee," *Abingdon (VA) Virginian*, October 9, 1863; Ward, *Public Executions in Richmond*, 89.

7. Porter asking Butler to retaliate: ORN, ser. 1, vol. 19, p. 186; Butler's refusal: OR, ser. 1, vol. 15, p. 567.

8. Arrival of 4th Louisiana Infantry: Wright, "Port Hudson, Its History, from an Interior View," *Daily True Delta*, August 2, 1863. I used Wright's accounts, which were published during the war by the *Daily True Delta*, but several versions of Wright's work were later edited and bound in book form. See, for example, Howard C. Wright, *Port Hudson: Its History from an Interior Point of View* (Baton Rouge: Committee for the Preservation of Port Hudson Battlefield, 1961).

9. Dixon, "William Y. Dixon Diary," William Y. Dixon Papers, LSU.

10. C. W. Read, "Reminiscences of the Confederate States Navy," *SHSP*, 1876, p. 361.

11. Few sources of masonry: Wright, "Port Hudson: Its History from an Interior View," *Daily True Delta*, August 2, 1863; destruction of Fort Pulaski: Schiller, *Fort Pulaski and the Defense of Savanah*, 22.

12. Wright, "Port Hudson: Its History from an Interior View," *Daily True Delta*, August 2, 1863.

13. Wright, "Port Hudson: Its History from an Interior View," *Daily True Delta*, August 2, 1863.

14. Wright on detached works plan: Wright, "Port Hudson: Its History from an Interior View," *Daily True Delta*, August 2, 1863; Ruggles's decision: OR, ser. 1, vol. 15, p. 567.

15. Confederate defensive plan and necessary soldiers and artillery pieces: Wright, "Port Hudson: Its History from an Interior View," *Daily True Delta*, August 2, 1863; limited troops used to defend New Orleans and Baton Rouge: Jones, *Historical Dictionary of the Civil War*, vol. 1, p. 534.

16. Enslaved laborers constructing fortifications: Wright, "Port Hudson: Its History from an Interior View," *Daily True Delta*, August 2, 1863; conflicting Confederate regulations on slave labor: Berlin, *The Destruction of Slavery*, part 1, p. 670; Confederate officials struggling with planters: Dubay, *John Jones Pettus, Mississippi Fire Eater*, 159.

17. Wright: Wright, "Port Hudson: Its History from an Interior View," *Daily True Delta*, August 2, 1863; southern whites avoiding day labor: Fitzhugh, *Sociology for the South*, 255; Confederate soldiers disdaining construction of fortifications: McPherson, *For Cause and Comrades*, 8; slaves constructing fortifications at Port Hudson: C. W. Read, "Reminiscences of the Confederate States Navy," *SHSP*, 1876, p. 361.

18. Breckenridge visiting Port Hudson: OR, ser. 1, vol. 15, p. 567;Taylor promising to send siege guns to Port Hudson: OR, ser. 1, vol. 15, p. 802.

19. Breckenridge leaving Port Hudson for Kentucky: Davis, *Breckinridge: Statesman, Soldier, Symbol*, 326; Ruggles and troops remaining at Port Hudson: OR, ser. 1, vol. 15, p. 803.

20. Confederate guerillas: Love, *Wisconsin in the War of the Rebellion*, 536; yellow fever among Union troops: Love, *Wisconsin in the War of the Rebellion*, 536; and Whitcomb, *History of the Second Massachusetts Battery*, 40; Confederate troops capturing Federal livestock: ORN, ser. 1, vol. 19, p. 785.

21. Butler evacuating Baton Rouge: ORN, ser. 1, vol. 19, p. 785; Federals aiding escaped slaves: Love, *Wisconsin in the War of the Rebellion*, 536.

22. OR, ser. 1, vol. 15, p. 803.

23. Federal gunboats offshore: OR, ser. 1, vol. 15, p. 130; city council request that Confederate troops stay outside city and De Baun's request that civilians evacuate : OR, ser. 1, vol. 15, p. 131.

24. Dixon: Dixon, "William Y. Dixon Diary," William Y. Dixon Papers, LSU;

newspaper report: "News of the Week," *Weekly Arkansas Gazette* (Little Rock, AR), September 13, 1862.

25. ORN, ser. 1, vol. 19, p. 181.

26. Confederate shore batteries at Port Hudson, *Essex* shelling earthworks, clashing with Confederate guerillas: ORN, ser. 1, vol. 19, p. 181; Confederate soldiers laughing at slave laborers: Wright, "Port Hudson: Its History from an Interior View," *Daily True Delta*, August 2, 1863.

27. C. W. Read, "Reminiscences of the Confederate States Navy," *SHSP*, 1876, p. 361.

28. OR, ser. 1, vol. 15, p. 556.

29. Smith, *Leaves From a Soldier's Diary*, 27–28.

30. Read: C. W. Read, "Reminiscences of the Confederate States Navy," *SHSP*, 1876, p. 361; Confederate soldiers and sailors fire at *Anglo-American*: ORN, ser. 1, vol. 19, p. 181; *Anglo-American* taking fire: ORN, ser. 1, vol. 19, p. 182; *Anglo-American* returning fire, sailing north: Read, "Reminiscences," 361; *Anglo-American* damage and casualties: ORN, ser. 1, vol. 19, p. 183.

31. Ruggles ordered to Jackson, MS: OR, ser. 1, vol. 15, p. 817; Van Dorn suggesting 2,500 men can defend Port Hudson, Beall left in command: OR, ser. 1, vol. 15, p. 804.

32. William Beall life and career: Eicher, *Civil War High Commands*, 123; and Sesser, "William Nelson Rector Beall," Encyclopedia of Arkansas, accessed May 18, 2022, https://encyclopediaofarkansas.net/entries/william-nelson-rector-beall-7849/; Beall skill and popularity: Harrington, "Arkansas Defends the Mississippi," 110; and "It is Now Positively Announced," *Washington (AR) Telegraph*, December 10, 1862; Wright: Wright, "Port Hudson: Its History from an Interior View," *Daily True Delta*, August 2, 1863.

33. Beall's census of Port Hudson garrison: OR, ser. 1, vol. 15, p. 804; Beall's limited manpower: Harrington, "Arkansas Defends the Mississippi," 110.

34. Beall revising defensive plan: Smith and Freret, "Fortification and Siege of Port Hudson," *SHSP*, 1886, p. 307; description of new defenses, troops deployed along Mississippi: Wright, "Port Hudson: Its History from an Interior View," *Daily True Delta*, August 2, 1863.

35. 12th Louisiana Heavy Artillery Battalion ordered to Port Hudson, less likely to suffer heat stroke and illness: Wright, "Port Hudson: Its History from an Interior View," *Daily True Delta*, August 4, 1863; 12th Louisiana experience at Yorktown, VA: Bergeron, *Guide to Louisiana Confederate Military Units, 1861–1865*, 11.

36. Paul de Gournay life and career: De la Cova, *Cuban Confederate Colonel*, 421; and Joslyn, "Well-Born Lt. Col. Paul François de Gournay Was the South's Adopted Marquis in Gray," *America's Civil War*, September 1995, 85.

37. De Gournay arrival: OR, ser. 1, vol. 15, p. 794; de Gournay disappointed

with fortifications: de Gournay, "Defending Port Hudson," in *Battles and Leaders of the Civil War*, vol. 5, p. 393; Wright: Wright, "Port Hudson: Its History from an Interior View," *Daily True Delta*, August 4, 1863; cannons left in Virginia: de Gournay, "Defending Port Hudson," 395; new clothing for de Gournay's men: de Gournay, "Received at Yorktown, April 1, 1862," Paul Francis de Gournay, Compiled Service Records of Confederate Soldiers from Louisiana, NARA; jacket type: Jensen, "A Survey of Confederate Central Government Quartermaster Issue Jackets," Military Collector & Historian, accessed July 25, 2021, http://www.military-historians.org/company/journal/confederate/confederate-2.htm.

38. Additional slaves, rapid progress: C. W. Read, "Reminiscences of the Confederate States Navy," *SHSP*, 1876, p. 361; soldiers versus slaves building fortifications, Minnich: Wright, "Port Hudson: Its History from an Interior View," *Daily True Delta*, August 2, 1863; and Minnich, "D'Gournay's Battalion of Artillery," *CV* 13, no. 1 (January 1905): 31; de Gournay's men obtaining tools: de Gournay, "Received at Yorktown, April 1, 1862," Paul Francis de Gournay, Compiled Service Records of Confederate Soldiers from Louisiana, NARA.

39. *Essex* on scouting expedition, returning fire at shore batteries, withdrawing, Porter's warning to Union high command: ORN, ser. 1, vol. 19, p. 182; Confederate bombardment from new shore batteries: Wright, "Port Hudson: Its History from an Interior View," *Daily True Delta*, August 2, 1863; and Minnich, "D'Gournay's Battalion of Artillery," *CV* 13, no. 1 (January 1905): 31.

40. Minnich: Minnich, "D'Gournay's Battalion of Artillery," *CV* 13, no. 1 (January 1905): 31; de Gournay: de Gournay, "Defending Port Hudson," in *Battles and Leaders of the Civil War*, vol. 5, 395; newspaper account: "More Hurt Than First Reported," *Natchez (MS) Daily Courier*, September 17, 1862.

41. Morgan: Dawson, *A Confederate Girl's Diary*, 186; Utley: John Utley, Compiled Service Records of Confederate Soldiers from Arkansas, NARA.

42. Hay arrival at Port Hudson hospital and death: Hewitt, *Post Hospital Ledger*, 1; Hay date of injury: W. A. Hay, Compiled Service Records of Confederate Soldiers from Tennessee, NARA; purchase of coffins and burial: E. H. Barnes, Confederate Papers Relating to Citizens or Business Firms, NARA; Villepigue death: "Death of Gen. Villepigue," *Daily Selma Alabama Reporter*, November 14, 1862; and Patrick, *Reluctant Rebel*, 53.

43. Ruggles on troops remaining in New Orleans: OR, ser. 1, vol. 15, p. 806; Ruggles's plan to march on New Orleans: OR, ser. 1, vol. 15, p. 807; General Beall's support: General Beall to General Ruggles, telegram, September 9, 1862, Confederate States Army Collection, LSU.

44. Whiting response to Ruggles: OR, ser. 1, vol. 15, p. 810; Ruggles response to Whiting: OR, ser. 1, vol. 15, p. 817.

45. OR, ser. 1, vol. 15, pp. 839–40.

46. OR, ser. 1, vol. 15, p. 141.

47. OR, ser. 1, vol. 15, p. 807.

48. Derbes, "Prison Productions," 47.

49. Dawson, *A Confederate Girl's Diary*, 233.

50. Dawson, *A Confederate Girl's Diary*, 234–35, 261.

51. "We Have a Letter," *Weekly Mississippian* (Jackson, MS), November 12, 1862.

52. 1st Alabama Infantry service: "First Regiment Alabama Infantry," Confederate Regimental History Files, 1st Alabama Infantry, ADAH; Smith, 1st Alabama journey to and arrival at Port Hudson: Smith, *Company K, First Alabama Regiment*, 37–38; Goble: Goble, "James A. Goble Diary," entry dated October 4, 1862, UALSC.

53. Smith: Smith, *Company K, First Alabama Regiment*, 39; Beall's report on 1st Alabama: OR, ser. 1, vol. 15, p. 841.

54. McMorries: McMorries, *History of the First Regiment, Alabama Volunteer Infantry*, 50; Goble: Goble, "James A. Goble Diary," entry date illegible 1862, UALSC; Thompson: Samuel Thompson to Wife, December 25, 1862, Samuel J. and Margaret Starnes Thompson Collection, BCAS; Hart: M. Hart to Brother and Sister, November 11, 1862, Miscellaneous Letters, Louisiana and Lower Mississippi Valley Collections, LSU.

55. Confederate reorganization: Gabel, *The Vicksburg Campaign*, 14; John Pemberton life and career: Eicher, *Civil War High Commands*, 423; Warner, *Generals in Gray*, 232; "Lt. General John C. Pemberton," National Park Service (website), accessed May 24, 2020, https://www.nps.gov/vick/learn/historyculture/general-john-clifford-pemberton.htm; and Smith, *Grant*, 222; Hay on Pemberton: Ballard, *Pemberton: The General Who Lost Vicksburg*, 122; Jefferson Davis on Pemberton: Cooper, *Jefferson Davis and the Civil War Era*, 46–47, 61.

56. OR, ser. 1, vol. 15, p. 840.

57. Bailey, "Joseph M. Bailey Memoir," 19, UAF.

58. Rives: H. Rives to R. T. Archer, November 1, 1862, John Pettus Correspondence and Papers, MDAH; Ruggles's conscription request: OR, ser. 1, vol. 15, p. 821.

59. August 1862 Port Hudson manpower reports: OR, ser. 1, vol. 15, p. 804; October 1862 Port Hudson manpower reports: OR, ser. 1, vol. 15, p. 841; manpower outside Port Hudson: OR, ser. 1, vol. 15, p. 841; field battery training: Patrick, *Reluctant Rebel*, 64.

60. Mayo report on artillery around Port Hudson, October 1862: OR, ser. 1, vol. 15, pp. 844–46; Mayo recommendations for siege batteries facing the Mississippi: OR, ser. 1, vol. 15, p. 844; Mayo recommendations for light artillery guarding overland approaches: OR, ser. 1, vol. 15, p. 845.

61. OR, ser. 1, vol. 15, p. 845.

62. Beall requesting permission to declare martial law: OR, ser. 1, vol. 15, p. 841; Campbell declining Beall's request: OR, ser. 1, vol. 15, p. 842.

63. Dederer: Nicholas Dederer to Son, January 30, 1863, Papers and Images of the American Civil War, GLI; Aiken: Henry Aiken to Mother, November 1, 1862, Henry T. Aiken Papers, UTBC; Bocker declaring Beedenham insane: Bocker, "Jacob Bocker Report on George Beedenham, October 16, 1862," George Beedenham, Compiled Service Records of Volunteer Union Soldiers Who Served in Organizations from the State of Louisiana, NARA; Beedenham experience in mental hospital: "Muster Roll, July and August 1864," George Beedenham, Compiled Service Records of Volunteer Union Soldiers Who Served in Organizations from the State Of Louisiana, NARA .

64. OR, ser. 1, vol. 17, pt. 2, p. 749.

65. Trade goods at Port Hudson, flow of people, Union spies: Wright, "Port Hudson: Its History from an Interior View," *Daily True Delta*, August 4, 1863; Texas cattle: Smith, *Company K, First Alabama Regiment*, 42; Goble: Goble, "James A. Goble Diary," entry date illegible, 1862, UALSC.

66. Wright: Wright, "Port Hudson: Its History from an Interior View," *Daily True Delta*, August 4, 1863; McMorries: McMorries, *History of the First Regiment, Alabama Volunteer Infantry*, 52.

67. Waterman: Waterman, "Afield Afloat," *CV* 7 no. 8 (August 1898): 390; supply boat: Christ, "*Homer*," Encyclopedia of Arkansas, accessed May 18, 2022, https://encyclopediaofarkansas.net/entries/fifteenth-12212/. The *Homer* was captured by the Union and then sunk during the Camden Expedition of 1864. The *Homer* shipwreck site was listed on the National Register of Historic Places on September 14, 2002. Smith: Smith, *Company K, First Alabama Regiment*, 43.

68. Proctor: Francis Proctor, Compiled Service Records of Confederate Soldiers from Arkansas; Moseley: William Moseley, Compiled Service Records of Confederate Soldiers from Arkansas; Roberts: Calvin Roberts, Compiled Service Records of Confederate Soldiers from Louisiana; and Stubbs: John Stubbs, Compiled Service Records of Confederate Soldiers from Alabama, all at NARA.

69. Evan to Sister and Mother and Niece, June 11, 1863, Rosemonde E. and Emile Kuntz Collection, DUL. Although Evan did not specify, the *Drover* he sailed on was almost certainly the side-wheel steam ferry displacing twenty-six tons, which was built in 1862 and sunk by its crew in 1864 in hopes of blocking the Red River. Gaines, *Encyclopedia of Civil War Shipwrecks*, 63.

70. Smith: Smith, *Company K, First Alabama Regiment*, 42; McNeilly: McNeilly, "Under Fire at Port Hudson," *CV* 27, no. 9, (September 1919): 337.

71. Hunger and spoiled food: Wright, "Port Hudson: Its History from an Interior View," *Daily True Delta*, August 4, 1863; purchasing food and fishing: Smith, *Company K, First Alabama Regiment*, 43; McNeilly: McNeilly, "Under Fire at Port Hudson," *CV* 27, no. 9, (September 1919): 337; Porter: Porter, "War Diary of W. C. Porter," 305.

72. Protesting poor rations: "A New War Cry," *Memphis Daily Appeal*, April 4, 1863; Butler Order No. 28: Underwood, *Women of the Confederacy*, 140.

73. McMorries, kangaroo courts, humorous camp newspapers: McMorries, *History of the First Regiment, Alabama Volunteer Infantry*, 51–52; molasses candy: McNeilly, “Under Fire at Port Hudson,” *CV* 27, no. 9(September 1919): 337.

74. Corn beer: Patrick, *Reluctant Rebel*, 65; local rum and destruction of stills: McMorries, *History of the First Regiment, Alabama Volunteer Infantry*, 51.

75. Patrick, *Reluctant Rebel*, 46, 48, 51–52, 54.

76. McNeilly: McNeilly, “Under Fire at Port Hudson,” *CV* 27, no. 9, (September 1919): 338; Porter: Porter, “War Diary of W. C. Porter,” 306.

77. McMorries, *History of the First Regiment, Alabama Volunteer Infantry*, 52.

78. Patrick’s residence in camp: Patrick, *Reluctant Rebel*, 47, 50; Eliza Goble’s arrival and residence in camp: Goble, “James A. Goble Diary,” entries dated June 1 and June 10, 1863, UALSC.

79. McNeilly, “Under Fire at Port Hudson,” *CV* 27, no. 9, (September 1919): 338.

3. My Thoughts Are Always of You

1. William Aldis to his wife, February 6, 1863, Aldis Collection, NYHS.

2. W. W. J. Magee to William Allen, December 16, 1862, William M. Allen Correspondence, LSU.

3. Risley, *Civil War: Primary Documents on Events from 1860 to 1865*, 147.

4. Removal of Butler: OR, ser. 1, vol. 15, p. 590; Banks’s political career and Army commission: Warner, *Generals in Blue*, 18; and Barney, *The Oxford Encyclopedia of the Civil War*, 22.

5. Banks’s defeat by Stonewall Jackson: Barney, *The Oxford Encyclopedia of the Civil War*, 23; Lincoln prioritizing politics with Banks appointment: Warner, *Generals in Blue*, 18; Butler alienating southerners: Warner, *Generals in Blue*, 61; Lincoln sending troops to Louisiana: OR, ser. 1, vol. 15, p. 590.

6. Van Alstyne: Van Alstyne, *Diary of an Enlisted Man*, 67, 70.

7. Flinn, *Campaigning with Banks*, 5.

8. Latture, ed., “Pinned Down Outside Port Hudson,” 48.

9. Clark, *The One Hundred and Sixteenth Regiment of New York Volunteers*, 44.

10. John Barnard to Sarah, December 25, 1862, John Barnard Papers, DUL.

11. Aiken: Henry Aiken to Father, December 6, 1862, Henry T. Aiken Papers, UTBC; Thomson: George Thomson to Mother, December 11, 1862, Papers and Images of the American Civil War, GLI; Ellis: Ellis, *The Twenty-Fifth Regiment Connecticut Volunteers*, 15. Ellis does not appear to have returned to the South after the war. He married, fathered a child, farmed, and died in 1918 at the age of seventy-eight or seventy-nine. He is buried in Rockville, CT. Samuel K. Ellis, Find a Grave (website), accessed July 27, 2021, https://www.findagrave.com/memorial/46487375/samuel-k.-ellis.

12. Federal navy scouting Confederate positions, firing on Confederate troops: ORN, ser. 1, vol. 19, p. 350, 352.

13. ORN, ser. 1, vol. 19, p. 350.

14. Federal navy conducting reconnaissance around Port Hudson: ORN, ser. 1, vol. 19, p. 351; 1st Alabama preparing for fight: Smith, *Company K, First Alabama Regiment*, 44.

15. Union naval commanders wary of Confederate positions on Mississippi around Port Hudson: ORN, ser. 1, vol. 19, pp. 351–54, quotation at 353.

16. Ransom: ORN, ser. 1, vol. 19, p. 352; Union ships withdrawing: ORN, ser. 1, vol. 19, p. 353; absence of batteries on west bank: ORN, ser. 1, vol. 19, p. 351; landing noted across from Profit Island: ORN, ser. 1, vol. 19, p. 352.

17. Second Union navy reconnaissance: ORN, ser. 1, vol. 19, p. 777; battle with Confederates: ORN, ser. 1, vol. 19, p. 778.

18. *Kineo* and *Katahdin* leaving Port Hudson: ORN, ser. 1, vol. 19, p. 778; Allen: F. L. Allen to William Allen, December 16, 1862, William M. Allen Correspondence, LSU.

19. Schley, *Forty-Five Years Under the Flag*, 37.

20. Smith, *Company K, First Alabama Regiment*, 45.

21. Confederates opening fire, *Winona* sheltering behind the *Essex*: ORN, ser. 1, vol. 19, p. 778.

22. ORN, ser. 1, vol. 19, p. 778.

23. Newspaper accounts of the battle: "Gunboats Repulsed at Port Hudson," *Natchez (MS) Daily Courier*, December 16, 1862; and "Skirmish on the River," *Memphis (TN) Daily Appeal*, December 17, 1862; Roe: ORN, ser. 1, vol. 19, p. 778.

24. Nathanial Banks taking command: Eicher, *Civil War High Commands*, 115; Butler accepting removal: OR, ser. 1, vol. 15, p. 614; Butler's farewell letter: OR, ser. 1, vol. 15, p. 610; Roe recommending earlier removal of Butler: ORN, ser. 1, vol. 19, p. 779; Butler taking new position: Eicher, *Civil War High Commands*, 156.

25. "General Banks Expedition," *Raftsman's Journal* (Clearfield, PA), December 17, 1862; "News of the Week," *Urbana (OH) Union*, December 31, 1862; "The Banks Expedition," *New York Herald*, December 21, 1862; "Mr. Seward as a Strategist," *Chicago Tribune*, December 22, 1862.

26. Banks headquarters: OR, ser. 1, vol. 15, p. 761; Banks reorganizing forces, appointing staff: OR, ser. 1, vol. 15, p. 611; reports on Confederate strength and reinforcements: OR, ser. 1, vol. 15, p. 614; actual Confederate strength from Port Hudson to Baton Rouge: OR, ser. 1, vol. 15, p. 841; Banks's promise for action: OR, ser. 1, vol. 15, p. 614.

27. "The Confederate Army," *Louisville (KY) Daily Journal*, December 17, 1862; "A Number of Persons," *Daily Delta* (New Orleans, LA), December 16, 1862.

28. Cannon: Cannon, *Inside of Rebeldom*, 65; Magee: W. W. J. Magee to William Allen, December 16, 1862, William M. Allen Correspondence, LSU.

29. Magee: W. W. J. Magee to William Allen, December 16, 1862, William M. Allen Correspondence, LSU; Patrick: Patrick, *Reluctant Rebel,* 65, 67, 69; Cannon: Cannon, *Inside of Rebeldom,* 67; Allen: F. L. Allen to William Allen, December 16, 1862, William M. Allen Correspondence, LSU.

30. Banks ordering Grover to recapture Baton Rouge: OR, ser. 1, vol. 15, p. 191; Banks expecting easy victory: OR, ser. 1, vol. 15, p. 613; Farragut sending ships to New Orleans: ORN, ser. 1, vol. 19, p. 352.

31. Alden, camps of Union soldiers and sugar mills: ORN, ser. 1, vol. 19, p. 761; Tiemann: Tiemann, *The 159th Regiment Infantry New York State Volunteers,* 17, 18; Ewer: Ewer, *Third Massachusetts Cavalry,* 49.

32. *Essex* shelling, transports unloading at Baton Rouge: ORN, ser. 1, vol. 19, p. 711; Gardner: Gardner, "A Yankee in Louisiana," 288; Confederate garrison retreating: OR, ser. 1, vol. 15, p. 191; US flag raised and Roe: ORN, ser. 1, vol. 19, p. 779.

33. Aldis: William Aldis to his wife, December 21, 1862; and William Aldis to his wife, February 6, 1863, both in Aldis Collection, NYHS.

34. William Smith to his wife, December 21, 1862, William A. Smith Letters, TUL.

35. Patrick, *Reluctant Rebel,* 66.

36. Grover not optimistic: OR, ser. 1, vol. 15, p. 191; Grover ordering earthworks, men concerned enemy not coming: Ewer, *Third Massachusetts Cavalry,* 53, 54; "contrabands" constructing fortifications: William Smith to his wife, December 21, 1862, William A. Smith Letters, TUL; Tiemann: Tiemann, *The 159th Regiment Infantry New York State Volunteers,* 17; Union reinforcements: OR, ser. 1, vol. 15, p. 1096.

37. OR, ser. 1, vol. 17, pt. 2, p. 801.

38. ORN, ser. 1, vol. 19, p. 430.

39. Cannon: Cannon, *Inside of Rebeldom,* 67; Thompson: Samuel Thompson to Wife, December 25, 1862, Samuel J. and Margaret Starnes Thompson Collection, BCAS; Porter: Porter, "War Diary of W. C. Porter," 307; Dixon: Dixon, "William Y. Dixon Diary," William Y. Dixon Papers, LSU.

40. Guest: Isaac Guest to Genl, December 18, 1862, Compiled Service Records of Confederate Soldiers from Arkansas, NARA. A note on the outside of Guest's letter notes that his request was approved and that his service with the Confederate army ended on January 6, 1863. Woodruff: Jasper Woodruff to Genl S. Cooper, January 2, 1863, Compiled Service Records of Confederate Soldiers from Arkansas, NARA. A note on the outside of Woodruff's letter notes that his request was approved and that his service with the Confederate army ended on January 7, 1863.

41. Confederate soldiers absent without leave: "Notice," *Weekly Arkansas Gazette* (Little Rock, AR), December 20, 1862; "Absences from the Army," *Natchez*

(MS) Daily Courier, December 27, 1862; cash rewards for deserters: "$30 Reward," *Natchez (MS) Daily Courier*, May 7, 1863; Mitchell deserting: E. G. Mitchell, Compiled Service Records of Confederate Soldiers from Arkansas, NARA; deserting Confederates surrendering: Park, "Diary of William Park," entry dated January 30, 1863, NLSC; Whitfield: Weitz, *More Damning than Slaughter*, 127.

42. William Thurman to Wife, December 26, 1862; and William Thurman to Wife, December 28, 1862, both in William Thurman Letters, TSLA.

43. Smith: William Smith to his wife, December 21, 1862, William A. Smith Letters, TUL; Aldis: Aldis, "Poem by William H. Aldis to his wife, December 21, 1862, Aldis Collection, NYHS; Barnard: John Barnard to Sarah, December 25, 1862, John Barnard Papers, DUL; Boyd: Louis Boyd to Wife, March 1, 1863, Louis Boyd Civil War Letters, FSA. Although the letter dates from March 1, 1863, Boyd complained that he had not received a letter for six months, which meant that at Christmas it had been roughly three months since he got a letter. On March 11, he wrote again to apologize, explaining that shortly after mailing his March 1 letter, he received two letters from her that had apparently been lost or delayed in the mail.

44. Clark, *The One Hundred and Sixteenth Regiment of New York Volunteers*, 46.

45. William Smith to his wife, December 29, 1862, William A. Smith Letters, TUL.

46. Gardner taking command: Wright, "Port Hudson, Its History, from an Interior View," *Daily True Delta*, August 5, 1863; Gardner life and career: Tucker, *American Civil War: The Definitive Encyclopedia and Document Collection*, 742; Gardner resigning from US Army: Franklin Gardner, April 7, 1861, "Letters from Officers and Enlisted Men of the Army," Letters received by the Adjutant General's Office, 1860–70, NARA.

47. Wright on Gardner: Wright, "Port Hudson, Its History, from an Interior View," *Daily True Delta*, August 5, 1863; Powers: Partin, ed., "Report of a Corporal of the Alabama First Infantry," 587; newspaper report on Gardner: "The Forces at Port Hudson," *Natchez (MS) Daily Courier*, January 15, 1863; Patrick on Gardner: Patrick, *Reluctant Rebel*, 71; Porter on reorganization of regiments: Porter, "War Diary of W. C. Porter," 308.

48. Union newspaper's view of Gardner: "Communications," *Portland (ME) Daily Press*, July 1, 1863; Hasbrouck: Jacob Hasbrouck to Rowena Hasbrouck, June 1, 1863, Jacob DuBois Hasbrouck Family Collection, HHSNP; Gregory: Erastus Gregory to Brother, June 13, 1863, Erastus Gregory Letter, PHP.

49. Gardner resignation: "Franklin Gardner," April 7, 1861, Letters from Officers and Enlisted Men of the Army, Letters received by the Adjutant General's Office, 1860–70, NARA; newspaper report on Gardner resignation: "Captain Franklin Gardner," *Alexandria (DC) Gazette*, May 15, 1861; accusation that Gardner abandoned his post: "Franklin Gardner," April 14, 1861, Letters

from Officers and Enlisted Men of the Army, Letters received by the Adjutant General's Office, 1860–70, NARA; accusation of slander: Jones, *Major General Franklin Gardner,* 71.

50. Beall at Port Hudson: OR, ser. 1, vol. 15, p. 627; Wright on Beall: Wright, "Port Hudson, Its History, from an Interior View," *Daily True Delta,* August 5, 1863.

51. Clustering heaviest artillery: Wright, "Port Hudson, Its History, from an Interior View," *Daily True Delta,* August 5, 1863; Gardner reporting additional fortifications needed, requesting equipment: OR, ser. 1, vol. 15, p. 913.

52. Gardner ordering Natchez planters to send slaves: "Provost Marshall's Office," *Natchez (MS) Daily Courier,* January 7, 1863; Natchez citizens requesting protection from governor: William Britton to John Pettus, September 2, 1862, John Pettus Correspondence and Papers, MDAH; Natchez family requesting exemption from request: James McCutchon to John Pettus, February 21, 1863, John Pettus Correspondence and Papers, MDAH; Buie sending slaves to Port Hudson: Confederate States, "Invoice for Engineer Service," Malcomb Buie Files, Confederate Papers Relating to Citizens or Business Firms, NARA.

53. Southern white men seeking to avoid conscription: Harding, *The Miscellaneous Writings of George C. Harding,* 332; Union army employing southern civilians: Cashin, *War Stuff: The Struggle for Human and Environmental Resources in the Civil War,* 45; southerners joining Union army: OR, ser. 1, vol. 15, p. 556; Montfort reporting on Confederate forces: OR, ser. 1, vol. 15, p. 1107; Otto serving as Union scout: Wetta, *The Louisiana Scalawags,* 54.

54. Park on escaped slaves: Park, "Diary of William Park," entry dated December 31, 1862, NLSC; Smith: William Smith to his wife, December 21, 1862, William A. Smith Letters, TUL; Union soldiers hiring former slaves: Ellis, *The Twenty-Fifth Regiment Connecticut Volunteers,* 54; former slaves joining Union army: OR, ser. 1, vol. 24, pt. 3, p. 157.

55. Federal authorities expecting assault on Port Hudson: OR, ser. 1, vol. 15, p. 614; and George Denison to Salmon Chase, December 25, 1862, in *Annual Report of the American Historical Association for the Year 1902,* vol. 2, p. 344; Banks awaiting draft animals: ORN, ser. 1, vol. 19, p. 420; Banks reporting on available troops: OR, ser. 1, vol. 15, p. 627; sick troops: Faust, *The 6th Michigan Volunteer Infantry in the Civil War,* 125; Van Alstyne: Van Alstyne, *Diary of an Enlisted Man,* 72.

56. Newspaper reports on Port Hudson's strength: "Port Hudson," *New York Herald,* June 12, 1863; Cunningham on Banks's delay: Cunningham, *The Port Hudson Campaign,* 18; Hewitt on Banks's delay: Hewitt, *Port Hudson Confederate Bastion* , 38.

57. Fowler, *Memorials of William Fowler,* 20.

4. I Should Have Resigned Long Ago

1. Louis Boyd to wife, March 11, 1863, FSA.

2. Morgan, letter to sister, March 8, 1863, John Morgan Papers, LSU.

3. Lincoln, "The Emancipation Proclamation," NARA (website), accessed on September 4, 2021, https://www.archives.gov/exhibits/featured-documents/emancipation-proclamation; Lincoln, "The Gettysburg Address," Division of Rare and Manuscript Collections, Cornell University Library (website), accessed September 4, 2021, https://rmc.library.cornell.edu/gettysburg/good_cause/transcript.htm; Lincoln, "A Letter From the President," *Daily National Intelligencer,* August 22, 1862.

4. Brooks: Louis Brooks to Friend, January 2, 1863, Papers and Images of the American Civil War, GLI; Park: Park, "Diary of William Park," entry dated January 12, 1863, NLSC; Brown: J. Harvey Brown to Wife, January 30,1863, J. Harvey Brown Letters, TUL; Dean: Charles Dean to Friend, December 7, 1862, HAU; Gregory: Erastus Gregory to Brother, June 13, 1863, Erastus Gregory Letter, PHP.

5. Halleck urging Banks to advance, adjutant general placing Banks in command of 19th Army Corps: OR, ser. 1, vol. 15, p. 636.

6. OR, ser. 1, vol. 15, pp. 639–40.

7. Banks regulating trade in Louisiana: OR, ser. 1, vol. 15, p. 616; Palfrey: Palfrey, "Port Hudson," *Papers of the Military Historical Society of Massachusetts,* vol. 8, p. 25; Banks suggesting return of slaves to southerners: "Address of Gen. Banks," *Portland (ME) Daily Press,* January 1, 1863.

8. "Address of Gen. Banks," *Portland (ME) Daily Press,* January 1, 1863.

9. African American newspapers denouncing Banks: Litwack, *Been in the Storm So Long,* 377; and "General Banks," *Liberator* (Boston, MA), April 3, 1863; Fauconnet: Fauconnet, *Ruined by This Miserable War,* 4.

10. Dargan: Dargan, "James Dargan Diary," entry dated June 21, 1863, CSUN; Dederer: Nicholas Dederer to Son, February 30, 1863, Papers and Images of the American Civil War, GLI.

11. Banks attempting to remove black officers: OR, ser. 3, vol. 3, p. 46; Crowder: Glatthaar, "The Civil War Through the Eyes of Sixteen-Year-Old Black Officer," 211; black officers receiving pay: Hollandsworth, *The Louisiana Native Guards,* 72.

12. Moors on lack of pay: Moors, *History of the Fifty-Second Regiment of Massachusetts Infantry,* 48; Park: Park, "Diary of William Park," entry dated January 12, 1863, NLSC.

13. Goble: Goble, "James A. Goble Diary," entry dated January 5, 1863, UALSC; Weaver: Daniel Weaver to Sister, January 26, 1863, Weaver and Gary

Family Papers, ADAH; 30-pounder Parrott rifle, "Lady Whitfield": Smith, *Company K, First Alabama Regiment,* 46.

14. Goble: Goble, "James A. Goble Diary," entry dated January 18, 1863, UALSC; Confederate mines: Rutherford, *America's Buried History,* 8.

15. Park, "Diary of William Park," entry dated January 5, 1863, NLSC.

16. Attempted ambush: Goble, "James A. Goble Diary," entry dated January 18, 1863, UALSC; *Essex* returning to Baton Rouge: Park, "Diary of William Park," entry dated January 18, 1863, NLSC; Union navy working against mines: Park, "Diary of William Park," entry dated February 19, 1863, NLSC.

17. Allen: F. L. Allen to William Allen, January 7, 1863, William M. Allen Correspondence, LSU; Broughton: Edward Broughton to Wife, January 31, 1863, accessed July 29, 2021, http://battleofraymond.org/letters.htm; 1st Alabama Infantry houses: Goble, "James A. Goble Diary," entry dated January 17, 1863, UALSC; 1st Alabama anticipating longer stay at Port Hudson: Hewitt, *Port Hudson,* 203.

18. Brooks: Louis Brooks to Sister, January 31, 1863, Papers and Images of the American Civil War, GLI; Van Alstyne: Van Alstyne, *Diary of an Enlisted Man,* 82; Peck: James Peck to Mother and Father, February 16, 1863, NYSMM; Moors: Moors, *History of the Fifty-Second Regiment of Massachusetts Infantry,* 48; Smith: William Smith to his wife, December 21, 1862, William A. Smith Letters, TUL.

19. Peck on funeral: James Peck to Mother and Father, February 19, 1863, NYSMM. In his reviewer report for this manuscript, Larry Hewitt wisely expressed skepticism about Peck's story of burying a man underwater. He pointed out that there was ample dry ground to the rear of Union positions. Hewitt might be correct, but the story remains in the manuscript because, even if it did not actually happen as Peck described, it is a primary source from a soldier produced during the war. The tale is therefore worth sharing, even if it is more folklore than fact.

20. Browne, "Remarks Accompanying Quarterly Report of Sickness of Army of the Gulf," *American Medical Times,* January 24, 1863, 40.

21. Buntly: G. W. Buntly to Brother, January 26, 1863, G. W. Buntly Collection, GLI; Weaver: Daniel Weaver to Sister, January 26, 1863, Weaver and Gary Family Papers, ADAH; Port Hudson hospital records: Hewitt, *Post Hospital Ledger,* 30–37.

22. Harmon: Harmon, "Memoir of J. W. Harmon," 15, TSLA; Cannon on digging ditches and drills: Cannon, *Inside of Rebeldom,* 68, 70; Patrick: Patrick, *Reluctant Rebel,* 71; Pettus ordering planters to provide slaves: "Military Order," *Natchez (MS) Daily Courier,* February 24, 1863.

23. Broughton: Edward Broughton to Wife, January 31, 1863, accessed July 29, 2021, http://battleofraymond.org/letters.htm; Thompson: Samuel

Thompson to Wife, January 7, 1862, Samuel J. and Margaret Starnes Thompson Collection, BCAS; Patrick: Patrick, *Reluctant Rebel*, 71.

24. Lawrence: Rufinia Lawrence to John Pettus, February 17, 1863, John Pettus Correspondence and Papers, MDAH; capture and death of Theodore Lawrence: Theodore Lawrence, Compiled Service Records of Confederate Soldiers from Mississippi, NARA; soldiers released to serve as overseers: Gardner, "Certificates of Disability, Transfers, and Miscellaneous Papers," HLHU.

25. OR, ser. 1, vol. 15, p. 923.

26. McGavock and Gower, *Pen and Sword*, 84.

27. Wailes: L. Wailes to John Pettus, February 24, 1863, John Pettus Correspondence and Papers, MDAH; Allen: F. L. Allen to William Allen, January 7, 1863, William M. Allen Correspondence, LSU; Walker: John Walker to Father, February 25, 1863, Samuel Walker Papers, ASA.

28. Whitfield: "Alabamians Fill up Your First Regiment," *Weekly Advertiser* (Montgomery, AL), January 1, 1863; hardships among new recruits: Smith, *Company K, First Alabama Regiment*, 46; Weaver: Daniel Weaver to Sister, January 26, 1863, Weaver and Gary Family Papers, ADAH.

29. McClung, *Three Years in the C.S. Army*, 11.

30. McClung, *Three Years in the C.S. Army*, 12–13.

31. McClung, *Three Years in the C.S. Army*, 13. There were at least three regiments that were all designated the 15th Arkansas Infantry. The 15th Arkansas Infantry that served at Port Hudson was also listed as the Fifteenth (Johnson's) Arkansas Infantry Regiment (for regimental commander Colonel Ben W. Johnson) to differentiate it from the two other 15th Arkansas Infantry regiments, one of which was also known as the Fifteenth (Northwest) Arkansas Infantry Regiment and the other of which was known as the Fifteenth (Josey's) Arkansas Infantry Regiment. Rushing, "Fifteenth (Johnson's) Arkansas Infantry," Encyclopedia of Arkansas, accessed May 18, 2022, https://encyclopediaofarkansas.net/entries/fifteenth-12212/.

32. United States, *Statistics of the United States*, 333.

33. Gardner reorganizing Port Hudson garrison: OR, ser. 1, vol. 15, p. 935; Gardner placing Smith in command of heavy artillery: OR, ser. 1, vol. 15, p. 943.

34. 9th Louisiana Partisan Rangers acting as couriers: OR, ser. 1, vol. 15, p. 948; cavalry positioned to cover overland approaches to Port Hudson: OR, ser. 1, vol. 15, p. 949.

35. Patrick: Patrick, *Reluctant Rebel*, 71; Vicksburg newspaper: "Our Most Serious Danger," *Vicksburg (MS) Daily Whig*, February 25, 1863; Memphis newspaper: "Shameful," *Memphis (TN) Daily Appeal*, January 23, 1863; Confederate inflation: Selcer, *Civil War America: 1850 to 1875*, 82.

36. Failure of commutation system: Wilson, *Confederate Industry*, 42; Confederate soldiers at Port Hudson awaiting uniforms: Patrick, *Reluctant Rebel*, 71; MS

civilians raising money to buy supplies: "The Wants at Port Hudson," *Natchez (MS) Daily Courier,* January 15, 1863; Quarles urging TN civilians to purchase goods for Confederate soldiers: "Col. Quarles," *Times Picayune* (New Orleans, LA), January 3, 1863.

37. Wright: Wright, "Port Hudson: Its History from an Interior View," *Daily True Delta,* August 5, 1863; Confederate officials disagreeing on defense of Port Hudson: Hewitt, *They Fought Splendidly,* 71.

38. Fauntleroy inspecting Port Hudson garrison: OR, ser. 1, vol. 15, pp. 943, 945.

39. Fauntleroy on quartermasters: OR, ser. 1, vol. 15, p. 945; Wright: Wright, "Port Hudson: Its History from an Interior View," *Daily True Delta,* August 4, 1863; Patrick: Patrick, *Reluctant Rebel,* 82.

40. OR, ser. 1, vol. 15, p. 945.

41. Morgan: Dawson, *A Confederate Girl's Diary,* 328; Steward: H. Steward, "Port Hudson, La," *True Democrat* (Little Rock, AR), March 25, 1863. While the press printed Steward's comments on March 25, the article notes that the information dated from February 27, 1863.

42. Morgan: Dawson, *A Confederate Girl's Diary,* 322; Fenner marriage: "Judge C. E. Fenner Dies," *Times Democrat* (New Orleans, LA), October 25, 1911.

43. Cannon: Cannon, *Inside of Rebeldom,* 68; Patrick: Patrick, *Reluctant Rebel,* 82; Allen: F. L. Allen to William Allen, March 4, 1863, William M. Allen Correspondence, LSU.

44. Patrick: Patrick, *Reluctant Rebel,* 83; Taylor: Meier, *Nature's Civil War,* 92; calomel: Chisolm, *A Manual of Military Surgery for the Use of Surgeons in the Confederate Army,* 18.

45. Porter: Porter, "War Diary of W. C. Porter," 309; Patrick: Patrick, *Reluctant Rebel,* 97.

46. OR, ser. 1, vol. 15, p. 671.

47. Badger: Algernon Badger to Father, March 22, 1863, Algernon Badger Family Papers, TUL; Hasbrouck: Jacob Hasbrouck to Rowena Hasbrouck, March 1, 1863, Jacob DuBois Hasbrouck Family Collection, HHSNP.

48. Dewey: Dewey, *A Memorial of Lt. Daniel Perkins Dewey,* 58; Curtis: Brainard Curtis to Father and Mother, February 24, 1863, HAU; Park: Park, "Diary of William Park," entry dated January 12, 1863, NLSC; Fyfe: Hewitt, *Port Hudson,* 38; Bean: DeLoss, *Wisconsin in the War of the Rebellion,* 550; Philbrick: William Philbrick to Friend, n.d., PHSHS.

49. Glatthaar, "The Civil War Through the Eyes of Sixteen-Year-Old Black Officer," 204, 210.

50. Banks's concerns about Port Hudson's strength, inexperienced troops: OR, ser. 1, vol. 15, p. 241; Banks planning indirect assault to control Red River: OR, ser. 1, vol. 15, p. 646; Banks planning to cut Port Hudson off from south and east, requesting additional troops and supplies: OR, ser. 1, vol. 15, p. 241.

51. Hasbrouck: Jacob Hasbrouck to Rowena Hasbrouck, March 1, 1863, Jacob DuBois Hasbrouck Family Collection, HHSNP; Fleming: Beifuss, ed., "The Diary of Sgt. John Fleming," 26.

52. Gardner: Gardner, "A Yankee in Louisiana," 274, 290; Dewey: Lloyd, *A Memorial of Lt. Daniel Perkins Dewey*, 60. Dewey never introduced his young sister to his pet. He died at the Battle of the Teche (April 14, 1863). Lloyd, *A Memorial of Lt. Daniel Perkins Dewey*, 118.

53. Fowler: Fowler, *Memorials of William Fowler*, 21, 23; Fleming: Beifuss, ed., "The Diary of Sgt. John Fleming," 26; Moors: Moors, *History of the Fifty-Second Regiment of Massachusetts Infantry*, 56.

54. Patrick, *Reluctant Rebel*, 96, 97.

55. Gardner and Pemberton discussing purchase of the *Essex*: OR, ser. 1, vol. 24, pt. 3, p. 645; failure of plot: OR, ser. 1, vol. 15, p. 269.

56. ORN, ser. 1, vol. 19, p. 644.

57. Farragut proposing combined arms offensive: ORN, ser. 1, vol. 19, p. 644; Farragut proposing to go with or without the army: Mahan, *Great Commanders—Admiral Farragut*, 211; Banks agreeing to plan, committing troops: Palfrey, "Port Hudson," *Papers of the Military Historical Society of Massachusetts*, vol. 8, p. 25.

58. Yeary, *Reminiscences of the Boys in Gray*, 158.

59. OR, ser. 1, vol. 15, p. 1005.

60. Harmon: Harmon, "Memoir of J. W. Harmon," 26, 27, TSLA; Morgan: John Morgan to Sister, March 8, 1863, John Morgan Papers, LSU.

61. Officer from 1st Alabama Volunteers: "Letter from Port Hudson," *Memphis (TN) Daily Appeal*, March 9, 1863; abolitionist prisoners: "The Prisoners," *Daily Selma (AL) Reporter*, January 6, 1863; rumors of Union desertion: "Port Hudson," *Montgomery (AL) Daily Mail*, February 7, 1863; comparison to Vicksburg: "Whilst Exulting O'er the Triumphs," *Vicksburg (MS) Daily Whig*, January 6, 1863.

62. Banks and staff arriving in Baton Rouge: Stevens, *History of the Fiftieth Regiment of Infantry, Massachusetts Volunteer Militia*, 65; attack on Bayou Sara picket post: OR, ser. 1, vol. 15, p. 280; Federals occupying Bayou Montesano: Ellis, *The Twenty-Fifth Regiment Connecticut Volunteers*, 6.

63. J. Harvey Brown to Wife, March 9, 1863, J. Harvey Brown Letters, TUL.

64. Kamphoefner, "Albert Krause to Parents and Brothers and Sisters, May 10, 1863," published in *Germans in the Civil War*, 205.

65. Townsend, *History of the Sixteenth Regiment New Hampshire Volunteers*, 73.

66. James Peck to Mother and Father, March 8, 1863, NYSMM.

67. Dargan, "James Dargan Diary," entries dated March 9, 1863, and March 10, 1863, CSUN.

68. Banks asking Farragut for gunboat: ORN, ser. 1, vol. 19, p. 650; Confederates at Camp Moore: George Shepley to Godfrey Weitzel, March 9, 1863, George Foster Shepley Papers, MHS.

69. Federal forces driving in Port Hudson's advanced pickets, Gardner

unsure of Federal strength: OR, ser. 1, vol. 15, p. 269; de Gournay estimate of river battery strength: de Gournay, "Defending Port Hudson," in *Battles and Leaders of the Civil War,* vol. 5, p. 396; Confederate cavalry prepared: "From Port Hudson," *Weekly Mississippian* (Jackson, MS), March 11, 1863.

70. Farragut arriving at Baton Rouge: ORN, ser. 1, vol. 19, p. 709; Boyd: Louis Boyd to Wife, March 11, 1863, FSA.

71. Loyall Farragut: Farragut, "Passing the Port Hudson Batteries," 1891, *Loyal Legion of the United States,* 315; Aiken: Henry Aiken to Mother, March 10, 1863, Henry T. Aiken Papers, UTBC.

72. Gardner to Pemberton on advance and supplies: OR, ser. 1, vol. 15, p. 263; Gardner preparing for Union ships: Waterman, "Afield Afloat," *CV CV* 7 no. 8 (August 1898): 390.

73. Griffin: McGavock and Gower, *Pen and Sword,* 84; Whitfield preparations: Smith, *Company K, First Alabama Regiment,* 48.

5. Gorgeous Yet Horrible

1. Waterman, "Afield Afloat," CV 7 no. 8 (August 1898) : 392.

2. Louis Boyd to Wife, March 15, 1863, FSA.

3. Cannon, *Inside of Rebeldom,* 77.

4. Gardner: OR, ser. 1, vol. 15, pp. 272, 273; Youngblood: Waterman, "Afield Afloat," 390.

5. Wright, "Port Hudson: Its History from an Interior View," *Daily True Delta,* August 5, 1863.

6. Ships in Farragut's fleet: ORN, ser. 2, vol. 1, p. 121; Farragut on ships' preparation: Boyton, *History of the United States Navy During the Rebellion,* 294; Boyd: Louis Boyd to Wife, March 11, 1863, FSA.

7. Farragut coordinating with Banks: ORN, ser. 1, vol. 19, p. 665; Banks's plans, Irwin: OR, ser. 1, vol. 15, p. 692; and Dyer, *Compendium: Regimental Histories,* 1110; Union army beginning advance: OR, ser. 1, vol. 15, p. 261; 1st Louisiana Union Cavalry acting as scouts, couriers: Algernon Badger to Father, March 22, 1863, Algernon Badger Family Papers, TUL; advance guard: Tiemann, *The 159th Regiment Infantry New York State Volunteers,* 23; Emory's Division: Stevens, *Fiftieth Regiment of Infantry—Massachusetts Volunteer Militia,* 66; Augur planning to follow: OR, ser. 1, vol. 15, p. 692; and Dyer, *Compendium: Regimental Histories,* 1110.

8. Irwin, *History of the Nineteenth Army Corps,* 78.

9. Stevens: Stevens, *Fiftieth Regiment of Infantry—Massachusetts Volunteer Militia,* 66, 67; Dargan: Dargan, "James Dargan Diary," entry dated March 12, 1863, CSUN.

10. Stevens: Stevens, *Fiftieth Regiment of Infantry—Massachusetts Volunteer Militia,* 67; Townsend: Townsend, *History of the Sixteenth Regiment New Hampshire*

Volunteers, 76; Rider: Rider, Diary of Claudius W. Rider, March 15, 1863, Claudius W. Rider Collection, NYHS; Union troops modifying, discarding winter clothing: Powers, *The Story of the Thirty-Eighth Regiment of Massachusetts Volunteers*, 53; Haskin: Haskin, *The History of the First Regiment of Artillery*, 547; Powers: Powers, *The Story of the Thirty-Eighth Regiment of Massachusetts Volunteers*, 52; Krause: Kamphoefner, "Albert Krause to Parents and Brothers and Sisters, May 10, 1863," published in *Germans in the Civil War*, 205; Dargan: Dargan, "James Dargan Diary," entry dated March 13, 1863, CSUN.

11. Metal vests: see, for example, "Wearing Breastplates," *Richmond Dispatch*, November 13, 1861; and "The Scientific American," *Vermont Journal* (Windsor, VT), November 16, 1861; Flinn: Flinn, *Campaigning with Banks*, 21; Plummer: Plummer, *History of the Forty-Eighth Regiment, M.V.M.*, 39.

12. Moors, *History of the Fifty-Second Regiment of Massachusetts Infantry*, 77.

13. Dargan: Dargan, "James Dargan Diary," entry dated March 14, 1863, CSUN; Townsend: Townsend, *History of the Sixteenth Regiment New Hampshire Volunteers*, 78.

14. Townsend, *History of the Sixteenth Regiment New Hampshire Volunteers*, 81.

15. Camp at Green's plantation: OR, ser. 1, vol. 15, p. 261; plantation belonging to Union supporter, top fence rails for firewood: Powers, *The Story of the Thirty-Eighth Regiment of Massachusetts Volunteers*, 53; Krause: Kamphoefner, "Albert Krause to Parents and Brothers and Sisters, May 10, 1863," published in *Germans in the Civil War*, 207; Morgan: Dawson, *A Confederate Girl's Diary*, 337.

16. Skirmishes with advancing Union troops: OR, ser. 1, vol. 15, p. 276; Gardner on skirmishes: OR, ser. 1, vol. 15, p. 272; Gardner on necessary supplies: OR, ser. 1, vol. 15, p. 271; supply boats unloading, departing: OR, ser. 1, vol. 15, p. 277.

17. Goble: Goble, "James A. Goble Diary," entry dated March 13, 1863, UALSC; *Essex* and mortar boats joining flotilla: ORN, ser. 1, vol. 19, p. 666.

18. Farragut's plan of attack: ORN, ser. 1, vol. 19, p. 666; Diggins: Diggins, *Sailing with Farragut*, 76; *Mississippi*'s side wheels offering protection: ORN, ser. 1, vol. 19, p. 667; *Essex*, mortar boats to bombard Confederate positions: ORN, ser. 1, vol. 19, p. 666; goal to run batteries, provide support to Vicksburg: ORN, ser. 1, vol. 19, p. 668; speed of ships: Boyton, *History of the United States Navy During the Rebellion*, 305; Farragut on Union guns: ORN, ser. 1, vol. 19, p. 669; gunboats to travel Red River, support Union forces at Vicksburg: ORN, ser. 1, vol. 19, p. 668; officers discussing plans, agreeing, returning to ships: ORN, ser. 1, vol. 19, p. 666.

19. Boyton, *History of the United States Navy During the Rebellion*, 296.

20. Waterman, "Afield Afloat," 390.

21. Port Hudson garrison preparing for action: Cannon, *Inside of Rebeldom*, 77; Boyd: Boyd, "Poem Book of James Addison Boyd," March 16, 1863, PHSHS.

22. Powers: Partin, ed., "Report of a Corporal of the Alabama First Infantry,"

589; bombardment beginning: OR, ser. 1, vol. 15, p. 276; Parish: William Parish to Wife, March 18, 1863, William Parish Letters, ASA; Morgan: Dawson, *A Confederate Girl's Diary*, 337; Union fleet out of range: OR, ser. 1, vol. 15, p. 271; Gardner: OR, ser. 1, vol. 15, p. 276; McMorries: McMorries, *History of the First Regiment, Alabama Volunteer Infantry*, 54; McNeilly: McNeilly, "Under Fire at Port Hudson," *CV* 7 no. 8 (September 1919): 338.

23. Drawing Union troops toward Confederate center: Wright, "Port Hudson: Its History from an Interior View," *Daily True Delta*, August 5, 1863; Tabor: Tabor, "Reminiscences of R. J. Tabor," 420.

24. Moors, *History of the Fifty-Second Regiment—Massachusetts Volunteers*, 79.

25. Algernon Badger to Father, March 22, 1863, Algernon Badger Family Papers, TUL. The Algernon Badger Family Papers includes a copy of a broadside titled "Col. Johnson's mounted men charging a party of British artillerists, 1813," which depicts a group of American cavalrymen killing dismounted British soldiers with their sabers. The significance of the broadside to Algernon's thoughts are unclear, but it is interesting that a man who believed his enemies "feared" his saber preserved only one piece of art in his papers, artwork that depicted soldiers killing enemies with sabers.

26. Moors, *History of the Fifty-Second Regiment—Massachusetts Volunteers*, 79.

27. Wright, "Port Hudson: Its History from an Interior View," *Daily True Delta*, August 5, 1863.

28. "Movements of the Infantry During the Late Attack," *Memphis (TN) Daily Appeal*, March 31, 1863.

29. Union soldiers too distant to aid Farragut: Irwin, *History of the Nineteenth Army Corps*, 79; Oberly: Oberly, "Aaron Oberly Diary," entry dated March 14, 1863, Aaron Shimer Oberly Papers, AUL.

30. Sunset: Clarke, *The Confederate States Almanac for 1863*, 14; Union fleet sailing north: ORN, ser. 1, vol. 19, p. 666.

31. Confederate sentries keeping watch: Cannon, *Inside of Rebeldom*, 78; James Boyd: Boyd, "Poem Book of James Addison Boyd," March 16, 1863, PHSHS; Confederates firing signal rockets: OR, ser. 1, vol. 15, p. 276; Louis Boyd: Louis Boyd to Wife, March 14, 1863, FSA; Waterman: Waterman, "Afield Afloat," 390; Cannon: Cannon, *Inside of Rebeldom*, 78; Griffin, 10th Tennessee Infantry: McGavock and Gower, *Pen and Sword*, 84; *Essex*, mortar boats opening fire: OR, ser. 1, vol. 15, p. 276; *Sachem* opening fire: Cunningham, *The Port Hudson Campaign*, 26.

32. Smith, *Company K, First Alabama Regiment*, 48.

33. Broom: J. Wes Broom to G. A. Bringham, March 27, 1863, TSLA; Waterman: Waterman, "Afield Afloat," 392; Powers: Partin, ed., "Report of a Corporal of the Alabama First Infantry," 590; Union fleet in range of heavy cannons: OR, ser. 1, vol. 15, p. 274.

34. Firing illuminating Federal ships, *Essex* firing at Confederate batteries: Waterman, "Afield Afloat," 392; Wright: Wright, "Port Hudson: Its History from an Interior View," *Daily True Delta*, August 5, 1863; sailors aiming at flashes from Confederate batteries: Park, "Diary of William Park," entry dated March 15, 1863, NLSC.

35. Boyd: Boyd, "Poem Book of James Addison Boyd," March 16, 1863, PHSHS; McMorries: McMorries, *History of the First Regiment, Alabama Volunteer Infantry*, 54; Broom: J. Wes Broom to G. A. Bringham, March 27, 1863, TSLA; Beauchamp: Andre Beauchamp to Wife, March 16, 1863," HAU; Waterman: Waterman, "Afield Afloat," 392.

36. Patrick, *Reluctant Rebel*, 105.

37. William Parish to Wife, March 18, 1863, William Parish Letters, ASA.

38. Louis Boyd to Wife, March 15, 1863, FSA.

39. Diggins: Diggins, *Sailing with Farragut*, 77; *Hartford* and *Albatross* escaping, rest of fleet missing: Boyton, *History of the United States Navy During the Rebellion*, 297.

40. Sailor on the *Richmond* describing battle: "The Fight at Port Hudson," *Harper's Weekly*, April 18, 1863; *Genesee* and *Richmond* floundering: Boyton, *History of the United States Navy During the Rebellion*, 299; ships steering toward 1st Alabama Infantry: McMorries, *History of the First Regiment, Alabama Volunteer Infantry*, 54.

41. Voices from the *Richmond*, Confederate gunners firing on *Richmond*: "Naval Attack on Port Hudson," *Memphis (TN) Daily Appeal*, March 20, 1863; McMorries: McMorries, *History of the First Regiment, Alabama Volunteer Infantry*, 54; *Richmond* and *Genesee* sailing south: Boyton, *History of the United States Navy During the Rebellion*, 300.

42. United States, *Medal of Honor Recipients 1863–1963*, 465, 508, 558, 599.

43. Confederates firing on *Monongahela*: Boyton, *History of the United States Navy During the Rebellion*, 306; steering equipment damaged: Oberly, "Aaron Oberly Diary," entry dated March 14, 1863, Aaron Shimer Oberly Papers, AUL; *Monongahela* damaged, ultimately sailing south: Boyton, *History of the United States Navy During the Rebellion*, 305, 306.

44. Confederates firing on *Mississippi*, ship running aground: Dabney, "The Sinking of the Mississippi," *CV* vol. 32, no. 5, (May 1924): 181; Griffin: McGavock and Gower, *Pen and Sword*, 84.

45. *Mississippi*'s crew seeking help from the *Essex*, *Essex* unable to locate tugboat, wounded left aboard burning ship: Park, "Diary of William Park," entry dated March 15, 1863, NLSC; crew setting fire to *Mississippi*: Dabney, "The Sinking of the Mississippi," 181; sailors captured: Wright, "Port Hudson: Its History from an Interior View," *Daily True Delta*, August 5, 1863; Brinn rescuing wounded men: ORN, ser. 1, vol. 19, p. 685; Brinn receiving Medal of Honor: United States, *Medal of Honor Recipients 1863–1963*, 387.

46. Burning ship's cannons firing, Confederates cheering: Dabney, "The Sinking of the Mississippi," 181; Cannon: Cannon, *Inside of Rebeldom*, 78; Morgan: Dawson, *A Confederate Girl's Diary*, 340; infantry claiming artillery set fire to ship: OR, ser. 1, vol. 15, p. 274; Mullins: David Mullins to Brother, March 21, 1863, Mullins Family Letters, BCA; end of firing: OR, ser. 1, vol. 15, p. 274.

47. Results of battle: ORN, ser. 1, vol. 19, p. 262; Alden: ORN, ser. 1, vol. 19, p. 770; *Mississippi* exploding: Dabney, "The Sinking of the Mississippi," 181; Badger: Algernon Badger to Father, March 22, 1863, Algernon Badger Family Papers, TUL; Banks blaming Farragut: Strother, *A Virginia Yankee in the Civil War*, 157; Farragut on operation: ORN, ser. 1, vol. 19, p. 667.

48. Diggins: Diggins, *Sailing with Farragut*, 79; Thayer: Thayer, "Report of Ammunition Expended by the Richmond," printed in Boynton, *The History of the Navy During the Rebellion*, vol. 2, p. 302; and James Thayer to His Friend, Thomas William Faulds Collection, NYHS.

49. Confederate losses: OR, ser. 1, vol. 15, p. 278; Morgan: John Morgan to Sister, March 8, 1863, John Morgan Papers, LSU.

50. Gardner estimate of Union losses: OR, ser. 1, vol. 15, p. 274; Powers: Partin, ed., "Report of a Corporal of the Alabama First Infantry," 590; Broughton: Edward Broughton to Wife, March 18, 1863, Battle of Raymond (website), accessed July 29, 2021, http://battleofraymond.org/letters.htm; Buntly: G. W. Buntly to Brother, March 16, 1863, G. W. Buntly Collection, GLI; Parish: William Parish to Wife, March 18, 1863, William Parish Letters, ASA; Cannon: Cannon, *Inside of Rebeldom*, 78; Thompson: Thompson, "History of the 35th Alabama Infantry Regiment," Regimental History Files, ADAH; Broom: J. Wes Broom to G. A. Bringham, March 27, 1863, TSLA; Boyd: Boyd, "Poem Book of James Addison Boyd," March 14, 1863, PHSHS.

51. Louisiana artillerymen mocking Banks: de Gournay, "Defending Port Hudson," in *Battles and Leaders of the Civil War*, vol. 5, p. 397; Wright: Wright, "Port Hudson: Its History from an Interior View," *Daily True Delta*, August 5, 1863.

6. Tired and Sick of Soldiering

1. Hazen Russell to Wife, March 28, 1863, NYSMM.

2. David Mullins to Brother, March 21, 1863, Mullins Family Letters, BCA.

3. Banks deciding to retreat to Baton Rouge: Strother, *A Virginia Yankee in the Civil War*, 157; 9th Louisiana Partisan Rangers attacking retreating soldiers: "Movements of the Infantry During the Late Attack," *Memphis (TN) Daily Appeal*, March 31, 1863; Ellis: Ellis, *The Twenty-Fifth Regiment Connecticut Volunteers*, 24.

4. Howe: Howe, *Passages from the Life of Henry Howe*, 41; Johns: Johns, *Life with the Forty-Ninth Massachusetts Volunteers*, 188; Peck: James Peck to Mother and

Father, March 15, 1863, NYSMM; Townsend: Townsend, *History of the 16th Regiment New Hampshire Volunteers,* 90; Krause: Kamphoefner, "Albert Krause to Parents and Brothers and Sisters, May 10, 1863," published in *Germans in the Civil War,* 208; Moors: Moors, *History of the Fifty-Second Regiment of Massachusetts Infantry,* 81; Russell: Hazen Russell to Wife, March 28, 1863, NYSMM.

5. Powers: Powers, *The Story of the Thirty-Eighth Regiment of Massachusetts Volunteers,* 55; Hart: John Hart to Son, April 16, 1863, USNA; Clark: Clark, *The One Hundred and Sixteenth Regiment of New York Volunteers,* 68; Johns: Johns, *Life with the Forty-Ninth Massachusetts Volunteers,* 188.

6. Strother: Strother, *A Virginia Yankee in the Civil War,* 158; Dargan: Dargan, "James Dargan Diary," entry dated March 15, 1863, CSUN.

7. Lambert: Lycurgus Lambert to Father and Mother, April 7, 1863, Papers and Images of the Civil War, GLI; Union cavalrymen deserting: "Just Arrived," *Vicksburg (MS) Daily Whig,* April 8, 1863; Fleming: Beifuss, ed., "The Diary of Sgt. John Fleming," 26. It is unclear why Olmstead attempted to desert to the Confederates. The Olmstead to whom Fleming referred was probably Conrad Olmstead, a Connecticut-born clerk whose official record lists him as being absent while serving at Baton Rouge. Olmstead successfully deserted in 1864 and was sentenced to two years at hard labor when he was caught. See Conrad Olmstead, Compiled Service Records of Volunteer Union Soldiers Who Served in Organizations from the State of New York, NYSA.

8. McMorries: McMorries, *History of the First Regiment, Alabama Volunteer Infantry,* 56; Powers: Partin, ed., "Report of a Corporal of the Alabama First Infantry," 591; Beauchamp: Andre Beauchamp to Wife, March 16, 1863, HAU. An examination of the Port Hudson post hospital ledger did not reveal any Union sailors, but the records might be incomplete, or the sailor may have been treated in a hospital other than the post hospital.

9. Powers: Partin, ed., "Report of a Corporal of the Alabama First Infantry," 591; Broughton: Edward Broughton to Wife, March 18, 1863, Battle of Raymond (website), accessed July 29, 2021, http://battleofraymond.org/letters.htm; Mullins: David Mullins to Brother, March 21, 1863, Mullins Family Letters, BCA.

10. Morgan: Dawson, *A Confederate Girl's Diary,* 340; Confederate newspaper coverage: "Brilliant Victory at Port Hudson," *Charleston (SC) Mercury,* March 17, 1863; "Naval Attack on Port Hudson," *Vicksburg (MS) Daily Whig,* March 21, 1863; "Queer," *Memphis (TN) Daily Appeal,* March 21, 1863; "Letter from Port Hudson," *Memphis (TN) Daily Appeal,* March 30, 1863; and "Naval Attack on Port Hudson," *Memphis (TN) Daily Appeal,* March 20, 1863; Sandlin: Alfred Sandlin to Wife, March 17, 1863, Alfred Sandlin Letters, EUL.

11. Northern newspaper coverage: "Very Important News," *New York Herald,* March 19, 1863; Hamilton: Hamilton, "The Fight at Port Hudson," *Harper's*

Weekly (New York, NY), April 18, 1863; Massachusetts soldier: "Letter from Baton Rouge," *Boston Herald*, April 2, 1863.

12. OR, ser. 1, vol. 15, p. 273.

13. Johns: Johns, *Life with the Forty-Ninth Massachusetts Volunteers*, 189; Krause: Kamphoefner, "Albert Krause to Parents and Brothers and Sisters, May 10, 1863," published in *Germans in the Civil War*, 208.

14. Krause: Kamphoefner, "Albert Krause to Parents and Brothers and Sisters, May 10, 1863," published in *Germans in the Civil War*, 209; Rider: Rider, Diary of Claudius W. Rider, Claudius W. Rider Collection, NYHS; Smith: William Smith to his wife, March 29, 1863, William A. Smith Letters, TUL; Peck: James Peck to Mother and Father, March 29, 1863, NYSMM; Dargan: Dargan, "James Dargan Diary," entry dated March 15, 1863, CSUN.

15. Van Alstyne: Van Alstyne, *Diary of an Enlisted Man*, 120; Krause: Kamphoefner, "Albert Krause to Parents and Brothers and Sisters, May 10, 1863," published in *Germans in the Civil War*, 207; Peck: James Peck to Mother and Father, February 12, 1863, NYSMM; Flinn: Flinn, *Campaigning with Banks*, 26.

16. "Movements of the Infantry During the Late Attack," *Memphis (TN) Daily Appeal*, March 31, 1863.

17. Farragut on Banks: ORN, ser. 1, vol. 20, p. 57; Cross: Bryant, "A Yankee Soldier Looks at the Negro," 42.

18. Dewey, *A Memorial of Lt. Daniel Perkins Dewey*, 71.

19. Federals initiate 1st Bayou Teche Campaign: OR, ser. 1, vol. 15, p. 275; southern civilians petition Gardner for troops: OR, ser. 1, vol. 15, p. 279.

20. Taylor defending western Louisiana: Taylor, *Destruction and Reconstruction*, 129; Confederates withdrawing, Federal pursuit: Cutrer, *Theater of a Separate War*, 199, 202.

21. Confederate morale high, Union troops demoralized: Cutrer, *Theater of a Separate War*, 202; Dederer: Nicholas Dederer to Son, April 29, 1863, Papers and Images of the American Civil War, GLI.

22. Wright, "Port Hudson: Its History from an Interior View," *Daily True Delta*, August 6, 1863.

23. Union gunboats firing on Port Hudson: OR, ser. 1, vol. 15, p. 279; Hart: John Hart to Wife, April 15, 1863, USNA; Confederates unloading supplies: OR, ser. 1, vol. 15, p. 279; Morgan: John Morgan to Sister, March 24, 1863, John Morgan Papers, LSU.

24. John Hart to Son, April 16, 1863, USNA.

25. Gardner sending detachments outside Port Hudson's defenses, Confederate scouts: OR, ser. 1, vol. 15, p. 276; Gardner on his objectives: OR, ser. 1, vol. 15, p. 275.

26. Goble: Goble, "James A. Goble Diary," entry dated March 24, 1863,

UALSC; Morgan: John Morgan to Sister, March 24, 1863, and Morgan to Sister, March 30, 1863, both in John Morgan Papers, LSU.

27. Stephens: William Stephens, Compiled Service Records of Confederate Soldiers from Arkansas, NARA; Swagerty: Lorenzo Swagerty, Compiled Service Records of Confederate Soldiers from Arkansas, NARA; southern civilians reporting sick Confederates: "War Department Ciphers Received From Mch. 26th 1863 to July 2, 1863," p. 4, Thomas Eckert Papers, HLAB; Gardner discharging sick soldiers, releasing others to work: Gardner, "Certificates of Disability, Transfers, and Miscellaneous Papers," HLHU; transfer of sick and wounded men to Clinton and Jackson, LA: Hewitt, *Post Hospital Ledger*, 53; Gardner noting shortage of wagons: OR, ser. 1, vol. 15, p. 1028.

28. Gardner reporting troop strength: OR, ser. 1, vol. 15, pp. 1031–32; Gardner ordering improvements to defenses, Wright on shortage or provisions: Wright, "Port Hudson: Its History from an Interior View," *Daily True Delta*, August 6, 1863.

29. Newspaper report on provisions: "Good News," *Weekly Advertiser* (Montgomery, AL), April 1, 1863; Goble: Goble, "James A. Goble Diary," entry dated April 4, 1863, UALSC.

30. Sturgis: Appleton Sturgis to Mother, April 3, 1863, Appleton Sturgis Papers, UKSP; Clark: Clark, *The One Hundred and Sixteenth Regiment of New York Volunteers*, 69; Crowder: Glatthaar, "The Civil War Through the Eyes of Sixteen-Year-Old Black Officer," 211; Smith: William Smith to his wife, March 29, 1863, William A. Smith Letters, TUL.

31. Holcomb: P. E. Holcomb to Major General N. P. Banks, April 27, 1863, Compiled Service Records of Volunteer Union Soldiers Who Served in Organizations from the State of Vermont, NARA; Holcomb slave ownership: US Slave Schedule for 1860, Harrison County, Texas; Holcomb on choosing patriotism over prejudice: Bryant, "A Yankee Soldier Looks at the Negro," 144; Holcomb commissioned as major: P. E. Holcomb, Compiled Service Records of Volunteer Union Soldiers Who Served in Organizations from the State of Vermont, NARA; Lancaster and Thrasher: The Murder of Oscar Chitwood, 104.

32. Russell: Hazen Russell to Wife, March 30, 1863, NYSMM; Cross: Bryant, "A Yankee Soldier Looks at the Negro," 143.

33. Glatthaar, "The Civil War Through the Eyes of Sixteen-Year-Old Black Officer," 213.

34. Aldis, "Poem by William H. Aldis, to his wife, April 23, 1863," Aldis Collection, NYHS.

35. Grierson attempting to distract Confederates along the Mississippi, Pemberton hoping to defeat Grierson: Gabel, *The Vicksburg Campaign*, 35; Confederate cavalry ride north from Louisiana, Gardner trying to block path to Baton

Rouge: Wright, "Port Hudson: Its History from an Interior View," *Daily True Delta*, August 6, 1863.

36. Bryant, "A Yankee Soldier Looks at the Negro," 143.

37. Flinn: Flinn, *Campaigning with Banks*, 66; Clark: Clark, *The One Hundred and Sixteenth Regiment of New York Volunteers*, 73.

38. Wright, "Port Hudson: Its History from an Interior View," *Daily True Delta*, August 6, 1863.

39. Wright crediting Gardner with reinforcement, troops hailing Gardner's return: Wright, "Port Hudson: Its History from an Interior View," *Daily True Delta*, August 6, 1863; Pemberton ordering Gardner to defend Port Hudson: OR, ser. 1, vol. 15, p. 1080; Davis telegram: McElroy, *Jefferson Davis: The Unreal and the Real*, 378.

40. Detachments bringing supplies, Gardner sending Arkansas infantry out to harass Federal forces: Wright, "Port Hudson: Its History from an Interior View," *Daily True Delta*, August 6, 1863; Goble: Goble, "James A. Goble Diary," entry dated April 24, 1863, UALSC.

41. Wright, "Port Hudson: Its History from an Interior View," *Daily True Delta*, August 6, 1863.

42. Wright, "Port Hudson: Its History from an Interior View," *Daily True Delta*, August 6, 1863.

43. Wright: Wright, "Port Hudson: Its History from an Interior View," *Daily True Delta*, August 6, 1863; Goble: Goble, "James A. Goble Diary," Entry Dated May 8, 1863, UALSC; McClung: McClung, *Three Years in the C.S. Army*, 17.

44. de Gournay taking cannons to Troth's Landing, Confederate cannons trading fire with Union mortar boats: Wright, "Port Hudson: Its History from an Interior View," *Daily True Delta*, August 6, 1863; 15th Arkansas Infantry supporting gunners: McClung, *Three Years in the C.S. Army*, 13.

45. McClung, *Three Years in the C.S. Army*, 16.

46. Wright, "Port Hudson: Its History from an Interior View," *Daily True Delta*, August 6, 1863.

47. Confederate casualty: Wright, "Port Hudson: Its History from an Interior View," *Daily True Delta*, August 7, 1863; Confederates reporting damage to mortar boats: "Port Hudson News," *Natchez (MS) Daily Courier*, May 12, 1863.

48. Palfrey, "Port Hudson," *Papers of the Military Historical Society of Massachusetts*, vol. 8, pp. 36, 37.

49. Van Alstyne, *Diary of an Enlisted Man*, 101 ; Perkins: Solon Perkins to his parents, brother, and sisters, May 31, 1863, Civil War Letters Collection, NYHS; Brooks: Louis Brooks to Friend, May 5, 1863, Papers and Images of the American Civil War, GLI.

50. Federal scouts, "contrabands" reporting small garrison at Port Hudson: "War Department Ciphers Received From Mch. 26th 1863 to July 2, 1863," pp.

186, 188, Thomas Eckert Papers, HLAB; Wadsworth: Charles Wadsworth to his mother, May 19, 1863, P. R. Chandler Papers: Wadsworth Family Correspondence, NYHS; Cahill: Thomas Cahill to Wife, May 12, 1863, Thomas Cahill Civil War Letters, SHU; Griffin: Eli Griffin to Wife, May 20, 1863, Eli Griffin Papers, UMBHL.

51. Wright, "Port Hudson: Its History from an Interior View," *Daily True Delta*, August 7, 1863.

52. Intelligence report to Banks: "War Department Ciphers Received From Mch. 25th 1863 to July 10, 1863," p. 188, Thomas Eckert Papers, HLAB; Beaufort: United States, *Medal of Honor Recipients 1863–1963*, p. 374.

53. Confederate cavalry reports Union approach, Gardner shifts forces to respond, Wright on Steadman's staff and preparations: Wright, "Port Hudson: Its History from an Interior View," *Daily True Delta*, August 7, 1863; Goble: Goble, "James A. Goble Diary," entry dated May 21, 1863, UALSC; Irwin: Irwin, *History of the Nineteenth Army Corps*, 170; Confederates using slave labor, offering cash to planters: "Notice to Planters," *Natchez (MS) Daily Courier*, May 19, 1863.

54. Wright, "Port Hudson: Its History from an Interior View," *Daily True Delta*, August 7, 1863.

55. Johnson moving regiment, building fortifications: Johnson, "Report of Benjamin Johnson," Confederate States Army Collection, LSU; size of Port Hudson garrison: OR, ser. 1, vol. 26, pt. 2, p. 10.

56. Jones, *Historical Dictionary of the Civil War*, 1125.

57. Wright, "Port Hudson: Its History from an Interior View," *Daily True Delta*, August 7, 1863.

58. Clark, *The One Hundred and Sixteenth Regiment of New York Volunteers*, 79.

59. Wright, "Port Hudson: Its History from an Interior View," *Daily True Delta*, August 7, 1863.

60. Wright: Wright, "Port Hudson: Its History from an Interior View," *Daily True Delta*, August 7, 1863; Clark: Clark, *The One Hundred and Sixteenth Regiment of New York Volunteers*, 80.

61. Wright, "Port Hudson: Its History from an Interior View," *Daily True Delta*, August 7, 1863.

62. Gardner ordering Steedman to oppose Federal advance: Steedman, "Official Report of Colonel J. G. W. Steedman," *SHSP*, 1886, p. 315; Gould: Thorpe Gould to Ned, June 6, 1863, Federal Soldiers' Letters Collection, UNC.

63. 9th Louisiana Partisan Rangers fighting delaying actions, Union work crews clearing forest: Wright, "Port Hudson: Its History from an Interior View," *Daily True Delta*, August 7, 1863; Krause: Kamphoefner, "Albert Krause to Parents and Brothers and Sisters, July 17, 1863," published in *Germans in the Civil War*, 207; newspaper report: "Battle at Port Hudson," *Times Picayune* (New Orleans, LA), May 24, 1863.

64. Louis Boyd to Wife, May 22, 1863, FSA.

65. Federals firing at Port Hudson defenders, gunboats shelling: Wright, "Port Hudson: Its History from an Interior View," *Daily True Delta*, August 7, 1863; letter to Farragut: Park, "Diary of William Park," entry dated March 24, 1863, NLSC.

66. Union skirmishers advancing: Wright, "Port Hudson: Its History from an Interior View," *Daily True Delta*, August 7, 1863; scouts encountering rebels in rifle pits: Hamilton, "The Siege of Port Hudson," *Harper's Weekly* (New York, NY), June 27, 1863.

67. Park, "Diary of William Park," entry dated May 24, 1863, NLSC.

68. Goble, "James A. Goble Diary," entry dated May 26, 1863, UALSC.

69. Union forces encircling Port Hudson: Clark, *The One Hundred and Sixteenth Regiment of New York Volunteers*, 83; Union gunboats in position, Union troops on west bank of river: Irwin, *History of the Nineteenth Army Corps*, 165.

70. Wright, "Port Hudson: Its History from an Interior View," *Daily True Delta*, August 9, 1863.

71. Wright, "Port Hudson: Its History from an Interior View," *Daily True Delta*, August 9, 1863.

72. Confederate garrison cut off: Bailey, "Joseph M. Bailey Memoir," 19, UAF; Evan: Evan to Sister and Mother and Niece, June 11, 1863, Rosemonde E. & Emile Kuntz Collection, DUL. Although Evan did not specify, the *Drover* he sailed on was almost certainly the side-wheel steam ferry displacing twenty-six tons, which was built in 1862 and sunk by its crew in 1864 in hopes of blocking the Red River. See Gaines, *Encyclopedia of Civil War Shipwrecks*, 63.

73. Van Alstyne, *Diary of an Enlisted Man*, 110.

74. New Hampshire infantry band playing: McGregor, *History of the Fifteenth Regiment New Hampshire*, 315; musicians working as stretcher bearers, medical orderlies: Flinn, *Campaigning with Banks*, 83–86.

75. Wright, "Port Hudson: Its History from an Interior View," *Daily True Delta*, August 9, 1863.

76. Johnson, "Report of Benjamin Johnson," Confederate States Army Collection, LSU.

77. Kennedy: Kennedy, "Diary of John A. Kennedy," *New York Times*, July 8, 1863; Union gunboats supporting infantry, Confederates repulsing attack: Wright, "Port Hudson: Its History from an Interior View," *Daily True Delta*, August 9, 1863.

78. Goble, "James A. Goble Diary," Entry Dated May 26, 1863, UALSC.

79. "John Henry, Civil War Soldier," Soldier's Record, Town of Chicopee Collection, CACPL.

80. Confederates improving fortifications: Steedman, "Official Report of Colonel J. G. W. Steedman," *SHSP*, 1886, p. 319; Kennedy: Kennedy, "Diary of John A. Kennedy," *New York Times*, July 8, 1863.

81. Confederates hearing Federal preparations, rumors of black Union soldiers: Steedman, "Official Report of Colonel J. G. W. Steedman," *SHSP*, 1886, p. 319; McClung: McClung, *Three Years in the C.S. Army*, 17.

82. Irwin, *History of the Nineteenth Army Corps*, 167.

83. Irwin, *History of the Nineteenth Army Corps*, 169.

84. War department urging progress: OR, ser. 1, vol. 15, p. 614; press condemning Banks: "The War," *New York Herald*, April 2, 1863; Banks justifying assault: Hoffman, *Camp, Court, and Siege*, 70.

85. Howe, *Passages from the Life of Henry Howe*, 48.

7. It Failed

1. Deforest, "Port Hudson: In the Trenches," *Harper's Weekly*, August 1867, p. 335.

2. McMorries, *History of the First Regiment, Alabama Volunteer Infantry*, 65.

3. McGregor: McGregor, *History of the Fifteenth Regiment New Hampshire*, 328; Clark: Clark, *The One Hundred and Sixteenth Regiment of New York Volunteers*, 87; Confederate garrison expecting attack: Wright, "Port Hudson: Its History from an Interior View," *Daily True Delta*, August 9, 1863; bombardment beginning, Steedman: Steedman, "Official Report of Colonel J. G. W. Steedman," *SHSP*, 1886, p. 319; Goble: Goble, "James A. Goble Diary," entry dated May 27, 1863, UALSC; Confederate artillery conserving shells: Irwin, *History of the Nineteenth Army Corps*, 169.

4. S. J. S. "The Field Hospital," *Daily Morning Drum Beat*, March 3, 1864, p. 8, NYSMM.

5. Weitzel ordering attack: Carpenter, *History of the 8th Regiment, Vermont Volunteers*, 114; Dwight's brigade in the lead: Irwin, *History of the Nineteenth Army Corps*, 169; Union soldiers expecting limited fight: Smith, *Leaves from a Soldier's Diary*, 24, 58; Federal regiments formed in columns: Irwin, *History of the Nineteenth Army Corps*, 169.

6. Six companies of 15th Arkansas Infantry sent to support Steedman: Johnson, "Report of Benjamin Johnson," Confederate States Army Collection, LSU; Steedman ordering advance: Steedman, "Official Report of Colonel J. G. W. Steedman," *SHSP*, 1886, p. 316.

7. Smith: Smith, *Leaves from a Soldier's Diary*, 59; McClung: McClung, *Three Years in the C.S. Army*, 17; Confederate small arms fire: Irwin, *History of the Nineteenth Army Corps*, 170; Union advance, Steedman ordering main line to hold fire: Steedman, "Official Report of Colonel J. G. W. Steedman," *SHSP*, 1886, p. 316; Hall: Hall, *Cayuga in the Field*, 116.

8. Steedman ordering concealed Confederate main line to fire, skirmishers to pursue retreating Union soldiers: Steedman, "Official Report of Colonel

J. G. W. Steedman," *SHSP*, 1886, p. 317; Kennedy: Kennedy, "Diary of John A. Kennedy," *New York Times*, July 8, 1863.

9. Park, "Diary of William Park," entry dated May 27, 1863, NLSC.

10. Union advance, Federal work crews and artillery following: Irwin, *History of the Nineteenth Army Corps*, 170; Peck: James Peck to Mother and Father, June 8, 1863, NYSMM.

11. Steedman ordering Confederate withdrawal, Confederates reforming original line: Steedman, "Official Report of Colonel J. G. W. Steedman," *SHSP*, 1886, p. 317; McClung: McClung, *Three Years in the C.S. Army*, 17; Edrington ordering artillery fire: Johnson, "Report of Benjamin Johnson," Confederate States Army Collection, LSU.

12. Confederate infantry rejoining artillery: Steedman, "Official Report of Colonel J. G. W. Steedman," *SHSP*, 1886, p. 317; Steedman ordering preparations for renewed attack: McMorries, *History of the First Regiment, Alabama Volunteer Infantry*, 64; Beall sending Confederate reinforcements north: Wright, "Port Hudson: Its History from an Interior View," *Daily True Delta*, August 9, 1863; Kennedy: Kennedy, "Diary of John A. Kennedy," *New York Times*, July 8, 1863.

13. Confederate foxholes concealed in natural terrain: Irwin, *History of the Nineteenth Army Corps*, 170; Union infantry faltering, Steedman ordering Confederates to open fire: Steedman, "Official Report of Colonel J. G. W. Steedman," *SHSP*, 1886, p. 320; Aldis: William Aldis to his wife, June 7, 1863, Aldis Collection, NYHS.

14. Weitzel ordering Thomas's brigade forward: Carpenter, *History of the 8th Regiment, Vermont Volunteers*, 114; Aldis: William Aldis to his wife, June 7, 1863, and June 30, 1863, both in Aldis Collection, NYHS.

15. Thomas's brigade under fire: Carpenter, *History of the 8th Regiment, Vermont Volunteers*, 114; Steedman shot: McMorries, *History of the First Regiment, Alabama Volunteer Infantry*, 64.

16. Steedman, "Official Report of Colonel J. G. W. Steedman," *SHSP*, 1886, p. 320.

17. Johnson and 15th Arkansas Infantry defending Fort Desperate, Steedman crediting artillery: Steedman, "Official Report of Colonel J. G. W. Steedman," *SHSP*, 1886, p. 320; Union shell striking Fort Desperate: Johnson, "Report of Benjamin Johnson," Confederate States Army Collection, LSU; Federal lines broken, retreating: Wright, "Port Hudson: Its History from an Interior View," *Daily True Delta*, August 9, 1863.

18. Deforest, "Port Hudson: In the Trenches," *Harper's Weekly*, August 1867, p. 335.

19. Wright, "Port Hudson: Its History from an Interior View," *Daily True Delta*, August 9, 1863.

20. Wright, "Port Hudson: Its History from an Interior View," *Daily True Delta*, August 9, 1863.

21. Deforest, "Port Hudson: In the Trenches," *Harper's Weekly*, August 1867, p. 335.

22. Deforest: Deforest, "Port Hudson: In the Trenches," *Harper's Weekly*, August 1867, p. 336; Wright: Wright, "Port Hudson: Its History from an Interior View," *Daily True Delta*, August 9, 1863.

23. Irwin, *History of the Nineteenth Army Corps*, 173, 174.

24. Wright on Native Guards: Wright, "Port Hudson: Its History from an Interior View," *Daily True Delta*, August 9, 1863; Kennedy on Native Guards: Kennedy, "Diary of John A. Kennedy," *New York Times*, July 8, 1863; Smith: Smith, *Company K, First Alabama Regiment*, 63; Turner: Turner, "May 27, 1863," The Siege of Port Hudson, a Civil War Diary, LCDAH.

25. Federals retreat under pressure: Waite, *New Hampshire in the Great Rebellion*, 381; Thomas ordering withdrawal, Weitzel hoping for reinforcements: Carpenter, *History of the 8th Regiment, Vermont Volunteers*, 114, 115; Federals pulling back, reinforcing their line at Fort Babcock: Irwin, *History of the Nineteenth Army Corps*, 170, 171.

26. Irwin, *History of the Nineteenth Army Corps*, 171, 172.

27. Irwin, *History of the Nineteenth Army Corps*, 172.

28. Banks ordering Sherman to attack: Irwin, *History of the Nineteenth Army Corps*, 177; Confederate troops watching Union advance: Wright, "Port Hudson: Its History from an Interior View," *Daily True Delta*, August 9, 1863.

29. Thorpe Gould to Ned, June 6, 1863, Federal Soldiers' Letters Collection, UNC.

30. Gardner, "A Yankee in Louisiana," 277.

31. Bailey, "Joseph M. Bailey Memoir," 20, UAF.

32. Confederates determined to get even: Bailey, "Joseph M. Bailey Memoir," 20, UAF; Duryee's Zouaves uniform: United States, *History of the Second Battalion Duryee Zouaves*, 17; Wright on uniforms: Wright, "Port Hudson: Its History from an Interior View," *Daily True Delta*, August 9, 1863.

33. Eli Griffin to Friend John, May 30, 1863, Eli Griffin Papers, UMBHL.

34. Rufus Dooley to Mother, June 16, 1863, IHS.

35. Hanaburgh, *History of the One Hundred and Twenty-Eighth Regiment*, 45.

36. Wright: Wright, "Port Hudson: Its History from an Interior View," *Daily True Delta*, August 9, 1863; Gould: Thorpe Gould to Ned, June 6, 1863, Federal Soldiers' Letters Collection, UNC.

37. Confederate firing: Wright, "Port Hudson: Its History from an Interior View," *Daily True Delta*, August 9, 1863; Gould: Thorpe Gould to Ned, June 6, 1863, Federal Soldiers' Letters Collection, UNC; Griffin: Eli Griffin to Friend John, May 30, 1863, Eli Griffin Papers, UMBHL.

38. Wright, "Port Hudson: Its History from an Interior View," *Daily True Delta*, August 9, 1863.

39. Thorpe Gould to Ned, June 6, 1863, Federal Soldiers' Letters Collection, UNC.

40. Trawick, "Col. Benjamin T. Pixlee, of Arkansas," *CV* 10, no. 7 (July 1902): 317.

41. Irwin, History of the Nineteenth Army Corps, 179.

42. Sutton: Mamie Yeary, Reminiscences of the Boys in Gray, 736.

43. S. J. S. on Federal advance, Confederate firing: S. J. S., "The Field Hospital," *Daily Morning Drum Beat*, March 3, 1864, p. 8, NYSMM; Clark: Clark, *The One Hundred and Sixteenth Regiment of New York Volunteers*, 89.

44. Hamilton: Hamilton, "The Siege of Port Hudson," *Harper's Weekly* (New York, NY), June 27, 1863; Plunkett: Charles Plunkett to Father, May 28, 1863, published in the *Pittsfield (MA) Sun*, June 11, 1863.

45. Frederick Deland rallying troops to fill ditch: United States, *Medal of Honor Recipients 1863–1963*, 419; exploding shells igniting brush, Confederates firing improvised material: Irwin, *History of the Nineteenth Army Corps*, 179, 181; Hamilton: Hamilton, "The Siege of Port Hudson," *Harper's Weekly* (New York, NY), June 27, 1863.

46. Federal commanders injured, troops forced to retreat: Irwin, *History of the Nineteenth Army Corps*, 179; Plunkett: Charles Plunkett to Father, May 28, 1863, published in the *Pittsfield (MA) Sun*, June 11, 1863.

47. Yeary, *Reminiscences of the Boys in Gray*, 736.

48. Smith: Smith, *Leaves from a Soldier's Diary*, 65; Turner: Turner, "May 27, 1863," The Siege of Port Hudson, a Civil War Diary, LCDAH; Hasbrouck: Jacob Hasbrouck to Rowena Hasbrouck, June 1, 1863, Jacob DuBois Hasbrouck Family Collection, HHSNP; Gale: Justus Gale to Sister, May 29, 1863, Justus F. Gale Correspondence, UVL.

49. Clark: Clark, *The One Hundred and Sixteenth Regiment of New York Volunteers*, 89; Waite: George Waite to George, June 10, 1863, George R. Waite Port Hudson Letter, LSU; S. J. S. thankful for field hospitals: S. J. S., "The Field Hospital," *Daily Morning Drum Beat*, March 3, 1864, p. 8, NYSMM; Oberly helping with wounded: Oberly, "Aaron Oberly Diary," entry dated May 28, 1863, Aaron Shimer Oberly Papers, AUL; overwhelming number of wounded Union soldiers: Irwin, *History of the Nineteenth Army Corps*, 181; Cross: Bryant, "A Yankee Soldier Looks at the Negro," 146.

50. Fewer Confederate casualties: Steedman, "Official Report of Colonel J. G. W. Steedman," *SHSP*, 1886, p. 325; Alexander: Alexander, "James Benton Alexander Diary," entry dated May 27, 1863, UNDSC; Bailey: Bailey, "Joseph M. Bailey Memoir," 20, UAF.

51. Wounded Union soldiers sent to Baton Rouge: Paine, "Charles Paine

Miscellaneous Papers," HLHU; Gould sent to Baton Rouge and New Orleans: Thorpe Gould to Ned, June 6, 1863, Federal Soldiers' Letters Collection, UNC; Griffin: Eli Griffin to Friend John, May 30, 1863, Eli Griffin Papers, UMBHL.

52. "Case, Major G. N. Lewis," in United States, *Medical and Surgical History*, vol. 2, pt. 1, p. 494.

53. Defeat degraded Union morale: Palfrey, "Port Hudson," *Papers of the Military Historical Society of Massachusetts*, vol. 8, p. 41; Plunkett: Charles Plunkett to Father, May 28, 1863," Published in the *Pittsfield (MA) Sun*, June 11, 1863; Park: Park, "Diary of William Park," entry dated May 27, 1863, NLSC; McGregor: McGregor, *History of the Fifteenth Regiment New Hampshire*, 328; Cross: Bryant, "A Yankee Soldier Looks at the Negro," 146; Gould: Thorpe Gould to Ned, June 6, 1863, Federal Soldiers' Letters Collection, UNC; Brown: J. Harvey Brown to Wife, June 8,1863, J. Harvey Brown Letters, TU. Brown recovered from his wound and briefly returned to duty. He died of illness at Brasher City, LA, on October 16, 1863. "Brown, James H.," New York, Civil War Muster Roll Abstracts, NYSA.

54. Griffin: Eli Griffin to Friend John, May 30, 1863, Eli Griffin Papers, UMBHL; Fowler: Fowler, *Memorials of William Fowler*, 44; Peck: James Peck to Mother and Father, June 8, 1863, NYSMM; Hanaburgh: Hanaburgh, *History of the One Hundred and Twenty-Eighth Regiment*, 47; Irwin: Irwin, *History of the Nineteenth Army Corps*, 181.

55. Smith: William Smith to his wife, May 8, 1863, William A. Smith Letters, TUL; Gale: Justus Gale to Sister, May 29, 1863, Justus F. Gale Correspondence, UVL; Lord: Charles Lord to Wife, May 29, 1863, Charles Lord Letters, PFL.

56. Wright: Wright, "Port Hudson: Its History from an Interior View," *Daily True Delta*, August 11, 1863; Goble: Goble, "James A. Goble Diary," entry dated May 31, 1862, UALSC; Turner: Turner, "May 28, 1863," The Siege of Port Hudson, a Civil War Diary, LCDAH; McMorries: McMorries, *History of the First Regiment, Alabama Volunteer Infantry*, 65.

57. Confederate newspaper coverage: "The Fight at Port Hudson," *Natchez (MS) Daily Courier*, June 5, 1863; "Victory at Port Hudson," *Charleston (SC) Mercury*, June 6, 1863; "Mobile," *Montgomery (AL) Daily Mail*, June 5, 1863; "We Give the Following Particulars," *Fayetteville Semi Weekly Observer*, June 8, 1863; "Telegraphic News from Mississippi," *Daily Dispatch* (Richmond, VA), June 6, 1863.

58. Confederates using captured rifles: Smith, *Company K, First Alabama Regiment*, 65; Wright: Wright, "Port Hudson: Its History from an Interior View," *Daily True Delta*, August 11, 1863; Confederate myth about drunk Union soldiers: Phillips, *Diehard Rebels*, 72.

59. Peck: James Peck to Mother and Father, March 15, 1863; and James Peck to Mother and Father, June 8, 1863, both at NYSMM.

60. Banks praising Native Guards: OR, ser. 1, vol. 26, pt. 1, p. 45; newspaper praising African American soldiers: "Nobly Done," *New York Tribune*, June 8, 1863; Maglathlin: Maglathlin, *Company I, Fourth Massachusetts Regiment*, 30; Edmond: John Edmond to Sister, June 1, 1863, Edmond Family Collection, NYHS; Buckley: Buckley, "Later from Port Hudson," *Boston Herald*, June 9, 1863.

61. Hoffman: Hoffman, *Camp, Court, and Siege*, 71; Cross: Bryant, "A Yankee Soldier Looks at the Negro," 147.

62. Kennedy: Kennedy, "Diary of John A. Kennedy," *New York Times*, July 8, 1863; Smith: Smith, *Company K, First Alabama Regiment*, 63; Goble: Goble, "James A. Goble Diary," entry dated May 30, 1863, UALSC.

63. Newspaper coverage of Native Guards: Wisley, "The Fight at Port Hudson," *Natchez (MS) Daily Courier*, June 5, 1863; and "Victory at Port Hudson," *Charleston (SC) Mercury*, June 6, 1863; Woods: Woods, "Memoir," John Henning Woods Papers, VT. Woods eventually escaped from a Confederate prison and served as a clerk in for the Union army. After the war, he moved to Missouri and died on March 5, 1901. "Unionist in Southern Lines: The Life of John Henning Woods," November 18, 2016, Virginia Tech Special Collections and University Archives (website), accessed July 28, 2021, https://vtspecialcollections.wordpress.com/2016/11/18/unionist-in-southern-lines-the-life-of-john-henning-woods/.

64. John Edmond to Sister, June 1, 1863, Edmond Family Collection, NYHS.

65. OR, ser. 1, vol. 24, pt. 3, p. 157.

8. Miserable in the Extreme

1. Dargan, "James Dargan Diary," entry dated June 1, 1863, CSUN.
2. Goble, "James A. Goble Diary," entry dated June 6, 1863, UALSC.
3. Smith, *Company K, First Alabama Regiment*, 66.
4. Smith, *Company K, First Alabama Regiment*, 67.
5. Banks and Gardner negotiate truce to remove dead and wounded: Irwin, *History of the Nineteenth Army Corps*, 185; Gardner accusing Federals of erecting a battery: OR, ser. 1, vol. 26, pt. 1, p. 515; Banks accusing Confederates of capturing wounded Union soldiers: OR, ser. 1, vol. 26, pt. 1, p. 516.
6. Turner, "May 27, 1863," The Siege of Port Hudson, a Civil War Diary, LCDAH.
7. Russell: Whitcomb, *Second Massachusetts Battery*, 48; Hanaburgh: Hanaburgh, *History of the One Hundred and Twenty-Eighth Regiment*, 48.
8. Deforest, "Port Hudson: In the Trenches," *Harper's Weekly*, August 1867, p. 336.
9. Smith, *Leaves from a Soldier's Diary*, 67.
10. Union attack immediately following truce: Wright, "Port Hudson: Its History from an Interior View," *Daily True Delta*, August 11, 1863; rainstorm: Tiemann, *The 159th Regiment Infantry New York State Volunteers*, 42.

11. OR, ser. 1, vol. 24, pt. 3, p. 353.

12. New Banks headquarters, additional artillery, troops arriving from surrounding area: Irwin, *History of the Nineteenth Army Corps*, 185, 186; Banks recalling troops: Pellet, *History of the 114th Regiment, New York State Volunteers*, 91; Banks requests troops from Grant: "War Department Ciphers Received From Mch. 25th 1863 to July 10, 1863, Page 194, Thomas Eckert Papers, HLAB; Van Alstyne: Van Alstyne, *Diary of an Enlisted Man*, 122; Billingshurst Requa Batteries: Faller, *The Indiana Jackass Regiment*, 140.

13. Hawkes: McMullen, "A Massachusetts Soldier at the Siege or Port Hudson, 1863," 319; regiment dwindling due to exhaustion and illness: McMullen, "A Massachusetts Soldier," 321; Gregory: Erastus Gregory to Brother, June 13, 1863, Erastus Gregory Letter, PHP.

14. Heat on march: Dargan, "James Dargan Diary," entry dated June 1, 1863, CSUN; injured soldiers in rear-echelon hospitals: Dargan, "James Dargan Diary," entry dated May 31, 1863, CSUN.

15. Charles Lord to Wife, May 29, 1863, Charles Lord Letters, PFL.

16. Stevens: Stevens, *Fiftieth Massachusetts Infantry*, 158; Federal positions and fortifications: Sneden, Robert Knox Sneden Diary, Siege of Port Hudson Map, 429, LOC, accessed October 16, 2021, https://www.loc.gov/item/gvhs01.vhs00139/.

17. Smith: Smith, *Leaves from a Soldier's Diary*, 66; Tiemann: Tiemann, *The 159th Regiment Infantry New York State Volunteers*, 42; Palfrey: Palfrey, "Port Hudson," *Papers of the Military Historical Society of Massachusetts*, vol. 8, p. 58.

18. Former slaves constructing Union fortifications: Irwin, *History of the Nineteenth Army Corps*, 219; Fauconnet: Fauconnet, *Ruined by This Miserable War*, 11.

19. Bryant, "A Yankee Soldier Looks at the Negro," 143.

20. Johns, *Life with the Forty-Ninth Massachusetts Volunteers*, 294.

21. Babcock, *Selections from the Letters and Diaries of Brevet Brigadier General Willoughby Babcock*, 23.

22. Confederates improving defenses, construction of loopholes: Wright, "Port Hudson: Its History from an Interior View," *Daily True Delta*, August 11, 1863; Johnson ordering additional line of rifle pits: Wright, "Port Hudson: Its History from an Interior View," *Daily True Delta*, August 12, 1863; Turner: Turner, "June 2, 1863," The Siege of Port Hudson, a Civil War Diary, LCDAH; Bailey: Baker and Parrish, *Confederate Guerrilla: The Civil War Memoir of Joseph M. Bailey*, 24.

23. Kennedy: Kennedy, *From Port Hudson to Cedar Creek*, 91; Perkins: Solon Perkins to his parents, brother, and sisters, May 31, 1863, Civil War Letters Collection, NYHS; Sturgis: Appleton Sturgis to Mother, June 8, 1863, Appleton Sturgis Papers, UKSP; Clark: Clark, *The One Hundred and Sixteenth Regiment of New York Volunteers*, 94; broad-brimmed straw hats: Johns, *Life with the Forty-Ninth Massachusetts Volunteers*, 313.

24. Hawkes: McMullen, "A Massachusetts Soldier at the Siege or Port Hudson, 1863," 321; day and night in the trenches: Tiemann, *The 159th Regiment Infantry New York State Volunteers*, 44.

25. McMorries: McMorries, *History of the First Regiment, Alabama Volunteer Infantry*, 65; Bailey: Baker and Parrish, *Confederate Guerrilla: The Civil War Memoir of Joseph M. Bailey*, 25.

26. Louis Boyd to Wife, May 31, 1863; and Louis Boyd to Wife, June 5, 1863, both at FSA.

27. Fowler, *Memorials of William Fowler*, 44, 45.

28. Perkins: Solon Perkins to his parents, brother, and sisters, May 31, 1863, Civil War Letters Collection, NYHS; Waite: George Waite to George, June 10, 1863, George R. Waite Port Hudson Letter, LSU; Gale: Justus Gale to Sister, June 7, 1863, Justus F. Gale Correspondence, UVL.

29. Solon Perkins life and career: Cowley, *Illustrated History of Lowell*, 187; Perkins: Solon Perkins to his parents, brother, and sisters, May 31, 1863, Civil War Letters Collection, NYHS.

30. OR, ser. 1, vol. 26, pt. 1, p. 180.

31. Alexander: Alexander, "James Benton Alexander Diary," entry dated May 30, 1863, UNDSC; Goble on desertion: Goble, "James A. Goble Diary," entry dated June 2, 1862, UALSC; Goble on southern courage: Goble, "James A. Goble Diary," entry dated May 31, 1862, UALSC.

32. Banks ordering Grierson to destroy Confederate cavalry, Grierson leading troops toward Clinton, LA: OR, ser. 1, vol. 26, pt. 1, p. 134; Curl: Curl, "The Fight at Clinton, LA," *CV* 13, no. 3 (March 1905): 122.

33. Confederate ambush at Comite River: OR, ser. 1, vol. 26, pt. 1, p. 135. Nims's Battery used Woodruff cannons, which were very light guns intended to keep up with fast-moving cavalry. They fired a 2-inch, 2-pound lead conical projectile or a 1-ounce load of antipersonnel canister shot. Lardas, *Roughshod Through Dixie: Grierson's Raid, 1863*, 27. Grierson's cavalrymen were armed with an assortment of weapons, including Smith, Union, and Sharps carbines. Grierson complained that he was unable to get ammunition for the Union and Smith carbines. He heard that there were Sharps carbines at New Orleans and requested permission to swap his Union and Smith carbines for the Sharps carbines. OR, ser. 1, vol. 26, pt. 1, p. 134. It does not appear that he was able to make the exchange before leading his men into battle on June 3.

34. Confederate double flanking maneuver: OR, ser. 1, vol. 26, pt. 1, p. 135; Grierson ordering artillery to cover withdrawal: OR, ser. 1, vol. 26, pt. 1, p. 136; Confederate forces advancing: Curl, "The Fight at Clinton, LA," *CV* 13, no. 3 (March 1905): 122.

35. Grierson ordering retreat: OR, ser. 1, vol. 26, pt. 1, p. 136; Confederates pursuing: Curl, "The Fight at Clinton, LA," 123; Ewer on death of Solon Perkins:

Ewer, *Third Massachusetts Cavalry*, 49; Perkins posthumously promoted: Solon A. Perkins, Compiled Service Records of Volunteer Union Soldiers Who Served in Organizations from the State of Massachusetts, NARA.

36. Logan reporting victory, casualties: OR, ser. 1, vol. 26, pt. 1, p. 181; Grierson's report: OR, ser. 1, vol. 26, pt. 1, p. 136; Curl: Curl, "The Fight at Clinton, LA," 123.

37. Deforest, "Port Hudson: In the Trenches," *Harper's Weekly*, August 1867, p. 334.

38. Gardner, "A Yankee in Louisiana," 278.

39. Hepworth: Hepworth, *The Whip, Hoe, and Sword*, 294; accuracy of shotguns and Civil War–era rifles: Wagner, *The Library of Congress Civil War Desk Reference*, 494.

40. George Thomson to Mother, June 7, 1863, Papers and Images of the American Civil War, GLI.

41. Erastus Gregory to Brother, June 13, 1863, Erastus Gregory Letter, PHP.

42. Tiemann, *The 159th Regiment Infantry New York State Volunteers*, 42.

43. Confederates conserving gunpowder, scavenging ammunition: Palfrey, "Port Hudson," *Papers of the Military Historical Society of Massachusetts*, vol. 8, p. 58; "Bounding Bet": Wright, "Port Hudson: Its History from an Interior View," *Daily True Delta*, August 11, 1863.

44. Confederates avoiding firing unless directly attacked: Wright, "Port Hudson: Its History from an Interior View," *Daily True Delta*, August 11, 1863; Smith: Smith, *Company K, First Alabama Regiment*, 69.

45. Banks and Farragut: OR, ser. 1, vol. 26, pt. 1, p. 100; Goble: Goble, "James A. Goble Diary," entry dated June 4, 1863, UALSC.

46. Stevens, *Fiftieth Massachusetts Infantry*, 158.

47. Johns: Johns, *Life with the Forty-Ninth Massachusetts Volunteers*, 294; Stevens: Stevens, *Fiftieth Massachusetts Infantry*, 158.

48. Park: Park, "Diary of William Park," entry dated May 28, 1863, NLSC; Hart: John Hart to Wife, June 7, 1863, HAU.

49. Townsend: Townsend, *History of the Sixteenth Regiment New Hampshire Volunteers*, 231; Whitehead: Latture, ed., "Pinned Down Outside Port Hudson," 49; Plummer: Plummer, *History of the Forty-Eighth Regiment, M.V.M.*, 39.

50. Erastus Gregory to Brother, June 13, 1863, Erastus Gregory Letter, PHP.

51. Babcock: Babcock, *Selections from the Letters and Diaries of Brevet Brigadier General Willoughby Babcock*, 25; Tiemann: Tiemann, *The 159th Regiment Infantry New York State Volunteers*, 44; Bacon: Bacon, *Among the Cotton Thieves*, 131, 155.

52. Johns, *Life with the Forty-Ninth Massachusetts Volunteers*, 296.

53. Louis Boyd to Wife, June 13, 1863, FSA.

54. Stevens, *Fiftieth Massachusetts Infantry*, 159.

55. John Hart to Wife, June 7, 1863, HAU.

56. Goble, "James A. Goble Diary," entries dated June 2, June 3, June 4, June 5, June 6, June 9, and June 12, 1863, UALSC.

57. Ingraham, "Port Hudson: The Forlorn Hope and the Siege," *National Tribune* (Washington, DC), February 13, 1902.

58. de Gournay: de Gournay, "Defending Port Hudson," in *Battles and Leaders of the Civil War*, vol. 5, p. 404; Beecher: Beecher, *Record of the 114th Regiment NYSV*, 196; Goble: Goble, "James A. Goble Diary," entry dated June 1, 1863, UALSC.

59. Maglathlin: Maglathlin, *Company I, Fourth Massachusetts Regiment*, 30; Tiemann: Tiemann, *The 159th Regiment Infantry New York State Volunteers*, 43; malaria among New Hampshire troops: Irwin, *History of the Nineteenth Army Corps*, 187; Johns: Johns, *Life with the Forty-Ninth Massachusetts Volunteers*, 300.

60. Washburn: Washburn, "Diary of Charles Washburn," entry dated June 11, 1863, HAU; newspaper coverage: "Suicide of Lieutenant Commander Hart," *Philadelphia Inquirer*, June 27, 1863; Hart buried with full Masonic honors: Halleran, *Freemasonry in the American Civil War*, 134; annual reenactment of funeral: Frances Spencer, "War Re-Enactment Tells Story of Brotherhood," *Advocate*, June 13, 2018, accessed December 24, 2021, https://www.theadvocate.com/baton_rouge/news/communities/st_francisville/article_e04c5df2-6e52-11e8-a007-87b2bd53cd1f.html.

61. Bell, *Mosquito Soldiers*, 81.

62. Confederate soldiers exposed to weather: Wright, "Port Hudson: Its History from an Interior View," *Daily True Delta*, August 11, 1863; Bailey on mosquitos: Baker and Parrish, *Confederate Guerrilla: The Civil War Memoir of Joseph M. Bailey*, 25; Goble: Goble, "James A. Goble Diary," entry dated June 2, 1862, UALSC; Smith: Smith, *Company K, First Alabama Regiment*, 68; Confederate doctors short of quinine, other medications: Wright, "Port Hudson: Its History from an Interior View," *Daily True Delta*, August 11, 1863; Johnson: Johnson, "Report of Benjamin Johnson," Confederate States Army Collection, LSU.

63. Turner: Turner, "June 3, 1863," The Siege of Port Hudson, a Civil War Diary, LCDAH; Goble: Goble, "James A. Goble Diary," entries dated June 7 and June 10, 1863, UALSC.

64. Beall and Gardner on potential deserters: OR, ser. 1, vol. 26, pt. 1, p. 146; Goble: Goble, "James A. Goble Diary," entry dated May 31, 1863, UALSC.

65. Van Alstyne: Van Alstyne, *Diary of an Enlisted Man*, 123; Confederates taking oath of allegiance: "Port Hudson," *New York Herald*, June 12, 1863; Gregory: Erastus Gregory to Brother, June 13, 1863, Erastus Gregory Letter, PHP; Johns: Johns, *Life with the Forty-Ninth Massachusetts Volunteers*, 313; Harris desertion: "Port Hudson," *New York Herald*, June 12, 1863; Hoffman: Hoffman, *Camp, Court, and Siege*, 72; Turner: Turner, "June 11, 1863," The Siege of Port Hudson, a Civil War Diary, LCDAH.

66. Goble, "James A. Goble Diary," entry dated June 12, 1863, UALSC.

67. Beecher: Beecher, *Record of the 114th Regiment NYSV,* 212; Gregory: Erastus Gregory to Brother, June 13, 1863, Erastus Gregory Letter, PHP; Dooley: Rufus Dooley to Mother, June 23, 1863, IHS.

68. Baker and Parrish, *Confederate Guerrilla: The Civil War Memoir of Joseph M. Bailey,* 23, 26; Goble: Goble, "James A. Goble Diary," entries dated June 4 and June 5, 1863, UALSC.

69. OR, ser. 1, vol. 26, pt. 1, p. 549.

70. Banks's view of nine-month men: Johns, *Life with the Forty-Ninth Massachusetts Volunteers,* 294; Waite: George Waite to George, June 10, 1863, George R. Waite Port Hudson Letter, LSU. Waite did survive the battle and returned home, receiving an honorable discharge on August 17, 1863, when his regiment's term of service expired. United States, *Roster, Muster Roll and Chronological Record of the Twenty-Sixth Regiment, Connecticut Volunteers,* 52.

71. Orders sending men into action: Carpenter, *History of the 8th Regiment, Vermont Volunteers,* 121; Gregory: Erastus Gregory to Brother, June 13, 1863, Erastus Gregory Letter, PHP. Erastus Gregory was killed in action on June 14, 1863. According to family folklore, Gregory was killed by a bullet that passed through a bible he carried in his pocket.

72. Wright, "Port Hudson: Its History from an Interior View," *Daily True Delta,* August 11, 1863.

73. Carpenter: Carpenter, *History of the 8th Regiment, Vermont Volunteers,* 121; Confederate defenders driving Union forces back: Wright, "Port Hudson: Its History from an Interior View," *Daily True Delta,* August 11, 1863; Turner: Turner, "June 11, 1863," The Siege of Port Hudson, a Civil War Diary, LCDAH; Goble: Goble, "James A. Goble Diary," entry dated June 11, 1863, UALSC.

74. Gardner: Gardner, "A Yankee in Louisiana," 279; Dooley: Rufus Dooley to Mother, June 21, 1863, IH; newspaper account: "Banks as a General," *New York Herald,* June 12, 1863.

75. Banks plans for attack: OR, ser. 1, vol. 26, pt. 1, p. 552; Farragut response: OR, ser. 1, vol. 26, pt. 1, p. 553; Maglathlin: Maglathlin, *Company I, Fourth Massachusetts Regiment,* 31.

76. Union soldiers constructing advanced fortifications: Van Alstyne, *Diary of an Enlisted Man,* 129; Dargan: Dargan, "James Dargan Diary," entry dated June 12, 1863, CSUN.

77. Bacon, *Among the Cotton Thieves,* 149.

78. Palfrey, "Port Hudson," *Papers of the Military Historical Society of Massachusetts,* vol. 8, p. 43.

79. Smith, *Company K, First Alabama Regiment,* 65.

80. Wright, "Port Hudson: Its History from an Interior View," *Daily True Delta,* August 11, 1863.

81. Banks demanding surrender: OR, ser. 1, vol. 26, pt. 1, pp. 552–53; Banks threatening massacre: Cunningham, *The Port Hudson Campaign,* 79.

82. Jackson on Gardner's response: Jackson, "An Account of the Occupation of Fort Hudson, LA.," 475; Gardner declining surrender: OR, ser. 1, vol. 26, pt. 1, p. 553.

83. Grover and Weitzel on Gardner: Bacon, *Among the Cotton Thieves*, 148; Wright: Wright, "Port Hudson: Its History from an Interior View," *Daily True Delta*, August 11, 1863; Smith: Smith, *Company K, First Alabama Regiment*, 70.

84. Smith: Smith, *Company K, First Alabama Regiment*, 69; Bacon: Bacon, *Among the Cotton Thieves*, 149.

85. Irwin, *History of the Nineteenth Army Corps*, 194.

86. Order of attack: Irwin, *History of the Nineteenth Army Corps*, 196; attackers carrying grenades: Palfrey, "Port Hudson," *Papers of the Military Historical Society of Massachusetts*, vol. 8, p. 45; Peck describing grenade: James Peck to Mother and Father, June 16, 1863, NYSMM; Ketchum grenades: Mountjoy, *Technology and the Civil War*, 50.

87. Waite, *New Hampshire in the Great Rebellion*, 382; and James Peck to Mother and Father, June 16, 1863, NYSMM. Waite wrote that each man got a single grenade. Peck states that he received three grenades. As was so often the case with equipment in Civil War armies, it is likely that different units and individuals receive different quantities of grenades.

88. Plans for attack finalized, late arrival of orders: Irwin, *History of the Nineteenth Army Corps*, 196; gunboat barrage beginning: Park, "Diary of William Park," entry dated June 14, 1863, NLSC.

89. Bacon, *Among the Cotton Thieves*, 154.

90. Powers: Powers, *The Story of the Thirty-Eighth Regiment of Massachusetts Volunteers*, 105; Paine ordering men to leave wounded on the field: Powers, *Story*, 106; 48th Massachusetts Infantry: Plummer, *History of the Forty-Eighth Regiment, M.V.M.*, 42; Barnard: John Barnard to Mary, June 19, 1863, John Barnard Papers, DUL; Sprague: Sprague, *History of the 13th Regiment*, 148; Moors: Moors, *History of the Fifty-Second Regiment of Massachusetts Infantry*, 174.

91. Turner: Turner, "June 13, 1863," The Siege of Port Hudson, a Civil War Diary, LCDAH; Johnson: Johnson, "Report of Benjamin Johnson," Confederate States Army Collection, LSU.

92. Sprague: Sprague, *History of the 13th Regiment*, 148; Barnard: John Barnard to Mary, June 19, 1863, DUL; Beecher: Beecher, *Record of the 114th Regiment NYSV*, 198; Willis: Willis, *The Fifty-Third Regiment*, 136.

93. Dargan, "James Dargan Diary," entry dated June 13, 1863, CSUN.

9. A Hell of a Fellow Long Enough

1. Sprague, *History of the 13th Regiment*, 156.

2. Turner, "June 14, 1863," The Siege of Port Hudson, a Civil War Diary, LCDAH.

3. Jackson, "An Account of the Occupation of Fort Hudson, LA.," 475.

4. Paine's order of attack: Irwin, *History of the Nineteenth Army Corps*, 196; Hosmer: Hosmer, *The Color Guard*, 188.

5. Hanaburgh: Hanaburgh, *History of the One Hundred and Twenty-Eighth Regiment*, 55; McGregor: McGregor, *History of the Fifteenth Regiment New Hampshire*, 338; Dargan: Dargan, "James Dargan Diary," entry dated June 14, 1863, CSUN; Beecher: Beecher, *Record of the 114th Regiment NYSV*, 204.

6. Powers, *The Story of the Thirty-Eighth Regiment of Massachusetts Volunteers*, 106.

7. Sprague, *History of the 13th Regiment*, 149.

8. Moors, *History of the Fifty-Second Regiment of Massachusetts Infantry*, 175.

9. Sprague, *History of the 13th Regiment*, 149.

10. Steedman noticing Federal forces: Steedman, "Official Report of Colonel J. G. W. Steedman," *SHSP*, 1886, p. 328; Federal gunners continuing bombardment: Willis, *The Fifty-Third Regiment*, 136; Sprague: Sprague, *History of the 13th Regiment*, 148; Turner: Turner, "June 13, 1863," The Siege of Port Hudson, a Civil War Diary, LCDAH.

11. Johns: Johns, *Life with the Forty-Ninth Massachusetts Volunteers*, 319; Dargan: Dargan, "James Dargan Diary," entry dated June 14, 1863, CSUN; Maglathlin: Maglathlin, *Company I, Fourth Massachusetts Regiment*, 30.

12. Willis, *The Fifty-Third Regiment*, 137.

13. Willis, *The Fifty-Third Regiment*, 137.

14. Bailey: Bailey, "Joseph M. Bailey Memoir," 22, UAF; Powers: Powers, *The Story of the Thirty-Eighth Regiment of Massachusetts Volunteers*, 106–7.

15. Hosmer, *The Color Guard*, 190.

16. Appleton Sturgis to Mother, June 15, 1863, Appleton Sturgis Papers, UKSP.

17. Union infantry: Steedman, "Official Report of Colonel J. G. W. Steedman," *SHSP*, 1886, p. 328; small force at Fort Desperate: Johnson, "Report of Benjamin Johnson," Confederate States Army Collection, LSU; Wright: Wright, "Port Hudson: Its History from an Interior View," *Daily True Delta*, August 12, 1863; Willis: Willis, *The Fifty-Third Regiment*, 137; percussion impact grenades failing to explode: Wright, "Port Hudson: Its History from an Interior View," *Daily True Delta*, August 12, 1863; Peck: James Peck to Mother and Father, June 16, 1863, NYSMM; advance continuing in spite of equipment failure: Smith, *Company K, First Alabama Regiment*, 70.

18. Confederates firing buckshot, Union advance continuing: Smith, *Company K, First Alabama Regiment*, 70; Confederates in reserve rifle pits firing: Wright, "Port Hudson: Its History from an Interior View," *Daily True Delta*, August 12, 1863; small section of Confederate line captured: Irwin, *History of the Nineteenth Army Corps*, 196; 53rd Massachusetts awaiting reinforcements: Willis, *The Fifty-Third Regiment*, 137; Union soldiers building breastworks with cotton: Powers, *The Story of the Thirty-Eighth Regiment of Massachusetts Volunteers*, 108.

19. Paine shot: Willis, *The Fifty-Third Regiment,* 137; Powers: Powers, *The Story of the Thirty-Eighth Regiment of Massachusetts Volunteers,* 106; Sturgis: Appleton Sturgis to Mother, June 25, 1863, Appleton Sturgis Papers, UKSP.

20. Latture, ed., "Pinned Down Outside Port Hudson," 48.

21. Dargan, "James Dargan Diary," entry dated June 14, 1863, CSUN.

22. Sprague, *History of the 13th Regiment,* 150–51.

23. Sprague: Sprague, *History of the 13th Regiment,* 152; Whitehead and the 28th Connecticut Infantry: Latture, ed., "Pinned Down Outside Port Hudson," 49.

24. Irwin, *History of the Nineteenth Army Corps,* 198.

25. Irwin, *History of the Nineteenth Army Corps,* 198.

26. Sprague, *History of the 13th Regiment,* 156.

27. Confederates retaking original line, Smith on grenades: Smith, *Company K, First Alabama Regiment,* 70–71; Goble: Goble, "James A. Goble Diary," entry dated June 14, 1863, UALSC.

28. Augur's feigned attack: Irwin, *History of the Nineteenth Army Corps,* 198; Alexander: Alexander, "James Benton Alexander Diary," entry dated June 14, 1863, UNDSC; Chamberlin: Chamberlin, "Diary of John Chamberlin," entry dated June 17, 1863, NYSMM.

29. Cunningham, *The Port Hudson Campaign,* 91.

30. Dwight ordering advance: Waite, *New Hampshire in the Great Rebellion,* 526; McGregor: McGregor, *History of the Fifteenth Regiment New Hampshire,* 338; infantry attack versus artillery bombardment: Smith, *Company K, First Alabama Regiment,* 71.

31. Willis: Willis, *The Fifty-Third Regiment,* 138; Steedman: Steedman, "Official Report of Colonel J. G. W. Steedman," *SHSP,* 1886, p. 329; limited water, Union troops firing when possible: Powers, *The Story of the Thirty-Eighth Regiment of Massachusetts Volunteers,* 109; Fox delivering water: United States, *Medal of Honor Recipients 1863–1963,* 438.

32. Appleton Sturgis to Mother, June 15, 1863, Appleton Sturgis Papers, UKSP.

33. Turner, "June 14, 1863," The Siege of Port Hudson, a Civil War Diary, LCDAH.

34. Trawick, "Col. Benjamin T. Pixlee, of Arkansas," *CV* 10, no. 7 (July 1902): 317.

35. Sprague, *History of the 13th Regiment,* 156.

36. Hosmer, *The Color Guard,* 192.

37. Powers: Powers, *The Story of the Thirty-Eighth Regiment of Massachusetts Volunteers,* 110; attempts to rescue Paine: Willis, *The Fifty-Third Regiment,* 138; Gardner on Paine: Gardner, "A Yankee in Louisiana," 280; Washburn tossing canteen, smoking cigar, Grover refusing truce: Willis, *The Fifty-Third Regiment,* 138.

38. Barnard, "John Barnard to Mary, June 19, 1863," DUL.

39. Dargan: Dargan, "James Dargan Diary," entry dated June 14, 1863, CSUN; Johns: Johns, *Life with the Forty-Ninth Massachusetts Volunteers*, 323–24.

40. Confederate ammunition running low: Steedman, "Official Report of Colonel J. G. W. Steedman," *SHSP*, 1886, p. 329; Bailey on Confederate sharpshooters: Bailey, "Joseph M. Bailey Memoir," 22, UAF.

41. Union soldiers escaping in darkness: Powers, *The Story of the Thirty-Eighth Regiment of Massachusetts Volunteers*, 110; Barnard: John Barnard to Mary, June 19, 1863, DUL; Goble: Goble, "James A. Goble Diary," entry dated June 14, 1863, UALSC.

42. Otis, A Report on Excisions of the Head of the Femur for Gunshot Injury, 109.

43. William Aldis, Case Files of Approved Pension Applications of Widows and Other Dependents of Veterans, 1861–1910, NARA.

44. Dargan, "James Dargan Diary," entry dated June 14, 1863, CSUN.

45. Dargan, "James Dargan Diary," entry dated June 14, 1863, CSUN.

46. Turner: Turner, "June 14 ,1863," The Siege of Port Hudson, a Civil War Diary, LCDAH; Goble: Goble, "James A. Goble Diary," entry dated June 14, 1863, UALSC; Morgan: Dawson, *A Confederate Girl's Diary*, 390; Wright: Wright, "Port Hudson: Its History from an Interior View," *Daily True Delta*, August 12, 1863.

47. Confederate newspaper coverage: "Telegraphic News," *Daily Dispatch* (Richmond, VA), June 19, 1863; and "Affairs at Port Hudson," *Memphis (TN) Daily Appeal*, June 25, 1863; Fentress: David Fentress to Wife, July 12, 1863, Maud C. Fentress Papers, UNT. Fentress wrote his letter three days after the fall of Port Hudson, which is another example of how news often traveled slowly during the Civil War.

48. Willis: Willis, *The Fifty-Third Regiment*, 139; Hardenbergh: James Hardenbergh to Sister, July 7, 1863, Hardenbergh Family Papers, MSUA; Park: Park, "Diary of William Park," entry dated June 15, 1863, NLSC; Irwin: Irwin, *History of the Nineteenth Army Corps*, 201, 204.

49. Hanaburgh: Hanaburgh, *History of the One Hundred and Twenty-Eighth Regiment*, 59; Townsend: Townsend, *History of the Sixteenth Regiment New Hampshire Volunteers*, 233.

50. Federal losses: Willis, *The Fifty-Third Regiment*, 139; Moors: Moors, *History of the Fifty-Second Regiment of Massachusetts Infantry*, 175; Irwin on losses: Irwin, *History of the Nineteenth Army Corps*, 201; Sturgis: Appleton Sturgis to Mother, June 25, 1863, Appleton Sturgis Papers, UKSP.

51. Chamberlin: Chamberlin, "Diary of John Chamberlin," entry dated June 14, 1863, NYSMM; Townsend: Townsend, *History of the Sixteenth Regiment New Hampshire Volunteers*, 233; Beecher: Beecher, *Record of the 114th Regiment NYSV*, 209; Barnard: John Barnard to Mary, June 19, 1863, DUL; Hosmer:

Hosmer, *The Color Guard*, 190; Clark: Clark, *The One Hundred and Sixteenth Regiment of New York Volunteers*, 95.

52. Sprague, *History of the 13th Regiment*, 161.

10. We Lay in the Ditches

1. McClung, *Three Years in the C.S. Army*, 18.

2. Caroline Smith to Her Husband, May 14, 1863, William A. Smith Letters, TUL.

3. Irwin, *History of the Nineteenth Army Corps*, 215.

4. OR, ser. 1, vol. 26, pt. 1, p. 56.

5. Hawkes: McMullen, "A Massachusetts Soldier at the Siege or Port Hudson, 1863," 323; Van Alstyne: Van Alstyne, *Diary of an Enlisted Man*, 133; Townsend: Townsend, *History of the Sixteenth Regiment New Hampshire Volunteers*, 237, 242; Barnard: John Barnard to Mary, June 19, 1863, DUL; Peck: James Peck to Mother and Father, June 24, 1863, NYSMM; Palfrey: Palfrey, "Private Journal of the Siege of Port Hudson," Palfrey Family Papers, HLHU.

6. Birge: Irwin, *History of the Nineteenth Army Corps*, 212; other volunteers for assault: OR, ser. 1, vol. 26, pt. 1, pp. 57–66.

7. Assault party gathering: Irwin, *History of the Nineteenth Army Corps*, 213; Fleming: Beifuss, ed., "The Diary of Sgt. John Fleming," 27.

8. Park, "Diary of William Park," entry dated June 15, 1863, NLSC.

9. Medical supply proposal, Banks ignoring truce offer: Irwin, *History of the Nineteenth Army Corps*, 204; comforting the wounded: Wright, "Port Hudson: Its History from an Interior View," *Daily True Delta*, August 12, 1863.

10. Wright: Wright, "Port Hudson: Its History from an Interior View," *Daily True Delta*, August 12, 1863; Bailey: Bailey, "Joseph M. Bailey Memoir," 22, UAF; Irwin: Irwin, *History of the Nineteenth Army Corps*, 204; Beecher: Beecher, *Record of the 114th Regiment NYSV*, 214; Goble: Goble, "James A. Goble Diary," entry dated June 15, 1863, UALSC.

11. Peck: James Peck to Mother and Father, June 17, 1863, NYSMM; Whitehead: Latture, ed., "Pinned Down Outside Port Hudson," 49; Bailey: Bailey, "Joseph M. Bailey Memoir," 22, UAF.

12. Rebel soldier to Van Alstyne: Van Alstyne, *Diary of an Enlisted Man*, 134; Wright, rival work crews: Wright, "Port Hudson: Its History from an Interior View," *Daily True Delta*, August 13, 1863.

13. Palfrey: Palfrey, "Private Journal of the Siege of Port Hudson," Palfrey Family Papers, HLHU; Cross: Bryant, "A Yankee Soldier Looks at the Negro," 147.

14. Irwin on blazing arrows: Irwin, *History of the Nineteenth Army Corps*, 221; Moors on setting cotton on fire: Moors, *History of the Fifty-Second Regiment of*

Massachusetts Infantry, 179; Skelton setting fire to cotton bales: Wright, "Port Hudson: Its History from an Interior View," *Daily True Delta*, August 13, 1863; Palfrey: Palfrey, "Private Journal of the Siege of Port Hudson," Palfrey Family Papers, HLHU; improvised incendiary bullets: Woodworth, ed., *Vicksburg Besieged*, 62; improvised explosives on night raids: Hanaburgh, *History of the One Hundred and Twenty-Eighth Regiment*, 49; Confederates burning houses at Port Hudson: Goble, "James A. Goble Diary," entry dated June 15, 1863, UALSC.

15. Palfrey: Palfrey, "Private Journal of the Siege of Port Hudson," Palfrey Family Papers, HLHU; construction of siege towers: Irwin, *History of the Nineteenth Army Corps*, 222.

16. Shielding Union artillerymen from Confederate sharpshooters: Irwin, *History of the Nineteenth Army Corps*, 223; Dooley distributing rifles: Rufus Dooley to Mother, June 16, 1863, HIS; Hanaburgh on "Arkansas Joe": Hanaburgh, *History of the One Hundred and Twenty-Eighth Regiment*, 49; Hardenbergh: James Hardenbergh to Sister, July 7, 1863, Hardenbergh Family Papers, MSUA.

17. Confederates digging tunnels, planting landmines: Wright, "Port Hudson: Its History from an Interior View," *Daily True Delta*, August 12, 1863; Wright on Confederate use of sharpened stakes: Wright, "Port Hudson: Its History from an Interior View," *Daily True Delta*, August 13, 1863.

18. Flinn, *Campaigning with Banks*, 83–86.

19. Clark, *The One Hundred and Sixteenth Regiment of New York Volunteers*, 98.

20. Unidentified Union Soldier to Friend Charley, July 1, 1863, HAU.

21. Van Alstyne on Banks: Van Alstyne, *Diary of an Enlisted Man*, 136; Chamberlin: Chamberlin, "Diary of John Chamberlin," entry dated June 18, 1863, NYSMM.

22. Wright on decrease in mortar fire: Wright, "Port Hudson: Its History from an Interior View," *Daily True Delta*, August 12, 1863; Park on end of bombardment, Banks request for targeted support, sailors' frustration: Park, "Diary of William Park," entries dated June 15, June 21, and June 28, 1863, NLSC; Boyd: Louis Boyd to Wife, June 5, 1863, FSA.

23. McClung, *Three Years in the C.S. Army*, 18.

24. Banks and conflict over terms of enlistment: Bowen, *Massachusetts in the War*, 147; Johns: Johns, *Life with the Forty-Ninth Massachusetts Volunteers*, 336; Barnard: John Barnard to Mary, June 19, 1863, DUL; Waite: George Waite to George, June 10, 1863, George R. Waite Port Hudson Letter, LSU; Peck: James Peck to Mother and Father, June 17, 1863, NYSMM.

25. Rufus Dooley to Mother, June 21, 1863, IHS.

26. Wife encouraging husband to return home: Caroline Smith to Her Husband, May 14, 1863, William A. Smith Letters, TUL; husband response: William Smith to his wife, June 9, 1863, William A. Smith Letters, TUL. We only have the exchange between William and Caroline because William wrote his

June 9th letter on the back of Caroline's letter of May 14. This is the only one of Caroline's letters that survives.

27. Whitehead: Latture, ed., "Pinned Down Outside Port Hudson," 48; Whitehead departure: John Bulkley Whitehead, 1898, Connecticut, Deaths, 1640–1955 database, FamilySearch (website), accessed June 11, 2020, https://www.familysearch.org/ark:/61903/1:1:F7VZ-8NY.

28. Officers living on elevated platforms, Johns on readjusting to feather beds: Johns, *Life with the Forty-Ninth Massachusetts Volunteers*, 311, 312; Van Alstyne on laundry: Van Alstyne, *Diary of an Enlisted Man*, 134; Smith: William Smith to his wife, May 8, 1863, William A. Smith Letters, TUL; Gale: Justus Gale to Sister, June 7, 1863, Justus F. Gale Correspondence, UVL.

29. Gale on sutler purchases: Justus Gale to Sister, June 19, 1863, Justus F. Gale Correspondence, UVL; Dargan on stealing from sutlers: Dargan, James Dargan Diary, entries dated June 15 and June 20, 1863, CSUN; Johns on sutlers: Johns, *Life with the Forty-Ninth Massachusetts Volunteers*, 311.

30. Wormy bread: Johns, *Life with the Forty-Ninth Massachusetts Volunteers*, 312; Whitney on poor rations: Laver, ed., "Where Duty Shall Call," 339–40.

31. Van Alstyne on Confederate deserters: Van Alstyne, *Diary of an Enlisted Man*, 134, 138; Wright on deserters: Wright, "Port Hudson: Its History from an Interior View," *Daily True Delta*, August 14, 1863.

32. Wright, "Port Hudson: Its History from an Interior View," *Daily True Delta*, August 13, 1863.

33. Taylor, *Destruction and Reconstruction*, 137, 138, 173.

34. Irwin, History of the Nineteenth Army Corps, 214.

35. Boyd: Louis Boyd to Wife, June 5, 1863, FSA; Van Alstyne on Confederate guerillas: Van Alstyne, *Diary of an Enlisted Man*, 136.

36. OR, ser. 1, vol. 26, pt. 1, p. 224.

37. Dooley on Confederate ambush of foraging party: Rufus Dooley to Mother, June 23, 1863, HIS; Gale on Brashear City raid: Justus Gale to Sister, July 1, 1863, Justus F. Gale Correspondence, UVL; Peck: James Peck to Mother and Father, June 30, 1863, NYSMM.

38. Dooley: Rufus Dooley to Mother, June 22, 1863, HIS; Dargan: Dargan, "James Dargan Diary," entry dated June 21, 1863, CSUN; Cahill: Thomas Cahill to Wife, June 13, 1863, Thomas Cahill Civil War Letters, SHU; Cahill's wife recommending he avoid combat: Margaret Cahill to Husband, June 21, 1863, Thomas Cahill Civil War Letters, SHU; Banks forbidding letters: Rufus Dooley to Mother, June 21, 1863, IHS.

39. Confederates repairing damage but unable to push Union forces back: Wright, "Port Hudson: Its History from an Interior View," *Daily True Delta*, August 13, 1863; Alexander: Alexander, "James Benton Alexander Diary," entry dated June 26, 1863, UNDSC.

40. Boyd fatigue with siege: Louis Boyd to Wife, June 26, 1863, FSA; Boyd in response to wife's accusation: Louis Boyd to Wife, June 13, 1863, FSA.

41. Confederate raid on battery 16; Irwin, *History of the Nineteenth Army Corps,* 221; Wright on prisoners carrying sandbags: Wright, "Port Hudson: Its History from an Interior View," *Daily True Delta,* August 13, 1863.

42. Dispatches, news arriving at Port Hudson: Wright, "Port Hudson: Its History from an Interior View," *Daily True Delta,* August 13, 1863; reports of Federals raiding Mississippi countryside: Turner, "June 27, 1863," The Siege of Port Hudson, a Civil War Diary, LCDAH.

43. Wright on Confederate response to news: Wright, "Port Hudson: Its History from an Interior View," *Daily True Delta,* August 13, 1863; de Gournay: de Gournay, "Defending Port Hudson," in *Battles and Leaders of the Civil War,* vol. 5, p. 407; Turner: Turner, "June 27, 1863," The Siege of Port Hudson, a Civil War Diary, LCDAH.

44. Confederates approach Fort Butler: Taylor, *Destruction and Reconstruction,* 143; fort defended by small Union garrison including convalescents: Bauer, ed., "Eyewitness Report on the Battle of Fort Butler," 206.

45. Confederates launching attack: Taylor, *Destruction and Reconstruction,* 143; Confederates surrendering: Bauer, ed., "Eyewitness Report on the Battle of Fort Butler," 207; Beecher: Beecher, *Record of the 114th Regiment NYSV,* 196.

46. Beecher, *Record of the 114th Regiment NYSV,* 217.

47. Palfrey, "Private Journal of the Siege of Port Hudson," Palfrey Family Papers, HLHU.

48. Union sharpshooters near Confederate lines, firing constantly: Wright, "Port Hudson: Its History from an Interior View," *Daily True Delta,* August 13, 1863; Confederate rolling grenades down gutter into Union lines: Wright, "Port Hudson: Its History from an Interior View," *Daily True Delta,* August 14, 1863.

49. Moors: Moors, *History of the Fifty-Second Regiment of Massachusetts Infantry,* 179; Dooley: Rufus Dooley to Mother, June 21, 1863; Rufus Dooley to Mother, June 27, 1863; and Rufus Dooley to Mother, June 28, 1863, all at HIS.

50. Wright on Union attack on main parapet, Confederate engineers constructing fallback positions: Wright, "Port Hudson: Its History from an Interior View," *Daily True Delta,* August 14, 1863; Alexander: Alexander, "James Benton Alexander Diary," entry dated May 27, 1863, UNDSC.

51. Park, "Diary of William Park," entry dated June 30, 1863, NLSC.

52. Wright, "Port Hudson: Its History from an Interior View," *Daily True Delta,* August 14, 1863.

53. Turner: Turner, "June 28, 1863," The Siege of Port Hudson, a Civil War Diary, LCDAH; Confederate capture of Dow: Irwin, *History of the Nineteenth Army Corps,* 216.

54. Confederates butchering mules, 1st Alabama response: "First Regiment

Alabama Infantry," Confederate Regimental History Files, 1st Alabama Infantry, ADAH; Wright on mule meat, rats: Wright, "Port Hudson: Its History from an Interior View," *Daily True Delta,* August 14, 1863; Bailey on diet and cooking methods: Bailey, "Joseph M. Bailey Memoir," 22, UAF; Goble: Goble, "James A. Goble Diary," entry dated June 6, 1863, UALSC; Ratcliff: Yeary, *Reminiscences of the Boys in Gray,* 631.

55. Wright on peas: Wright, "Port Hudson: Its History from an Interior View," *Daily True Delta,* August 14, 1863; Julian on peas: Julian, "The Early Life and War Record of George H. Julian," published in John Ridgdon, *Historical Sketch and Roster, AL 49th Infantry Regiment,* Ebook; Turner, "June 30, 1863," The Siege of Port Hudson, a Civil War Diary, LCDAH.

56. Ingraham, "Port Hudson: The Forlorn Hope and the Siege," *National Tribune* (Washington, DC), February 13, 1902.

57. Goble: Goble, "James A. Goble Diary," entry dated June 29, 1863, UALSC; Gardner on starving deserters: Gardner, "A Yankee in Louisiana," 281; Smith: William Smith to his wife, June 29, 1863, William A. Smith Letters, TUL; Kennedy, *From Port Hudson to Cedar Creek,* 97.

58. de Gournay: de Gournay, "Defending Port Hudson," in *Battles and Leaders of the Civil War,* vol. 5, p. 404; crowded Confederate hospital: Hewitt, *Post Hospital Ledger,* 100–102.

59. Wright on Confederate use of beer, tobacco, and sumac leaves: Wright, "Port Hudson: Its History from an Interior View," *Daily True Delta,* August 14, 1863; Ingraham: Ingraham, "Port Hudson: The Forlorn Hope and the Siege," *National Tribune* (Washington, DC) February 13, 1902.

60. Banks on Union army's morale problems, mutiny: OR, ser. 1, vol. 26, pt. 1, p. 14; Dargan: Dargan, "James Dargan Diary," entry dated June 29, 1863, CSUN. Fort Jefferson, located in the Dry Tortugas of the Florida Keys, was an infamously harsh military instillation. Today it is best known for serving as a prison for Confederate president Jefferson Davis after the war. Hitchcock, *Dry Tortugas National Park,* 114.

61. Dargan on mutiny and treatment of mutineers: Dargan, "James Dargan Diary," entry dated June 30, 1863, CSUN.

62. Clark on Banks's handling of expired enlistments: Clark, *The One Hundred and Sixteenth Regiment of New York Volunteers,* 98; Dargan on Banks's treatment of mutineers: Dargan, "James Dargan Diary," entry dated June 30, 1863, CSUN; rumors of mutiny circulating in Union ranks: Park, "Diary of William Park," entry dated June 15, 1863, NLSC.

63. Louis Boyd to Wife, July 1, 1863, FSA.

64. Irwin on Confederate raid on Springfield Landing: Irwin, *History of the Nineteenth Army Corps,* 216; Townsend on raid: Townsend, *History of the Sixteenth Regiment New Hampshire Volunteers,* 233; arrival of *Essex*: Park, "Diary of William Park," entry dated July 2, 1863, NLSC.

65. Goble, "James A. Goble Diary," entry dated July 2, 1863, UALSC.

66. Wright, "Port Hudson: Its History from an Interior View," *Daily True Delta*, August 14, 1863.

67. False rumors of Union attack on July 4: Turner, "July 4, 1863," The Siege of Port Hudson, a Civil War Diary, LCDAH; Hanna delivering water: United States, *Medal of Honor Recipients 1863–1963*, 455; Chamberlin: Chamberlin, "Diary of John Chamberlin," entry dated June 17, 1863, NYSMM; Hardenbergh: James Hardenbergh to Sister, July 7, 1863, Hardenbergh Family Papers, MSUA.

68. Kennedy, *From Port Hudson to Cedar Creek*, 105.

69. Park, "Diary of William Park," entry dated July 4, 1863, NLSC.

70. Goble, "James A. Goble Diary," entry dated July 5, 1863, UALSC.

71. Boyd committing to wait patiently: Louis Boyd to Wife, June 26, 1863, FSA; Boyd out of patience: Louis Boyd to Wife, July 5, 1863, FSA.

72. Rufus Dooley to Mother, July 5, 1863, IHS.

73. Park, "Diary of William Park," entry dated July 5, 1863, NLSC.

74. Turner, "July 6, 1863," The Siege of Port Hudson, a Civil War Diary, LCDAH.

75. Union troop strength by end of June: Irwin, *History of the Nineteenth Army Corps*, 217; Hawkes: McMullen, "A Massachusetts Soldier at the Siege or Port Hudson, 1863," 323; heat and rain depleting Union soldiers: Irwin, *History of the Nineteenth Army Corps*, 217; Ellis: Ellis, *The Twenty-Fifth Regiment Connecticut Volunteers*, 54.

76. Beecher on inadequate medical care: Beecher, *Record of the 114th Regiment NYSV*, 219; Moors helping at hospital: Moors, *History of the Fifty-Second Regiment of Massachusetts Infantry*, 179; Union navy sending surgeons, evacuating soldiers: Park, "Diary of William Park," entry dated June 28, 1863, NLSC.

77. Dargan, "James Dargan Diary," entry dated July 1, 1863, CSUN.

78. Browne on feigning illness: Browne, "Remarks Accompanying Quarterly Report of Sickness of Army of the Gulf," *American Medical Times*, January 24, 1863, p. 40; Barnard: John Barnard to Mary, June 19, 1863, DUL; Banks ordering officers in hospitals to return or resign: Nicholas Dederer to Son, June 23, 1863, Papers and Images of the American Civil War, GLI; doctors authorizing medical discharges: "Dederer, Nicholas," New York, Civil War Muster Roll Abstracts, 1861–1900, NYSA.

79. Irwin, *History of the Nineteenth Army Corps*, 217.

80. Van Alstyne: Van Alstyne, *Diary of an Enlisted Man*, 139; Whitehead: Latture, ed., "Pinned Down Outside Port Hudson," 49; Griffin: Eli Griffin to Wife, June 30, 1863, Eli Griffin Papers, UMBHL; Johns: Johns, *Life with the Forty-Ninth Massachusetts Volunteers*, 337; Moors: Moors, *History of the Fifty-Second Regiment of Massachusetts Infantry*, 181.

81. James Hardenbergh to Sister, July 7, 1863, Hardenbergh Family Papers, MSUA.

82. Beecher, *Record of the 114th Regiment NYSV,* 210.

83. Frank to Murray, July 8, 1863, HAU.

84. Babcock, *Selections from the Letters and Diaries of Brevet Brigadier General Willoughby Babcock,* 23.

85. Justus Gale to Sister, June 7, 1863, and Justus Gale to Sister, June 19, 1863, both in Justus F. Gale Correspondence, UVL. Gale never returned home, dying of chronic diarrhea in Baton Rouge on September 19, 1863. "Collection Overview," Justus F. Gale Correspondence, UVL.

86. Confederate soldiers present for duty in May and June: OR, ser. 1, vol. 26, pt. 2, p. 98; Confederate soldiers present for duty in July: OR, ser. 1, vol. 26, pt. 1, p. 144; Confederate artillery damaged: Wright, "Port Hudson: Its History from an Interior View," *Daily True Delta,* August 14, 1863; Confederates painting logs to look like cannons: "Quaker Gun Mounted on Bluff of Port Hudson," photographed by McPherson and Oliver, Library of Congress (website), accessed December 27, 2021, https://www.loc.gov/item/2010647768/.

87. Turner, "June 25, 1863," The Siege of Port Hudson, a Civil War Diary, LCDAH.

11. The First Time I Felt Sorry for the Brave Fellows

1. Van Alstyne, *Diary of an Enlisted Man,* 146.

2. Wright, "Port Hudson: Its History from an Interior View," *Daily True Delta,* August 15, 1863.

3. Van Alstyne on Union response to fall of Vicksburg: Van Alstyne, *Diary of an Enlisted Man,* 144; Wright on Confederate response: Wright, "Port Hudson: Its History from an Interior View," *Daily True Delta,* August 15, 1863.

4. Beall to Gardner on anticipated Union assault: OR, ser. 1, vol. 26, pt. 1, p. 148; Turner on anticipated assault: Turner, "July 7, 1863," The Siege of Port Hudson, a Civil War Diary, LCDAH.

5. Turner, "July 8, 1863," The Siege of Port Hudson, a Civil War Diary, LCDAH.

6. Gardner sending officers to negotiate surrender: Wright, "Port Hudson: Its History from an Interior View," *Daily True Delta,* August 15, 1863; Turner on surrender: Turner, "July 8, 1863," The Siege of Port Hudson, a Civil War Diary, LCDAH.

7. de Gournay, "Defending Port Hudson," in *Battles and Leaders of the Civil War,* vol. 5, 409.

8. Wright, "Port Hudson: Its History from an Interior View," *Daily True Delta,* August 15, 1863.

9. Gardner, "General Orders No. 61," July 8, 1863, Confederate Collection, BABM.

10. Wright on meeting of Union and Confederate troops, Union food delivery to Confederates: Wright, "Port Hudson: Its History from an Interior View," *Daily True Delta*, August 15, 1863; Peck: James Peck to Mother and Father, July 10, 1863, NYSMM; de Gournay: de Gournay, "Defending Port Hudson," in *Battles and Leaders of the Civil War*, vol. 5, p. 409; Gardner: Gardner, "A Yankee in Louisiana," 283.

11. Daniels brothers and Graham escaping: Martel, "The Escape of Captain Joe and Lieutenant Dock Daniel," *Arkansas Historical Quarterly* 6, no 3. (Autumn 1947): 341; Arkansas lieutenants escaping: Sesser, "Eighteenth Arkansas Infantry, https://encyclopediaofarkansas.net/entries/eighteenth-arkansas-infantry-12093/ "Encyclopedia of Arkansas, accessed May 18, 2022.

12. Testimony of John Bryant to Judge George Bond, September 30, 1863, George W. Bond Files, Confederate Papers Relating to Citizens or Business Firms, NARA.

13. Coleman on Bryant: Testimony of James Coleman to Judge George Bond, October 12, 1863; Greaves on Bryant, missing items: Testimony of Erasmus Greaves to Judge George Bond, September 10, 1863; Leonard on missing items: Testimony of Richard Leonard to Judge George Bond, September 17, 1863, all in George W. Bond Files, Confederate Papers Relating to Citizens or Business Firms, NARA.

14. Wright on Confederates preparing to surrender: Wright, "Port Hudson: Its History from an Interior View," *Daily True Delta*, August 15, 1863; de Gournay: de Gournay, "Defending Port Hudson," in *Battles and Leaders of the Civil War*, vol. 5, p. 410.

15. Andrews leading Union column: Wright, "Port Hudson: Its History from an Interior View," *Daily True Delta*, August 15, 1863; Chamberlin: Chamberlin, "Diary of John Chamberlin," entry dated July 9, 1863, NYSMM; Van Alstyne: Van Alstyne, *Diary of an Enlisted Man*, 146.

16. Wright on Gardner and Andrews exchange, conclusion of ceremony: Wright, "Port Hudson: Its History from an Interior View," *Daily True Delta*, August 15, 1863; de Gournay on Gardner and Andrews exchange: de Gournay, "Defending Port Hudson," in *Battles and Leaders of the Civil War*, vol. 5, p. 410.

17. Van Alstyne, *Diary of an Enlisted Man*, 146.

18. Clark, *The One Hundred and Sixteenth Regiment of New York Volunteers*, 106.

19. Diggins, *Sailing with Farragut*, 94.

20. Park, "Diary of William Park," entry dated July 9, 1863, NLSC.

21. Enlisted Confederates paroled: Wright, "Port Hudson: Its History from an Interior View," *Daily True Delta*, August 15, 1863; Goble: Goble, "James A. Goble Diary," entry dated July 7, 1863, Turner: Turner, "July 11, 1863," The Siege of Port Hudson, a Civil War Diary, LCDAH. Turner walked home with several of his comrades. He returned to service the next year and surrendered with the

final remnants of the 39th Mississippi Infantry at Fort Blakely, AL. W. S. Turner, Compiled Service Records of Confederate Soldiers Who Served in Organizations from the State of Mississippi, NARA.

22. Bailey escape: Bailey, "Joseph M. Bailey Memoir," 22, UAF; parole request for Brand: Weitzel, "G. Weitzel to General Banks, July 9, 1863," Compiled Service Records of Confederate Soldiers from Louisiana, NARA; Sutton: Yeary, *Reminiscences of the Boys in Gray*, 736.

23. Alfred Sandlin to Children, August 11, 1864, Alfred Sandlin Letters, EUL. Alfred Sandlin survived the war and was released from prison on June 12, 1865. Alfred Sandlin, Compiled Service Records of Confederate Soldiers from Mississippi, NARA.

24. Goble and spouse requesting help: Goble, "James A. Goble Diary," entry dated July 7, 1863, UALSC; final diary entry: Goble, "James A. Goble Diary," entry dated August 13, 1863, UALSC.

25. Wright, "Port Hudson, Its History, from an Interior View," *Daily True Delta*, August 2–16, 1863; and Wright, *Port Hudson: Its History from an Interior Point of View* (Baton Rouge: Committee for the Preservation of Port Hudson Battlefield, 1961).

26. Support for Confederacy: Howard Cushing Wright to His Mother, 1861, Howard Cushing Wright Collection, NYHS; death and eulogy: "de Gournay," Howard Cushing Wright Collection, NYHS.

27. Confederate losses at Port Hudson: OR, ser. 1, vol. 26, pt. 1, p. 144; Graves: Yeary, *Reminiscences of the Boys in Gray*, 279. Union losses: Richter, *Historical Dictionary of the Civil War and Reconstruction*, 674.

28. Confederates paroled and imprisoned: OR, ser. 1, vol. 26, pt. 1, p. 642; civilian employees also paroled: Cunningham, *Port Hudson*, 121; Beecher: Beecher, *Record of the 114th Regiment NYSV*, 226.

29. Clark, *The One Hundred and Sixteenth Regiment of New York Volunteers*, 106.

30. Sutherland, *African Americans at War*, 647.

31. Kidder refusing to obey African American Union soldier: "Charges and Specifications," Charges, United States Army Colored Infantry Regiment, 81st, UAF; Kidder career: Henry Kidder, Compiled Service Records of Union Soldiers from Arkansas, NARA.

Conclusion

1. Woods, "Memoir of John Henning Woods," VTU.

2. Fauconnet, *Ruined by This Miserable War*, 11.

3. Milton Chambers to Brother July 17, 1863, Milton Chambers Letters, UAF.

4. Christ, *Civil War Arkansas*, 142.

5. Daniel, "Larry Daniel, author of *Conquered: Why the Army of Tennessee Failed*," *Impediments of War: The Civil War Talk Radio Companion*, podcast, Episode

1733, accessed July 5, 2021, https://www.impedimentsofwar.org/singleshow.php?show=1733.

6. Woods, "Memoir of John Henning Woods," VTU.

7. Sherman on fighting southerners: United States, B. F. Wade, and Daniel Wheelwright Gooch, *Report of the Joint Committee on the Conduct of the War at the Second Session, Thirty-Eighth Congress*, vol. 1 (Washington, DC: GPO, 1865), 161; Sherman's willingness to sacrifice soldiers: Simpson and Berlin, eds., *Sherman's Civil War*, 660.

8. "About," Port Hudson State Historic Site (website), accessed December 26, 2021, https://www.lastateparks.com/historic-sites/port-hudson-state-historic-site.

9. "Port Hudson National Cemetery," National Cemetery Administration, US Department of Veterans Affairs (website), accessed December 26, 2021, https://www.cem.va.gov/cems/nchp/porthudson.asp#gi.

10. Ellis, *The Twenty-Fifth Regiment Connecticut Volunteers*, 24.

Appendix

1. This information was taken from ORN, ser. 1, vol. 19, pp. 666–69; NavSource Naval History: Photographic History of the US Navy (website), https://www.navsource.org/archives/search.html; Dictionary of American Naval Fighting Ships, Naval History and Heritage Command (website), https://www.history.navy.mil/research/histories/ship-histories/danfs.html; Cunningham, *The Port Hudson Campaign*, 23; and Hewitt, *Port Hudson, Confederate Bastion*, 74.

2. Wright, "Port Hudson: Its History from an Interior View," *St. Francisville Democrat*, 26.

3. OR, ser. 1, vol. 15, p. 1027.

4. OR, ser. 1, vol. 15, p. 1033.

5. OR, ser. 1, vol. 38, p. 143.

6. OR, ser. 1, vol. 26, pt. 1, p. 529.

Selected Bibliography

Archival Collections

ADAH Alabama Department of Archives and History
Confederate Regimental History Files, 1st Alabama Infantry
History of the 35th Alabama Infantry Regiment
Weaver and Gary Family Papers
AUL Auburn University Library
Aaron Shimer Oberly Papers
ASA Arkansas State Archives
Samuel Walker Papers
William Parish Letters
BABM Boston Athenaeum, Boston, MA
Confederate Collection
BCA Bedford County Archives, Shelbyville, TN
Mullins Family Letters
BCAS Butler Center for Arkansas Studies, Little Rock, AR
Samuel J. and Margaret Starnes Thompson Collection
CACPL Chicopee Archives, Chicopee Public Library, Chicopee, MA
Town of Chicopee Collection
CSUN California State University at Northridge
James Dargan Diary
DUL Duke University Libraries, Durham, NC
John Barnard Papers
Rosemonde E. & Emile Kuntz Collection
EUL Emory University Libraries, Atlanta, GA
Alfred Sandlin Letters
FSA Florida State Archives Tallahassee, FL
Louis Boyd Letters
GLI Gilder Lehrman Institute of American History, New York, NY
G. W. Buntly Collection
Papers and Images of the Civil War
HAU Heritage Auctions Dallas, TX
Andre Beauchamp Letter
Brainard Curtis Letters
Charles Washburn Diary
Frank Letter
Friend Charley Letter

HHSNP Historic Huguenot Street, New Paltz, NY
Jacob DuBois Hasbrouck Family Collection
HLAB Huntington Library, Art Museum, and Botanical Gardens, San Marino, CA
Thomas T. Eckert Papers
HLHU Houghton Library, Harvard University, Cambridge, MA
Charles Paine Miscellaneous Papers
Franklin Certificates of Disability, Transfers, and Miscellaneous Papers
Palfrey Family Papers
IHS Indiana Historical Society Indianapolis, IN
Rufus Dooley Letters
KSHS Kansas State Historical Society Topeka, KS
Orville Chester Brown Collection
LCDAH Lauderdale County Department of Archives and History, Meridian, MS
The Siege of Port Hudson, a Civil War Diary
LOC Library of Congress, Washington, DC
Photographs by McPherson and Oliver
Robert Knox Sneden Diary, Siege of Port Hudson Map
LSU Louisiana State University, Baton Rouge, LA
Confederate States Army Collection
George R. Waite Port Hudson Letter
John Morgan Papers
Louisiana and Lower Mississippi Valley Collection
William M. Allen Correspondence
William Y. Dixon Papers
MDAH Mississippi Department of Archives and History Jackson, MS
John Pettus Correspondence and Papers
MHS Maine Historical Society Portland, ME
George Foster Shepley Papers
MSUA Michigan State University Archives, East Lansing, MI
Hardenbergh Family Papers
MSUK Murray State University, Murray, KY
William J. Stubblefield Diary
NLSC Newberry Library Special Collections, Chicago, IL
William Park Civil War Journal
NYHS New York Historical Society New York, NY
Aldis Collection
Civil War Letters Collection
Claudius W. Rider

Edmond Family Collection
Howard Cushing Wright Collection P. R. Chandler Papers
Thomas William Faulds Collection

NYSMM New York State Military Museum and Veterans Research Center, Saratoga Springs, NY
Beat the Drum—Brooklyn and Long Island Fair for the Benefit of the US Sanitary Commission Records, New York Public Library Archives, New York, NY
Civil War Letters of Hazen Russell
James H. Peck, Jr., Letters
John Newton Chamberlin Diary

NYSA New York State Archives, Albany, NY
New York, Civil War Muster Roll Abstracts

NARA National Archives and Records Administration, College Park, MD
Case Files of Approved Pension Applications of Widows and Other Dependents of Civil War Veterans
Compiled Service Records for Union and Confederate Soldiers
Confederate Papers Relating to Citizens or Business Firms
Index to Pensions 1860–1934

PFL Patten Free Library, Bath, ME
Charles T. Lord Letters

PHP Pamplin Historical Park and the National Museum of the Civil War Soldier, Petersburg, VA
Erastus Gregory Letter

PHSHS Port Hudson State Historic Site, Jackson, LA
Poem Book of James Addison Boyd
William Philbrick Letter

SHU Sacred Heart University, Fairfield, CT
Thomas Cahill Civil War Letters

TSLA Tennessee State Library and Archives, Nashville, TN
Letter from J. Wes Broom
Memoir of J. W. Harmon
William Thurman Letters

TUL Tulane University Library, New Orleans, LA
Algernon Badger Family Letters J. Harvey Brown Letters
William A. Smith Letters

UAF University of Arkansas at Fayetteville, Special Collections
Joseph M. Bailey Memoir
Milton Chambers Letters
Charges, United States Army Colored Infantry Regiment, 81st

UALSC University of Alabama Library, Special Collections, Tuscaloosa, AL
James A. Goble Diary
UKSC University of Kentucky, Special Collections, Lexington, KY
Appleton Sturgis Papers
UMBHL University of Michigan, Bentley Historical Library, Ann Arbor, MI
Eli A. Griffin Papers
UNC University of North Carolina, Southern Historical Collection, Chapel Hill, NC
Federal Soldiers' Letters Collection, Gould Letter
UNDSC University of Notre Dame, Notre Dame, IN
Thomas Benton Alexander Diary
UNT University of North Texas, Denton, TX
Maud C. Fentress Papers
USNA United States Naval Academy, Annapolis, MD
John Hart Letters
UTBC University of Texas, Briscoe Center, Austin, TX
Daniel Ruggles Papers
Henry T. Aiken Papers
UVL University of Vermont Libraries, Burlington, VT
Justus F. Gale Correspondence
VT Virginia Tech, Blacksburg, VA
John Henning Woods Papers

Newspapers and Periodicals

Alexandria Gazette
Boston Herald
Charleston Mercury
Chicago Tribune
Confederate Veteran (abbreviated as *CV*)
Daily Dispatch
Daily National Intelligencer
Daily Selma Alabama Reporter
Daily True Delta
Harper's Weekly
Liberator
Louisville Daily Journal
Memphis Daily Appeal
Natchez Daily Courier
New York Herald
New York Times
Philadelphia Inquirer
Pittsfield Sun
Portland Daily Press
Raftsman's Journal
Richmond Dispatch
Southern Bivouac
Southern Historical Society Papers (abbreviated as *SHSP*)
Times Picayune
Times Democrat
True Democrat
Urbana Union
Vermont Journal

Vicksburg Daily Whig
Washington Telegraph
Weekly Advertiser
Weekly Arkansas Gazette
Weekly Mississippian

Government Publications

Chisolm, Julian John. *A Manual of Military Surgery: For the Use of Surgeons in the Confederate States Army: with an Appendix of the Rules and Regulations of the Medical Department of the Confederate States Army*. Richmond, Va.: West & Johnston, 1861.

Confederate States of America. *Army Regulations, Adopted for the Use of the Army of the Confederate States, in Accordance with Late Acts of Congress*. New Orleans: Bloomfield & Steel, 1861.

Confederate States of America. *Laws of Congress in Regard to Taxes, Currency and Conscription, Passed February 1864*. Richmond: James E. Goode, 1864.

Hitchcock Susan L Beth Wheeler Byrd and United States. Dry Tortugas National Park Garden Key Cultural Landscape Report. Atlanta Ga: Cultural Resources Division Southeast Regional Office National Park Service, 2011.

Tennessee. *Tennesseans in the Civil War: A Military History of Confederate and Union Units with Available Rosters of Personnel*. Nashville, TN: Civil War Centennial Commission, 1964.

Union Army. *A History of Military Affairs in the Loyal States, 1861–65, Records of the Regiments in the Union Army, Cyclopedia of Battles, Memoirs of Commanders and Soldiers*. Madison, WI: Federal Pub. Co., 1908.

United States. *Medal of Honor Awards 1863-1963: Hearing Before the Subcommittee on Veterans Affairs of the Committee on Labor and Public Welfare United States Senate Eighty-Eighth Congress First Session on S. 1046 a Bill Relating to Medal of Honor Recipients October 9, 1963*. Washington D.C: United States Government Printing Office.

United States. *Revised United States Army Regulations of 1861*. Washington, DC: Government Printing Office, 1863.

United States, B. F. Wade, and Daniel Wheelwright Gooch. *Report of the Joint Committee on the Conduct of the War at the Second Session, Thirty-Eighth Congress*, vol. 1. Washington, DC: Government Printing Office, 1865.

United States. Statistics of the United States, (including Mortality Property, Etc.) in 1860. Washington, DC: Government Printing Office, 1866.

United States. The Census of 1860. Washington, DC: Government Printing Office, 1899.

United States. *The Medical and Surgical History of the War of the Rebellion (1861–65)*. Washington, DC: Government Printing Office, 1870.

United States. *The War of the Rebellion: Official Records of the Union and*

Confederate Armies. Washington, DC: Government Printing Office, 1899. (abbreviated as OR)

United States. *The War of the Rebellion: Official Records of the Union and Confederate Navies*. Washington, DC: Government Printing Office, 1899. (abbreviated as ORN)

Published Primary Sources

Babcock, Willoughby, and Willoughby M. Babcock. *Selections from the Letters and Diaries of Brevet-Brigadier General Willoughby Babcock of the Seventy-Fifth New York Volunteers: A Study of Camp Life in the Union Armies During the Civil War.* Albany, NY: University of the State of New York, 1922.

Bacon, Edward. *Among the Cotton Thieves*. Detroit: Free Press Steam Book & Job Printing House, 1867.

Bailey, Joseph M. Confederate Guerrilla: The Civil War Memoir of Joseph M. Bailey. Edited by T. Lindsay Baker. Fayetteville: University of Arkansas Press, 2007.

Bauer, Craig, ed. "Eyewitness Report on the Battle of Fort Butler." *Louisiana History* 45, no. 2 (Spring 2004) 201–208.

Beecher, Harris H. *Record of the 114th Regiment, N.Y.S.V.* Norwich, NY: J. F. Hubbard Jr., 1866.

Beifuss, Ronald, ed. "The Diary of Sgt. John Fleming." *Military Images* 5, no. 2 (September–October 1983) 26–27.

Brown, Spencer Kellogg, and George Gardner Smith. *Spencer Kellogg Brown: His Life in Kansas and His Death as a Spy, 1842–1863, as Disclosed in His Diary.* London: W. Heinemann, 1903.

Bryant, William. "A Yankee Soldier Looks at the Negro." *Civil War History* 7, no. 2 (1961) 133–148.

Cannon, J. P. *Inside of Rebeldom: The Daily Life of a Private in the Confederate Army.* Washington, DC: National Tribune, 1900.

Carpenter, Geo. N. *History of the Eighth Regiment Vermont Volunteers, 1861–1865.* Boston: Press of Deland & Barta, 1886.

Clark, Orton S. *The One Hundred and Sixteenth Regiment of New York State Volunteers: Being a Complete History of Its Organization and of Its Nearly Three Years of Active Service in the Great Rebellion. To Which Is Appended Memorial Sketches and a Muster Roll of the Regiment, Containing the Name of Every Man Connected with It.* Buffalo: Printing House of Matthews & Warren, 1868.

Clarke, H. C. *Clarke's Confederate Household Almanac: For the Year 1863, Being the Third Year of the Independence of the Confederate States of America.* Vicksburg, MS: H. C. Clarke, 1863.

Davis, Jefferson. *The Rise and Fall of the Confederate Government.* New York: D. Appleton and Co, 1881.

Dawson, Sarah Ida Fowler Morgan. *A Confederate Girl's Diary*. Boston: Houghton Mifflin Co., 1913.

de Gournay, Paul. "Defending Port Hudson." In *Battles and Leaders of the Civil War*, vol. 5, edited by Peter Cozzens, 392–409 . Urbana, IL: University of Illinois Press, 2002.

Dewey, Daniel. *A Memorial of Lt. Daniel Perkins Dewey, of the Twenty-Fifth Regiment Connecticut Volunteers*. Hartford, CT: Case, Lockwood & Co, 1864.

Diggins, Bartholomew. *Sailing with Farragut: The Civil War Recollections of Bartholomew Diggins*. Edited by George S. Burkhardt. Knoxville: University of Tennessee Press, 2016.

Ellis, Samuel. *The Twenty-Fifth Regiment Connecticut Volunteers in the War of the Rebellion: History, Reminiscences, Description of Battle of Irish Bend, Carrying of Pay Roll, Roster*. Rockville, CT: Press of the Rockville Journal, 1913.

Ewer, James Kendall. *Third Massachusetts Cavalry in the War for the Union*. Maplewood, MA: W. G. J. Perry Press, 1903.

Fauconnet, Charles Prosper. *Ruined by This Miserable War: The Dispatches of Charles Prosper Fauconnet, a French Diplomat in New Orleans, 1863–1868*. Edited by Carl A. Brasseaux and Katherine Carmines Mooney. Knoxville, TN: University of Tennessee Press, 2013.

Farragut, Loyal. "Passing the Port Hudson Batteries." In *Addresses Delivered Before the New York Commandery of the Loyal Legion of the United States, 1833–1891*. New York: New York Commandery, 1891.

Fitzhugh, George. *Sociology for the South; Or, the Failure of Free Society*. Richmond, VA: A. Morris, 1854.

Flinn, Frank M. *Campaigning with Banks in Louisiana, '63 and '64: And with Sheridan in the Shenandoah Valley in '64 and '65*. Boston: W. B. Clarke, 1889.

Fowler, P. H. *Memorials of William Fowler*. New York: A. D. F. Randolph & Co., 1875.

Gardner, Henry R. "A Yankee in Louisiana: Selections from the Diary and Correspondence of Henry R. Gardner." Edited by Kenneth Shewmaker and Andrew K. Prinz. *Louisiana History* 5, no. 3 (Summer 1964): 271–95.

Glatthaar, Joseph. "The Civil War Through the Eyes of Sixteen-Year-Old Black Officer." *Louisiana History* 35, no. 2 (Spring 1994): 201–16.

Grant, Ulysses. *Personal Memoirs of U. S. Grant, Two Volumes in One*. New York: C. L. Webster, 1894.

Halleran, Michael Anthony. *The Better Angels of Our Nature: Freemasonry in the American Civil War*. Tuscaloosa: University of Alabama Press, 2010.

Hall, Henry, and James Hall. *Cayuga in the Field: A Record of the 19th N.Y. Volunteers, All the Batteries of the 3d New York Artillery, and 75th New York Volunteers Comprising an Account of Their Organization, Camp Life, Marches, Battles, Losses, Toils and Triumphs in the War for the Union, with Complete Rolls of Their Members*. Auburn, NY: Truair, Smith & Co., Printers, 1873.

Hanaburgh, D. H. *History of the One Hundred and Twenty-Eighth Regiment, New York Volunteers (U.S. Infantry) in the Late Civil War.* Poughkeepsie, NY: Enterprise Pub. Co., 1894.

Harding, George C. *The Miscellaneous Writings of George C. Harding.* Indianapolis: Carlon & Hollenbeck, Printers, 1882.

Hepworth, George H. *The Whip, Hoe, and Sword.* Freeport, NY: Books for Libraries Press, 1971.

Hewitt, Lawrence L., and Arthur W. Bergeron, eds. *Post Hospital Ledger, Port Hudson, Louisiana, 1862–1863.* Baton Rouge, LA: Le Comite des Archives de la Louisiane, 1982.

Hoffman, Wickham. *Camp, Court and Siege: A Narrative of Personal Adventure and Observation During Two Wars, 1861–1865, 1870–1871.* London: Sampson Low, 1877.

Hosmer, James Kendall. *The Color-Guard: Being a Corporal's Notes of Military Service in the Nineteenth Army Corps.* Boston: Walker, Wise, 1864.

Howe, Henry Warren. *Passages from the Life of Henry Warren Howe: Consisting of Diary and Letters Written During the Civil War, 1861–1865.* Lowell, MA: Courier-Citizen Co., Printers, 1899.

Irwin, Richard Bache. *History of the Nineteenth Army Corps.* New York: G. P. Putnam's Sons, 1892.

Jackson, Crawford. "An Account of the Occupation of Fort Hudson, LA." *Alabama Quarterly* 18, no. 4. Winter, 1956, 474 - 485.

Johns, Henry T. *Life with the Forty-Ninth Massachusetts Volunteers.* Pittsfield, MA: for the author, 1864.

Johnston, Bradley. *A Memoir of the Life and Public Service of Joseph E. Johnston: Once the Quartermaster General of the Army of the United States, and a General in the Army of the Confederate States of America.* Baltimore: R. H. Woodward & Company, 1891.

Kamphoefner, Walter D., and Wolfgang Johannes Helbich, eds. *Germans in the Civil War: The Letters They Wrote Home.* Chapel Hill: University of North Carolina Press, 2006.

Kennedy, Charles Washington. *From Port Hudson to Cedar Creek: The Civil War Letters of Charles Washington Kennedy.* Edited by Edward Steers Jr. Scotts Valley, CA: CreateSpace Independent Publishing Platform, 2015.

Kundahl, George G., ed. *Confederate Engineer: Training and Campaigning with John Morris Wampler.* Knoxville: University of Tennessee Press, 2000.

Landry, Christophe. *Slave Narratives of Louisianans Living in Texas.* Baton Rouge: Louisiana Historic and Cultural Visas, 2017.

Latture, Richard, ed. "Pinned Down Outside Port Hudson." *Quarterly Journal of Military History* 16, no. 4 (Summer 2004): 48–49.

Laver, Tara, ed. "Where Duty Shall Call: The Baton Rouge Civil War Letters of William H. Whitney." *Louisiana History*, 46, no. 3 (Summer 2005): 333–70.

Love, William De Loss. *Wisconsin in the War of the Rebellion: A History of All Regiments and Batteries the State Has Sent to the Field, and Deeds of Her Citizens, Governors and Other Military Officers, and State and National Legislators to Suppress the Rebellion.* Chicago: Church and Goodman, 1866.

Maglathlin, Henry B. *Company I, Fourth Massachusetts Regiment, Nine Months Volunteers, in Service, 1862–3.* Boston: Press of G. C. Rand & Avery, 1863.

McClung, Richard. *Three Years in the C.S. Army.* New York: Bowden Group, 2013.

McMullen, Glenn. "A Massachusetts Soldier at the Siege or Port Hudson, 1863." *Louisiana History* 26, no. 3 (Summer 1985) 313–26.

McGavock, Randal W. *Pen and Sword: The Life and Journals of Randal W.* McGa*vock.* Edited by Herschel Gower. Nashville: Tennessee Historical Commission, 1959.

McGregor, Charles. *History of the Fifteenth Regiment, New Hampshire Volunteers, 1862–1863.* Concord, NH: I. C. Evans, 1900.

McMorries, Edward Young. *History of the First Regiment, Alabama Volunteer Infantry.* Montgomery, AL: Brown Printing Co., Printers, 1904.

Moors, J. F. *History of the Fifty-Second Regiment, Massachusetts Volunteers.* Boston: Press of G. H. Ellis, 1893.

Otis George Alexander. *A Report on Excisions of the Head of the Femur for Gunshot Injury.* Washington: Gov. Print. Off, 1869.

Palfrey, John. "Port Hudson." *Papers of the Military Historical Society of Massachusetts,* vol. 8. Boston: Military Historical Society of Massachusetts, 1910.

Partin, Robert, ed. "Report of a Corporal of the Alabama First Infantry." *Alabama Historical Quarterly* 20 (Winter 1950): 583–600.

Patrick, Robert. *Reluctant Rebel: The Secret Diary of Robert Patrick, 1861–1865.* Edited by F. Jay Taylor. Baton Rouge: Louisiana State University Press, 1959.

Plummer, Albert. *History of the Forty-Eighth Regiment, M.V.M. During the Civil War.* Boston, MA: Press of the New England Druggist Pub. Co., 1907.

Porter, William Clendenin. "War Diary of W. C. Porter." Edited by J. V. Frederick. *Arkansas Historical Quarterly* 11, no. 4 (Winter 1952): 286–314.

Powers, George Whitefield. *The Story of the Thirty-Eighth Regiment of Massachusetts Volunteers.* Cambridge, MA: Dakin and Metcalf, 1866.

Repp, Celeste, and William Little Park. *Two Civil Wars: The Curious Shared Journal of a Baton Rouge Schoolgirl and a Union Sailor on the USS* Essex. Edited by Katherine Bentley Jeffrey. Baton Rouge: Louisiana State University Press, 2016.

Risley, Ford. *Civil War: Primary Documents on Events from 1860 to 1865.* Westport, CT: Greenwood Pub. Group, 2007.

Ripley, Eliza McHatton. *From Flag to Flag: A Woman's Adventures and Experiences in the South During the War, in Mexico, and in Cuba.* New York: D. Appleton, 1896.

Roman, Alfred. *The Military Operations of General Beauregard in the War between the States 1861 to 1865: Including a Brief Personal Sketch and a Narrative of His Services in the War with Mexico, 1846–8.* New York: Harper, 1884.

Schley, Winfield Scott. *Forty-Five Years Under the Flag.* New York: Appleton, 1904.

Scott, H. L. *Military Dictionary.* New York: Can Nostrand, 1861.

Sherman, William T. *Sherman's Civil War: Selected Correspondence of William T. Sherman, 1860–1865.* Edited by Brooks D. Simpson and Jean V. Berlin. Chapel Hill: University of North Carolina Press, 1999.

Smith, Daniel P. *Company K, First Alabama Regiment, or, Three Years in the Confederate Service.* Gaithersburg, MD: Butternut Press, 1885.

Smith, George Gilbert. *Leaves from a Soldier's Diary: The Personal Record of Lieutenant George G. Smith, Co. C., 1st Louisiana Regiment Infantry Volunteers (White) During the War of the Rebellion; Also a Partial History of the Operations of the Army and Navy in the Department of the Gulf from the Capture of New Orleans to the Close of the War.* Bethesda, MD: University Publications of America, 1990.

Sprague, Homer B. *History of the 13th Infantry Regiment of Connecticut Volunteers, During the Great Rebellion.* Hartford, CT: Case, Lockwood, 1867.

Stevens, William B., William C. Eustis, and Solomon Nelson. *History of the Fiftieth Regiment of Infantry, Massachusetts Volunteer Militia, in the Late War of the Rebellion.* Boston: Griffith-Stillings Press, 1907.

Strother, David Hunter. *A Virginian Yankee in the Civil War: The Diaries of David Hunter Strother.* Chapel Hill: University of North Carolina Press, 1961.

Tabor, R. J. "Reminiscences of R. J. Tabor." *Southern Bivouac* 3 (May 1885) 420.

Taylor, Richard. *Destruction and Reconstruction: Personal Experiences of the Late War.* New York: D. Appleton and Co, 1879.

Tiemann, William F. *The 159th Regiment Infantry New York State Volunteers, in the War of the Rebellion, 1862–1865.* Brooklyn, NY: W. F. Tiemann, 1891.

Townsend, L. T. *History of the Sixteenth Regiment, New Hampshire Volunteers.* Washington: N. T. Elliott, 1897.

Underwood, John Levi. *The Women of the Confederacy: In Which Is Presented the Heroism of the Women of the Confederacy with Accounts of Their Trials During the War and the Period of Reconstruction, with Their Ultimate Triumph Over Adversity. Their Motives and Achievements as Told by Writers and Orators Now Preserved in Permanent Form.* New York: Neale Pub. Co., 1906.

Van Alstyne, Lawrence. *Diary of an Enlisted Man.* New Haven, CT: Tuttle, Morehouse & Taylor Company, 1910.

Waite, Otis F. R. *New Hampshire in the Great Rebellion: Containing Histories of the Several New Hampshire Regiments, and Biographical Notices of Many of the Prominent Actors in the Civil War of 1861–65.* Claremont, NH: Tracy, Chase & Co., 1870.

Watkins, Sam. *"Co. Aytch": Maury Grays, First Tennessee Regiment, or a Side Show of the Big Show.* Chattanooga, TN: Times Print. Co, 1900.

Whitcomb, Caroline Elizabeth. *History of the Second Massachusetts Battery (Nims' Battery) of Light Artillery, 1861–1865.* Concord, NH: Rumford Press, 1912.

Willis, Henry A. *The Fifty-Third Regiment Massachusetts Volunteers: Comprising Also a History of the Siege of Port Hudson.* Fitchburg: Press of Blanchard & Brown, 1889.

Wright, Howard C. *Port Hudson: Its History from an Interior Point of View.* Baton Rouge: Committee for the Preservation of Port Hudson Battlefield, 1961.

Wyeth, John A. *With Sabre and Scalpel: The Autobiography of a Soldier and Surgeon.* New York and London: Harper & Bros., 1914.

Yeary, Mamie. *Reminiscences of the Boys in Gray, 1861–1865.* Dallas, TX: For the author by Smith & Lamar Pub. House, M. E. Church, South, 1912.

Secondary Sources

Ballard, Michael B. *Pemberton: The General Who Lost Vicksburg.* Jackson, MS: University Press of Mississippi, 1999.

Barnett, Gene. "The Glorious Old Fifteenth: A History of the Fifteenth Alabama Infantry Regiment in the Confederate States Army." PhD diss., Auburn University, 1995.

Barney, William L. *The Oxford Encyclopedia of the Civil War.* New York: Oxford University Press, 2011.

Bell, Andrew McIlwaine. *Mosquito Soldiers: Malaria, Yellow Fever, and the Course of the American Civil War.* Baton Rouge: Louisiana State University Press, 2010.

Bergeron, Arthur W. *Guide to Louisiana Confederate Military Units, 1861–1865.* Baton Rouge: Louisiana State University Press, 1996.

Boynton, Charles. *The History of the Navy During the Rebellion.* New York: D. Appleton, 1867.

Cashin, Joan E. *War Stuff: The Struggle for Human and Environmental Resources in the American Civil War.* New York, NY: Cambridge University Press, 2018.

Christ, Mark K. *Civil War Arkansas, 1863: The Battle for a State.* Norman: University of Oklahoma Press, 2010.

Cooper, William J. *Jefferson Davis and the Civil War Era.* Baton Rouge: Louisiana State University Press, 2008.

Cova, Antonio Rafael de la. *Cuban Confederate Colonel: The Life of Ambrosio José Gonzales.* Columbia, SC: University of South Carolina Press, 2008.

Cutrer, Thomas W. *Theater of a Separate War: The Civil War West of the Mississippi River, 1861–1865.* Chapel Hill: University of North Carolina Press, 2017.

Derbes, Brett. "Prison Productions: Textiles and Other Military Supplies at the Louisiana State Penitentiary in the Civil War." *Louisiana History* 55, no. 1 (Winter 2014): 40–64.

Dobak, William A. *Freedom by the Sword: The U.S. Colored Troops, 1862–1867.* Washington, DC: Center for Military History, 2013.

Dubay, Robert W. *John Jones Pettus, Mississippi Fire-Eater: His Life and Times, 1813–1867.* Jackson: University Press of Mississippi, 2008.

Dyer, Frederick H. *A Compendium of the War of the Rebellion.* Bethesda, MD: University Publications of America, 1991.

Eicher, John H., and David J. Eicher. *Civil War High Commands.* Stanford, CA: Stanford University Press, 2001.

Faust, Eric R. *The 6th Michigan Volunteer Infantry in the Civil War: A History and Roster.* Jefferson, NC: McFarland & Company, Inc., 2020.

Foote, Shelby. *The Civil War, a Narrative: Fort Sumter to Perryville.* London: Pimlico, 1986.

Gabel, Christopher R. *Staff Ride Handbook for the Vicksburg Campaign, December 1862–July 1863.* Fort Leavenworth, KS: Combat Studies Institute, US Army Command and General Staff College, 2001.

Gallman, Matthew J., and Gary W. Gallagher, eds. *Lens of War: Exploring Iconic Photographs of the Civil War.* Athens: University of Georgia Press, 2015.

Hanks, Abby. "Josie Fernandez," The Encyclopedia of Arkansas. (website), accessed July 27, 2021, https://encyclopediaofarkansas.net/entries/josie-fernandez-13780/.

Hine, Clark, Darlene, and Earnestine Jenkins, eds. *A Question of Manhood: A Reader in U.S. Black Men's History and Masculinity.* Bloomington: Indiana University Press, 1999.

Harrington, Fred Harvey. "Arkansas Defends the Mississippi." *Arkansas Historical Quarterly* 4, no. 2 (1945): 109–17.

Hattaway, Herman, and Archer Jones. *How the North Won: A Military History of the Civil War.* Urbana: University of Illinois Press, 1983.

Hearn, Chester G. *The Capture of New Orleans 1862.* Baton Rouge, LA: Louisiana State University Press, 1995.

Hewitt, Lawrence L. *Port Hudson, Confederate Bastion on the Mississippi.* Baton Rouge: Louisiana State University Press, 1994.

———. *Port Hudson: The Most Significant Battlefield Photographs of the Civil War.* Knoxville: University of Tennessee Press, 2021.

Hollandsworth, James G. *Louisiana Native Guards: The Black Military Experience During the Civil War.* Baton Rouge: Louisiana State University Press, 1995.

Hunter, G. Howard. "Politics of Resentment: Unionist Regiments in the New Orleans Immigrant Community." *Louisiana History* 44, no. 2 (Spring 2003): 185–210.

Jensen, Leslie D. "A Survey of Confederate Central Government Quartermaster Issue Jackets." The Company of Military Historians. Accessed July 25, 2021. http://www.military-historians.org/company/journal/confederate/confederate-2.htm.

Jones, Michael. *Major General Franklin Gardner: Hero of the Siege of Port Hudson.* Scotts Valley, CA: CreateSpace Independent Publishing Platform, 2018.

Lancaster, Guy, ed. The Encyclopedia of Arkansas (website). https://encyclopediaofarkansas.net/.

Lancaster, Guy, and Christopher Thrasher. *The Murder of Oscar Chitwood in Hot Springs Arkansas.* Chicago: Arcadia Publishing, 2022.

Litwack, Leon F. *Been in the Storm So Long: The Aftermath of Slavery.* London: Athlone, 1980.

McElroy Robert McNutt. *Jefferson Davis; the Unreal and the Real.* New York: Harper & Brothers, 1937

McPherson, James M. *Battle Cry of Freedom: The Civil War Era.* New York: Oxford University Press, 1988.

McPherson, James M. *For Cause and Comrades: The Will to Combat in the Civil War.* New York: Oxford University Press, 1997.

McWhiney Grady, and Perry D. Jamieson. *Attack and Die: Civil War Military Tactics and the Southern Heritage.* University, AL: University of Alabama Press, 1982.

Mendoza, Alexander. *Chickamauga 1863: Rebel Breakthrough.* Santa Barbara, CA: Praeger, 2013.

Mountjoy, Shane. *Technology and the Civil War.* New York: Chelsea House Publishers, 2009.

Noe, Kenneth W. *The Howling Storm: Weather, Climate, and the American Civil War.* Baton Rouge: Louisiana State University Press, 2020.

Gaines, W. Craig. *Encyclopedia of Civil War Shipwrecks.* Baton Rouge: Louisiana State University Press, 2008.

Perello, Chris. *The Quest for Annihilation: The Role and Mechanics of Battle in the American Civil War.* Bakersfield, CA: Strategy & Tactics Press, 2009.

Phillips, Jason. *Diehard Rebels: The Confederate Culture of Invincibility.* Athens: University of Georgia Press, 2010.

Reed, Merl Elwyn. *Louisiana's Transportation Revolution: The Railroads, 1830–1850.* Baton Rouge: Louisiana State University, 1957.

Rutherford, Ken. *America's Buried History: Landmines in the Civil War.* El Dorado Hills, CA: Savas Beatie, 2020.

Skipwith, Henry. *East Feliciana Louisiana Past and Present. Baton Rouge: Reprinted by Claitor's Book Store for East Feliciana Pilgrimage and Garden Club Clinton La.],* 1971.

Smith, Jean Edward. *Grant: A Biography.* Newtown, CT: American Political Biography Press, 2014.

Sutherland, Daniel E., ed. *Guerrillas, Unionists, and Violence on the Confederate Home Front.* Fayetteville: University of Arkansas Press, 1999.

Sutherland, Jonathan. *African Americans at War: An Encyclopedia.* Santa Barbara, CA: ABC-CLIO, 2004.

Wagner, Margaret, Gary W. Gallagher, and Paul Finkelman. *The Library of Congress Civil War Desk Reference.* New York: Simon & Schuster, 2002.

Ward, Harry M. *Public Executions in Richmond: Virginia, A History, 1782–1907.* Jefferson, NC: McFarland & Company, Inc., 2012.

Warner, Ezra J. *Generals in Gray: Lives of the Confederate Commanders.* Baton Rouge: Louisiana State University Press, 2013.

Weitz, Mark A. *More Damning Than Slaughter: Desertion in the Confederate Army.* Lincoln: University of Nebraska Press, 2005.

Wetta, Frank J. *The Louisiana Scalawags.* Baton Rouge: Louisiana State University and Agricultural and Mechanical College, 1978.

Wilson, Harold S. *Confederate Industry Manufacturers and Quartermasters in the Civil War.* Jackson: University Press of Mississippi, 2005.

Wilson, Joseph T. *The Black Phalanx; A History of the Negro Soldiers of the United States in the Wars of 1775–1812, 1861–'65.* Hartford, CT: American Pub. Co, 1890.

Woodworth, Steven E., and Kenneth J. Winkle. *Atlas of the Civil War.* New York: Oxford University Press, 2004.

Yearns, W. Buck. *The Confederate Congress.* Athens: University of Georgia Press, 1960.

Index

Page numbers in **boldface** refer to illustrations.